A Handbook For Light Workers

By David Cousins
Edited by Jean Prince

Barton House

Original material by David Cousins. Edited by Jean Prince
Book design and typesetting by David Bowles
Cover illustration by Ivan McGrath. Cover photograph by Gwenan
Printed and bound by Guernsey Press, Channel Islands

A Handbook For Light Workers

© David Cousins 1993

ISBN 1-85588-599-9 (Paperback)

The moral right of David Cousins to be identified
as the author of this work has been asserted

British Library Cataloguing in Publication Data:
Cousins, David
Handbook For Light Workers, A
I. Title
133

Additional copies of this book can be ordered direct from the publisher:
priced at £12.99 each. Please add £3.00* UK p&p for
the first book plus an additional £2.00* for each book thereafter.

*the above p&p rates apply to the UK only. For overseas airmail orders:
To Europe please add £5.00 sterling p&p *per book.*
To the rest of the world please add £8.00 sterling p&p *per book.*

Credit-card orders welcome: Access, Visa, Mastercard,
Eurocard, etc. (sorry *NOT* Switch, Amex or Diners).
Call our order line anytime on 01803-835593 or FAX 01803-833464
Overseas call (+44) 1803-835593 or FAX (+44) 1803-833464

Orders by post to: Barton House, PO Box 6, Dartmouth, TQ6 9YE
Enclose your credit card details or a cheque/PO/bank draft
made payable to *'Barton House'* in UK pounds sterling.

**Barton House, The Networking Publisher, PO Box 6,
Dartmouth, TQ6 9YE.   01803-835593 fax 01803-835210**

Distributed to the booktrade in the UK by:
Airlift Book Company. UK bookshops only call 0181-804-0044.

Distributed to the booktrade in North America by:
*New Leaf Distributing, 401 Thornton Road, Lithia Springs, Georia 30057-1557
US/Canadian bookshops only call (707) 948 7845.*
(NB: If you have difficulty obtaining additional copies via a North American bookshop, quote this source)

For details of workshops audiotapes and readings by David Cousins, please write to him directly:
c/o 26 Pensylvania, Llanederyn, Cardiff, CF3 7LN, UK.

DEDICATION

To my wife Linda,
for her patience, humour, understanding
and flexibility in allowing me to pursue my quest.

ACKNOWLEDGMENTS

To all the elves
who have given me the opportunity
through practical experience, to view their systems
and to invoke within the sharing of energy the informational
patterns which are presented within this book.

CONTENTS:
CHAPTERS

.

CONTENTS: MEDITATIONS

EDITOR'S PREFACE

This book was spoken by David onto tapes in Wales, then transcribed and written in Normandy, France. As I learnt to merge with David so that his energy worked through me, it became clear we had a karmic contract to bring this book into form, and David said, "By merging our vibrations we can create a package of energy that can work for us in a karmic way. It will also help the pattern of energy, information and love which you are bringing into your physical place. In some ways there is, I feel, a deep significance in tapping into this subject matter in your home in France, because the French and British have a history which has been discordant, so possibly in our own ways, we are bringing these two nations together."

This book is for those who have enough courage to embrace and welcome change in their lives. From my own experience during the 15 months it took to complete this book, I can assure you that change is guaranteed!

Right from the beginning, whatever copy I typed and worked on, that subject manifested in my life. It was clear that not only was I helping to bring this book into written form, but the book was using me to demonstrate how it will change readers' lives on all levels.

As I worked on the chapter which says, "...*The* miracle, if you want it, if you really need it, can actually come about," miracles happened around me.

When I worked on the chapter on thought forms, all my old thought forms jumped up and stared me in the face. Situations were created, in rapid succession, to reflect my old thoughts and conditioning - and then I was shown how quickly I could transmute those with the new meditations coming through.

A month later, I worked on the chapter 'Health and Diet'. It says, "A lot of Light workers are experiencing back problems. Back means stubborn. It is the body saying it is time to change."

And in true form to my pattern of 'living' the book, a vertebra in my lower back went out of alignment. I spent several days flat on my back, looking at the ceiling, reflecting on what my body was telling me. Some days later I thought I had the message. I was surprised that my back was still in spasm, so I stayed with it and looked more deeply. I realised I had only got half the message. When I grasped the full meaning behind what my back was saying, the spasm subsided and my spine started to realign.

Still wanting to keep my back straight, I devised a new typing position. I put my computer on the sofa and knelt in front of it with my bottom resting on a meditation stool. I asked God to help with the healing of my spine, then I switched on a new tape from David and typed, "If you kneel down in a form of prayer, by that simple act of kneeling you activate the prayer-force energy..."

And so it continued.

As I typed the words, "It takes a lot of honesty and courage to release what you assume is part of your reality," my computer screen wouldn't produce the words. The keyboard was working, the cursor was moving but left a blank space instead of the words I was typing.

I tried various commands. The words suddenly flashed on the screen. I moved the cursor to correct the sentence and the words disappeared. For ten minutes I was caught in frustration, trying to escape from the situation I was in. I said aloud, "What is this sentence saying? What do I need to hear so much the computer won't let me move on? OK, whatever it is I am willing to listen!" As I touched the keyboard, the words I had previously typed suddenly appeared on the screen: "It takes a lot of honesty and courage to release what you assume is part of your reality because you have been used to it in the past."

I sat and thought. When I finally affirmed my willingness to release my old reality, I resumed typing and the computer worked perfectly!

As I worked with the meditations and practised them with situations in my life, the shifts and healings were often so rapid I can only call them miracles. Just days after David gave me the new healing meditation (Meditation 53), a spark from a match flew up and burnt my left eye. I couldn't see but was told, "It's OK. You can heal this." I sat and repeated the new meditation all day. The next morning I woke up and was stunned to find my eye had totally healed. No pain. No burning. No redness. Two days later I tripped and stuck a piece of metal in my right eye! I was temporarily blinded. Again I was told, "It's OK. You can heal this."

Once more I sat all day working with the healing meditation, and within 48 hours my eye was totally healed. My sight was undamaged. My eye was back to normal. I know this experience was just to show me both the power of the meditation, and the power of self-healing we are all now able to bring through.

The book was rewritten several times. New meditations were brought through. New copy added. Existing copy was refined. At each stage I could feel the stream of energy becoming more gentle. Yet more powerful within the gentleness. The more I learnt to merge with David, the more my own reality opened to new levels. There were days when I jumped in and out of different realities - and at times I wasn't sure if it was 1992 or 1994! My clairvoyant and telepathic abilities burst wide open and a break was needed while I integrated the inner shifts and my energy system adjusted to the change.

I spent the summer in the garden and grounded myself. In October I started the final rewrite. In peace and solitude, surrounded by fields in rural Normandy the final energy stream of the book came pouring through. For David this was all quite normal, and he just chuckled when I told him of my adventures!

With the text barely finished, the right publishers said 'yes' to the book. Everything fell smoothly into place. Their intuition said the timing for this book was *now*, and pushed it through an unusually fast production programme. With their enthusiasm the book was launched within a few months - in October 1993, the exact publication date forecast by David two years earlier.

As I look back I can see how the book has woven a new tapestry for my life. Everything looks and feels very different and very new. Refreshingly new. On a physical level, I came to France to help renovate an old Normandy house with the vision of starting a retreat centre. As I finished the last pages of the book, I received the message, "You can go now." So I am preparing to walk a new path. My life changes are not an exception - just an example of how this book will also change you!

Enjoy the change. Surrender to it and, like me, you will be a very different person in a year's time!

Jean Prince
July 1993

DAVID COUSINS:
A SHORT AUTOBIOGRAPHY

I was born in 1948, in a place called Llwynpia in the Rhondda Valley, Wales. The mountains and streams were my favourite childhood playground where I developed a very special connection with nature.

I incarnated into a psychic family. My mother was a natural clairvoyant and every time someone in the family died she would have advance warning, usually in the form of her mother who would materialise in front of her. My grandmother, grandfather and my great-grandfather, all on my mother's side of the family were also naturally psychic - so family life for me was a genetic training ground which I have capitalised on.

I became aware of my own psychic abilities as a young child, and in keeping with most psychic children I was often ill - I had every childhood sickness going, plus some mysterious illnesses no-one could explain. I also had constant migraine which manifested as extreme stomach pains. Doctors at that time couldn't find the cause; they said I ate too quickly and often put me on hot water fasts for several days.

My clairvoyant ability focused when I was 10 years old. I had scarlet fever which made me go blind for three days and my eyesight never fully recovered. I became very short-sighted, but being a proud 10 year old I wouldn't wear glasses. As I couldn't see people I learnt to identify them by 'feeling' them, and without consciously realising it I developed my ability to psychometrise people.

We lived in an old Welsh house where I often experienced psychic phenomena - noises, tapping, doors opening and closing. In my early teens I could feel spirits in the house, and could hear their boots as they walked next to me.

I left school at 15, worked as a carpet salesman in a departmental store then, when my parents moved to Surrey, I took a series of uneventful jobs in the south of England - driving large vehicles, working in a garage.

Although clairvoyance and psychic abilities were a natural part of my life, I didn't do anything to develop this until I was 21 when I became aware of various mediums. As a result of this I joined a development circle. At that time, this was within the spiritualist movement. After a period of two years in the development circle, I spent some time working the circuit of the spiritualist churches.

At 21 I married, moved back to Wales, and became a milkman. The job was ideal; the physical work carrying crates of milk helped to keep me earthed as a lot of high frequency energy was coming through me. It also gave me time to do readings, absent healings and work with my own development circles.

To amplify my earthing I became interested in most aspects of physical sport, especially the various martial arts and parachuting. I also worked in a local mental hospital for five years which gave me a crash course in communication of an unusual kind, since my job there was part of a recreational team to stimulate and motivate those who had been engaged for some time in the apparatus of the mental hospital programming.

I had a lot of experiences with entities through my mediumistic work. I remember one day during my milk round, feeling something targeting my solar plexus. Stopping my milk van, I looked around astrally and saw nine dark figures all cording into my solar plexus chakra. I looked closer and saw that the nine were a thought projection of one dark-robed figure who was standing in the astral distance. By targeting that dark entity with unconditional love through the focus of the Daisy Chain meditation, I successfully ensured that the manifestation of energy he was projecting towards me was neutralised and he was suitably banished.

I have always had an energy system that attracts people in. The large Mind-Body-Spirit Festivals were a good training ground to develop my capacity to bring energy through as I did clairvoyant readings for 10 hours a day, continuously for several days. I always remember the first Mind-Body-Spirit Festival I worked at. At the end of the first day, I sat on the seafront at Brighton, as high as a kite, eating a bag of fish and chips, and felt as if I was sizzling with the residue of excess energy that was still, to a degree, pouring through me!

When changes in the milk industry offered me the option to leave, I did so. I was then 38. The next two years were spent building up my clairvoyant and healing ability and at 40 I started leading workshops and it all expanded from there.

I now do four to five hours of clairvoyant work throughout most weekdays together with absent healing. I also give workshops most weekends, either in the UK or within Europe.

With the expansion of the high frequency energies I now work with, I find I need to earth myself. But because of my slightly older age, I do so in a much more gentle way working more with the elements in nature out in the fresh air, in the mountains or by the seaside, combining that with a little weight training and yoga, with the occasional T'ai Chi and swimming.

The way I work clairvoyantly is quite specific. I have a territory that is limited to certain linear time periods where I work with individuals such as Jean, or with organisations, or with the music I use in my workshop settings.

The vibration I work with gives me access to certain information. From a karmic point of view I have to be invited into a space before I can access information. In a way, there is a massive computer 'up there' which will give access - once you have the right password. These passwords give access to certain types of information on all levels.

I work with various sub-alignments of energy, and as I tap into that I allow it to happen. You could say I channel the information, as the words fall out of my mouth as I speak. Sometimes I listen to myself talking, which is quite a funny experience. But I invariably have a feeling of rightness. I have always felt I have the ability to be anything I have ever wanted, so I can also see into all aspects of life.

The akashic records are a form of knowing and information from them is given on a 'need' basis. If I look at the akashic records of someone's past lives, say Egyptian lives, I don't see all those lives, I just see what is necessary for the information needed at the time. That information - as a vibration - can then be amplified through my system. Sometimes it is like a blast as high frequency energy comes through. But most times it is slowed down and suitably sedated, because if I give people too much information within the emotional and mental levels, it encourages old habits to come up again. So within the series of alignments I work with, guides tell me what each person needs to become aware of. The manifesting frequency coming through then goes through a series of filters in my body and the person is only fed what is necessary. The akashic records are there as a series of encoded vibrations that are given to me. But for me to be able to receive them, I have to maintain the high level of a spiritual athlete working on the physical, emotional and mental planes.

From a channelling point of view I have access to everything - as we all have. But my remembrance of how we do it is a little bit more accurate than most people's. Because of the training I have had, and through long-term sessions of bringing energy through I can actually maintain a state of confidence and a state of holding the energy for a lot longer than most people, which puts me in a very useful setting for the work I need to do on a global basis working with nationalities as well as individuals.

I also work with Earth energies, neutralising the mind viruses and negative energies on all levels.

My feeling is that the tide is changing. The lonelier days are over, even though we still have to face the fury of the intellectual lobby and those who have vested interest in the emotional climate in the planet. It is now a very fine line we are beginning to tread. Therefore the information we give needs to be adequate for the time, but not too far in advance.

The higher frequency of the new energies coming into the planet are mutating everyone - whether they are aware of it or not. Fourth dimensional energies are imprinting on third dimensional physical bodies, and the vibratory core of people, on a cellular level, now has to rise. Everyone's medium abilities are being developed and these new Light pulsations are giving people a whole new reality. Everyone is changing and that change is happening now.

The timing of this book is important as it will help people work with and adapt to those changes. By using these meditations as a series of telephone numbers you will gain access to the new information about yourself and about the society in which we now live.

As you change, this book offers you the opportunity to become part of the group, to join the cosmic dance and be part of the new alignment which is known as the 'mind of one'. Teacher guides can reach you and individual guides can come closer. Astral interference can be understood, worked with and released. You can then go through the lower static astral levels and start to tap into the higher ones.

As you do that, you can use your natural abilities as there is only one rule now - that is you have no limitation in any shape or form.

A lot of Light workers are now coming up to the point of waking up. So the time has come to introduce a note of harmony - and the signpost of this book represents the signpost for the way home. Home being the 'mind of one'. As more people recognise that the Age of the Individual is over and the Age of the Group is here, we can have spontaneous healing and a feeling of tenderness and understanding that is necessary for you to become aware of who you are. Not the human in the human shell, but the immortal with access to your immortality.

So this book is a direct line to Avataric energy - a way to God's doorstep.

David Cousins
July 1993

INTRODUCTION

The planet Earth, as an entity in its own right, is becoming aware of its soul. Mother Earth is also moving from the third dimension into the fourth dimension. As this note of initiation takes place and the planet's soul begins to reflect this and moves closer to the physical plane, through the various subtle levels of matter, the vibrations of the planet are reflecting the immensity of this change.

As the planet restructures and its vibration heightens and becomes more focused in relation to the purpose that its soul is now demanding, so physical life forms on Earth, in all their diversity, also have to hear that change by adapting, changing, and becoming.

Although the planet has already become fourth dimensionalised on an astral level, the planet on a physical level, and humanity in the main, are still polarised in the third dimension.

Third dimensional reality is reflected in Chernobyl, deforestation, our feudal system and the artificial component of fear which is still deliberately cultivated. All these third dimensional aspects no longer have credence in the fourth dimension and will sooner, rather than later, have to go.

Fourth dimensional reality brings the capacity for us all to be telepathic, aware of the inner planes, and able to merge and meld with the mineral, plant and animal kingdoms as we all vibrate in unison, in the more total way that the New Age is demanding.

As fourth dimensional reality begins to focus and dominate and becomes the new key note - not only for the planet itself, but for all life forms who choose to remain here - the Earth will have the capacity to absorb more Light particles directly into her mass.

But to do this she needs us - the vast network of Light workers. In fact, the whole reason for human form on Earth at this time, is to interpret and partially digest these cosmic Light energies and pass them to the planet as she is not yet in a position to directly interpret them by herself. By passing these energies through human form, the planet can use this Light and distribute it on whatever level she requires.

This pattern is, of course, not so much a long-term event as short-term one which is already upon us.

At this time, Light workers - whom I call cosmic elves - are meeting this challenge by moving into a different frequency where life and the Universe take on a totally different meaning.

This book is, in essence, dedicated to those who are beginning to wake up and see. Dedicated to those who are starting to recognise the true essence of the Cosmic Christ, and beginning to acknowledge that all life, in particular humanity as a whole, is now working, melding and moving into a space where a deep love, harmony and purpose await.

And so in our own way, two hard-working little elves, Jean and myself, have actually invoked within this book a pattern of information, a pattern of opportunity to help you see more clearly.

We have also planned a campaign so that as you work with the exercises and meditations in this book, they will help you not only to stabilise your energy system, but will also give you a better awareness of this new reality.

So instead of feeling lost, abandoned, or forgotten, you can recognise that you are part of a large cosmic family which is now in a position to serenade and support you, and give you the identification you need to move on into a new polarity of understanding.

Understanding, of course, comes in many shapes and forms. The understanding is for you to define by personal experience, and by your capacity - under your karmic heading - to resonate with the vibrations or overtones of these words, with the thought forms behind them, and with the concentrated essence which this book offers you.

Working with this book will speed up your karma. You will be working with prosperity on all levels. Each meditation is a trigger mechanism that will push you into a new level of reality where you will have an opportunity to become yourself.

The trick is to know you have access to everything already. You just haven't remembered it. This book is therefore about remembering. Remembering who you are. Remembering the informational circuits you can use and being aware of the capacity love has to change everything. And to specifically recognise that fear is artificial and has to be transmuted in its totality.

So I invite you to freely participate in what is offered, by selecting and working with the areas of energy which you feel are appropriate to you, for your life's experience.

If you wish to use the keys wh   re in this book - which, of course, you will have to find! - th   en up the doorways that give you access to the subtle leve   your anatomy on both the inner and outer planes, in a way that can restore your harmony and your confidence in your own cosmic self.

With these keys you can also open up the gateway to the essence of your soul, which can then flow unhindered into your physical personality and in so doing, give you a better understanding of life, the Universe and everything that is currently unfolding around us.

This book is a pathway, an interdimensional doorway. It is both an indicator and a protective mechanism. It will enable you and all Light workers to participate in the bounty of what is to come. It is a probability of what the future will bring and is, therefore, a series of equations or key notes which will allow you to have a supporting mechanism to go over the abyss of doubt, fear and despair - and on the other side, when your vibrations have shifted sufficiently, you will then be in a position to harvest the land of milk and honey.

HOW TO USE THIS BOOK

When you start to work with the meditations in this book, you will find yourself shifting to a different level of being where you see and experience a whole new reality.

As you start to work with that reality, through the focal point of unconditional love, you will find your old need to suffer will be totally banished from your expectancy and your life purpose. Then, as you move off the ray of suffering onto the ray of love, harmony, power and joy, you can perceive and consciously live - physically, emotionally and mentally - on a whole new level of freedom.

This shift is akin to describing the human race as being blind, then as you start to work with the exercises in this book you start to see - and in full colour! In fact, many of you will already have started to intuitively perceive this - in which case you probably find that life presents you with difficulties as those who are still blind do not relate to what you are doing.

If you are ready to take this step - and the fact that you are reading this book means, on one level, you are - you will have to apply effort, discipline and perseverance.

Working with these meditations and moving into a new reality could also be described as the old you breaking both your legs. The old you is dependent on crutches while healing takes place, but once your legs have healed, you find yourself still depending on those crutches, on the support mechanism of those sticks, which are not really supporting you at all, but keeping you slow and bound up in old concepts and old conditions.

As the New Age energies come in they dispose of those crutches for you. As you try to walk on your own without them and try out your muscles, you may start to wobble. But as you improve, with effort, your muscles become stronger and firmer. You will quickly find that you start not only walking, but running down the intuitive pathway of life in a way that will enable you to link into the joy, love, power and beauty now waiting for you.

But to do this you have to try. At first you might think that some of the meditations in this book are a little complicated, or that they require a discipline that doesn't fit in with your busy schedule. If you think this, it is only your old thought forms that are resisting the shift you are about to make, for the human race has been conditioned to accept reality from an intellectual and emotional viewpoint.

When the going gets tough, don't give into the younger side, the primitive side, the saboteur side of you which has influenced your life to date. Just remind yourself that you are the butterfly! So even though the grub, as you might perceive yourself, is on one level frightened of the change - the great change that will enable you to fly - this metamorphosis is something you are now here to achieve.

Become that butterfly, that focal point of Light, grasp your own personal power and as you do that you can create your own destiny.

* * *

A Handbook For Light Workers represents a thought form which could best be described as a 'preprogrammed shell' with a frequency input inside it. As you read this book and cord into it, and as everyone else also reads it, you will all contribute energy in your own unique way.

As you become more flexible you will link into the teacher guides behind the energy input of this book. And as you allow its vibration to open your space, your awareness will also begin to flow more freely, and will be placed into the appropriate frequency setting within the thought form of this book.

Therefore, the next person who reads this will have an advantage. As more people read it, as more people are transformed, the vibration frequency behind this book will change. The people who read it at a later stage will have an even better advantage. As its thought form continues to grow, and as you and others work with the meditations, the frequency input of the magnetic, solar, angelic and astral energies will create a platform - a 'hall of learning'.

A person who then picks up this book, in say five to ten years after publication, will look at the meditations and these will flow into their space in a very easy and specific way.

So this book is a bit like a crystal skull. It is a preprogrammed event for the future as well as for the now. Therefore, each time you tap into this book and its frequency vibration, your heart will open in a unique and beautiful way.

While you may think you are doing these meditations to work just on yourself and on your own soul's path, in reality you are adding your frequency input to the thought form of this book, which will help many, many other people to wake up and move forward.

The *Key Aspects Of Meditation Work* form the foundations of the main meditations. If any of these are new to you, take time to practise them. When a main meditation sequence starts, "Bring white Light down through the top of your head and root yourself in," and goes on to say, "...put on your Light body," it is important that you know what to do and can easily flow into this before moving onto the main part of that particular meditation.

The text of this book includes information on the new energies coming into the planet, and how this is changing our lives here on Earth. I have covered all the topics of particular interest to Light workers and to those people who are waking up and seeking a better understanding of the new reality we are moving into. At the end of each chapter you will find meditations specifically relating to that text.

The meditations cover a wide range of topics including:
    How to raise your own vibrational pattern;
    How to detoxify your body and release negative energies;
    How to transmute thought forms that have a limiting effect
    on your life;
    How to test your guides;
    How to cleanse your computer and television;
    Advanced meditations to transmute personal karma.

In some chapters you will find several different meditations to work with one specific aspect, such as 'How to locate and transmute negative energies in a room'. So you have multiple choices.

We do this rather than being specific and saying, "This is the meditation to use. It has to be done this way!" The reason for this is that each meditation has its own governing note. As you become more aware of the energy within yourself and within the book as a whole, you will find yourself specifically gravitating towards the meditation with the key note that represents the quickest way for you to move from A to B.

It is also important for your intuitive potential to start working, so when you look at any meditation and think, "Oh, that looks good, but I'd like to do it subtly differently," then work with your intuitive sense of what is right for you.

Some meditations are aimed at helping you develop the flexibility to move your vibration up and down so that you can take advantage of situations, karmic and otherwise, as and when they are introduced into your field of awareness.

You will also find many different meditation practices to help you raise your vibration, long-term. As you work with those higher frequency energies you will start to remember and will find more diverse information starting to come in. You can then work freely with the group unconsciousness, and hence have access to any and all the information you need at any one point in time. This means, of course, that intuitively you can have the answer to any equation you are presented with at any time, now or in the future.

Other meditations will take you in and out of your meditative state to help you become more flexible. This flexibility is important since meditation, within most people's life, will start to become a natural 24 hour-a-day way of living, rather than just an isolated half-an-hour's meditation sitting down.

To sit down and meditate in order to bask in the God flow will no longer be necessary. As more people become cosmically rather than linearly orchestrated they will have the capacity, within their inner vision, to stretch their current moment of linear time into a thousand years of cosmic time.

Many Light workers are in fact already doing this. They are also finding that meditation, in the conventional way, is becoming more difficult because they have so much data coming in. Therefore they need to have active meditations as a natural part of their everyday physical life, as well as working in a meditative state within their astral, mental and spiritual orbit.

These meditations are therefore aimed at stretching you and moving you into the space where meditation becomes your whole linear life. As you work, walk, talk and do everything that is a normal part of your day, it will be one ongoing meditation.

As this happens and you develop the capacity to be in many places at once, and move in and out of the inner planes, then everything you do physically will have its symbolic reference elsewhere. How you live your life in every moment will have more meaning and become more important, both on a personal and planetary level.

You will then start to live, and become, the love of the God force that will be reflected in your behaviour and your attitude towards people.

As many of you will want to continue working with these meditations on an ongoing basis, and will want to create your own meditation programme, you will also find a full index of meditations at the back of the book for easy reference. In this index, meditations are listed under subject headings. This will help to give you an overview of the different meditations you can use for any one aspect and you can then choose the one that is right for you on that day.

If you are new to some of the terms used in this book, such as 'slow frequency energy', 'logos', and 'star gateways', you will find these covered in greater detail in the Glossary at the back of the book. All such terms are starred* when they first appear in the text. The Glossary is offered to you, both as a source of reference, and for those who wish to go deeper into the meaning of things.

KEY ASPECTS
OF MEDITATION WORK

In this section you will find all the aspects of meditation work that are regularly incorporated within the main meditations. Rather than repeat these sections over and over again, we give them in detail here, and then merely refer back to them where appropriate.

If any of these aspects of meditation are new to you, take time to practise them, so that when a main meditation sequence starts, "Bring white Light down through the top of your head and root yourself in," you will immediately know what to do, and can quickly flow into that before moving onto the main part of that meditation.

If you read one of the main meditations and find an aspect you do not know or fully understand, then come back to this section and practise that part before going back to the main meditation.

1. Bringing down white Light

When you first start to meditate the aim is to slow down your physical vibration, since many people's chakra* centres (*see Glossary under *chakras*) are far too open and are receiving conflicting patterns of vibrations - both slow and high. In this way a lot of people's vibrational pattern is higgledy-piggledy, and often their etheric and astral vibrations are too quick, or too high for their physical body.

The result is they attract slow frequency energy* which basically hangs on within their physical orbit creating pain, misalignment and problems within their physical body.

If you dash straight into meditation, you speed everything up straight away and put too much emphasis on the organs that are too slow. You also put a lot of pressure on the chakras that might already be in a point of disharmony, which increases your inner conflict.

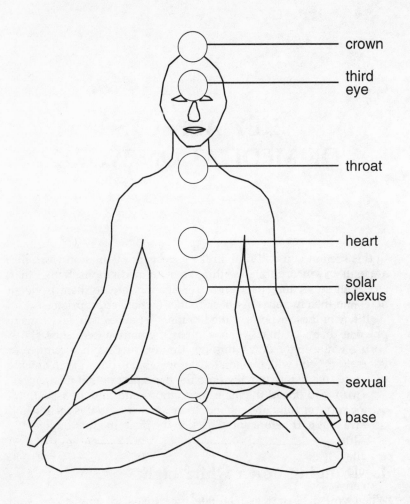

crown

third eye

throat

heart

solar plexus

sexual

base

The chakra centres

By slowing down your physical vibration to a slower frequency than you normally use, your muscles relax, your chemical factory stops being apprehensive, and you release any stress and anguish. As you do that, you get rid of a lot of treacly magnetic energy that tends to hang on in different chakra centres and within your auric field as a whole, and you remove the subliminal particles of thought interference from outside your auric space.

So instead of dashing straight into a meditation with your vibration all over the place, you slow it down first, then gradually raise your vibration again, but this time with everything in harmony.

In this way you don't stress any part of you, but bring it gently up to the right operating temperature. Rather like starting a car in a low gear then gently moving up through the gears, rather than screaming straight up to top gear and putting a lot of stress on the engine!

Slowing down your vibration

To initially slow down your vibration, sit with your back in straight physical alignment, with your weight balanced centrally. Rectify any bad posture so that your chakra centres are well aligned. Then focus on your breathing and start to breathe in and out in a steady rhythm. It doesn't matter whether you breathe in for a count of three and out for a count of three, or in for a count of seven and out for a count of seven. That depends on your own lung capacity and what feels comfortable for you. What is important is that you find your own natural steady rhythm, and breathe consciously with a steady breath cycle.

Now use your visualisation to take your awareness down to your base chakra, to slow your vibration down even further. As you then tap into the main part of this exercise, your vibration will automatically rise again, but this time with the chakra centres vibrating in harmony rather than in conflict with each other. In this way you have team effort rather than one individual chakra taking the strain for the lazy ones!

Although this isn't mentioned at the beginning of all the main meditations, breathing rhythmically to slow down your vibration should become a natural practice and should be done before going into any meditation in this book.

Bringing down white Light

Having found a comfortable position, found your natural breathing rhythm and slowed down your vibration, visualise white Light coming down through the crown chakra, which is the highest vibrational point within your body form. So always bring white Light in through your crown chakra as you are aiming for the best and the most beautiful!

Visualise the white Light flowing down through your body into each of your seven main chakra centres from the crown, down through the third eye, throat, heart, solar plexus, sexual centre and into your base chakra.

If you wish, in this practice session, you can visualise each chakra centre as being empty, then each one filling up with white Light as the Light flows into that chakra. As it does, use your awareness to also breathe into that chakra. As you do this, the centre into which you are breathing will become warm and eventually hot. As it becomes hot you will know that the centre has now filled with white Light and it is time to pass onto the next chakra centre.

If you have not done this before, take time to practise this and feel, sense or imagine the vibration of white Light flowing through each chakra centre, starting with the crown chakra and working down to the base chakra, until all your centres are full and linked into each other with this inflow of white Light.

2.   Rooting yourself in

Think of the rooting system of a tree. Now use your visualisation to imagine roots coming from your feet, going down into the planet and spreading out, just like the roots of that tree. As this happens, imagine your main taproot as something akin to a tail coming out of the base of your spine. Your roots are now the drawing mechanism that will enable you to draw up into your body the positive frequency, or vibration, of the female essence of Mother Earth.

As both your taproot and side roots go down into the planet, start to feel and be aware of a response from the planet flowing into your space. You can visualise this as your roots linking into an area of water, deep within the planetary core, that represents love, healing and the subtle Earth energy-cum-power.

As your roots tap into this Earth energy, feel it, sense it, and taste it as an expression of the higher energy of unconditional love. As you start to draw this energy up into your roots, visualise it as a colour flowing through them and up into your physical body. The colour that you need to work with will be the colour that intuitively comes into your mind. This can be any colour including black or white, since both black and white are the composite of many colours. As every colour has its own vibration and sound, the colour that you intuitively choose and draw up through your roots will represent the right vibration for you at that time. As you progress with your meditation practice, the colour you draw up through your roots will change as your own vibration changes.

We rarely spend enough time linking into the Earth. So working with this exercise, linking yourself into the essence of the planet, will not only give you stability but will also feed you with healing energy in a way that is very beneficial.

This exercise of rooting yourself in also anchors you before starting other meditation work.

3. Bringing down white Light and rooting yourself in at the same time

Imagine a rose that has not fully opened - it is still in bud form, waiting for the stimulus of the food input from Mother Earth. Waiting for the sun to help it grow, and waiting for the fulfilment of the imprint that is genetically within that rose.

In the same way, when you meditate and visualise roots going from your feet down into the planet, you are drawing up the Source of life that Mother Earth gives us. By bringing white Light down through the top of your head, you are also linking into the higher principle and resonating with the sunshine. In essence, you become that rose.

When you bring white Light down through the top of your head and root yourself in, you are linking into the higher and lower, linking into the essence of the Father energy of Heaven which the white Light represents, and the essence of the Mother energy of the planet. You are merging both aspects and by combining these energies you become neither male nor female, neither father nor mother, but rather a composite of everything that is best for you at that time.

4. Black healing meditation

This meditation is used as a positive focus to transmute, release and get rid of any unwanted slow frequency energy that is collecting within both your inner and outer auric space. Your inner auric space, which most people call the aura, surrounds the body in a rugby ball shape. It should be uniform in shape spreading out three to four feet (1-1.3m) around your body in all directions - above, below and out on either side. Your outer auric space, which I call the buffer zone, lies beyond that. This buffer zone normally prevents negative energy and energy interference coming into your aura, providing you are in good health. This buffer zone should normally spread out to about 15 feet (4.5m) around your aura. Both the aura and the buffer zone make up your auric space in its totality which, for the average person, would be about 18-19 feet (5.5-5.8m) around the body in all directions.

But a lot of people's buffer zone can be as thin as six to nine inches (15-22 cm), or even only half an inch (1 cm). Sometimes they have no buffer zone at all! It can also be distorted, so when astral entities touch the outer sheaf of your auric wall they can easily move in, like a sheep mite, and destructive tendencies can then take place.

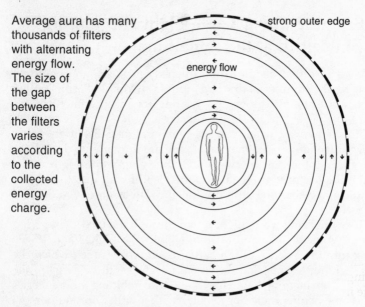

Average aura has many thousands of filters with alternating energy flow. The size of the gap between the filters varies according to the collected energy charge.

strong outer edge

energy flow

strong aura of a healthy person

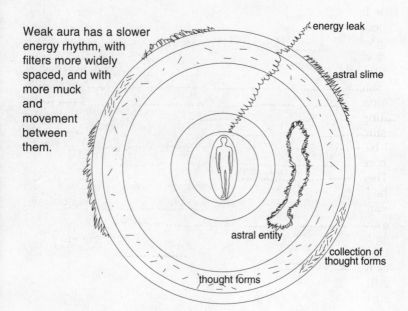

Weak aura has a slower energy rhythm, with filters more widely spaced, and with more muck and movement between them.

energy leak

astral slime

astral entity

collection of thought forms

thought forms

weak aura of a sick person

The aura and buffer zone

Black, as used in this book and in this meditation is the sum total of all colours which represent harmony, health and power. Unfortunately a lot of people tend to consider black as negative and a bit down-market. We have been taught, from long ago, that darkness is something to fear. When night-time or darkness comes, our vision contracts, we can't see, and fear of the unknown comes in. But this is an artificial, self-induced thought form, deliberately magnified by minds that should know better.

In reality, black is a very warm, healing and earthy current. It is a very positive, healing and beautiful way of working with Earth energies.

Black is also a descriptive term used to describe a certain wavelength, or frequency, and in itself is neither positive nor negative, until it is actually charged by the input of will orientation.

The black vibration is also slow compared to the quick vibration of white, or of Light. Therefore, by using black in a constructive way, you can actually rearrange the structure of any atoms that might be carrying far too much negative energy, and remove that negative charge in a very systematic, specific and safe way.

To do the black healing meditation

Sit or lie with your back straight and your chakra centres nicely aligned. Take a few deep breaths to slow down your vibration, then bring white Light down through the top of your head and into your heart chakra centre, then root yourself into the Earth. For this meditation you just bring the white Light into your heart centre at this stage, because as white Light comes into your heart chakra, a dominant signal is released which will go up and down the body creating a stabilising pattern of energy from the heart centre. If you are stuck in any of your lower chakra centres, your dominant signal will be emotional, therefore by stabilising your energy from the heart centre the whole vibration of your body can be lifted.

Then draw the healing black energy up from the female essence of the Earth, and into your roots. If this energy does not flow freely upwards, you can use your in-breath to draw the black vibration upwards, bringing it a little higher with each in-breath. As you bring the black vibration up through your roots and into your toes and feet, be aware of the feeling of harmony and health which the black represents, which you are now drawing into your body.

Allow the black energy to flow up your legs and visualise it filling the lower part of your body. Visualise the black energy flowing into all the major organs in the lower part of your body - sexual organs, intestines, kidneys, etc.

As the black energy flows up your body, symbolise any irregularities - any aches, pains, any problems of a physical or emotional nature - as ice cubes. Each time the black energy comes to an ice cube, focus on that, allowing the warm black energy to wash over it, like a wave coming in and out. As it does, visualise the ice cube gradually melting and see the melted ice being absorbed by the black. Then continue drawing the black energy higher up your body.

Continue to use your in-breath to draw the black energy up through your body in this way, dissolving any other ice cubes as you go, and visualise the black energy flowing up through your upper body, into your spleen, liver, lungs and heart. See it flowing up into your shoulders, then down into your arms and fingers, and also flowing up into your head. Be aware of it flowing into every part of your internal mechanism, including hair follicles and fingernails!

Having done that, visualise the black energy flowing out of the pores of your skin into your inner and outer auric space.

Then move your focus back to the white Light coming in through the top of your head, and amplify that Light by indicating to your higher self that you are ready to receive a lot more energy, recognising that you have an abundance of it external to yourself at all times. Feel that abundance of white Light energy manifesting and amplifying above your head. As the white Light amplifies, feel it flowing through the top of your head and down through your body like wave after wave, like sea waves coming into an estuary. This washes all the black energy out of your body and out of your auric space.

You do this entire sequence of bringing black energy up, filling your body, absorbing any irregularities and washing it out with white Light, twice more, making three times in all.

If you cannot bring the black energy all the way up your body during the first session, you can stop whenever you start to feel tired, or stuck, and flush the black energy out with white Light. Then repeat the meditation again the next day and continue doing this daily until you can completely fill up your body with black healing energy.

After you have done this as an initial cleansing meditation, you can do it regularly as an ongoing cleansing practice, last thing at night. With practice you will find that you will be able to do each complete sequence in about 20 seconds, although initially it may take a lot longer.

You can also do it as a cleansing focus during the day, wherever you are - even in the supermarket waiting at the check-out!

5. How to put on your Light body

Your Light body represents an archetypal pattern which can be an eagle, a snowy white owl, a hawk, an Indian bear, or a polar bear. In older times these archetypal patterns were used by medicine men and medicine women to help them when they went questing or seeking on the inner planes. These archetypal patterns represent the older essences of wisdom which have been used as vehicles in the conscious, subconscious and superconscious minds over the years. All the animals suggested are appropriate, and the archetypal pattern which you use in your meditations will be intuitively chosen by you, depending on the meditation and your individual need, although the eagle is the one most people still readily identify with. (You can also use a dolphin if you feel drawn to that, but it is usually best to keep it earthly.) To put on your Light body, the full sequence is:

Bring down white Light

First bring white Light down through the top of your head and root yourself in.

Accept your archetypal pattern

Visualise three points of pure white Light forming a triangle coming down and resting slightly above your head and behind your back. These points of Light will expand and wrap around you, enveloping you, a bit like putting on a cloak of power, or like the old monks putting on their hood - but in this case the hood represents the focal point of energy of the archetypal pattern you are using.

You then accept your archetypal pattern. If it is an eagle, you visualise an eagle's head coming over your head, with your arms becoming wings and your body becoming covered with feathers. If you accept the archetypal pattern of a bear, then a bear's head will come over your head, your arms will become paws and your body will be covered with fur.

Build up an energy charge in your heart centre

Physically fold your arms in front of you and cross them over your chest, with your palms facing towards you, and your hands or wrists laying one on top of the other over your heart chakra, depending on which position you find most comfortable. As you physically do this, visualise it as you crossing your wings or paws depending on which archetypal pattern you are wearing.

Now refocus on the white Light that is flowing in through the top of your head and into your heart chakra, and start to build up an energy charge in your heart chakra.

When you first bring white Light down through the top of your head and into your chakras at the start of this meditation, most people only bring it down through the outer aspect of their chakra centres. To build up the energy charge in your heart centre you work more deeply and more specifically as follows: visualise your heart chakra as being split into nine levels. As white Light comes down into your heart chakra, visualise it going down to the bottom level, filling up that level, then travelling up through the eight levels above - like the upward flow of water in a fountain. When the white Light has filled up all nine levels - just like that fountain - it flows out of the top of your heart chakra and flows down the outer aspect of your heart centre. In this way your heart centre becomes filled with a continuous stream of white Light, which will build up into a charge of white Light energy.

You need to allow time for this energy charge to fully build up. Because not only are you building up a frequency energy charge that will spontaneously dissolve negative energies and thought forms when that energy charge is projected, but this is also a process of self-healing as the energy charge is one of unconditional love.

When you initially do this exercise it might take up to 20 minutes to build up this package of energy, but with practice you should be able to do it in just five to six seconds. As with everything else, practice is the key!

As the white Light increases, you might feel a build-up of heat in your heart centre itself. You may feel the heat reflecting in your hands as they rest over, or close to your heart chakra. You may also feel a sensation of warmth creeping up your body, starting at the bottom chakra centre and moving up into your heart chakra - and your body might become quite hot.

Projecting your energy charge as a triangle of white Light

You then physically open your arms - but visualise this as opening the wings or paws of your archetypal pattern. As you do this, focus your will and visualise the white Light that you have built in your heart centre radiating out as a shaft of power or Light. See it flowing into and linking your third eye and both palms of your hands to form a triangular focus of energy.

You then project this triangle of Light, which is an energy focus of unconditional love, into whatever thought form or aspect of energy you are working with.

You project your triangular focus of energy by whacking it into whatever aspect you are working with, in short thrusts lasting five seconds. You don't have to hold this energy for any longer. What should happen is that as you allow your energy charge to flow in, it should interact fairly quickly to transmute and dissolve whatever negativity you are working with.

By using your will to manifest and project this triangle of unconditional love energy, you can change energy from a slow frequency into a high frequency vibration. You also give your own energy system a lift in whatever way is necessary for you at that particular time.

It is important to always project your energy in a triangular focus with the point upwards as the triangle represents a new input of the shape of the atoms that is to come, so represents both the new system coming in now and our future DNA*.

If this type of meditation is new to you, you may find that you need to practise this exercise several times, maybe even ten times or more, before you fully experience the power of the triangular focus of energy flowing through you. So if you do it a few times and think you are not feeling anything, continue with your practice, and one day it will just happen.

To practise working with your triangle of Light

1. You can practise this meditation by working on your food to raise its vibration before you eat it. To do this, you look at the meal you are about to eat and use your intuition to sense the package of energy that your meal represents. Then use your will and energy, through this meditation sequence, to project your triangle of white Light at the meal to raise its vibration. As you eat that food, the results will be self-evident.

2. You can also practise this meditation by cleansing objects in a room. Look around the room you are in and focus on any specific object, or area of the room which offends your feeling of rightness. Recognise that what you see or feel is an area of energy manifesting in a way that is unacceptable to your energy system.

If you are not yet able to feel energies, just work intuitively. Bear in mind that you cannot imagine anything that is not there, as the term 'imagination' is the vehicle which gives us access to the group unconsciousness. So by using your intuition and imagination you will naturally tap into the package of energy you are working with, and with practice will start to feel, see, sense, or even smell that energy formation within your awareness.

Now practise targeting that object, or area of the room, by projecting your triangular focus of energy into the heart centre of that energy formation. If you find it difficult at this stage to feel or see the heart centre of the energy formation - although this is something you will start to do as you work through this book and open yourself to this reality - then just send your triangular energy formation towards the object or area you are working on.

Continue to whack your triangle of energy into this one spot until you feel or sense the energy change as the tempo changes. You can then work on each corner of the room in turn, and you will find that the whole room will vibrate differently. Although you can work on the whole of the room at once, it is best to initially just focus on one place at a time.

Your first practice session may take about 20 minutes as you feel your way round the room. But as you progress you will find yourself looking at the room, zapping the energy in one clean sweep, and transmuting it in just five to ten seconds. Recognise that you don't have any limitation within linear time and you will find you do it quicker and quicker.

Charging yourself up

If you start to get tired while projecting your triangle of white Light, you are using far too much of your own physical energy. So every time you feel your physical energy slowing down a bit - you might feel this as a coldness in your heart centre - close your wings or paws and recharge yourself up. Then continue to project your triangle of white Light energy.

The very act of charging yourself up is achieved by the understanding within yourself that, as you close your wings or paws, you are actually opening up your crown chakra to an input of high frequency Light which will automatically give you healing, understanding, information - and the flexibility to allow the energy to build up again to a point that is acceptable for you.

To come out of the meditation

To end each practice session, you come out of your meditation by contracting the white Light back into your heart centre. Then contract your roots back from the planet and close down your chakra centres. To close down your chakras, which should be done at the end of every meditation, you visualise each one as a little gold rose. Then reverse the growth process seeing each rose going into a bud, and from a bud shrinking down to a point of white Light. Then visualise a small Celtic cross - an equal-sided cross within an outer circle - over each chakra centre and shrink each Celtic cross down to a point of white Light, which will seal and protect the chakras.

With practice you can speed up this closing down process by merely closing your wings (by folding your arms) and your chakras will then automatically close down. But until you are sure that you are closed down in this way it is best to work with closing each individual chakra using the rose process as above.

Bringing your astral body back

During meditation, your astral body normally drifts away a little and as you come back out of your meditation, there can be a tendency for your astral body to be out of alignment with your physical body.

In fact most Light workers' astral body is sitting a good six inches (15 cm) or more above the top of their head most of the time. So their astral body is not in their body at all, even during their normal waking day! And during meditation they are even more out of alignment. When your astral body is not fully aligned with your physical body, you are at a disadvantage as you are in a position where astral nasties can have a good nibble at you!

At the end of every meditation make sure your astral and physical bodies are aligned, by think of your feet and your fingers as being physically magnetised. Your astral body will then, like iron filings being drawn to a magnet, automatically flow back in through your whole body and will be centred and anchored by the magnetic pull of your fingers and feet.

As you feel your essence coming back into your body in this way, deepen your breathing so that more oxygen goes around your body, and become aware of the sounds of everyday living.

You should adopt the practice of centring and anchoring your astral body at the end of all meditations.

As you progress with working with your Light body

1. At the end of some meditations we suggest you keep your Light body on as a protective sequence which can be spontaneously reactivated when needed. If you then do another meditation which says, "Put on your Light body," in essence all you need to do is refocus on your Light body and reactivate it. You will know when you are at this stage because whatever archetypal pattern you have chosen will flow into your space without any resistance when you need to reactivate it. You should also be able to imagine it, feel it, taste it, smell it. There should be no resistance and no strain involved in reactivating your Light body. It should just be like slipping your feet into a very comfortable pair of slippers.

2. In all the main meditations in this book, we refer to this triangular focus of energy as being white. But as you progress and become intuitively aware of what vibration you need to work with for each different meditation, you may feel the colour of your triangle changing from white to pale blue or gold. Colour has a sound, and each sound is a frequency of multiple particles coming in, so depending on the frequency you are working with, the colour can change.

3. As you progress further you can also start to adopt the various vibrations which the shamanistic robe gives you, instead of the archetypal patterns.

Your shamanistic robe

The shamanistic robe is another form of Light body which you may sometimes intuitively feel is more appropriate for you, depending on the meditation and vibrations you are working with. The vibration of the shamanistic robe tends to drop your vibration down to your solar plexus chakra or below and is more useful to ground Light workers who are having difficulty in being earthed.

The term shamanistic robe is used to describe a vibratory package which is, in the main, third dimensionalised. But as the vibration on the planet begins to rise, the fourth dimension shamanistic robe will come into its own. Since most Light workers, within their vibratory core, are not balanced in a true sense within their physical, etheric, astral and mental bodies, initially using a third dimensional shamanistic robe, will bring the forgotten key notes back into their conscious awareness.

In older lives, most Light workers have had shamanistic journeys as wise old men or wise old women, living as the hermit, prophet, or seer. These have often been lives of great importance to help cement the physical and spiritual together. By working with shamanistic robes you can focus on those golden moments of the third dimensional age and rescue the cream of the third dimensional shamanistic experience, and use that as a focal point to develop the new fourth dimensional shaman experience.

The third dimensional shamanistic robe can be described as a highly decorated one which can change colour at will, since each colour is really a series of encodements, a series of sounds to help you to remember.

The fourth dimensional shamanistic robe will be a robe of white Light only. That white Light will be the higher key note of multiple dimensional time which will become the new vision you will work with.

The third dimensional shamanistic robe represents stability, strength, power of an old kind. So initially working with the third dimensional shamanistic robe is akin to a ballet dancer doing exercises to develop their muscles and gain the physical strength to do the subtle movements which require more intuitive skill.

The third dimensional shamanistic robe is, in the main, the vibrational form of animals that will stabilise and counteract any astral energy flow detrimental to your purpose as you move through this physical incarnation to a better understanding of the purpose of life in its totality.

Whereas the archetype of, say the American bear is very earthy, the shamanistic robe of the American bear has a different vibration and is a working pattern of Light molecules held together by conscious will, interpreted by experience. With practice you will start to feel the difference in their vibrations.

For example, if you work with a Light body that is the archetype of the American bear you will feel or sense its primeval strength and rawness. If you work with the shamanistic robe of the American bear, it will have a different vibration and you might find the brown colour of the bear will start to transmute, and flecks of gold or rainbow colours might form within its fur. As that happens, the archetypal pattern becomes activated by the higher knowledge of what the bear represents, not only genetically, but also by the way it brings in cosmic energies and transmutes them in relation to the planetary need, and our need as well.

All forms carry an energy charge that might be loosely defined as positive or negative. As you work with Light, all forms can basically be cleansed and then become Light-focused. By initially using third dimensional shamanistic robes, by accepting those of a slower frequency and heightening their vibration, you are basically stripping slow frequency toxic energy and stabilising the energy of the planet in a much more unique way and as such, preparing these robes for others who will be following you along the path.

This is akin to having a robe of office that has become particularly dirty because of abuse and the parties it has been to. Then taking it to the dry-cleaners to purify it, so that the next person who wears it will have something untainted. So as Light workers work more in conscious harmony with each other, becoming aware of the telepathic overtoning of the shamanistic robe, and aware that each time they enhance an energy charge with love and trust, the more that vibration will become an exclusive pattern for use by those who have access to that specific club. This is the club of unconditional love.

Initially, to get used to the shamanistic robe, you have to work through the third dimensional charge, before you can activate the fourth dimensional charge, and then use both in harmony together.

As you become aware of the different vibrations of Light bodies and shamanistic robes, you can start to intuitively tune in to the energies of the day as you wake up each morning. You can then open up your esoteric wardrobe of Light bodies and shamanistic robes, select the one you intuitively feel you might need during the day, and put it on so that you are in a state of preparation.

Like any wardrobe, you need to be flexible, because each day brings a different vibratory pattern of energy. Your physical, emotional and mental biorhythms will be slightly different to yesterday, and the vibrations of the planet, the sun spots* and the more distant planets will all magnetise or neutralise to a degree the vibration which might be confronting you on that day.

But with intuitive practice, you become a bit like the martial art expert who anticipates no problems, but is always prepared and aware that he has the capacity to deal with anything that may come in. His automatic reflexes then take over. In the same way you develop lightning reflexes in relation to the Light body or shamanistic robe you might suddenly need.

All these Light bodies are patterns, thought forms, specifically created for a particular performance. If you are an ice-skater, you go to the rink equipped with the ice-skating apparatus. If you are a rock-climber then you need different equipment. Likewise with Light bodies, you need different ones for different situations. To help you get to know them it is a good idea to practise changing to different Light bodies for different meditations rather than becoming dependent on just one particular archetypal pattern. In this way you will get to know the different vibrations of each Light body, and will start to clairvoyantly see, sense, feel or taste each one - depending on the sense range available to you at the time. With practice you will be able to easily change Light bodies, and choosing the right one in any one particular moment will simply become an intuitive feeling of rightness.

By experimentation, and by finding the right note within yourself, you will quickly discover the Light body or shamanistic robe that represents the best note of energy for you each day.

If you have been working with the archetypal pattern of an eagle and are at the stage where you keep it on as a protective sequence, then come to a meditation where you need a more earthy archetypal pattern such as the polar bear, take a moment to close down your eagle Light body, before adopting the Light body of the polar bear.

6.   How to fully close and open your chakra centres

The chakra system is a living thing - a bit like jellyfish in the sea, continually opening and closing, continually sampling their plankton. If they sample something nice they can open up and have more of it. If they sample something rotten they should close down fast. But a lot of people's chakras get stuck, maybe through spasm or shock during childbirth or childhood, then their centres are really, on one level, wide open to abuse. Usually these people are not aware of this until they try to close them and find they can't.

When some people first start to practise closing down their chakras they find they can't close down all their chakra centres, or they can only hold them closed for a short space of time. If chakra centres are not closed properly, then negative astral energy can get a foothold and cause little ruptures. By learning to close your chakra centres you will create a mechanism that will intuitively and automatically close them when you come into any congested area which might be harmful to your system.

Some Light workers think that if they close down all their chakras they are closed down and cannot radiate love and Light. This is an illusion.

Light can still radiate out from all your chakra centres, irrespective of whether they are closed or not. Basically your chakras are a series of filters which filter outward and, to a degree, filter inward as well. These filters will stop you from becoming harmed by energy interference coming in, but at the same time will allow an energy surge of Light and unconditional love to spontaneously flow out when needed.

Your chakra filters are karmic filters. They retain memories through the vibrational pattern of desire. A lot of these filters hold within them the vibratory levels of slow frequency energy which might be sitting within the wrong chakra centre. This can happen through trauma in a past life, during which the interchange of energies between the victim and tyrant entered the chakra sequence offered by the evolution of the people concerned and the placement of psychic energies available at the time. A person who had a bloodthirsty death, for example, might have received physical abuse and an emotional input of anger, rage or fantasy from the attacker. If that energy entered the solar plexus but wasn't released through the throat centre in the form of screaming - maybe because the victim had partially left their body, then the emotional solar plexus energy would stick in the throat.

Likewise if a person was tortured by people wanting information, and refused to speak, their emotional solar plexus energy which again needed release through sound would also stick in the throat centre. Whereas if the victim screamed or did speak out, the emotional sound could have been released.

In a karmic sense, this energy would eventually have to be released and given back to the tyrant. So a person in this life with throat cancer, who has to have his vocal cords removed, could well be the old attacker. His therapist who has to offer patience, understanding and sufficient love to teach the cancer patient to coordinate muscles in order to learn a new type of speech, may well be his old victim. Therefore the therapist has the opportunity to forgive, while the cancer patient might experience different types of fear as the old karmic energy is released back into his throat centre.

In this way misplaced energy which is clogging up a chakra filter as a slow energy sequence, might have been in that centre for several lives, rather than just in this particular lifetime. But as all karmic contracts are now up for renegotiation, you can now transmute any misplaced energy in any of your chakras, rather than holding onto it until it can be transmuted when the right karmic opportunity presents itself. In this way you can move forward much quicker.

If your chakra filters are clogged up and haven't been cleansed for a long time, then as you bring white Light into your chakras, and radiate that Light out through them, it is a bit like blasting congested soot from a chimney.

Then as you practise these meditations you will be able to strengthen your inner muscles so that your chakras open and close in harmony with each other, physically, mentally, etherically and astrally, rather than opening and closing out of sequence.

Because of a lack of training, when some Light workers send out a lot of high frequency energy, the response time of closing down the centres afterwards is slow. Therefore the closing down process needs to be practised and speeded up, so that chakras can be closed down within a split second, rather than taking three or four minutes, or not actually closing down at all.

Most people can't open their chakras either, or can't open them as fully as they should, therefore they have a small banding that they tend to live and work within, which is a limitation.

If you are not closing down fully, you are in a position of vulnerability. If you are not opening your chakras fully, you are not maximising the energy and power you could bring in. It is only by practising and expanding the opening and closing processes within each chakra, working with your inner vision, that you become aware of any limitations within your chakra centres, and can then work to release them.

To practise closing down your chakras

To close down your chakras, visualise each one as a little gold rose, and reverse the growth process back to a bud then to a point of white Light as explained in the closing down process for the previous meditation.

Alternatively, you can close down each centre by shrinking the frequency of each chakra down to the size of a black triangular button, which is given in Meditation 8, 'How to button up your chakra centres'.

To practise opening your chakras

To practise opening your chakras, start with your base chakra. Take your awareness into that chakra and see it as a little round circle, which is your base chakra in its closed sequence. Around that are ten circles, expanding in sequence, each one a little bigger than the one inside it.

Bring white Light down through the top of your head and into your base chakra. Take a deep breath in, and as you breathe out use your will and visualisation to push the chakra outwards, as if you were blowing up a balloon. Expand it outwards as far as you can go, and see it filling up with white Light as it expands. Initially you may only be able to expand the chakra out to say level five, although many Light workers will be able to expand each chakra out as far as level seven or eight. Hold that base chakra open as you breathe in and out, for five breath cycles, and with each out-breath see if you can push it out further. At the same time try to feel the centre becoming charged up and more expansive as you keep it pushed out.

Then reverse the process by relaxing and contracting your chakra as you breathe in and out. Visualise the white Light contracting down as you focus on the bottom end of the vibration within that chakra and in this way your auric muscles become more focused in relation to what your will is demanding. As you contract that chakra, see if you can close it down to a zero rating, then hold it in that closed sequence for five breath cycles and repeat the full sequence.

Then move up through all the other chakra centres, repeating this sequence with each chakra. With practice you will be able to fully open up each chakra to level ten, and close it down fully to zero. When you reach this stage you can then practise keeping it open at level ten for a few breath cycles, then close it down using the reverse process, and hold it in a closed position for a few breaths.

If you stand in front of a full-length mirror, you can focus on each centre in turn, and intuitively observe which chakra centre is misbehaving. You may be able to intuitively see if any centre is stuck open in spasm. Even if you can't see your chakras at this stage, regular practice, learning to both fully open and fully close your chakra centres is still important.

7. How to charge up each chakra centre

As you progress with these techniques, you may like to work more specifically at charging up each individual chakra. This can be done as part of a practice session when working with your Light body and projecting your triangle of Light, or it can be done as a separate session.

If you are doing this as a separate practice session, start as always by bringing down white Light through the top of your head. Then root yourself in and put on your Light body.

Now take your awareness down to your base chakra and visualise that chakra as an empty container being split into nine levels, with level one at the bottom and level nine at the top.

In the same way that you filled up your heart chakra with white Light when building up your energy charge with your Light body (Meditation 5), you bring white Light down through the top of your head into the bottom level of your base chakra and fill that level up with white Light. The white Light now starts to flow upwards, just like water flowing upwards in a fountain, and you visualise the white Light flowing upwards through your base chakra, filling up all nine levels. The white Light continues to flow upwards into the bottom level of your sexual chakra centre, which you again visualise as being split into nine levels. As the white Light flows up, it again fills all nine levels. Allow the white Light to continue flowing upwards in this way, filling up all nine levels of each chakra with white Light.

Once you have filled up all the chakras, you visualise the energy you have built up flowing out from the top of each chakra into the inner and outer aspects of your auric space, washing off any dirt or slow frequency energy which might have collected there. The white Light then flows out into your auric space. By doing this, the buffer zone around your auric space will also be purified. Quite often your buffer zone will be polluted even though the chakras may be relatively clear, so this washes your whole auric space and helps to clear any irregular rhythm which might be there.

When you have completed this, come out of your meditation in the same way as at the end of the practice session for putting on your Light body, by contracting the white Light back into your heart centre, contracting your roots back from the Earth, and closing down all your chakra centres.

Variation:

As an alternative practice, you can do this meditation as a basic breathing exercise. Start as before, bring white Light down through the top of your head, root yourself in, and put on your Light body. Again visualise each chakra being split into nine levels. Move your focus to the bottom level of your base chakra. Breathing at a steady rhythm, breathe in as you focus on level one, breathe out as you focus on level two then repeat this sequence twice more, making three breath cycles. As you do this, visualise level one filling up with white Light.

Then do another three in- and out-breath cycles, breathing in through level two and out through level three as you fill up level two with white Light. Then repeat this series of three breath cycles, breathing in through level three, out through level four, as you fill up level three with white Light. In this way you move up through all the levels. On level nine you breathe in through level nine and out through the top of the chakra, making a total of 27 breath cycles in all for the base chakra.

You then move up to the sexual chakra and repeat the whole sequence, and move up through all the chakras in the same way.

When you have completed this, you continue your steady breathing as you visualise the white Light flowing out into your auric space, washing off any slow frequency energy as before and come out of the meditation in the same way as before.

8.   How to button up your chakra centres and contract your aura as a protective sequence

This exercise will help to contract your auric field from wherever it is, to about 18 inches (45 cm) around your body. This is a good exercise to practise regularly, so that you can quickly button up your chakra centres and contract your aura as you go into a supermarket, or large group of people where there might be a lot of stress or slow frequency negative energy.

Auras continually expand and contract depending on the need of the moment. But the aura of people taking medication or drugs is often in a stagnant state, neither expanding nor contracting properly. Quite often people who have had anaesthetic will also have a stagnant aura for a period of three to four days after the operation, and this puts them in a position of vulnerability.

With continual practice, this meditation will programme your chakra centres and aura to automatically respond and contract whenever you go into a situation where you are being threatened.

With this meditation you will be working with each chakra centre in turn, starting with the crown chakra. You will be visualising each chakra centre on a one to three level basis, i.e. visualising each chakra as having three levels one behind the other. You will then be contracting the tension, or frequency within each level down to the size of a black button. In your visualisation, the black button should be in the shape of a triangle with the point upwards.

As an aid to help you understand the meditation, first draw three equal circles, about six inches (15 cm) in diameter. Cut out each one, then colour each one a different colour, but keep them all pale shades. For example, you can make one circle pale blue, and the others pale yellow and white. Now cut out a small triangle of cardboard the size of a button and colour it black. Lay the three circles one on top of each other, place the little black triangle in the centre of the top circle with the point upwards, and push a pin through the centre of the triangle and the circles behind that.

The three circles represent the three levels within each chakra centre, one behind the other, and the black triangle at the front is the size of the contracted frequency you will bring each level down to.

Using this as a working guide start the meditation. To do this, first think of white Light coming in through the top of your head and flowing down through each of your chakra centres in turn. Now visualise roots from your feet going down into the ground. The roots should be nice and slinky, and black in colour.

Starting with the crown chakra, visualise this as having three levels, one behind each other. Then visualise the energy in the first level darkening and use your will to contract the frequency of that level and bring it down to the size of the black triangle in your illustration. You then repeat this with the other two levels behind that, until all three levels are the size of the black triangle.

In this way you are contracting the multi-frequency levels of each chakra so that the whole chakra is nicely buttoned up. This will make it very difficult for any slow frequency energy to infiltrate your chakra system.

Initially, it might help you to do this meditation with two friends. You lay down on the floor and the other two dowse to see where your auric field is. Then do the meditation, and get your friends to dowse and test you again to see if you have contracted your aura. Take it in turns to do this so that you all get the opportunity to dowse and sense other people's auras.

Don't be surprised if after a day with this book your aura has expanded! But your total auric space, including your buffer zone, should normally be about 18 feet (5.5m) around your body in all directions.

9.   Exercise to move into your chakra centres

Within the vibratory gateways of each chakra centre are multitudes of informational notes you can tap into. Tuning into this information has to be done totally intuitively. You can't prepare for it, but your intuition will tell you which chakra centre you need to tune into at any one point in time. So just focus specifically on whichever chakra centre feels right for you to work with, and allow the information that you need to flow.

To do this, bring white Light down through the top of your head, visualise it flowing through all your chakra centres, then root yourself in, linking yourself into the higher and the lower. As you do this, your physical vibration will slow down, getting rid of stress and tension.

Then in your visualisation, drop your awareness down to your base chakra. Using your will and visualisation, move up through your chakra centres, through the subtle planes of awareness to find the right octave where you will find the gateway you need to go through to knowledge, understanding and informational law.

To help you understand this, think of the analogy of going up in a lift. In your visualisation, see a lift with the lift door level with your base centre. The lift door will open and you step inside and push the right button in your awareness that says, for example: "Right, today I need to work with my solar plexus."

The lift door then closes and the lift takes you to the floor level with your solar plexus chakra. As the lift door opens you will normally be met by your guide, or a representative, who will indicate in their own way what it is that you need to do, or know.

It could well be that you just need to wait, contemplate, and be open to what comes through before going back down in the lift. Or you may have some additional work to do, or some folk to meet in your awareness who can share with you the symmetry of the information you are linking into.

Only work with one chakra within each session, as the concentration required for this exercise is initially quite difficult for most people. If you try to push yourself too fast, and try to work with more than one chakra in each session, you may burn off too much energy and will start to feel tired.

To end the meditation, as a general rule irrespective of what chakra centre you have been working with, it is best to find the point of reality within yourself that represents your own personal area of peace. For Light workers this would normally be within the bottom part of the heart chakra centre.

So just allow your awareness to concentrate on the bottom part of your heart chakra for a few seconds. Then, still based within that point of harmony within your heart centre, you amplify the Light coming in through the top of your head, and visualise it flowing down your body through each chakra. Allow the Light to help you see or feel any rightness or wrongness within the chakra centre you have been working with.

Now become aware of your roots and your earthing mechanism. The best way to do this is to take your awareness into your feet and feel your feet expand and become heavy.

With your feet nicely rooted you can now make sure your astral body is back and fully aligned. As mentioned before at the end sequence of *How to put on your Light body*, your astral body normally drifts away a little during meditation and as you come back out of your meditation, there can be a tendency not to be astrally centred within your physical body.

To remind you of the visualisation technique to make sure your astral and physical body are aligned: think of your feet and your fingers as being magnetised and your astral body will then, like iron filings being drawn to a magnet, automatically flow back into your body. It will be centred and anchored by the magnetic pull of your fingers and feet.

As you feel your essence coming back into your body, deepen your breathing and become aware of the sounds of everyday life.

Then make sure that each chakra centre is closed down, because often in one's rush to come out of the meditation you might have inadvertently left a doorway open. If any centres are still a little open, visualise them closing like the rose becoming a bud then a point of white Light. Bless and dedicate them to Light and understanding, and to the protection of your higher self. If you wish you can also visualise a little cross of white Light over each chakra centre and shrink each cross down to a point of white Light, which will seal and protect your chakras.

10. Making intuitive decisions

In many of the meditations in this book, we tell you to intuitively ask your higher self for required information. If you initially feel unsure about the responses you get, remember that you can't imagine anything that isn't there!

Intuitive excellence is based on the first impression you get. So stay with your first impression. Often when people start to get intuitive flashes they tend to dismiss them and think it is just their mind playing tricks on them. They allow doubt and logic to argue with that intuitive insight. But the only way to develop your intuitive excellence is to always assume that what you are getting is accurate. Then have enough love for yourself to trust your first intuitive impression, and know that what you are getting is, in fact, an accurate interpretation from your higher self. With this work, there is no limitation except the limitation your thoughts and old conditioning place upon you. It is now time to step beyond limitation and wake up to your full potential.

In some meditations we give you an either/or aspect to do. In these cases it is up to you to decide which aspect is right for you - remember each time you make an intuitive decision you are allowing your higher self to guide you along the best path for you.

11. Traffic light dowsing

You can use this method as a tool to help you make intuitive decisions. To understand the principle of traffic light dowsing simply think of traffic lights - red, amber and green. Using this analogy, your higher self can show you the right response for your intuitive decision process, by giving you a 'yes' (green), 'no' (red) or 'maybe' (amber) in reply to your question.

You can use this method of intuitive dowsing for many things, such as choosing the best food for your optimum health. For example, if you are buying apples, intuitively ask your higher self for a traffic light response and you might be surprised to find that the apples which look absolutely gorgeous give you a red 'no' response. This could mean they have been irradiated or sprayed with chemicals. An amber light might be an indication that the apples have been magnetically stored for too long in one place, the vibration in the apples might simply be on a nuisance level, or there might be a bug inside. If all the apples give you a red response, go elsewhere and only buy apples with a green 'yes' light over them which tells you these are the best ones for you.

You can also do this to select foods which will give your body the right balance of vitamins. For example, if you think there is a lack of B vitamins in your diet, look around at the choice of food available and choose the food which you see or feel gives a green 'yes' response.

You can also use traffic light dowsing for any specific decision, such as when is the best time of day for you to meditate (see below). You can even ask your higher self when is the best month to go on holiday, using the red, amber, or green response to help you choose the month when you will have enough prosperity and so on.

If you use this system in your daily life you will enhance your confidence as you will be constantly linked to your higher self. This will allow a much clearer input of energy to resonate from the Source to yourself.

12. Intuitive dowsing to find the best time of day to meditate

As planetary and Earth energies are constantly changing, the best time of day for you to meditate may be different every day.

At different times during the day and evening, and during the weekly and monthly cycles, planetary conditions sometimes connive so that the biorhythms in both the planet and the cosmos actually create a package of energy that produces static like a snowstorm. This is difficult to penetrate.

On those days it would be best to just concentrate on physical exercise and earthing your physical vehicle. When the reception is better, that is the time for you to tune in.

In this way you follow the law of least resistance. Instead of burning up a tremendous amount of effort and energy - as happens if you rigidly meditate at the same time every day irrespective of conditions - you can tune in and know when it is best to meditate, rather than just feeling you want to, or should do.

So first thing in the morning, when you wake up, ask your higher self whether it is right for you to meditate that day. Use traffic light dowsing for your answers. If you get a green 'yes' response, then ask yourself which time of day is best to meditate. For example, you can ask, "Would it be best for me to meditate at 7am today?" If you get a red 'no' response then ask, "Would it be best for me to meditate at 8am today?" If you again get a red 'no' response, repeat the question for each hour that you are able to meditate, according to your day's schedule, until you get a green 'yes' light.

In this way you will coordinate all the best vibrations available for you that day.

13. How to cleanse a crystal

To cleanse a crystal, soak it in a mixture of one pint (half a litre) of water, a dessertspoon of sea salt and a teaspoon of cider vinegar for a minimum period of one hour. Cider vinegar seems to speed up the absorption of negative energy into the sea salt. If you don't have any cider vinegar you need to soak it in just sea salt and water for much longer - at least eight hours, or ideally overnight.

By doing this your crystal will be cleansed and freed of a lot of magnetic energy. Then bless and dedicate your crystal to put your own particular stamp on it.

14. How to dedicate and bless a crystal

There are many ways to dedicate and bless a crystal, but you may like to try one of the following ceremonies:

First ceremony

In this ceremony, hold the crystal in one hand, or if it is a large crystal hold your left hand by the left side of the crystal, and hold your right hand over the top of it.

Then bring white Light down through the top of your head, and visualise this as bringing down the male aspect of the Father God. Visualise roots coming out of your feet, going into Mother Earth, and in this way you link yourself into the female aspect of the planet.

Allow the white Light coming down through the top of your head and into your heart chakra to build up in your heart centre. Now move your awareness into your solar plexus centre, allowing the white Light to also flow into your solar plexus chakra. You will then be presented with a symbol specifically for this crystal and dedication ceremony. This symbol may be different for each crystal, so each time you do this ceremony, be open to a new symbol being presented to you, if necessary.

Take this symbol up into your heart chakra. Enlarge it and place a duplication of this symbol in both hands and feet. Now visualise the white Light flowing from your heart down both arms into your hands, and flowing down into both feet. This will amplify the symbol which will in turn amplify the energy pattern required for this specific ceremony. You are not building up a triangle of Light as you do when you work with your Light body, you are just passing an energy charge directly from your heart, into your hands and feet.

This white Light then passes out from your hands into the heart centre of the crystal. If you find it difficult to feel or sense where the heart centre of the crystal is, just pass the Light into the centre of the crystal itself. As you do that, dedicate and bless the crystal to truth, Light and understanding - bearing in mind you are also passing in the unconditional love you are bringing in, through your heart chakra, in the form of white Light.

As the white Light passes into your crystal you should feel warmth being expressed in the crystal at the point where your hands are. This warmth usually manifests in two to three minutes. If your crystal feels cool, continue to pass white Light into it until it feels warm. You might also feel a tingling from the ground energies or a slight tightening around your crown chakra as you work with the Light energy during this dedication and blessing ceremony. This is quite normal, so just allow these sensations to flow through you.

Once the dedication and blessing ceremony is complete you contract the outer symbol in your hands and feet, feeling the symbols contracting and moving up through your arms and legs into your heart centre, where they will be absorbed into the bigger symbol. This bigger symbol will then drop back down into your solar plexus centre where you visualise it as a buckle on a golden belt, which you attach round your waist. Each time you want to energise the crystal, you just amplify the symbol which you are wearing around your waist. The symbol might change if you have a specific type of energy to bring through which requires a speciality role, but in general your symbol should remain active throughout the rest of your life.

Second ceremony

Stand or kneel in front of a candle, facing north. Then light the candle. Bring white Light in through the top of your head, and put on your Light body.

Now link into the host of Light workers symbolised as the Cosmic Christ who will be standing directly behind you. Feel this energy of the Cosmic Christ as the sun's energy flowing in through the top of your head and into your heart centre. You will feel a tremendous strength, warmth and vitality building up in you as a whole. So you will have both the white Light of the Father God, and the unconditional love of the Cosmic Christ coming through the top of your head and into your heart chakra.

Hold your hand over the crystal, and visualise the Light of the Cosmic Christ, which is an outpouring of unconditional love, flowing from your heart centre, down into your hand, and out into the heart centre of the crystal.

Then dedicate your crystal to love, freedom, right use of will, understanding and knowledge. Bless it with whatever words come naturally into your mind, depending on your intuitive impressions and your understanding and belief of the God force.

Alternatively you can just ask for the blessing of the spiritual hierarchy or the Cosmic Christ to seal the energies of your crystal.

After the crystal has been dedicated and blessed it will be protected and sealed from any negative energies which an external force might send towards it.

The advantage of doing this is that any negative energy being directed towards the crystal will then be bounced back to the person who is sending it, and their higher self will be ever so pleased, although the personality might be very cross.

To dedicate and bless a candle

Use the sequence in the second dedication and blessing ceremony above, but hold your hand in front of the candle, with your palm facing the candle, so that your white Light energy passes from the palm of your hand into the candle flame.

15. Dowsing with a dowser or crystal

To practise dowsing, first choose the dowser you would like to work with. This can be a personal slim crystal with a point on the end which hangs on a chain, or any slim object suspended on a length of string, or cord, about six to nine inches (15 - 22 cm) long. If you are using a crystal on a neck chain, fold the chain in half.

Hold the chain or cord between the thumb and first finger of your right hand if you are naturally right-handed, or in your left hand if you are left-handed. Your dowser should now be suspended about six inches (15 cm) below your fingers.

First of all practise getting a 'yes' and 'no' response from your dowser. The best way to do this is to simply ask your dowser to give you a 'yes' response. Your dowser should then move in a clockwise or a backward and forward movement. Then ask for a 'no' response and the dowser should then move in an anticlockwise or sideways movement.

If, initially, you find the dowser doesn't respond or move, sit down and hold your dowser about six inches (15 cm) over your right knee if you are right-handed, or over your left knee if you are left-handed. Then again ask for your 'yes' response. The dowser should then move as above. Then repeat over the other knee for your 'no' response.

Having established which movement is your own 'yes' and 'no', now practise using the dowsing as a technique. You can do this by asking simple questions that have a 'yes' or 'no' answer. Explore your way around this and you will find it is a lot of fun!

Now try some dowsing hunting. This is a term used to find irregular patterns of ground energies. To do this, walk very slowly about your room, or garden, and as you walk very slowly the dowser will move in a straight line, back and forth, normally away from your body and back again. But if you hit any irregular patterns of energy, it will either swing in the direction of where that is flowing, or will swing in a spiral.

You can then step to one side and ask if it is an underground flow of water, a ley line, or a distorted ground energy.

If you want to go into this more deeply, some good books on dowsing are listed in the Appendix.

16. How to find your centre of balance, the polarity point or hara within your body

The hara* is normally referred to as the energy centre, or physical point of balance, which is static within the body, at the navel just below the belly-button. But the hara I refer to is the point of balance, or centre of gravity, that moves around and, therefore, might be in any part of your physical body or your subtle network of bodies.

For the sake of definition the hara is a term I use to indicate a level of energy vibrating at a certain frequency. The hara, therefore, is a package of energy which can be applied to and found in a cell, an organ, or even a larger body form like the Earth. But within the human body as a whole, the hara is a placement setting which is a focal point where a person - through discipline and perseverance - can focus their will and have feed-back. This gives them the capacity to assess what their vibration is actually doing within the particular part of their body they are focusing on.

But most Light workers when initially working with this, sense their hara within their chakra system. The hara, your polarity point, moves up and down through your chakras and shows you whether you are vibrating too high or too low, or whether in fact you are at the right vibrational level for a Light worker.

The ideal positioning of the hara for the New Age person, when you are into your power and bringing through high frequency energy, is in the middle or lower part of your heart chakra. When you are human and therefore not radiating energy in a specific high frequency sequence, your hara should be in the middle or top part of your solar plexus chakra. In any of these positions you will be at peace with yourself and in a state of neutrality.

With your hara in the middle or lower part of the heart chakra, or in the top or middle part of your solar plexus, you are at a point of balance. You can then use this as a reference point when looking at your main organs and see if the hara of any particular organ is at the same vibratory note. If, for example, your kidneys are under strain, either chemically or from astral pollution, the hara of your kidneys will reflect that stress by being in a lower position than the nicely balanced hara in your chakra system.

The hara for Light workers should not be in the emotional lower part of the solar plexus chakra or in any of the lower chakras. And certainly not above the heart because the frequency would then be far too high, you would be vibrating out of key with the planet, and your earthing would not be adequate.

People with too much high frequency energy coming into their body, and those people with extraterrestrial memories, are usually vibrating far too high. This is reflected in their hara which will be sitting in their throat centre, or their third eye. Clairvoyantly you can see their astral body is out of alignment, with their astral feet level with their physical knees.

General physical symptoms of this can manifest as a feeling of being light-headed, and sometimes with a slightly raised blood pressure. Depending on the person's vibration this might also manifest as low blood pressure, an inability to concentrate or to remember simple things - people's names for example - or a feeling of being in many places at once. It can also manifest as feeling unhappy, lonely, rejected, frustrated, or a feeling of irritation with other people being physically too near you. It can also result in an inability to do physical exercise - almost as if your will has been eroded - yet feeling deliciously better once physical exercise has been done.

Other physical symptoms can include being physically underweight, a lack of appetite, allergies to foods, sensitivity to weather and its movements which might manifest as headaches, and migraine in all its forms.

If you are vibrating too high, work with the following meditation to practise dropping your hara down to your base chakra. It will then sit there for a short while before automatically moving up again. By doing this regularly, you can bring your overall vibration down to the right level for you. Practising the meditation to button up your chakras and shrink the three levels within each chakra down to a small black triangle will also help. (Meditation 8)

People who are, in the main, aggressively violent will be vibrating too low and their hara will be in their base centre or in the bottom part of their sexual chakra centre.

To help you visualise your hara, symbolise your chakra system as being a thermometer, with your hara moving up and down in the same way that mercury moves up and down a thermometer. Then to find out where your hara normally sits, intuitively feel into your chakra system first thing in the morning as you wake up. If you prefer you can use the traffic light dowsing and see which chakra centre gives you a green light. This will show you where your hara is.

Then check again during the day to see what your hara is doing, as your hara and your vibration will move up and down depending on what you do and the stimulus around you.

17. How to raise and lower your centre of balance, your polarity point or hara

With all life forms the centre of balance, or hara, can be in any particular chakra centre, depending on the evolution of the life form, be it on the inner or outer planes.

If you want to communicate with an aspect of awareness whose vibration is higher or lower than yours, you have to raise or lower your vibration by raising or lowering your hara, to match their frequency. Communication can then take place. Angels, for example, normally vibrate within their third eye. A large dog which is aggressive would normally be vibrating in his base chakra. By raising and lowering your hara, you can adjust your vibration to match whatever life form you want to communicate with. Below are two exercises to help you do that. It is important to practise this so that when you come to a meditation to connect with nature or any life form, you will be able to drop or raise your vibration to match their frequency.

Just because you are working with love energy, don't assume you can contact all life forms through your heart chakra. If a tree for example is solar plexus activated, then trying to contact that tree through your heart centre will create a distortion of energy that will block communication. It will be a bit like trying to speak Chinese to a French waiter. You won't get very far!

First exercise

This exercise is done in a swimming-pool, or can be done in the sea. As you put your feet into the water or walk into the shallow end, try to feel which chakra centre is being activated. This will tell you where your hara or point of balance is at that moment.

As you go deeper into the water, the natural human response is to keep one's head above water, so your centre of gravity will automatically work its way up through each chakra centre and will normally rest in the throat chakra while you are swimming.

If you float on your back your hara will normally move down to your heart centre.

If you swim underwater, your hara will normally drop down to your base chakra as you go down. If you have difficulty swimming underwater, assuming you have no conscious fear that you are aware of, then obviously your centre of gravity is staying at a higher chakra level which is stopping you from going under.

So move around the swimming-pool or in the sea, swimming, floating and diving and see if you can feel your hara moving up and down. Initially this is done intuitively, although with concentration you may immediately feel some sensation within your body.

Second exercise

This exercise is done merely by using your intuitive awareness to see in which chakra centre your hara is active. This will show where your hara is sitting within your body at that time. You will then use your will and power of visualisation to move your hara up and down.

First of all bring down white Light and root yourself in. Then intuitively look to see where your hara is. You can use the traffic light dowsing technique to give you a green light over the chakra where the hara is active.

When you have your intuitive response as to where your hara is, visualise a horizontal line being drawn through your body at that point. See all your body beneath that hara point as being flooded with colour from planet Earth. The best colour to use here is sky-blue. So from the hara down your body would be sky-blue, and from the hara up the colour is a representation of the vibration coming in through your higher chakra centres which is normally white, or possibly gold or pale pink. Your intuition will guide you as to what colour is right for you to use.

Then take a deep out-breath, and as you breathe out visualise your hara dropping downwards in your body. Or visualise it being pushed down by your out-breath. As your hara drops down, it pushes all the sky-blue colour downwards and all your body which is now above the hara fills up with your chosen higher colour. As you breathe out, also feel your body becoming relaxed and heavy.

Then take a deep in-breath and visualise yourself becoming lighter, as if you were floating upwards. At the same time try to visualise your hara floating up your body, pushing all your higher colour up with it, and as it does, all your body below your hara fills up with sky-blue.

Continue to practise this exercise, moving your hara up and down, visualising your lower and higher colours moving up and down with the hara until you can actually sense or feel your hara moving. At first you will just be working with your power of visualisation and may feel nothing. But be patient. It may take some time before your perception of your hara moving comes into play. Until then just work with visualisation and know and trust you are using your will to actually move your hara up and down, thereby raising and dropping your vibration.

As you start this practice, you may initially find it easy to drop your hara all the way down to your base chakra, but find it difficult to move it up higher than your throat centre. If this happens, don't force it. With practice your flexibility will improve and the aim is to eventually move your hara all the way from the base chakra to the crown chakra, and back again.

Grounding yourself

If ever you feel a bit light-headed after any meditation, you can ground yourself merely by intuitively asking yourself where your hara is. Then focus your awareness on that chakra centre, and using your visualisation drop your hara down to your base chakra. Your hara will stay down in your base chakra for a little while and will then automatically go back up to its correct sequence within your body.

Working with ground energies

The exercise above is also useful if you are working with ground energies, although on this occasion you drop your hara all the way down to your feet. To practise this, you can visualise dropping your hara down to your feet - seeing it dropping or flowing downwards - or you can just take your awareness down into your feet. With practice you will find the variation that works best for you.

Then do a meditation on your feet by releasing all the miles you have ever walked from the feet themselves, then visualise your feet becoming transparent and expanding to about six feet (2m). This will have the effect of opening up the minor chakra centres* in your feet quite nicely!

Now visualise roots from your feet going down into the Earth. Visualise your roots acting as antennae through which you are able to pick up and feel the vibrations you need to harmonise with. This can be crystalline structures, archetypal patterns of fire, earth, air and water, or you can link into all the streams, all the oceans of the world, depending on the ground energies you want to work with.

CHAPTER 1
THE SOUL'S JOURNEY

In the beginning, when the soul is at the Source within the God formation, it is part of the 'ocean of life' which is the unity of everything - the God force. Within that ocean of life a continual process occurs whereby a vibration sends a little ripple in one direction and reality undergoes a subtle change. When that happens the 'ocean of life' gets whipped up by the atmosphere and is whisked up into the air where it separates into different little droplets of divinity.

When that happens, a soul within one of those 'droplets' awakens. It becomes aware of itself as a separate entity, even though it is still part of the overall package that is the Source, and becomes aware of sensation outside of itself. In order to interpret that sensation, the soul creates vehicles which are the subtle bodies.

To begin with the soul only creates minor subtle bodies, but as it does it is drawn away from the Source into different levels of reality. As it becomes more focused in that reality, it has more sensation and creates more subtle bodies.

In this way the soul gradually moves further and further away from itself, which is the Source, which is one and the same, as we are God even though we have forgotten that.

As the soul starts its downward journey, spiralling down through different realities, it becomes aware of the capacity to be in more than one place at once. It then starts to split itself up and creates an aspect of itself which starts its own journey, in turn developing its own unique personality.

The stage at which a soul actually splits depends on the individual soul. Some tend to be stubborn, holding the vestige of vibrations within a nucleus of three aspects. Others actually split themselves spontaneously - it depends how quickly they become aware of each other and how quickly they become aware of other souls like themselves.

As a general rule, most souls split themselves into seven aspects very quickly during the start of the downward journey. They then use the capacity to split each of these main aspects as an 'optional extra' when they have moments of particular difficulty to overcome.

Each soul aspect* might take millions and millions of years, and several millions of lives to complete its downward journey.

As they travel down through the various levels, each soul aspect picks up on various states which can be termed the more refined forms of extraterrestrial life. They 'clothe' themselves in different vehicles in order to interpret the vibrations and experiences within each state. So a lot of extraterrestrial lives in gaseous, crystalline and angelic forms would have been experienced in order to give a soul aspect enough growth, or 'Brownie points' to be able to incarnate into Earth.

During the downward journey each soul aspect also picks up a lot of static or magnetic energy which is termed desire. This desire makes the soul aspect addicted to matter and takes it further and further down into the grosser levels.

During the downward journey soul aspects also become aware of other soul aspects similar to themselves. These soul aspects band together in different coloured units, or family units, which make up a soul family. As each soul family collects more data they tend to share karmic notes to help each other through difficult spots and basically to speed up their whole endeavour.

Slowly, over millions of years, each soul aspect comes down through the mental levels into the astral or emotional kingdom, and continues journeying downwards until it comes to the grossest one - the combination of the first, second and third planes - which is the physical plane in which we now find ourselves.

As it hits the physical plane it has to clothe itself again by experimenting with the variations found here. It does this by working in a spiral through all the permutations of the mineral kingdom, then all the permutations of the plant kingdom, and continues in this way through the animal kingdom.

Therefore, in essence cats and dogs are young soul aspects working their way towards human incarnation, and are the highest vibration in animal form which is why they have a high degree of intelligence. Quite often domesticated animals will learn a lot as they mimic the vibratory core their masters bring. Since they are kept in an artificially immune environment they don't have to cultivate their wild instincts which then get blunted. This allows them to fully absorb the vibration of their human hosts and to feed off the emanations which humans give to their younger 'brothers and sisters'.

When a soul aspect has earned the right to move into the top echelon in matter, which is the human body, it can then start to clothe itself in the most refined vehicle it has to play with during its full journey, since it is only in the human kingdom that a soul aspect can experiment with free-will.

One could describe this downward spiral by using the analogy of losing your memory, then waking up one morning and finding yourself in a wigwam. As you look outside you see strange territory. At first you just sit there and take it all in, but after a while you pluck up enough courage to go outside and explore.

As you start to do so you develop new skills in order to survive. You come back each night to your wigwam with that newly acquired information, and as you get more adventurous you feel the urge to go further and further afield. The further away you go, the less opportunity you have to get back to your wigwam each night.

Then, as the wanderlust becomes fiercer, you finally leave your wigwam altogether. You start to travel over mountains and lakes, cross deserts and continents and, because of the stimulus these adventures bring and through the people you meet, you tend to forget where you came from. On the way you give 'birth' and those aspects of yourself travel off on their own journeys.

Finally you come to a massive ocean which you might try to cross, but find that you can't. The ocean becomes a barrier and you have to stop your journey.

This is what has happened in the main to everyone currently on Earth. During their downward journey they have forgotten where they came from and now have to remember again. This takes some doing because all the stimulus encountered as we worked further and further away from the Source has blocked out those memories.

For most soul aspects that massive ocean, that final barrier is, in reality, the slowest or grossest plane which is the physical one in which we are now living.

When a soul aspect comes into the physical plane and works through the permutations of minerals then moves on into the plant life, it forgets all about its experiences in the mineral kingdom. When it goes from plant life into animal life it forgets the plant kingdom. When it goes from animal into human it forgets the animal kingdom. But in essence a soul aspect is still a composite unit of everything that has passed before. The remembrance is still there in a latent form and can still be activated. So within each soul aspect multiple impressions build up to a point of crisis before it is thrown forward into a different vibration. Only when a soul aspect has burnt up all the permutations and moved on, will it be content.

This is why devas*, elementals, angelic states, and extraterrestrials to some degree, all want to come in as a human vehicle, since it is only within the human vehicle that emotional states can be experimented with.

As the DNA moves into a more specific vibratory pattern where it can support more high frequency life forms, the contract of building up the new DNA structure which some souls have agreed to work through, can help those who have not yet started this evolutionary process and so the genetic experiment is on an ongoing basis.

Because of the complexity and beauty of the DNA structure, physically, etherically and in the more subtle states, those who are outside this 'system' at the moment realise it is only through the human vehicle that one can become God realised and complete the circuit. Therefore, our extraterrestrial neighbours are watching this 'experiment' with interest and some trepidation!

But the Earth chapter is just one experiment. There are other factors involved in a soul's full cycle as this Earth is just one of three earths! This Earth is 50% head and 50% heart, whilst the other two earths are more 75% head and only 25% heart. These therefore have a more intellectual focus.

These other earths are not in our time zone. They share parallel time zones. Although their culture and vibratory essence are very similar, they don't actually share our same time frame. But they do sit in a similar orbit within a similar solar system since duplications are normally in threes.

There are three permanent atoms which create the soul in unison, so the 'three' continually haunts the creative process.

In some ways this Earth is the 'finishing school' which is why it is so popular, and why the Earth's population is now the most it has ever been.

The soul's full cycle

The soul's full cycle is for all its aspects to go from the Source which is a timeless zone, into outer time, working down through the various levels into gross physical matter, then working in an upward spiral back to the Source where the soul aspects merge and blend back into one.

To fully understand this, think of a point which is the Source. From that point are millions of different circles radiating outwards, each gradually getting wider and wider and on the furthest one is planet Earth in outer time.

At the start of its downward journey, if a soul aspect was near to the Source looking towards outer time at evolving species, it might recognise a need it has for its evolution. It would then gravitate through these millions of radiating circles into outer time on Earth where it would attach itself to a structure, or personality to collect the information needed for its evolution.

On the downward journey the different aspects of each soul pick up magnetic energy known as desire. During the Earth chapter, each soul aspect has to become desireless.

During the early part of the Earth chapter a soul aspect has a fascinating way of oscillating to an opposite frequency in different lifetimes, and always does this to extremes - just like the swing of a pendulum. So if a soul aspect has a life of great power, it will swing in the opposite direction having a life of being powerless. A lifetime of great poverty will follow a lifetime of great wealth. Great happiness will follow great sorrow. And so on. As it permutates back and forth, the swing of the pendulum gradually slows down and the soul aspect then starts to have lives of great importance, one after the other.

As the pendulum slows down a lot of unfinished business can be dealt with, and the aspects of the soul draw nearer to each other as they deal with the quota of experiences they were allocated. In this way the soul aspects work through the desire they collected on the downward journey, and slowly become desireless.

Once they become desireless, they can start to move back up from the physical plane through the various planes of awareness, into the etheric and so on. But even though a soul aspect might have dropped the physical desire, it might still find that it has astral desire to contend with!

On the upward journey, soul aspects start to release all the illusions which on the downward journey they took on as being real within their human perception of reality. As they release these illusions they can then refine their apparatus and start to move further in again, in ever decreasing circles as they move nearer to the Source.

Within the fullness of creation the various permutations of the soul aspects with all their experiences eventually merge into a concentrated cycle, becoming more and more closely interwoven until they can blend and merge back into one. They can then return home once again.

The average soul essence takes approximately 8,400,000 lives in which to complete this full circuit. The more stubborn souls might take considerably longer since this is a free-will universe. Therefore we are allowed to make mistakes. If someone is continually stubborn, continually making the same mistakes, then the number of lives required to reach the point of efficiency and understanding might be considerably more. Some souls cheat when they hit the fourth plane and have to go back to square one. So most of these lives are taken within the free-will zone, and the length of time for each soul's full journey depends on the permutations necessary for the soul itself.

A lot of people with their understanding based within linear time think there is a start and a finish to a soul's cycle, but this is not so. All the lives of all the soul aspects run at the same time, because the life of the now has a knock-on effect on what we call the lives of the past and what we perceive as the lives of the future. But it could well be that the human personality of the life in the future, looking backward in time in a linear sense, might recognise the difficulty of a younger aspect of itself, and might be motivated to go back in time to help out that segment of itself. This sometimes although rarely occurs the other way round!

Soul mates

On average, most people living on Earth at this time are working with 50 subtle bodies on the inner planes, whereas most Light workers have between 92 and 212 subtle bodies on the inner planes.

The soul, when it is at the Source, is concentrated into the first 30 levels - or the first 30 subtle bodies. On these 30 levels your soul is complete, after which it normally fragments into seven aspects during its downward journey. Each aspect can be male or female charged, with an opportunity to split itself into the opposite polarity. So if one of the seven aspects is a male strand, this can split into its opposite polarity, which would then be a female aspect. It is these aspects of the same soul who then incarnate into matter, and it these aspects of the same soul which most people refer to when they say, "I want to meet my soul mate."

A lot of people think their soul mate is one special person of the opposite sex. But soul mates are the seven main aspects which result from the soul splitting itself during its downward journey. So, in theory, if your soul has split into seven aspects, and all seven aspects have split into their opposite polarities, you could have 14 aspects of your soul incarnating into Earth, each incarnating into a different body during the same Earth time. So you could have 14 soul mates down on Earth!

A twin soul, or twin flame, is the opposite polarity of one of these seven aspects who have split themselves. So, if your soul has split itself into 14 aspects and all 14 have incarnated, you could in theory, have 14 soul mates here on Earth, but as you will be half of one of the seven main aspects, you will only have one twin soul.

In practice what usually happens is that only five soul aspects, or five soul mates, incarnate into physical matter. They may incarnate into both male and female bodies, or sometimes into all male, or all female bodies. The others stay on the astral realms to 'watch the shop' so to speak, working with 'management upstairs' in a way that can influence and give you the opportunity to move forward far quicker. Or they may be working in a different dimensional frequency field, and may even be in a different part of the Universe.

If any of the five aspects who have incarnated have chosen to split into their opposite polarity, their twin soul usually lives on the inner planes or on another dimensional level.

So when you think about your soul's purpose, it is good to remember that you, the physical person, are not the total representation of your soul, but just one aspect of that soul. Therefore, although every action you take and every thought you have affect your specific Earth life and contribute to your evolution, your thoughts and actions also affect all the other aspects of your soul who might be living in physical form in another country at the very time you are reading this book.

When most people talk about a soul's journey, they are really talking about the journey of one soul aspect. For in reality a soul in its entirety will be taking many journeys concurrently. Therefore to help you understand the intricacies of a soul's full journey, when we talk about a soul, we are talking about the essence of the soul, the soul in its entirety. When we talk about a soul aspect we are talking about one of the fragmented parts of the soul essence. Each soul aspect normally has a different number of subtle bodies, as each aspect is developing independently of the others.

One other point to remember is that each soul aspect will develop its own unique personality. No two aspects will be the same. Each aspect of the soul might become a specialist in different transmutation techniques through the unique experiences it has had. Even though it will share these experiences with the other aspects of its own soul, it will in essence still be identified in a very special way.

Therefore some aspects of each soul will be more versed in certain interpretations. Those who are 'better at it' will take the forefront and become the 'leaders of the pack' by setting new standards which are necessary for the overall experiences to be cultivated.

The quota of 8,400,000 lives which each soul has for its full cycle, is split up between its 14 aspects. Some aspects of the soul will live their Earth chapter on the physical plane while others work in different dimensional fields or different universes. Soul mates can best be described as facets of a multi-faceted jewel. By placing each facet within a different permutation on earth, the soul essence gains multiple variations through the individual experiences of each aspect and spontaneously collects a massive amount of data, far more than it would get if it were experiencing life in all its forms through just one aspect, or one vehicle. In this way the soul is very creative, is always expanding, and never static.

So a soul mate can be described as an aspect of the 'central tree of life'. It is this central tree of life which bonds the same impulse from the soul to the various soul aspects who are the outer manifestations physically in matter.

Sometimes all five aspects, or soul mates, will live within close proximity to one another. When a soul brings two of its aspects together, the soul loses a lot of its flexibility within the permutations of concentrated Earth life, and loses out on the opportunities and experiences it can have when the different aspects live far apart.

Therefore the soul prefers to keep each aspect well away from each other. So soul mates are normally spread out around the planet in order to give the soul the multiple permutations within the various time space settings that are appropriate for its needs.

When someone does meet their soul mate it is an event of great importance. The soul's purpose in bringing two aspects of its soul together is to create an energy flow to shift misaligned energy, mainly astrally, and to unclog some of the subtle network of energy inputs. This only happens when there is a lot of karmic business to be resolved. When it does happen, a terrific amount of high frequency energy will result and the two soul mates have a tremendous impact of energy on and in each other's space. Then, depending on the threshold of each individual aspect, the required change can take place.

So a meeting of soul mates only happens to those who are sufficiently developed to maintain and hang onto the high frequency energy, who have the courage to change, and are karmically ripe within the essence of their soul life.

This is why a lot of people have an urge to meet their soul mate - the higher aspect of themselves recognises that once the vibrations come to a point of efficiency, a lot of sorting out can be done.

In olden days when someone met an aspect of their soul it was always as a result, in the personality setting, of unfinished personal karma which was very difficult to contend with and work through, hence the need for it. Through their meeting quite a lot of unfinished personal karma was transmuted on the spot, which gave those two soul aspects in matter a pretty rough time. The longer the soul mates stayed together, the more magnetic energy would build up, and the two physical entities that represent the same soul input, the same 'tree of life' would burn each other up. The result was that one or both people concerned would die.

Today there is a lot of illusion and glamour around meeting a soul mate. Normally the motivation to meet a soul mate is for a perfect partner. But to meet a soul mate these days is not for personal gratification, or for a mating process to take place. It is more a bringing together for work, mainly on the inner planes, so that the whole soul family can move forward into a much more concentrated essence of what is required.

Therefore soul mates today really only meet when the vibrations of the soul group move more into harmony and when they have a need of that joint venture, because the age of the individual is over, and the age of the group is now the dominant factor.

When you do meet a soul mate you can usually recognise them by the pattern of energy interchange - which is not always love and joy! Sometimes you just belong so totally you can swop in and out of each other's bodies with no resistance at all. At other times you just

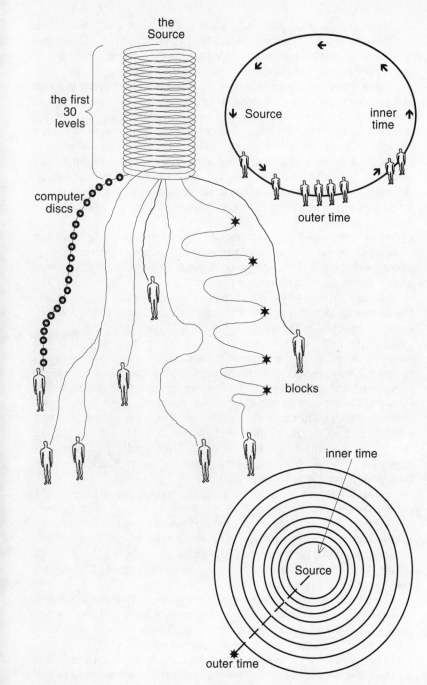

The soul's downward journey

hiss and think this isn't a friendly meeting at all. And of course there is often a lot of attraction, usually physical, emotional and mental. If you have been through the permutations of the lover, wife, husband, mother or father in past lives, you have a terrific bonding to that person when you meet, and feel so happy just to be with them again. As you allow this pattern of love to flow over you, it is a great temptation - if you are feeling a bit dissatisfied with your current partner - to get rid of that one and change over to the new person you have just met.

A lot of people who succumb to this say, "Oh, I've met my soul mate and I have to work with them." Yet working with a soul mate is difficult, and living with them is even more so, as the impact of energies can be so ferocious that living together is almost impossible for any length of time, without special provision on an energy level having been brought in.

Because of the needs of the group, Light workers who do meet a soul mate can now move through the magnetic attraction and then raise their vibration up to a higher level. They then have an old friend with whom they have been through the permutations of desire, and once they forget about desire they can work unhindered within their group purpose.

It is because of the demands of the New Age, because of the initiation within humanity as a whole, that more individual aspects of the same soul are now coming together, so that the point of burning can be applied to the various 'boils' within society. The high frequency energy generated can then open up multiple sequences. In this way, the sound of the unspoken word, the sound of the unconscious love of the Cosmic Christ can be released in its totality and these people - these soul groups - will become loudspeakers, a bit like a political party touring around singing out its promises! These soul groups will then serenade the future voters.

But it is only when the evolution of the individual soul has reached a pitch where individual aspects can match each other's high frequency energy input, can they start to work together in a concentrated and specific way. As they eventually get very near to each other, working within physical matter through telepathy, through astral alignment, they will know specifically and on a conscious level what each other is doing.

This normally only manifests when they are coming to the end of their Earthly cycle. That is, of course, assuming that the soul chooses to manifest the five aspects at that vibration, at the same time and place setting. This is again something of a rarity. As soon as each aspect of the soul has received its attunement to the higher aspects, and therefore the personal karma has been physically transmuted, it normally gravitates on to transmute astral karma - and possibly might not come back down to Earth into physical matter again.

Sometimes the five aspects of the same soul will incarnate at different times during one Earth lifetime. Some aspects of the soul may incarnate when other aspects are already adults. This increases the multiple permutations of possible Earth experiences.

Only on rare occasions will a soul aspect or soul mate incarnate into the same family where one of the parents, or one of the other family members is already part of the same soul. When this takes place it is for a speciality contract. It could well be that similar aspects of the same soul will agree to a set sequence of lives where they will live in close proximity to each other in order to build up a special energy thrust that is more than useful for themselves in human form, for the soul essence itself and for all those working with them on the inner planes. But because of the difficulties and tremendous pressure that will be brought to bear during the physical life, this is not something many engage in!

If you met your twin soul, the other half of your soul aspect, as someone of the opposite sex, you would have a perfect expression of yourself - which would make life extremely comfortable! But the opportunity to experience that permutation is very, very, very rare. As the soul is ever hungry for new experiences, and new creative sensations, it may play this scenario out at some time, just for the experience. That scenario may take place on the Earth plane or in some other reality.

But as the soul itself is not usually willing to give up the play tools it has created, quite often the twin soul will be motivated to work within the subtle anatomy* on the inner planes rather than meeting in physical form.

Quite often, when I look at the akashic records of individuals who have physically met their twin soul and merged in a physical sense during an Earth lifetime, I can see it was a tremendously traumatic shock when one of them died. In essence, the aspect left on Earth feels as if they have found themselves then lost themselves. This creates a future limitation where it will only go a short distance from the planet after physical death, and will incarnate fairly quickly as it is still in a state of grief. That grief then has to be worked through its system during the next lifetime.

This can manifest as a constant urge to commit suicide when there is no apparent reason. Or the twin soul aspect, as a child, may put itself in a position of risking death as it is subconsciously still seeking its twin soul. This soul aspect might come back down in a series of sharp encounters which might bring home the point of their loss, which they need to release, as their illusion of loss is so deep. I am told it is akin to having your heart ripped out, as in one sense you lose your favourite esoteric teddy bear.

While this is happening the soul aspect stagnates and can't move on. So, again, this is not a scenario that many souls engage in.

Soul alignments

A soul alignment is a package of energy, akin to a series of soul sounds, which the soul needs to freely pass from its essence down to the personality structures of the soul aspects in their totality, both within the inner and outer planes. Each soul sends out soul 'sounds' which have to be negotiated within the subtle bodies. Bear in mind that not all these subtle bodies are duplications of the physical - a lot of them are entirely different which gives the soul the flexibility to manifest in different planes of reference and also in different universes if it needs to gain the information it can gather from there.

So when an alignment takes place, energy passes freely from the soul down through the many permutations of subtle bodies into the physical personality. A total alignment happens fairly rarely, and occasionally may take thousands and thousands of Earth years to pass freely from the top to the bottom.

To go deeper into soul alignments let us think of each aspect of the soul as being a computer disc. This is a generalisation of the permutations of subtle bodies that each soul aspect has available. Each computer disc has a high note and a low note - the threshold above and below. Each disc has to be balanced by male and female input, male and female lives. Each disc is split into ten main planes, and each main plane split into a further ten sub-planes* so you have 100 sub-planes in total on each computer disc.

Each computer disc, each aspect of the soul, also has the capacity to hold between 20 and 200 life experiences. It is a bit like the soul saying to each particular aspect, "Here is the menu, here is £200 (or 200 lives), go down to the market-place of life to collect the experiences for us all and for the banquet to come." Now the average person currently down here would need to go down to Earth and spend all of their £200 (or 200 lives) to collect the experiences they required for their computer disc to be balanced.

But older soul aspects, having a better understanding through their craftiness of having come down to Earth in the permutations of matter more often, build up a better understanding within the various subtle levels as well as within the outer levels. They do this by getting together with others like themselves in a sort of cooperative. This cooperative within the permutations of the contractual life of brother, father, mother, sister, friend, enemy, teacher - and lover since one must have a bit of fun when one is down here! - would speed everything up and give them more oomph on the inner planes.

So where the average soul aspect has one life in ten that is important, and nine lives to assimilate what that tenth has brought about, they would need to live the full 200 lives in order to gain the experiences needed. But those soul aspects who are a little older and a little wiser can achieve a point of balance within their computer discs in far fewer Earth lives - in fact, in about 25 to 35 lives instead of the 200 lives allocated.

That means they may possibly have a residue of 165 lives worth of energy left over. So what they do with that energy is to negotiate for other computer discs far more wide-reaching to make their evolution more complete.

Occasionally they have to mark time by working with younger aspects of their soul, maybe for ten or twelve years, or whatever time it takes to bring these younger pupils up to a pattern where they can accept more responsibility within themselves. This helps to bring them to a point of balance within the network of the soul on all levels. When this happens the older aspect will accept some of the responsibilities or burden from the younger aspects, who may be a little lost or having a hard time, by sharing their emotions or karmic burden. If it is possible to regulate the energy in this way it makes the release of the problem in the younger component far easier.

While marking time with its younger soul aspects, the older soul aspect will also work with other aspects from other souls to whom they are contracted, to also help these souls raise their vibration and get to a point of vibratory efficiency. By helping both the younger aspects of themselves and other souls in this way, they can fulfil their own contract and move on.

A good example of this is the Master Jesus who, when he came in, had to mark time working with selective souls whom we know as his disciples. As their vibration was fulfilled, he was then released. He could then move on into a greater frequency whilst, at the same time, passing on some of the structural information - his ideas and concepts - and gifting these disciples with the polarity point that enabled them to use his energy in a much more specific way.

We all do similar work with smaller groups, sometimes on the inner planes and sometimes on the outer planes, absorbing higher key notes* as they come in. We then drop that high note down to a lower vibration so that the soul group can absorb its essence. As we drop the vibration of a high note down to the lower operating frequency of the soul group, this has a knock-on effect and the whole group can move forward.

The soul's contract

As the overall contract with each soul aspect is to raise its vibration during each Earth lifetime, in theory you come in at a certain vibration when you are born and your ideas, concepts, thoughts and, of course, your actions should increase that vibration before physical death. When you die you leave one permanent physical atom behind as a nucleus, or memory bank of all that you have experienced and achieved.

Your one permanent atom is left behind at the highest threshold within the frequency accord, which is the frequency point within the many millions of sub-planes where it naturally gravitates to. This one permanent atom is implanted with your encodement and will sit in a subtle ring-pass-not within that frequency until your house note, or the 'calling card' activates the encodement and recalls it into the structure of planet Earth for your next incarnation. It is normally only the essence of the individual soul aspect to whom that one permanent atom belongs, who can call that atom back into being.

When that one permanent atom is recalled it will then release the permutations of memories, ideas, concepts and the inherent 'thunder' which is the experiences from your past lives, into your subconscious and superconscious mind as you reincarnate.

By leaving one permanent atom behind in this way, you don't lose any time in form building when you incarnate back into matter. You just pick up from where you left off. This means that the vibration in your current Earth body is the highest it has ever been.

This permanent atom is an ongoing contractual arrangement which all soul aspects tend to have within the dialogue of life. This means that for the Earth chapter you would contract to build up the vibratory pattern within that atom over say 10 million years and your soul contracts would be accumulated during that time. So it is unlikely your higher self will allow you to take your one permanent physical atom and use it on a different time space frequency because of the irregularities which could result from that, until the evolution within yourself was sufficiently high enough for the vibration to pass safely into a new etheric mix.

The akashic record

The akashic record is the total of the experiences of the soul unit held within the key notes of each computer disc. This allows you to draw energy and information as and when it is appropriate for your need.

The average Light worker at this time has access to approximately the bottom 20 computer discs within the essence of their soul in its entirety. As each computer disc has the ability to experience 200 lives, the average Light worker would therefore have access to the awareness of approximately 4,000 lives, both male and female.

Incorporated into this are the two to three percent extraterrestrial lives a lot of Light workers have had. The soul aspect also has the awareness of the permutations of contractual lives of the whole group, which is roughly 20 times greater than the actual lives they have experienced. This is a result of the cooperation of younger soul aspects who have banded together with the various soul families they are contracted to work with. The sum total of life experiences which a Light worker has access to can therefore be up to 80,000.

On top of that should be added the equivalent of the experience of another 15,000 lives through opportunist karma - being in the right place at the right time, or in the right place at the wrong time! Quite often, soul aspects have the capacity, through their curiosity, to do the wrong thing rather than the right thing, as there are no hard and fast rules.

A soul aspect is also often sent off to collect specific data, or to experience a specific key note - which might be peace, freedom or power. How it actually collects that data and the time it takes to collect it is immaterial. Each soul aspect is also free to encounter what other experiences it chooses along the way.

If a soul aspect tries something new on the way and develops an addiction to that experience, be it power or sex, the addiction might take the soul aspect out of sequence with what it actually came down to collate and collect.

But the soul itself will peer suspiciously, and excitedly, at this new development, which might take 200 to 300 Earth lives depending on the new people and problems encountered, and the new karmic contracts - pleasant and horrid - which are invoked as this soul aspect goes off at a tangent. This happens all the time!

One aspect of the soul might take several million years to collect the necessary data, and might still be having fun while all the other soul aspects have finished their missions. If one aspect of a soul has been gone a long time and hasn't come back, then the soul itself might be motivated to send other aspects down to find it. They will then try to speed up the permutations within the life experiences of the one who is 'lost' to create a greater gravitation back to the soul.

In essence this might sound easy. But often it is not! You could describe this rescue mission by using the analogy of two parents going to a circus with 30 kids. Some are theirs, some belong to various friends. So they all go off to the circus where the parents buy all the goodies to make the kids' visit enjoyable. They see the show, then go back home again.

There they do a head count and find they have only got 29 kids! Not realising there is a problem, the kids have all run off to play. So the parents have to go and find them, bring them all back in, look carefully to see who is there and find out who has been lost.

They then have to get together with the higher aspects to decide what the next procedure should be. By this time the circus has moved on, so the parents have to find out if the kid has gone with it. When they finally catch up with the circus, if the kid is not there, they realise it may have hitched up with another family. So this entails another hunt. All in all, it might take some time to catch up with the lost kid - the lost soul aspect - and encourage him to come home!

In a similar way during your own journey, you are constantly coming to crossroads where there are no signposts. And you have to make a choice! The route you take will either bring you more lives and more karma, or it might shorten the experience which is necessary for you to go through.

Each soul aspect has a 'finger in the pie' not only in the physical experimentation going on with conscious choice on planet Earth, which is built into their karmic contract, but also within the various computer discs and the diversity of life vehicles they are using. This creates not only physical karma but astral karma as well. The result is we have far more diversity than we currently think. The astral levels for example are 50 times larger than the physical and there is an awful lot more space, with various types of entities and various forms of awareness manifesting and working through different creative inputs.

To put this into focus

Let us take a look at the average contract the soul aspect would find itself immersed in when it incarnates into matter.

The individual aspect of the soul residing on the inner planes will be absorbing the phenomenon of matter on Earth. It will be having a good time, enjoying its esoteric cup of tea and putting a few esoteric bets from the esoteric betting shop upstairs on those in matter. It will possibly be working with various other soul aspects who have already incarnated, or generally just having a holiday on the inner planes, when all of a sudden the soul aspect who is ready to incarnate will start to feel a little sleepy. The last conscious thought is, "Oh no, it's not time already, is it?" and magnetically the soul aspect is drawn down to Earth eventually ending up in this little bundle of fun called a baby person.

Between the cup of tea and the baby, the soul aspect has various choices. The main choice is the parental menu of the day. So it looks at the data, the akashic record memories and the karma which is calling it back as a magnetic package in a geometrical pattern. This aspect of the soul looks at the various parents available within the planet and tries to match the pattern it requires with those parents currently on Earth.

Having located the parents who are necessary for its formation, the soul aspect then moves closer to them. It magnetises the sperm and egg as they come together, drawing into that space the one permanent physical atom it left behind on its last journey. The parents then contribute their DNA to build the physical essence or life body the individual soul aspect requires. That soul aspect will also have ancestral memories coming in, both male and female, both positive and negative, plus the akashic record memories.

By choosing their parents the soul aspect will also have to deal with their emotional dumping - their fears, phobias and to a degree their aspirations.

The choice of parents will also affect their choice of society. If a soul aspect is born in London it will take on the thought forms, ideas and local customs manifesting as energy in that place, which are stamped on their 'esoteric hide' when they are born. A bit like being stamped 'Made in Great Britain'.

By choosing a particular society the soul aspect will of course have to put up with the liquid concrete of the educational programme - and it is nice to see within most Light workers now, large cracks are appearing in that concrete!

Soul aspects also know that by choosing a certain parental focus they can influence their path in that lifetime. For example, if a soul aspect was contracted to come down and experience leukaemia, it would know the odds of survival, and therefore the length of its Earth life, would be far less with parents in Mexico, than if they chose parents in a country where there was excellent medical care.

As soul aspects become wiser and are capable of merging with higher vibrations, they remember more and choose more wisely. But younger soul aspects often choose unwisely. They might incarnate into a life with tremendous difficulties - a bit like treading on super glue, then realising what they have done when it is too late, because they are stuck! This younger soul aspect is then continually caught up in round after round of incarnations where it can't free itself from the magnetic attraction of the package it is going through. This is when the rescue mission has to be carried out by the soul family.

When making all these decisions, the soul aspect also has access to the flavour of the month - the planetary alignments which influence the characteristics of the astrological star sign it is born under. This creates a handicap within a handicap, although it does offer certain assets as well.

It also chooses a specific time and place for its actual birth. Quite often, coming into this exact entrance point will be ley lines and geopathic stress points which place the soul aspect in a position of advantage or disadvantage depending on what is needed in that particular cycle.

Into this equation will also go the cosmic biorhythms from all the outer planets which have an effect on the Earth. For example, the rhythm of the moon, depending on whether it is at a high or low point will affect the astral life of the soul aspect as it comes in.

In addition to the intricate interplay of the effect from these planets, from the ley lines which might be positive or negative, and from the geopathic stress points, you might have the added input of the magnetic energy from the mother herself who might also be geopathically stressed. On top of all this, the biggest shock to the baby is the break of its telepathic link with its mother, which occurs when it is physically born.

All these inputs at the time of physical birth make up a set of auric equations which make each particular life either easier or more difficult, depending on the calculations and the timing which the soul aspect chose. Quite often the soul aspect might get the timing wrong, or there might be deliberate interference from those physically in matter - an accident creating an early birth, or an induced birth - which might prevent the soul aspect from coming in at the exact time it chose. So it might come in too soon, or too late, which causes initial problems for the soul aspect who then tries to unscramble the vibrations it needs.

Quite often this soul aspect may find that throughout its whole lifetime it is always behind or always in front. If the soul aspect has prearranged to meet people at certain times, then quite often a lot of the people will not be met in that particular lifetime.

As a result, the soul aspect may be so frustrated it might try to cut short its Earth life. Suicide then takes place, sometimes deliberately and sometimes inadvertently. The soul aspect will then reconsider what went wrong when it leaves the physical plane, reincarnating very quickly to do a catching up job.

Magnetic energy patterns required for the experiences during that lifetime are also contracted before incarnating. The soul aspect agrees at what time and what place those energy patterns will come in and is contracted to achieve a certain vibration before it meets that energy pattern. But if during the course of everyday life the physical personality of the soul aspect has drifted away from its main alignment and has not achieved the required vibrational increase, or is not in the right place at the right time, the energy pattern will still come down! This will have a negative instead of positive impact, as the new energy of a higher frequency will impact into the slower frequency energy the physical body is still using. A disruptive pattern is created within the chakra centres and the aura is sometimes ruptured. Quite often you have the phenomenon of accidents - right place, wrong time - as a lot of magnetic energy within the auric space has to be spontaneously released as the higher frequency energy comes in.

Occasionally if the soul aspect in human form has gone way out of alignment, this new energy comes in at what will now be totally the wrong place and wrong time. The resulting accident could be fatally damaging. Death would occur through the force and impact of all this high frequency energy on the slow frequency vibration which the personality has actually gone into.

On the other hand if the physical personality has reached the agreed vibration, and is in the right place at the right time when this new input of energy comes in, they will have more joy and more spontaneous understanding of the life situation as a result of bringing this energy through. Prosperity on all levels of life would then become easier.

Occasionally, by intuitively following your nose you can actually follow the guiding current the soul essence is sending down. You will then find the permutations of moving from one vibration to another are fairly easy. Instead of having head-on crashes with the train because you are on the wrong track, you can go whistling past on a higher vibration safely out of harm's way.

Although you may aim to always be on the right track at the right time, you can never do this all the time. The permutations deliberately handicap you to ensure you collect the necessary frequency responses the soul requires.

All these factors mixed together create the conscious conditioning all soul aspects have to go through as they come down to Earth. This is a bit like putting a brown paper bag over your head. But most of those connected with the 'mind of one' are now prepared to break free from this, from the heritage the past has brought and the pattern of old thought forms which make up the very nature of existence.

Some soul aspects growing on the spiritual levels will choose to incarnate just to experience abortion in order to gain the necessary astral information required before their next full physical incarnation. Guides in particular do this as their vibrations are quite high and they need to practise dropping their vibration. Although guides do incarnate back into Earth, it is very difficult for them and is not a pleasant experience. It is a bit like jumping into manure, holding your nose and hoping for the best!

For similar reasons a soul aspect might choose to incarnate into a severely handicapped body. It will specifically choose this if its evolutionary cycle does not allow it to manifest within normal human life. But by incarnating into a severely handicapped body it can create a useful anchor point without being fully physically present while it deals with the necessary astral manifestations.

An advanced soul who has a very refined vibration might also decide to incarnate into the body of a brain-damaged child, or a mongoloid child, specifically for the purpose of allowing the chosen parents to experience love and compassion in this way, which they might need in order to speed up their evolution. Or it may choose to incarnate into a body which is a mess purely for the experience of working through great physical difficulties, while at the same time healing lots and lots of people who come into its life.

Many people down here on Earth right now are actually beautiful Light beings who have not had the opportunity of an emotional background on Earth. So they have gravitated down here to gain the experience of pain and suffering - because if a soul has never suffered any emotional trauma, they are missing out on a unique experience which is needed for their evolution.

In our illusion we might pity the life of a severely handicapped child, or someone we perceive as experiencing a lot of suffering, but in reality that soul aspect has chosen the perfect experience for its evolution and growth.

If this experiment on planet Earth is carried out within the fullness of time, and I think it will be, then everyone will want to have a bit of it! So the permutations of our experience will have a knock-on effect as this expands throughout the Universe. What we are currently trying to achieve on Earth is an experiment in free-will which affects all life forms within the destiny of the frequency we are currently working in.

If you have three perfect lives and don't do anything wrong then you won't need to reincarnate and come back to Earth again. The trouble is, because of the handicaps we undertake when we come down, the angle of entry, the type of body we choose and the permutations within our contract, it is very difficult to have three perfect lives. We are all now at the stage where intuitively we can choose to only do the right thing. But to do that requires courage and total honesty, and quite often we opt for the easier road.

If someone on the higher planes says to you before you incarnate, "OK, we will evolve you in this life. But you will have to lose all your family, lose all your wealth, your health will deteriorate and over the next 20 years you will suffer physically. Will you accept it?"

The average soul aspect would say, "No, thank you!" So they spread out your contract and in one life you might have the loss of your family. In the next you might suffer the physical problems in your body. And so it goes on through several lives.

We are all in the cycle of reincarnation, and within the permutations of Earth lives we have got to balance the computer disc which represents humanity as a whole. There is the computer disc which holds the individual experiences, the computer disc which holds the experiences of the soul group, the computer disc which holds the planetary experiences, and so on. So the permutations are quite wide. But it is not just the individual person who has to balance the computer disc of humanity, but all of planetary life which also has to work in this way.

Spiralling home

When the soul is at the Source it is at a radioactive core. As it starts its downward journey it loses its radioactivity. As it moves down through the various subtle planes it actually creates a new radioactive shield and comes into the physical plane with its three permanent atoms which are radioactive and hold within them the soul essence.

To understand this, visualise the three permanent atoms in the shape of a triangle. The top point is the blending or completion of the multiple cycles of the 'everything' which represents the experience for the soul in its completion. The bottom two points represent the male and female expression of that completion. Therefore the richness and diversity of life, through the male and female, eventually have to merge creating the essence of the three vibrating in one space.

When the Earth cycle is complete, the soul takes that completed cycle and moves into a different system where it can once again release essences of itself, working with a different rhythm, creating a different point of harmony in its own unique way.

When you understand this you can move into the reality of knowing we are immortal and there is no end, just a continuance. When we have moved through the permutations of this planet we have the opportunity to move on into a different planetary focus and cycle where we can evolve into greater aspects of purity our soul requires.

So it is a continuous moving forward for every soul. Moving on into different planets, different universes, as we spiral our way back home.

Avatars

Avatars are God in matter, or God more specifically in a physical form. The soul contract and soul journey of an Avatar is different in as much as Avatars never come down voluntarily, but are commanded to come down by the five Perfect Masters of the God force, who are the door keepers of the whole creation within our reality as we know it.

The Avatar was the first one to become God realised. Because he was the first he was forever bound up to look after everyone else. So until everyone else has also become aware of itself and also becomes God realised, then the Avatar will be our eternal shepherd.

So the physical incarnation of an Avatar is always pre-commanded by group need, and only when humanity comes to a crisis point, such as now, are the physical incarnations of Avatars necessary. This necessity is assessed by the five Perfect Masters who are always here on Earth in physical form and therefore will always assess the 'soup of the day'. When the 'soup' is coming nicely to the boil, they send out this group change which represents the five, which will basically draw down the Avataric energy to manifest in its own way that which is necessary.

But since linear time and everything down here on Earth is an illusion, the God force of the Avatar in matter has foreknowledge of the time when it will be necessary for him to come back.

When an Avatar perceives a shredding of the veil, which happens when the race as a whole comes to an extreme octave and moves from one major cycle to another - as it is doing right now - there is a preordained set of sequences where he knows he will be needed. This is where Avatars indicate quite clearly that they will come back in another personality mode, and sometimes give the exact time sequence in between each life setting. Sathya Sai Baba for example has already told his devotees when he will leave this physical incarnation and the exact year when he will next incarnate as Prema Baba.

There are always five aspects of the Avataric God force down here in physical form at any one time, in addition to the five Perfect Masters. Each Avatar, very much like us, passes through the ring-pass-not, is subjected to the same clauses of spiritual amnesia and has to be woken up. With an Avatar the waking up process is achieved by two of the five Perfect Masters physically appearing in his or her space to remove the veils and allow a remembrance to take place. Normally, in a short space of time, the three other Perfect Masters also appear in the physical space of the Avatar to complete the waking up process so that he or she can fully realise who they are - God in matter.

This is where the Avatar in physical form can have a lot of problems. With Meher Baba for example, the vibration of the God force as it came through was so intense he developed a habit of bashing his head against a wall in order to alleviate the pressure, and in so doing lost all his teeth through the vibration of the banging. This indicates the difficulty of accepting the knowledge that you are God but being limited by karma. The karma in this instance is the karmic charge being placed on all life forms physically living on the planet, which the Avatar has agreed to pass through his system in order to orchestrate a new beginning.

With the young Babaji in Italy, the youngest aspect of the Avataric God force here on Earth at this time, only part of him has woken up. Until he fully wakes up and can fully remember, he is on a personal level finding it immensely difficult. Many of those who have met him have noticed he is in a great deal of turmoil in a number of ways, so he needs the perpetual love of the group coming in.

This gives you some idea of the degree of suffering the Avataric energy brings within the human structure. This also clues us into the quality of suffering deliberately chosen by those who are more evolved, in order to transmute and raise the vibration of the planet.

All Avatars suffer. Even those whom we perceive as not suffering do in fact suffer. But do bear in mind that suffering is an illusion. Therefore suffering is just a soap opera played for the need of others external to the Avatars themselves.

If you look at the historical pattern of Sathya Sai Baba, you will see he has deliberately taken on manifestations of suffering from time to time to physically bring a point home to those who are working through his quality of love. All Avatars do this. They physically take on the necessary components of suffering to illuminate the people they are working with.

Of course one has to bear in mind that every physical action by an Avatar has a manifestation astrally and etherically. Each simple action they take talks to us about the momentous task being done on the inner and outer planes as well.

Avatars still have to live within the limitation of the physical body and still have to go through the birth/baby cycle because it is symbolic. If you look at an Avatar's life cycle everything they do, including their teaching, is symbolic. They each work within a theme under the umbrella setting they have responsibility for. Not just for the human kingdom but for all kingdoms. In this way there is a multiple frequency input from all different levels which is going to open up lots and lots of doorways, and this is why we only understand a small proportion of what their work really is.

Each Avatar will have a specific personality. Sathya Sai Baba is in essence creative, whereas Meher Baba wasn't. Meher Baba did a lot more inner focusing with a small minority of people, whereas Sathya Sai Baba works more externally with the manifestation of his creativity, and creates little shock waves with what he does.

Some Avatars we don't even know about. They incarnate and to us seem to be ordinary people leading an ordinary life. But in reality it is anything but ordinary. Everything they do is symbolic. If they physically work with the local drains, they are really working with the drains of humanity and the drains on the lower astral levels as well. Not all Avatars work with miracles creating Light and love. Quite often it is the hidden Avatars working with hidden substances who are also creating a powerful pattern of change.

Of the five aspects of the Perfect Masters in physical matter on Earth, two always have a high profile, and three do not. Mother Meera is one of the Perfect Masters currently with a high profile because she is bringing in a necessary high vibration, and is invoking in her own way a very intense programme to speed up the evolution of everyone who is privileged to come into her space.

CHAPTER 2
THE AWAKENING

Over the years Light beings have come down to stimulate and move us into a new capacity of understanding so that the way forward can be shown. By their personal example and by their very existence they raised the vibration of those around them. They also offered ideas and concepts that made an interesting alternative to the 'menu' dominant at that time.

Light beings who came down to raise the vibration of humanity include Buddha, the Master Jesus and the more recent Avatars such as Meher Baba, Babaji and Sathya Sai Baba. Their contracts always hold the same focus - to raise the vibration of the planet, to invoke and to move all planetary life forms into a new shift or emphasis. This happens through personality experience as people 'earn the right' to physically meet aspects of divinity who can invoke the necessary patterns of change to give those who are more human a new framework to operate within. As this framework expands people can handle and hold a lot more Light energy. This shift has been taking place over the last 2,000 years.

Over the last 125 years Light frequencies have also been manifesting in a specific way to stimulate Light workers and bring them up to a point of remembrance.

This awakening process gathered momentum in the 60's when music started to have encodements put into it to help wake up more Light workers. So when music, such as the Beatles, woke people up at breakfast, it also genetically woke up the latent DNA and punched people into a different encodement that genetically stimulated their body to remember. Their chakra centres were transmuted and realigned. Their vibration was raised, and a mutation started to take place.

These encodements were done subliminally by the spiritual hierarchy and music writers themselves were not aware of this happening. But as the inspirational focus of the music writer formed, a subliminal particle of Light was implanted into their inspirational expression, and Light from planetary focuses was tuned into that music. In this way a subliminal vibratory note was implanted. This is one of the reasons people are still addicted to 60's music, and keep on playing it over and over again.

The encodement in music is still happening as much, if not more than it was 30 years ago, especially through the opera being sung by tenors such as Luciano Pavarotti and Placido Domingo who are currently allowing their sound to be heard on a worldwide basis. A new wave of this energy formation also started to come in and resonate in the spring of 1993.

As a Light worker it is now important to become intuitively aware of the vibrational pattern behind music, and what it is doing to you. Some music has an extremely negative effect. Heavy jazz and rock, which can be very destructive, are alright for brief moments if you need to be earthed, but not most of the time if you want to be in a state of grace.

New key notes

In the 60's, when this mutation began, it stimulated Light workers in a way that allowed them to absorb Light particles. This enabled them to draw into their essence advanced information encoded within the structure of the planet, and allowed certain key notes to be released.

As Light workers absorbed the essence of those key notes into their creativity and sent out a rhythm of truth which vibrated through the subtle mechanisms of thought, in a form of telepathic overture, it helped to awaken others like themselves.

Since the 60's there have also been a series of key notes coming into the planet to activate the circuitry within the genetics of our bodies. As these different key notes of harmony continue to come in, they help to build up our vibrations until we go through the various thresholds necessary for us to remember our cosmic heritage, our immortality, and to remember where we actually live.

As these key notes continue to rise, they also affect the structure of our planet, and the planet itself is now communicating with us in a variety of different ways.

Crop circles are one of the forms of magnetic key notes being offered to us. They are coming in as a new communication structure, in a form of encodement. Through these crop circles, an implantation of energies is also being put into the Earth to help raise our vibration and make us think in a different way. Some crop circles which appeared in 1992 took on the patterns of the trigger mechanism of the star gateway* opening, known as the 11:11, which occurred on 11th January 1992.

A lot of Light workers are also being genetically encoded. This is done through the focus of meditation when a frequency vibration allows unconditional love to come in, and their genetic encodement to be breached. In this way Light particles trigger off a form of cellular structural realignment. The space between their atoms is realigned to create more space, more energy movement, so that old memories can be reactivated in a way that helps them move up to a different rhythm. This new rhythm also has implantations of energy which creates rhythms of magnetic energy that activates anyone who physically comes into their presence - something akin to a very contagious spiritual virus!

In certain parts of the planet, such as America, crystals are now being activated to help raise the vibration of that country. America is a relatively young nation. They do not have a lot of karmic history in this round, so they have the opportunity of also raising the vibration of the planet as a whole, and Americans will start to come into their own around 1998 or 1999.

At the moment America is going through a materialistic decline which can be symbolised as the base chakra of the American continent drawing up a lot of slow frequency magnetic energy from the Earth. The race riots which have been going on for many years, and the intolerance within the races as a whole, is a reflection of this slow frequency energy being flushed to the surface in a very specific and fundamental way. This is going to get somewhat worse until enough people care sufficiently to form themselves into counter-groups to rectify the point of imbalance.

This can only come about when the individual American accepts responsibility for America as a whole, rather than just being concerned with their particular vested interest.

When sufficient Americans exhibit increased intolerance for the corruption, greed and limitations of the corporate family, and as individuals band together to raise public awareness and public support, they will then raise the presentation of group understanding. In this way, a gradual sweeping change of energy will affect the whole American nation.

The ground energies will play their part by releasing structural slow frequency energy* for transmuting, and by raising the energy potential within the people sitting above those crystalline structures or clusters.

Part of the effect of all this is that more and more people will become mediumistic, and will start to channel in a much more specific way - this is already being seen in many parts of America.

In this way the third eye of the American race will be opened. Their heart centres are already in the process of opening more and more, and therefore a sense of caring rather than isolation and separation will begin to dominate throughout the race.

Star gateways

On 14th February 1992 a new star gateway opened which created another new alignment. On this date a new vibratory pattern came into the planet.

As this star gateway is mainly of a karmic nature, it is much more slippery than the 11:11, so a lot of people may not have picked up on this one. Although 14th February 1992 may have gone unnoticed by many folks, its impact for Light workers is important as this was the trigger date, or trigger mechanism, when the karmic pattern within the planet changed. A new opportunity is now offered to all of us to release personal karma through meditation, inner work, and through the right activation of the will, rather than having to 'live out' the experiences normally required to clear and release karma in a physical manner.

Karma comes on several different levels. You can have personal karma of a physical nature only, and also have emotional, mental and spiritual karma. If you make the right changes emotionally, the impact of karmic energy you were due to physically collect will no longer be necessary. The same applies mentally and emotionally.

It is now the time when personal karma has got to go! You can then move on to work with your friends on group and planetary karma. You will then be strong enough, as part of the corporate unit, to raise the vibrations of both yourself and your group on the inner planes, and share that with your spiritual family.

Although the karmic pattern within the planet totally changed in February 1992, that change can be symbolised as an oil tanker which takes a little while to stop. So the drive, or the expectancy of the masses, took approximately a year and a half for the new vibrations to impact into the conscious understanding of those who are more intuitively alert to the changes coming into our planet. This happened around August 1993.

As the karmic contract which the planet has with humanity is now changing, a lot of karmic contracts with folk currently down here are being renegotiated. This means that more promotion can actually be in-built into the human form and though, karmically, those working with Light previously had the brake placed on them, in February 1992 it was taken off.

You can equate this in a symbolic way to the comparison of previously counting on your fingers and toes, and now counting much faster using a computerised calculator. So from the 14th February 1992, the 'computer' was switched on. It is now in operation! And those who decide to take up that overture will find their karmic intent, be it personal, group or planetary, can be moved forward far quicker than ever before.

A meditation programme which can be used, on an ongoing basis, to work with this new opportunity to release personal karma is given in Meditation 20 at the end of this chapter.

Opportunist karma is either being in the right place at the right time, or being in the right place at the wrong time. This gives the opportunity of freedom of choice to be applied since karma has various tides, ebbs and flows. These karmic tides have a tight and specific schedule. It is only when the right focal point of inner plane cooperation brings about physical planetary alignment, that karmic tides can be focused in a slightly different way.

Prior to the event of February 14th 1992 these karmic tides were tightly focused and allowed very little conscious freedom of choice for those with contractual patterns within the field in which their karma was being expressed. Therefore, Light workers could not consciously work with the impact of that karma since their awareness was denied the freedom of choice of opportunist karma within that cycle.

But since February 14th 1992 Light workers can now have the conscious understanding, intuitively as well as intellectually, to realise what has happened, and should now be able to make the right decisions about events which manifest within their space, based on that knowledge.

Since karma in general is very much like a dragging mechanism - somewhat like sailing in a boat with multiple anchors that get snagged as you drag them along - the average person has an awful lot of slow frequency energy which needs to be disposed of. But for most Light workers, personal karma is now relatively small although there are some lumpy bits in places which still need to be cleared. This is where the opportunist karma of the future can bring that lumpy aspect in, this time working with the conscious cooperation of yourself, rather than being herded along by karmic events which have previously pushed you into karmic situations you may not have been willing to deal with.

Most Light workers are now being made aware that problems are in fact opportunities and something to acknowledge and consciously work with. By taking off the blinkers of conditional thinking imposed by society, and changing your thought forms around problems, you can start to see a problem as an asset in your life rather than a limitation. By welcoming a problem with this new way of thinking you can move through it far quicker than with the old way of reckoning.

The old predictions

A structural pattern, a crossroads is coming around 1993/4. This means that as the vibrations build, if enough of us haven't raised our vibration and made the movement into the space where we need to be, some of the more rotten predictions might become part of our reality.

These earthquakes and tidal waves are, to my mind, totally unnecessary if we recognise we are now part of fourth dimensional reality. As energy follows thought, if we consciously work with the higher frequencies of unconditional love, recognising it is now time to become reunited through the laws of faith and trust, we can neutralise these predictions.

The need to suffer is only in the mind, as humanity has been physically programmed, both genetically and emotionally, to accept the worst. We all came in on the ray of suffering which is a preprogrammed pattern all Light workers have to go through in order to raise their vibration. And we all incarnated through the ring-pass-not, the band of blue energy around the planet which gives us a bad case of spiritual amnesia.

The way we can awake from that amnesic state is by attaining group consciousness. We do this by meeting the right people at the right time, and becoming aware of the telepathic mind merge that is now possible as we physically meet within groups, and more specifically through the networking which is now a hallmark of Light workers everywhere.

It is time to move off the ray of suffering onto the ray of love and joy. It is time for remembering, for activation. As this new Light energy of the Aquarian cycle comes in, with that Light energy you can attract to you other Light workers who are activating things in different ways. In this way you help each other to move forward.

Fulfilling your contract

If your guides are near you, they will now be pushing you to reach out to as many people as you can, to bring about a structural change in their awareness and help them to wake up. You do this by not only teaching but just by physically being.

If you are standing at a bus-stop, your vibrations will be affecting the person who comes to stand next to you. So if you run for the bus and just miss it, instead of getting frustrated or angry, stop and look to see who comes along to stand next to you. Open your awareness and you may find that you were deliberately made to miss that bus so that this person could catch you up, stand next to you and get a boost from your vibrations and energy which will help them to move on. If you approach life in this way then everything takes on a new meaning. So be aware of which check-out you take at the supermarket. Don't just choose the shortest queue but intuitively look to see which check-out girl needs your energy, and look to see who comes to join that queue after you.

The same applies if you travel on trains or the underground. Be conscious of which seat you sit in as you will be magnetising that seat with your energy. The next person who comes along and sits in that seat after you may think, " Oh, it feels so good to be sitting down," but really they are feeling good because they are being fed by your energy and your higher vibrations.

If you are intuitively in the right space, you can send out waves of comfort, peace and understanding as you travel in the rush hour. This will help to neutralise a lot of the slow frequency negative energy in an anaesthetic sense. To do this, you have to deliberately cultivate the right attitude, bringing in love, peace and harmony, in order to help raise the vibrations of everyone around you.

This waking up and activation process is now happening in many ways: many Light workers have, in past lives, been crystal singers. A crystal singer is a person whose vibratory capacity was sufficient to bring in cosmic sounds, and to translate those sounds vibrationally through the etheric versions of their physical body on the inner planes. In this way they influenced not only crystal structures within the crystal alignment of the planet, but also the vibratory hue of thought forms and ground energies like ley lines and geopathic stress points.

A lot of these crystal singers left behind sounds that have been held in bondage in certain parts of the planet. These sounds have been waiting to be reactivated at the right time - which is now. This is why Light workers who were crystal singers in past lives now have gypsy feet and feel motivated to travel extensively. In essence, they are being motivated to physically return to the parts of the planet where these sounds have been held. They then reactivate those sounds, at the same time activating their own system, by simply physically being over the sites where they left the sound in previous lives.

This reactivation allows an encodement to take place within their DNA which gives them telepathic access to a whole vibratory input of knowledge which could not come through their system until this activation took place.

As a Light worker reactivates a part of the planet in this way and spreads the gospel, more Light workers are intuitively drawn to that place where they harmonise with each other. They in turn are also activated, and can then re-engage the contracts agreed to in past lives, which are now ready to be implemented as part of the 'new revolution'.

When these Light workers physically return to the place where they can be activated, various etheric skins are removed. Their bodies then etherically interpret Light particles in a much more direct way, through working with devic or angelic forms. They can also start to resonate with Light and start to accept Light as a form of intuitive and physical food.

This is already beginning to happen, and is one of the reasons why more and more Light workers are refining their diets. Many Light workers are now finding they no longer want or can no longer digest the foods they used to enjoy. Some are experiencing difficulties absorbing physical food, for their bodies now recognise they need something entirely different, therefore there is often a great deal of confusion as the old conditioning of the past struggles to maintain its dominance over new physical eating habits that are trying to come through.

We all have contracts to fulfil which are linked to this current awakening and transition into the Aquarian Age. This is why there is now a call for all Light workers to raise their vibrational pattern so that contracts made in past lives can be activated, and their purpose in this lifetime fulfilled.

For example, you might have made a contract with a Light being 25 lifetimes ago who said, "I want to meet you at a certain time in the future for a special purpose. But you have to have a body vibration that is sufficient for my needs."

You may have agreed to that, and slaved away for the past 24 lives to achieve the right body vibration in preparation for this encounter. Then along comes this Light being, who might not have actually come onto this planet before, and if your vibration is right, your contract can be fulfilled.

This may be in the form of direct channelling as is happening with the being 'Lazaris' who communicates through a Light worker in the States. In this way communication can come through to give humanity precise information with a quality of love that is fairly unusual. But this can only happen when the timing and vibration are right.

A lot of inspirational thought is now being channelled by those on the inner planes. This can be seen in the numerous New Age books that are being published, offering the alternative view from beings who are more extraterrestrial. These beings, who come from inner space and inner time have, at one time or another, resonated with the planet and now have the capacity to merge with us again. They work directly with those in human form who are in tune with them and who have the capacity, through telepathy, to channel their readings.

This inspirational pattern is also permeating the various sciences and the whole educational programme. In fact, all folk involved with producing new ideas and concepts for companies and major organisations are actually receiving new inspiration of an extremely diverse nature!

So your contract might be to do with bringing through specific information in a particular way. It might be connected with structural healing. Or it might be to absorb slow frequency negative energy thought forms - in fact, many Light workers are here on the planet with a specific contract to help raise the vibration by absorbing slow frequency energy and thought forms.

A lot of Light workers are also here with contracts to be 'fear teachers' - to help people overcome their fears and move to a vibrational frequency higher than the slow frequency vibration of fear. But to become a fear teacher we have to first run through our own fears, which can result in sensitivity and insecurity. By facing our fears we not only transmute them, we also transmute the group fear which has accumulated through the collective build-up of fears and thought forms on the inner planes as well.

Your life purpose does not necessarily have to be the fulfilment of some great environmental project. Consciously transmuting slow frequency energies and working with your own fears may look, on the outer surface, as if your life is ordinary. But the role you are playing is, in fact, very vital to the greater plan on Earth.

Transmuting slow frequency energies can be done through a normal healthy body. But some Light workers, both adults and children who have agreed to work with planetary energy, take on cancer or leukaemia in order to draw that negative energy into their system. Small children who have cancer or leukaemia, may have deliberately chosen to take that particular path in order to absorb large amounts of slow frequency energy. This is a deliberate act of love for the planet. As they absorb the negative energy and their body starts to break down and 'die' they can also teach their parents and society a great deal about unconditional love, rather than the conditional love which only identifies with the form and the need to hang onto the personality.

Once their system has absorbed as much negative energy as they can handle, they transmute it by the process of their physical death.

Quite often people with cancer are in fact sleeping over negative ley lines or geopathic stress points which allows them to absorb the negative energies which are slowing down the evolution of the planet. As they physically die these areas of negative stress also completely disappear. This is their gift to the planet.

During the next thousand years the main core of vibratory Light workers who are currently down here - and most of you, since you have acknowledged the vibration in this book and responded to it by reading it, are part of that core - will reincarnate very quickly after each Earth life. This main core of Light workers have had about 75% of the Earth lives they contracted to do, so in the year 3000 most of you will still be here, in a different vibratory vehicle, but your presence will still be needed within the planet, since this is part of your contractual arrangement.

New corporate wave

There are now sufficient Light workers and disciples on the planet, working freely within the public domain, with enough Light workers infiltrated into all the major organisations: the governments, the banking system - and even the Mafia!

A lot of these Light workers haven't yet been activated, but the process of awakening is under way and a lot of activation will be seen between now and the end of 1996. In 1997 the equivalent of the 'cosmic brain' will be activated which means that every cell in your body will have a 'remembrance'.

As Light workers are activated, this new corporate wave of Light beings will impact into our now, and also into the future of humanity as a whole. As this happens they will start to rock the boat in the organisations within which they are working, and these organisations will start to fragment. Structures will break down and there will be a total and positive change in everything that represents civilisation.

Therefore the grossness of civilisation - the various uncivilised acts we regard as normal expression - will then be demolished very quickly.

As humanity wakes up to a greater realisation of the intuitive quality of life, and as that manifests it will in its own way ensure that the 'weeds in our garden of life' can be removed and those who are bound up in negative organisations can be disrobed and thrown out! Then those Light beings who are reaching for their own personal power - mainly in a group formation under the mantle of the Cosmic Christ energies - will ensure that only the best remains and everyone will enjoy a new package of energy, and the prosperity that is necessary for well-being and life in a fundamental and specific way.

This should be accomplished by the year 2008. The planet will then move forward into a new vibratory pattern which will fully embrace the New Age we term the Age of Aquarius.

So as the pattern of energy begins to build, especially between now and 1996, and as the understanding begins to dawn on the minds who are connected with the 'mind of one' - who then become the spiritual leaders, the spiritual teachers of the planetary folk - so it is that a new order is beginning to form and the spiritual revolution is well on its way.

* * *

The Awakening: meditations

18. Meditation programme to help raise your vibrational pattern

A useful way to raise your vibration is to utilise natural law or natural energy - a bit like sailing with the breeze behind you.

To do this you work with the Great Invocation, saying it in series of 13s during the five-day period when the moon is most active. This is the two days before the full moon, the full moon day, and the two days after the full moon.

The Great Invocation, which is the update of the Lord's Prayer released into humanity in the late 30's, can be used irrespective of background or creed. It is a dominant energy package of the Cosmic Christ which is continuously going out. Therefore working with the Great Invocation in the way described below will give you a boost in a high frequency way and will increase your vibrational field.

Using this positive source of energy will also ensure that freedom can enter your space in a much more specific way than through using some of the older and outdated meditation techniques, which involve continual use of older style mantras to make chakras wider and more powerful. But because of the new polarity of Light, most people's chakra centres are too open. So some of the older mantras have become a hindrance, rather than a help.

It is particularly important to work with the Great Invocation during the full moon as the full moon energy stimulates and releases energy in the sexual and base chakras. This lower chakra energy comes under the heading of tyranny, fear and old conditioning. But by utilising the power of the Great Invocation, it pushes that energy of fear and old conditioning up through the lower chakras into the heart centre where it can be transmuted and used in a much more positive and specific way. In this way biorhythms of a positive nature will dominate.

The Great Invocation Full Moon Programme:
To remind you, this five-day programme is done during the two days before the full moon, on the day of the full moon and on the two days after the full moon.

Start first thing in the morning of day one and say the Great Invocation 13 times, one after the other as a gentle continuous chant, which makes one cycle. You then repeat this cycle another 12 times during that day making a total of 13 cycles in all for day one.

Then repeat this full day's programme of 13 cycles on each day over the next four days making a five-day programme for that full moon.

This five-day programme is then repeated over the next 12 consecutive full moons, making a total programme over 13 full moons.

Versatility is the key here as, due to commitment within your work or daily rhythm, you might initially find it difficult to verbally chant and count the full 13 cycles of the Great Invocation each day during the five days of the full moon. If so, I suggest that you prerecord a full day's programme of 13 cycles onto a cassette tape. Then carry your cassette recorder and earphones with you during the five days of the full moon, and whenever you find yourself in any situation where you can 'plug in' - in a traffic jam, on a train travelling to and from work, or even waiting at the supermarket check-out - you can switch your tape on and work through your 13 daily cycles in this way. You can also play the tape as a pre-sleep introduction - depending on your partner!

You will find that you can chant one cycle of 13 Great Invocations in about eight minutes. So you could prerecord 10 cycles on a 90-minute tape, leaving the other three cycles to chant yourself first thing in the morning and before you go to sleep. Or you can prerecord all 13 cycles onto a 120-minute tape.

Although on one level this is a bit like intuitive cheating, using a cassette recording of the Great Invocation can still create the required vibration. If you use the recorded version for this exercise you will find that although you are just listening to yourself saying the Great Invocation, your real awareness will be coaxed into a new position where the higher vibration of love, comfort and healing that you need can still take place, and the telepathic overture of this invocation will come into its own.

You will then find yourself inspired to say it yourself, outside of your normal time sequence. For example, you might find yourself waking up in the early hours of the morning, about 3am and feel the need to allow the Great Invocation to run through your mind - without the cassette tape - and possibly even want to chant it out aloud. When this starts to happen, recognise that your higher self has given you a little nudge to wake up and sacrifice some sleep in order to give yourself a boost in the high frequency way that is achieved when you verbally chant the Great Invocation. When this happens you will know you have broken through your subconscious limitations and are working directly with the Source.

Depending on where you are, you can of course chant the Great Invocation out loud, while listening to the prerecorded tape. This allows you to drive your car, do your housework, or washing up, while chanting the Great Invocation without having to count each cycle of 13. The prerecording does the counting for you!

If you are doing the programme verbally, and counting each cycle, you can thread 13 beads onto a cord and tie it into a continuous loop. Choose one large bead and 12 smaller beads, then as you chant each Great Invocation you can use the beads to count, and focus all your attention on the words and vibration of what you are saying.

Initially you may think this programme requires too much discipline and dedication. So let me explain the reasons why fulfilling the 13 moon cycle is important. Then your higher self may nudge you into making the necessary commitment!

By chanting the Great Invocation in series of 13s, over 13 full moons, you restructure any disharmonious packages of energy within your space and within your physical environment - your car, your place of work, your home - and you also utilise natural law to your advantage by working with the magnetic law associated with the number 13 which is a very high vibrational number.

The vibration from the 13 sequence creates a key note which has the capacity to introduce octaves of Light to unscramble the circuitry of the subtle anatomy. As the subtle anatomy holds the soul's experiences collected through the journeys of interdimensional time, by using this particular 13 sequence and activating this vibration you open your access into the 13th plane.

The 13th plane is where neither Light nor dark exists, but where entities called Devic Lords live who can be called into your space. These Devic Lords have immense power and will respond to your call when you work with this Great Invocation programme in series of 13s, as the spiritual hierarchy have already negotiated with the Devic Lords and placed an advance order for those willing to make the effort and the journey by working with the programme.

Therefore the response to the vibration of the Great Invocation is a preordained amplification of energy which the spiritual hierarchy have actually applied for. By working with this programme in series of 13s, you create the right encodement and vibration which these Devic Lords will amplify, and you create a 'calling card' for the energies of unconditional love, healing, harmony and joy.

As these Devic Lords will automatically respond to the sound of the Great Invocation, you could describe this programme as creating spontaneous prosperity! So 13 is far from being unlucky as the 'misinformation service' would like us to believe. It is in fact a very lucky vibration and number.

The Great Invocation also has a very high energy vibration. If anyone tries to use the Great Invocation in a fundamentally negative way, they will have their energy system neutralised and find it immensely difficult, or even impossible, to keep up the vibratory chant. If they do manage to enforce the vibration and invoke the Devic Lords, through applying group will, a payment will be demanded directly from them. This payment is normally in the form of speeding up their karma and energy life form on the physical, etheric and astral levels. This will move them into a point of surrendering their energy in this particular lifetime.

If you are going to invoke anything there is always a payment! When you use the Great Invocation with a positive focus, the payment is met by the spiritual hierarchy. They will accept what you are negotiating for, and you will become aware of a mind meld, a merge of energy, where telepathy rules. To become telepathic you have to merge with at least one other person, and by doing that, you become totally aware of them and they become totally aware of you. You can't hide anything from each other or manipulate each other's system. The result is you have a very exclusive club where only those with sufficient high frequency - in this case unconditional love - can actually get in.

So by making the effort, by invoking the 13th rule, and using the encodement which the Great Invocation brings, the Devic Lords will come into your space and give your energy a boost in whatever way is necessary for your development under the headings of personal, group and planetary karma.

Therefore the Great Invocation is a bit like an elder brother or sister taking you to a football match and paying for you to go in, so you can enjoy all the excitement and all the fun of the game with everyone else who is there!

The discipline needed to complete this programme over a continuous 13 moon cycle is worth the effort as you can enhance your energy pattern, amplify your circuitry and bring together any vibrational fragmentation in your body. This will increase your capacity to handle and hold energy, will raise your vibration and move you into a whole new tempo. In the main this means that sooner, rather than later, you will experience a direct flow of Avataric energy and will be able to communicate directly with God.

As you start to work with this programme, you will begin to release the energy of old conditioning and thought forms. You may get physical symptoms of unloading in the form of energy cleansing - a cold or flu, or rushing to the toilet.

Initially you might be aware of something happening, and be a bit apprehensive because these thought forms won't want to leave you willingly. So they might amplify their signal and fear in any of its forms may become apparent. Dreams may also become rubbish dreams as you throw out of your subconscious the outdated packages of magnetic energy that become unacceptable to your system as your vibration moves up.

You might also get flashbacks to older times when the full moon was to your disadvantage. The people around you might also 'hiss'. These might be folk who have a slow frequency vibration with astral entities feeding off them, who will seek to interpret this programme in a down-market or occult way. But it is only their fear talking.

You may have emotional symptoms of vulnerability, loneliness, fear, a feeling of unloading your destiny and a speeding up within yourself, and spiritually feeling that you don't belong to the human family. But all these symptoms will tend to fade, and as you come out into the sunlight, doubt and fear in its totality will cease to be an issue.

You will then experience a mental sharpness, and may develop an ability to feel or see inside yourself in a much more focused way.

During this programme you will say the Great Invocation 169 times on each day of the five-day programme, making a total of 845 Great Invocations during each full moon. Over the 13 full moon cycle you will complete 10,985 Great Invocations which will bring you up to the point of efficiency although you will find that, after just three months of using this programme, your vibration will start to alter and go up.

90% of the people who complete this programme should totally transmute the negative overtures of fear and old conditioning and should not be bothered by that ever again. But there will be the stubborn 10% - the sulky old souls - who might find they need to do this programme three times! But these are just a minority few. These are people who are a bit behind in their karmic contract, but working with this programme will still be to their advantage and will help them to speed up their evolution within this lifetime.

The Great Invocation

From the point of Light within the Mind of God
Let Light stream forth into the minds of men.
Let Light descend on Earth.
From the point of Love within the Heart of God
Let Love stream forth into the hearts of men.
May Christ** return to Earth.
From the centre where the Will of God is known
Let purpose guide the little wills of men -
The purpose which the Masters know and serve.
From the centre which we call the race of men
Let the Plan of Love and Light work out
And may it seal the door where evil dwells.
Let Light and Love and Power restore the Plan on Earth.

**NB. *Many religions believe in a World Teacher, knowing him under such names as The Lord Maitreya, the Imam Mahdi, and the Messiah, and these terms are used in the Hindu, Muslim, Buddhist and Jewish versions of the Great Invocation.*

To obtain a free copy of the Great Invocation, printed on a small card suitable to keep in your purse or wallet, write to 'Invocation Distribution' at the address given in the Appendix - Sources.

* * *

Releasing Personal Karma

Following are three meditations we offer to help you release personal karma. The first meditation helps you decord from personal karma by working with the energy pattern of white Light, bringing it down through the top of your head into your heart centre, filling both your physical and dream body.

The second is an ongoing meditation programme which should be done regularly, over a 13 or 18 month period. *This is one of the most important meditations in this book.* It is offered to those who are ready to take this step and make the commitment to themselves. The reward for all Light workers who are ready for this is that, within 18 months you can free yourself of all unfinished personal karma which you are currently working with. You can then move into a whole new rhythm.

The third meditation offers a choice for those who might not need to, or want to do the 18 month programme. You might want to just target the hard-core memories, or past-life experiences that are particularly troublesome and are creating an imbalance in your system. If this is the case, you might find this particular meditation useful to 'dig into' a very precise problem or past life sequence, in order to transmute and release that imbalance of energy quite quickly.

Some people might also prefer to look at each past life sequence in turn. Some might want to deal with one specific aspect very quickly, then settle down into a more gentle rhythm and enjoy the overall process of the main 13 to 18 month programme, rather than go into the overall process with 'raging toothache' in one particular area.

Remember that each meditation has a governing note, and your intuition will help you to gravitate towards the meditation which holds the key notes that are right for you.

19. First meditation to release personal karma by working with your dream body

This meditation is done last thing at night when you are tucked up in bed and ready to go to sleep.

First of all, visualise white Light coming down through the top of your head, through your crown chakra, and travelling down into your heart chakra. Then visualise roots going down into Mother Earth.

As the white Light flows into your heart centre, visualise this expanding out from your heart centre, flowing up and down your body. The aim is to allow your whole body to fill up and reflect this Light which represents the flames of centralised truth. In this way your whole body will manifest as white Light. Initially, when you start this, you might only be able to project this Light a short way out from your heart centre, but with continual practice and effort, you will be able to fill your whole physical body with Light.

As your physical body fills with white Light, all the negative subliminal patterns, karmically and otherwise, within your subtle anatomy will start to be released. During your sleep time your dream body will reflect what is happening, and initially may take on different colours, some murky, and some quite nice. But as you continue to work with this meditation each night, you will find the white Light starting to be reflected within your dream body. Then, not only will you have greater clarity in your dreams and a better remembrance taking place, but if you perceive yourself within your dream life, you will find that your heart centre - irrespective of how you are portrayed in that dream - will also start to fill with white Light. As white Light, in its own way, spreads throughout your dream body, all the colours within your dream body will dissipate and be transmuted. Your dream body will become purer. It will become whiter and whiter, until your whole dream body radiates white Light as well.

This manifestation of white Light within your dream body will only start to happen after you have managed to fill your whole physical body with white Light, prior to going to sleep.

By doing this on a regular basis each night you will resolve and restore some of the imbalance of energies within your subtle bodies which might have been collecting there for centuries and centuries.

If you don't have access to your dream life this could be for a number of different reasons. It might well be that your guides have instigated a filter mechanism if, for example, in childhood you were too open to psychic interference during your dream state. As a protection, access to your dream life is then normally denied. Or the arrangement of your atoms, and polarisation of your life purpose might demand that you have no conscious knowledge of your dream life at this particular time. But things will become far clearer as you will soon have a lot more personal choice in relation to all facets of your life.

If you don't dream you can still work with this meditation. When you start to fill your physical body with Light before going to sleep, this will mirror a reflection within your subtle anatomy. That reflection will take on different colours in the same way that your dream body does, which will give you a series of coloured 'pointers'.

Then as you work with this meditation, and as the white Light starts to permeate throughout your physical body, you will find that all colours reflected within your subtle anatomy will start to be transmuted.

When your physical body becomes totally white, and when all the colours reflected in your subtle anatomy have been filtered out, the mirror image within your subtle body will reflect the purity and whiteness of your physical body. You may then find that you have access to your dream state, since the vibration of white Light energy will have interacted with your subtle anatomy.

20. Full meditation programme to release personal karma

This meditation encompasses many parts - first you can deal with, and transmute, any slow frequency energy that is causing physical problems. This also helps you to focus on your subtle anatomy and get in touch with what your body is saying, not only about problems in this life time, but also about problems from past lives which you are still carrying in your body and which need to be removed.

In the main vision of this meditation you work with your 'darker twin' who represents any unfinished karma within the various planes you are working in, as well as any concentrated thought forms you might be unaware of.

You will also be working with all the members of your family, and any other person physically in your life with whom you have unfinished karma. This sequence also gives you a specific way of knowing when the karma between you and each person you work with, is finished.

This is followed by the sequence which works with any thought form or any energy pattern under the umbrella of 'limitation'.

There is no limit to how much you can do in any one meditation other than the limitations you personally set yourself. Initially you may try too hard and try to do everything at once. If you start to feel tired, then recognise that you have overstepped the mark, although if you keep charging yourself up as explained then you should not lose energy.

Once you start to work with this and tap into old thought forms, the meditation will act a bit like a vacuum cleaner and will suck all the 'gunk' out of you! You may even find areas of weakness you haven't come into contact with before. So the amount you should attempt at any one time is the amount you feel happy with, recognising there is no time limit with this - if you want to take a few years to work with all your personal karma, then that is OK.

As you see, this meditation has a far-reaching effect and can be very open-ended. You can use this format to work with anything that is an irritant in your life and release that energy quite quickly, moving your life into a new octave.

Initially you may want to record the full meditation onto tape. You can then play it as a guided meditation. Alternatively a prerecorded tape set of this meditation programme, led by the author, is available from the address at the back of this book. If recording the meditation for yourself, leave sufficient gaps of silence to allow time for yourself to do the various steps. Then you won't be rushing the actual meditation in order to keep up with your tape.

An outline of this meditation sequence is given first, to give you an overview of the full sequence. As it is important for you to understand the full meaning and essence behind this meditation, you should read the *full* meditation before you attempt to work with this.

Preparation

As part of this meditation sequence you will be doing the black healing meditation. You will be working with your Light body, building up an energy charge in your heart centre, and projecting that Light out in a triangular focus. You will also be working with the hara, or point of balance within your chakra centres. If you are not clear about any of these aspects, they are all given in detail in *Key Aspects Of Meditation Work*, so refer back to them and practise these techniques before going into the full meditation. See: Meditation 4 - Black healing meditation; Meditation 5 - How to put on your Light body; Meditation 16 - How to find your centre of balance, the polarity point or hara within your body.

Outline of meditation

Bring white Light down through the top of your head and root yourself in. Do the black healing meditation to cleanse the body. Next focus on your heart centre and build a shaft of white Light which, in your visualisation, goes out from your heart centre as a bridge forming 29 steps into a plateau in a space setting with stars all around.

In your visualisation, walk over the 29 steps onto the plateau where you will see a bonfire. You walk into that fire which represents protection and healing, and remove any slow frequency energy from your body, working through your body from the outer layer of skin to the soft tissue, muscles and skeletal structure.

Then put on your Light body. Beyond the flames visualise your darker twin who represents all your hate, doubt, anger and negative emotions. You project white Light in a triangular focus into your darker twin's heart centre to transmute all that he or she represents. Continue to project your white Light until the darker twin becomes transparent and merges with you in the fire.

In the same way, you can then work with any members of your family with whom you have unfinished karma. Again put them outside the flames and transmute any karma by projecting your white Light.

You can also work with any thought forms or energy patterns which come under the umbrella of limitation. You do this by symbolising the thought form as a shape, then project your triangle of white Light into that thought form to transmute the energy package.

Full meditation sequence

You can do this meditation last thing at night when you are tucked up in bed and feel nice and safe. Alternatively, if meditating in this mode sends you to sleep, then do it as a meditation proper.

1. Bring down white Light and ground yourself

First think of a point of white Light, pencil thin, coming down through the top of your head, linking into each of your main chakra centres, linking you into Heaven. Then visualise roots coming out of your feet, going down into the planet linking you with Mother Earth. Make the colour of your roots whatever colour feels intuitively right.

2. Black healing meditation

Now do the black healing meditation, breathing in black energy, bringing it up through your roots into your body to absorb any imbalance of energy, then flush that out with the white Light coming down through the top of your head.

3. Build up white Light in your heart centre

Focus again on the white Light coming into your heart and build up an energy charge of white Light in your heart centre.

4. Building the bridge

Visualise a shaft of white Light going from your heart into a plateau which you imagine in front of you. This plateau should be in a space setting, like a flat asteroid, with stars all around. Each star represents a cosmic gypsy*. These beings are 50 miles (80 km) high, 25 miles (40 km) across, with wing spans of 75 miles (120 km). Each one will have a different colour focus, but initially you may just see them as stars as a whole.

Visualise your shaft of Light going from your heart into the plateau as a bridge with 29 steps. Each step should be clearly defined as each one has a specific vibration. The 29 steps represent the 29 subtle vehicles of your lower self. Each of these 29 subtle vehicles will in essence have positive and negative frequencies within them.

Each step also represents a filter mechanism which has a colour and therefore a keynote or sound. Initially, when you first do this meditation, the steps may be transparent, but as you do the meditation more and more you will become aware of the colour in each step. When you walk on each step a vibrational package of energy will be released which you walk through. This vibrational filter package will absorb from your own negative frequencies, the seed thoughts, the notes of doubt or fear that might be inbred within your body. In this way you will release some of the subtle imbalances of energy within your various bodies as you walk over each step and respond to its colour and frequency vibration.

This filter mechanism will happen even if you are not fully aware of it. If your clairvoyance is adequate you may sense, feel, or see the different colour formations of each step. You may not sense or feel anything at all. But by thinking this bridge into existence, by focusing on it in your visualisation, energy will follow thought and you will create a structural thought form* of some complexity. Therefore by simply walking over this bridge within your visualisation, you will automatically filter off subliminal negative imprints you might still be working with.

The vibrational package of your 29 steps will also deny access to astral entities, or structural thought forms who might try to follow you into this new setting.

Occasionally, as you project your beam of white Light and form your bridge there might be inner resistance to you moving, in your awareness, from one level to another. So don't be alarmed if you see or feel some of the steps on your bridge missing, or if the bridge is blocked or comes to a dead end. This merely represents an inner obstacle or imbalance that your conscious, or subconscious mind has not specifically focused on.

If this is the case, concentrate and direct your energy into the part of the bridge that is incomplete. Then, as your superconscious mind directs the energy accordingly, the bridge formation will rectify itself.

To do this, focus on the incomplete part of the bridge and symbolise that part as having three lenses. Each lens should be approximately 6 feet square (2m square) and transparent. If any or all of the lenses have any colour at all, then visualise your arms and hands stretched out sideways, and visualise the white Light coming in through your crown chakra, flowing down through all your chakras into your base chakra, then flowing back up into your heart centre, and from your heart flowing along both arms into your hands. In this way the white Light forms a cross. You then project shafts of Light in this cross formation into the first lens. As the white Light flows in, the lens will clear and you will see the second lens behind that. You repeat this with the second and third lens. When all three lenses are clear, the missing sequence in your bridge should then be rectified and you will have your 29 steps.

It is important that your bridge is complete, so do not proceed further with the meditation until the bridge mechanism is fully in place.

5. Going into the fire

When your bridge is complete, walk over it and come down into the plateau where you will see a large bonfire, 50 feet (15m) high and 25 feet (7.5m) across. The fire represents purity, self-healing and unconditional love. It is also the force of the collective will of your group on the inner planes. When you start working with this meditation, the bonfire will be seen as white Light.

Walk into the fire, and the first thing you will be aware of is a growing sense of well-being. Just allow the flames to flow around you as you breathe in the flame of life, and breathe out the wisdom and harmony that will bring you the insights you need.

If you have a fear of fire and find the thought of walking into fire difficult to work with, bear in mind that this fire is just a symbol of something which can transmute energy. It is a symbol of purity. It will reduce to its basic essence the package of energy which all who go into it must confront. It also represents protection and healing, so just see this fire as a safe, healing Light you will sit in.

6. Removing any slow frequency energy from your body

It is advisable to do this part of the meditation prior to the larger vision of the meditation which begins with Step 8. This section is where you can deal with and transmute any slow frequency energy causing physical problems in the body. It also works with any problems from past lives which you might still be carrying in your body and now need to be removed.

By doing this section and the following Step 7 you can also build your vibration. You may well choose to stick with just this part for a while, and move onto the main part of the meditation later on. Practising Steps 6 and 7 will be a bit like learning your lines on the stage. You keep going over the same bit until you get it right. In this way you build up better 'muscles' which will make working with the main part of the meditation a lot easier.

If however you find a great deal of reluctance to do this part in the way described, then move onto Step 8. I recognise that a lot of people don't want to do the basics - they just want to move onto the good bits! Having said that, remember you have to get rid of the sludge first so that your vibration can go up and be maintained at the new frequency note. Also I should add here that in Step 9 you will be looking at the 'darker twin' aspect of yourself, which is the sum total of everything. That everything will imply a lot of things which on a conscious level you may not be able to tap into until you have got used to the various filters your mind is using, and have enough courage to take them off. Working with Steps 6 and 7 will help you to remove those filters. Once you have taken those filters off, you can then have a good look at your darker twin. If you skip this part and choose to dive straight into the main part of the meditation, it will be like trying to grapple with your darker aspect in one go. So it comes back to personal choice!

If you do choose to get rid of the sludge then you just sit in the fire and allow it to burn off all your clothing which symbolises the burning away of old ideas, misinformation, and expectancy.

Some Light workers may find their clothes transmute quite quickly, and will only need to repeat this part again in future meditations, when it feels appropriate.

But sometimes old habits die slowly! So although you may dissolve your clothing in one meditation and move freely onto the next step, when you come back to this part in your next session, you might find some clothes are still active on your body. If so, continue to repeat this part regularly which will help to transmute the old ideas and build your confidence.

Once all your clothing goes you can have a good look at your physical body. You might see scar tissue, old wounds from a previous life, and you may get flashbacks to that lifetime. Allow the flames to heal any outer imbalance which is apparent, and as it does, you might have more flashbacks to older time periods. As this happens, use the unconditional love of the fire as a focus, and allow the fire to work as a demolishing pattern of energy. As old thought patterns from flashbacks of past lives come up, they are there to be released and not to be dwelt upon. Therefore they are on one level relatively unimportant, and should be released as quickly as possible. See this as your old thoughts being on a blackboard, and you merely rub them out - so your flames are the blackboard rubber and your demolishing focus.

If all your clothing doesn't burn off, stay in the fire until it does. You might have to repeat the meditation up to this point for a few weeks until all your clothing burns away. Clothing also symbolises fear of the unknown and fear of dealing with structural energies which you need to focus on. So there may be some resistance to working through this. A resistance to transmuting all your clothing might also be due to magnetic and structural imbalances on an astral level, and you might have astral entities who are deliberately cultivating fear within your own thought forms.

By repeating this daily, you will eventually burn off all your clothing and will gain a sense of well-being. If you work with the meditation up to this point only, then come out of the meditation as explained in Step 12.

7. Physical release mechanism

Once you have fully completed Step 6, take off your skin and look at your muscle fibres and soft tissue. You can also look into your capillaries, into each major organ - you can even travel up your arteries and look at your cholesterol level. You are just questing, basically looking for any dark energy. Each organ and every part of your body should be viewed as pure and white, so any dark lumpy bits or any peculiar patterns which you may even see as geometric symbols, can be transmuted by visualising the fire moving into that part and burning away the dark energy.

Having done that, you then remove all your soft tissue and look at your skeleton. Take a close look and if there is any inflammation in the joints, you can transmute that as well, using the fire to burn it away.

8. Put on your Light body

You now accept your archetypal Light body. Just allow your intuition to guide you as to which archetypal pattern you need to adopt today.

9. Dealing with your darker twin

With your Light body on, focus on the white Light coming down through the top of your head into your heart centre and build up your energy charge in your heart centre. Looking at this on a percentage basis, your energy charge should reach a minimum of 90%. Use your intuition to tell you when you are ready. When you get up to this 'hot point' look outside of the bonfire, and visualise your darker twin, who represents all your hate, doubt, anger and negative emotions, standing 45 feet (13.5 m) away. He or she will be jet-black and will represent a duplication of yourself but a lot older -

about 400 years old. A bit like a warty old hag! The skin should be really black, and you can visualise the body as being a bit deformed if you wish. In fact any current problems you might have, physically or emotionally, can be registered within the appearance of your darker twin.

For those who have clairvoyant focus you can also look at the individual cordings linking you with your darker twin.

You then open the wings or paws of your archetypal pattern. As you do this, visualise a shaft of Light coming out from your heart centre, linking your third eye and both palms of your hands to form a triangular focus of energy. This triangle can be pale blue, gold or white. Every frequency vibration has a colour and, therefore, you intuitively choose the colour which feels right for you, depending on the frequency vibration you are working with. You then whack this triangle of energy into the heart centre of the darker aspect of yourself. It should interact fairly quickly. The intensity of the black in your darker twin should start to fade and he or she will start to slowly shuffle towards you. As it does, it should start to get younger and the colour should continue to fade until it is transparent.

In this way you are using your will to transmute and draw out fear, misinformation, and ignorance in its totality until in essence the life-blood of all that is negative, which is represented by your darker twin, is neutralised. This is when the form becomes transparent.

The actual pattern of releasing the triangular focus of energy is in short thrusts lasting five seconds. You don't have to hold this energy for any longer. Each time you whack the energy in for five seconds you look to see if your darker twin has changed in any shape or form. If at any point, you project your energy for five consecutive sets of five seconds and your darker twin has not changed or becomes static, you stop here. Then leave it a minimum of 12 hours or until the next day before repeating the meditation. Ideally this should become a daily meditation, rather than just once or twice a week. To come out of the meditation, read Step 12.

If you come to a level where, for whatever reason, part of you is not willing to release any more energy then your darker twin will stop moving. It will remain static. Come out of the meditation and come back to this the next day. Continue to work with this on a daily basis, whacking in your triangle of Light for 25 seconds a day. If your darker twin seems to be stuck, continue working with this on a daily ongoing basis, sending in your 25 seconds of Light energy and know that you will still be removing energy. Your darker twin may remain static for several months - maybe even six months - then suddenly your darker twin will move forward.

Your aim is to continue working daily with this meditation until you bring this darker aspect of yourself right up to the flame. By then it should be totally transparent and should be the age of a one-month old baby. You then bring this transparent baby aspect of yourself right into the flame and allow it to merge with you in its totality. Once you have achieved this, you will know that the karma, or the initial package you are working with under this karmic heading has been resolved and transmuted.

However, this darker aspect which is a manifestation of many thought forms and many hidden - and possibly known - desires, will have a latent intelligence. So in its own way it will be motivated to preserve its energy system, and might even try to get into the fire with you while it is still black and old. If this happens, bear in mind that what you are seeing is a reflection of many particles which need to be transmuted, and therefore you must be totally ruthless in your relationship with your darker aspect.

You therefore keep it at a distance. Do not allow it to come near you, irrespective of how it is manifesting, until its colour starts to fade. Just continue to focus on sending in unconditional love as you systematically whack in your triangle of energy until the colour becomes transparent.

As you stand in the flames of your fire and continue to whack your triangle of energy into your darker twin, the essence of your will and the power of your group family on the inner planes will automatically flow through you to intensify the Light you are projecting at your darker twin.

If you start to get tired, you are using far too much of your physical energy. Every time you feel your physical energy slowing down a bit, and you might feel this as a coldness in your heart chakra, just close your wings or paws, and recharge yourself up. Then continue to project your triangle of Light energy once again. The very act of charging yourself up is achieved by the understanding within yourself that, as you close your wings, you are actually opening up your crown chakra to an input of high frequency Light which will automatically give you healing, understanding, information and, of course, the flexibility to allow the energy to build up to a level which is acceptable for you.

So while you are in the flames, you are like a battery attached to the mains - a trickle charge is in place so that energy systematically continues to flow into your body.

If during this meditation your thoughts drift and side-track, part of you will still be carrying on the exercise on whatever level is necessary. The drifting mechanism is tapping into alternative realities as you become more multi-dimensional. If this happens, once you become conscious of drifting, just bring your focus back and continue from where you were in the meditation.

Most people who are just waking up will need to do this part of the meditation regularly over a period of 18 months, as this is the normal time frequency to get your 'muscles' into a sort of harmonic convergence - it is also the karmic cycle most people are working with. If you have already been working with Light, or have been doing a lot of meditation, you may only need to work with this over a period of 13 months. The 13 or 18 month time period is something you have to intuitively decide for yourself.

It is recommended that you work with your darker twin as an ongoing programme for a minimum of 13 months. Even if you have the capacity to dissolve all the darkness in your darker twin in any earlier session you may find when you repeat the meditation, say three nights later, your darker twin might be back again but subtly different. You might then see it as the opposite sex to what you are. In fact, it might totally change and you might see this darker aspect of yourself not as a very old, but as a very young aspect, just nine or ten years old who is intensely evil.

By working with this for a minimum of 13 months you will find a collection of data, which are the different karmic packages stored in your body being presented to you in whatever way is appropriate to your individual need.

By working with this over 13 months you will also be working with the vibration of the number 13 as discussed in Meditation 18, 'To raise your vibrational pattern', earlier in this chapter. In addition, you will also benefit from the power of the cosmic cycle where the sum total of the planets, as they spin through their oscillating fields, has a knock-on effect within the cosmic biorhythms within your subtle bodies. This helps to release the overall pattern you might be working through at that time.

By systematic use you will be able to spontaneously bring your darker aspect into the flames and release any peculiar energy which might be manifesting through it during that meditation session. When you have reached this stage, you will know you have also freed yourself of the particular aspect of karma which was reflected in the current darker twin within that meditation session.

The important thing is to discipline yourself to do this meditation regularly as it is one of the most important meditations in this book. This particular meditation will also make you aware of alternative states of reality that will sneak in during each session. With ongoing practice you will also become aware of multi-dimensional time, not only in past-life frequencies but also future lives, parallel lives, as well as factual and actual lives. So it will speed everything up for you quite nicely!

10. Decording from the karma with your family and other people in your life

In this part of the meditation, you can work with anyone in your physical family, and anybody physically in your life with whom you have any relationship, be it positive or negative. You can also work with a family member who has died as their thought forms may still be active and linked into any emotional dumping set up during your childhood.

Whereas the darker twin is worked with over 13 to 18 months, working with anyone in this section is done over shorter periods of three months for each person.

For this, do Steps 1 to 8, then initially put all the people you want to work with outside the fire. Look to see where they are standing and start working with those nearest to the flames first, working systematically and dealing with those furthest away last.

If you are working with a family member, look at the cordings between you, which might look a bit like garden hose pipes with teeth on the end. Then visualise that person as a specific colour. Remember that each colour represents a specific vibration, so work intuitively and your higher self will tell you what colour to use.

Once again charge up your triangular focus of energy and freely project it from your heart into the heart chakra of the person you are working with. By encouraging this interaction through the unconditional love you are placing in their heart centre, you can burn off any cordings between you.

In this section, as you project your triangular focus of energy, it will form 29 triangles one within the other. Each one will be a different frequency corresponding to the frequencies of the 29 steps in your bridge. As each step and frequency has its own colour, so each triangle will also have a different colour. When working with a member of your family, you just amplify the appropriate triangle and colour which corresponds to the vibrational charge of the person you are targeting. Again work intuitively, and you will know which triangle to amplify. Some people might osculate with all 29 triangles, in which case the whole combination of colour and sound frequency of all 29 triangles - healing, love, etc. - will be amplified and projected all at the same time.

As you amplify and project the appropriate triangle of energy into their heart chakra in five bursts of five seconds each, all their colour should fade, even if the colour is really pleasant. They should then become transparent and start to move towards you. As they slowly move towards you, they won't get younger as your darker twin did but will remain a constant age. The only exception here is when, occasionally, a family member represents something linked to your childhood, and they might get younger.

When the person you are working with has become transparent, they will move into the flames and merge with you. When this happens, you will know that all personal karma between you and that person has been transmuted.

If the person isn't willing to deal with the karma between you, as you pass your triangular focus of energy into their heart centre they won't respond and will actually move away from you until eventually they disappear over the horizon. Or they might turn their back on you. This is an indication that the timing is not right. If this happens, continue to work regularly with that person, passing your triangle of energy, which represents your unconditional love, into their heart centre and this will build up as an energy charge. When the cosmic, biological, or soul timing of that person is right, they will turn to face you and the accumulation of energy which you have been passing into their heart will be released into their being.

If that person was stuck in their karmic cycle, as the build-up of your Light energy is released into their heart centre, this may trip their karmic cycle and speed them up. This may help to bring them up to a point where you can help to free them up, and at the same time move yourself into a place of greater freedom.

If for whatever reason, the person you are working with becomes transparent, comes into the flames with you, but will not merge with you, this means the astral karma - the subtle patterns of energy on a higher plane - in relation to that person still has be transmuted. So although on a physical level your personal karma with this person will have been transmuted, the astral karma still needs to flow down and be transmuted. This will happen naturally, so continue working with that person, sending your triangle of Light into their heart chakra. You may find that while the astral karma is being transmuted, that person just dances in the flames with you. This is a positive indication of energy movement, and once that energy or cycle has been completed, that person will totally merge with you.

If you work with someone in your physical family who has died and who, for whatever reason, is stuck in the lower astral planes and unable to move on, they may also come into the flames and dance with you. In the same way continue to work with them by sending your triangle of energy into their heart chakra. In this way you will be systematically healing them. You will create a vibration of energy that will continue to get stronger and stronger, day by day, until your energy charge transmutes and releases the energy pattern which has been holding them in the Earth's orbit. They will then be free and able to move onto a different level of development and awareness. This will be your parting gift to them.

11. Working with specific thought forms or energy patterns

In this section you will be dealing with specific negative thought forms and emotions within yourself which come under the umbrella of limitation. Although on one level this part of the meditation is a duplication of the darker twin, it can be symbolised as looking at an Olympic athlete running round the track, then seeing that athlete with X-ray vision, seeing all the sinews, muscles, arteries and every minute aspect which contributes to the effort of that Olympic run.

By splitting up your karma into specific areas, and working with each section, you also have a much better understanding of what is taking place with your darker twin. Each time you systematically dispose of your darker twin, a new cycle of energy will replace the old package which has been transmuted and other darker twins, subtly different, may come in. As this happens, thought forms and packages of energy may come in which aren't specifically encased within your darker twin. And that is a new ball game!

Therefore this part of the meditation is the other half of the equation. You can work with this as a continuation within any session after Steps 1 to 10. In this part you work with any specific thought form and dominant emotional pattern which is a bit of a nuisance. You can also work specifically with any limiting emotion, be it loneliness, pain, anger or fear.

You can also work with your bank if you want to! And you can work with any thought form that intuitively offends you. If you want to work with, say violence in its totality, or rape for the female or male aspect, you can symbolise each of these as a thought form and work with that.

You can symbolise a thought form in several different ways. One way is to visualise the thought form as an egg-shaped energy form - or any shape that intuitively presents itself to you. Then give that shape seven chakra centres, splitting each one up into three: a bottom, middle and top. If you find visualisation difficult, you can draw an egg shape on a piece of paper, colour it, and give it seven chakras, splitting each one into three as before. The idea is to create a shape or symbol that represents the thought form, which will give you a working dialogue to get a 'reading' showing where within that thought form you need to focus your energy.

To explain how this works, let us take loneliness as an example. Visualise the thought form of loneliness as a shape - let us assume it is an egg shape. Put that egg shape outside of the fire and give it a chakra system with each chakra split into three, a bottom, middle and top. Then look to see which chakra centre is active - we call this the active point of balance, or hara - which will show you where loneliness is being activated within that thought form. You do this intuitively. With practice, most people can do this quite easily and it just becomes a very natural intuitive feel of where the pattern of energy is coming into that thought form.

For most people, loneliness is activated within their own sexual chakra centre. So the sexual centre in their egg-shaped thought form will reflect this and will also be the active point. Once you have located the active chakra, look closer and see whether loneliness is coming in through the bottom, middle or top part of the sexual centre.

If, for example, loneliness is coming in at the bottom part of the sexual centre, you charge up your triangle of Light energy and project that into the section *just above* that, which will be the middle section of the sexual centre. Project your triangle of energy for a maximum of five bursts of five seconds each. This should push the hara up to that section. As linear time is an illusion, 25 seconds in total is enough for each section to move the vibration up.

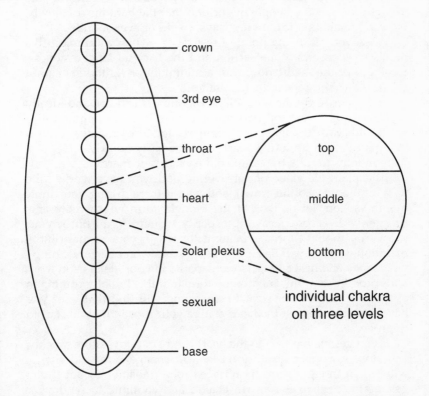

Egg-shaped energy form with seven chakras

Once the hara has moved up to the middle section, you project your triangle of energy into the section just above that, which is now the top part of the sexual centre. Repeat the above sequence, projecting your triangle of energy into that section for a maximum of five bursts of five seconds. Once again this should move the hara up to that section. Move your focus up to the solar plexus and start to project your energy into the lower section of the solar plexus chakra. Continue in this way to systematically move the hara up through all the other chakras.

In this way you are using your energy input to improve the vibration of that thought form, heightening it, pushing it further up, and raising its active point of balance.

The upward movement of this active point of balance is normally fairly quick, and as you whack your triangle of energy in, you should get a fairly spontaneous response by the hara moving upwards. But there is always an exception! In practice, the hara will move up fairly quickly for most people, but depending on the thought form, some people might find that the hara moves slowly, or even remains static for a few days, weeks or even months.

When you reach any point of resistance - when you project five bursts of energy into one section and the hara no longer moves - come out of the meditation, wait a minimum of 12 hours, or until the next day and repeat the meditation.

The aim is to get the hara all the way up to the heart, and ideally to move it up to the top part of the crown. It is also important to work with each thought form regularly for three months, even if you get the hara up to the heart or above fairly quickly, as it takes three months to fully transmute old packages of energy.

To explain the value of persevering until you have worked the hara all the way up to the crown, and held it there during your three month session, let us look at the thought form which represents prosperity. Everybody has a prosperity thought form. But if your prosperity thought form is being activated in your sexual centre, that thought form will be lacking energy and won't be very strong - which may manifest as a lack of prosperity in your life. As you work with prosperity in this meditation format, if it is initially coming in at the top half of your sexual centre, you will find that once you have moved it up past the heart chakra your prosperity will start to improve.

If you get the hara up to the heart centre or above quite quickly, and stop working with it, not a lot will change if the old energy within that thought form hasn't been fully transmuted. But if you get the hara up to the crown chakra and continue to send your triangle of energy into it and keep it energised during the three-month session, your prosperity will then dramatically change in a very specific way. During this three-month period, any colour within your thought form will also disappear and your thought form will become transparent as the old negative vibration gets starved!

Prosperity can be physical, emotional, or mental, so you can split it up into each of these segments and work individually with each segment, or you can just lump it all into one and work with it in its entirety.

Keep a list and write down all the thought forms you are working with. You can work with up to 40 in any three-month session. Put them in order of importance and as you work with each one, note where you end the meditation. So if, in your meditation with loneliness, you got the hara to move up to the middle section of the solar plexus centre, note that and the date.

If you start working with any thought form, especially if it is an old package, and for some reason you don't repeat this exercise within a two-week period, you may find that when you go back to the meditation again, the old package of energy has flowed back down towards the level where it was before. So if you don't continue to work with your chosen thought form on a regular basis it will take a lot longer to move the hara up - and it will be like going three steps forward and two steps back!

So continue to work with each thought form on a regular basis in this way. Exercise patience, perseverance and discipline, recognising that irrespective of what pattern you are being presented with, the vibration of your positive thought input will create a change for the better, and the pattern will change once the hara hits the heart centre.

Suggestions for the energy patterns you can work with:

a) physical problems

You can use this meditation format to work with all negative and limiting thought forms around your body and health. You can work with any physical problem or disease, be it the common cold, cancer, arthritis or AIDS.

If, for example, you have gall-stones, you can symbolise the gall-stones as a thought form. See it as an egg shape, give it a chakra system and see where the hara, or active chakra is within that thought form. Then work with this meditation sequence in the same way as in the example for loneliness. This will create a healing of the thought form that caused the gall-stones. Depending on your personal karma, the gall-stone problem itself may also be healed, although you may still have to have them physically removed by a surgeon if you need that experience as well. But the underlying thought form which created the gall-stones will have been transmuted and the gall-stones themselves should not come back.

You can also target the genetics of your body by looking at any genetic weakness you are aware of through family history, be that migraine, arthritis, or a susceptibility to heart problems. Again symbolise that disease as a thought form, and work to release the imbalance by moving the hara and vibration within that thought form upwards as before. It is important to do this with any genetic weakness, as a lot of them are now in a very active format. This has been caused by a cumulative input of inbreeding because of the basic formation of the genetics now in the planet, and the frequency vibration from different races blending into a point of disharmony.

We all have a self-healing mechanism - our immune system - on the physical, etheric, astral and mental levels, and on a soul level as well! Occasionally this self-healing mechanism is at a point of inactivity either from a series of irregular energy flows, or because of a trauma from a past life. Sometimes the self-healing mechanism of the individual cell has been manipulated - and cancer is a good example of this. Therefore, by symbolising your self-healing mechanism as a thought form in its own right, it would be useful to push the hara of that thought form upwards to help underpin the self-healing work you are doing in a much more conscious way.

The same can be applied to unconditional love. Most people have very little unconditional love coming into their lives. They live under an illusion, thinking the love they have is unconditional when it is really conditional. By targeting unconditional love as a thought form and pushing the vibration upwards, true unconditional love can reach a point of activation where it flows into all levels of your being.

b) material possessions

If you have a fear of being burgled, especially if your home has already been burgled, that fear is a thought form. Fear of being physically assaulted is another thought form. So is fear of death. By using this meditation sequence you can neutralise all these thought forms which may be limiting you and holding you back.

Motor-cars are also thought forms. They tend to attract a build-up of magnetic energy and when the build-up goes over 30%, the activation and implosion of that energy creates an accident. This meditation can transmute any negative energy in your car to ensure you don't drive around in a car which is liable to attract an accident to you!

c) environment

Any problem in your local environment can be worked on in the same way. For example, if the plants in your garden won't grow, you can target the weeds, negative ley lines, geopathic stress, or any magnetic package of energy which might be interfering with their growth.

If you don't know what is specifically wrong, you can still work with the problem in general by just labelling it 'any harmful energy in my garden'.

12. To come out of the meditation

At whatever stage of the meditation sequence you decide to finish your current session, you come out of the meditation by bringing your awareness back to the fire. Fold the wings or paws of your Light body, which closes your aura and in its own way is a very nice way to protect yourself. So if, for example, you have been targeting astral entities as a thought form, they won't be able to reapply themselves as your aura will be closed through the focus of closing your Light body around you.

After closing down your aura you can keep your Light body on as a constant companion. In this way you build up an awareness of it being there, so whenever any threat or any negative energy tries to come into your space, you can immediately think of your Light body, and activate it. In this way it becomes a permanent asset or protection.

Now go back over the 29 steps on the bridge between the plateau and your heart. Each step should dissolve as you walk over them. This closes down the frequency entrance points you opened when you first went over the bridge.

When you come back over the bridge, it may appear to be far shorter than when you first went over it. Occasionally you may even feel the frequency in each step as being different from when you went over them. This is quite normal. When you initially create the bridge and go over the steps, you are expanding your consciousness and pumping a lot of energy into the thought form of the bridge in order to focus it. But once you have done the meditation - irrespective of whether you have done one section or the full sequence - you will have transmuted and subtly balanced some energy in a variety of different ways. You will, therefore, be subtly different when you come back over the bridge. So know that this is a normal process and just be kind to yourself.

When you first do this meditation and come back over the bridge, take your time, focus your awareness and tune into the sequence of each step. Then if you find some of the steps are subtly different compared to when you first went over them, you will know you have made an energy movement.

As this realignment of energy takes place, it occasionally takes a good three days in Earth time for the energy to settle back down into a new rhythm.

When you have come back off the bridge, go back into your heart centre which you visualise as a golden rose. You then reverse the growth process, seeing the rose go into a bud, then into a point of white Light which you seal with a Celtic cross. Then visualise that completely disappearing as well. Now close down all your other chakras in the same way, then come back into your physical body.

When you next repeat the meditation you will find everything is subtly different. As you continue to work with this exercise and tune into your higher self, becoming more balanced, your inner strength will grow and your reality within Earth time will alter very quickly.

As you progress with this meditation you can vary it in the following ways:

Variation 1:

As you progress, you can start to intuitively alter the colour of the bonfire to match any frequency when there is an intuitive need to work with a special vibration. Bear in mind that each vibration is a colour encodement, and each encodement might be particles of many million frequencies. Although initially the white Light of the bonfire will be the swamping mechanism, you can intuitively change the fire to a specific colour frequency if an old memory or emotional package responds to it. For example, if your intuition guides you to change the colour of the fire to indigo, you may find that unresolved difficulties will be transmuted much quicker.

White Light is in essence a combination of all colours, but in a general high frequency note. As your intuition develops, the recognition of when to change that colour will naturally take place. So although you will start by visualising the bonfire as white Light, you will find your higher self will be well aware of what the physical personality is trying to manifest, and as such, the data will be there for you to tap into. It is a bit like putting a password into a computer and then having multiple options as to what programme you want to tap into. So as you progress with this meditation, do allow your intuitive essence to alter the frequency according to your need.

Variation 2:

As you progress, you may also find that when you return back over the bridge, you have a feeling there are no longer any specific steps. This is because each time you do the meditation everything speeds up and the steps close up like a concertina. You can then return over the bridge very quickly. As you continue working with this programme and expand your consciousness, you will also find it easier to project into multiple dimensional aspects of yourself and into multiple dimensional time. You will then find it gets easier and quicker to go and come back over the bridge.

Variation 3:

When it feels intuitively right to do so, you can vary the *black meditation* in Step 2 by working with rainbow colours instead of black. This is a higher vibrational alternative.

To do this, root yourself in with emphasis on your taproot which will come down from your spine like a tail. This will vibrate with the divinity of Mother Earth and drink her essence. Using the same meditation sequence as in the *black meditation* you now draw rainbow colours up through your roots and into your body.

These rainbow colours will transmute and heal any irregularities within the inner aspect of your body, so again symbolise any aches, pains or problems as ice cubes which are melted by the rainbow colours. When your body is full of rainbow colours, these colours will flow out through the top of your head and flow down all sides of your body like a fountain.

You can also do this as a healing meditation in its own right last thing at night just going off to sleep. In this case, you may find you can only bring the vibration of the rainbow colours up to the sexual chakra centre before drifting off to sleep. But that is OK as, subconsciously, you will continue to work with the meditation on the inner planes, and will continue to bring the colours higher during your sleep state.

21. Third meditation to release old karma from past lives

This meditation is specifically focused with the aim of releasing any old personal karma from past lives which is still within the essence of yourself, and creating an ongoing problem in this lifetime.

For example, a lot of people becoming alcoholic in this lifetime have had previous lives as a shaman. In that lifetime they used the drugs equivalent to alcohol to induce a stupor or dull their nervous system, so that entities or shaman energies could then enter into their space and communicate with them, without the personality getting in the way. These people still have that dominant thought form within them. It is a very sticky thought form which needs to be specifically targeted. So these people may want to work specifically with alcoholism and its association with past lives.

If this is the case you may find, for example, that when working with thought forms in the previous meditation programme, alcoholism or past shaman memories might be at the bottom of your list of thought forms to be worked with, as opposed to number one. This particular meditation will be useful to get rid of that specific problem, so that you can move on into a new sense of freedom.

This meditation is also useful if you are being subjected to psychic attack since this normally tunes into the bottom three chakra centres where psychic attack takes place, or if you are being targeted by any organisation within your physical life, such as a satanic group. This is also a particularly useful meditation if you meet up with a soul mate where you have a negative energy charge between you which has to be transmuted. When a soul brings two aspects of itself together in one place there is usually a lot of personal karmic 'flavouring' added to the proceedings.

Meditation sequence

With this exercise you start, as always, by visualising white Light coming down through the top of your head, rooting yourself in, and putting on your Light body. Then visualise all your main chakra centres as being external to yourself and visualise each one being split into three - bottom, middle and top.

In your visualisation go and sit outside your base chakra. Then choose two people you wish to invite in to help you transmute your karma. This may be an Avatar, plus someone else you trust and have a close affinity with.

For each person intuitively choose a colour that represents their energy system. If for example one of the two people you have chosen is an Avatar, and you intuitively feel that silver is the colour which symbolises his or her energy system, put on an imaginary silver glove onto your right hand. The glove should be fairly long, coming up to your elbow.

If you feel that purple represents the energy power of the other person you have invited in, put a long purple glove on your left hand.

In this way each of their energy systems is represented as a package of energy, fitting over one of your hands. Initially you can use the colours given here in this example. But ideally allow your intuition to guide you so that the vibration of the colours you work with match the vibration of the energy systems of the people you have chosen. With practice you will spontaneously know what colours to use.

Then invite in the karmic package you want to work with. You visualise this karma as a ball of light coming out from the lower section of the base centre opposite which you are sitting. As the ball comes out, all you do is grab it with your hands. As you do, the white Light which is coming in through the top of your head comes down into your heart, down your arms and into your hands. You blend this white Light with the energy colour of the two people your gloves represent. This combination of energy will then dissolve the ball. It should just go, like a puff of smoke, or you may feel a cracking sensation - and it is gone!

Then repeat this, dissolving the ball that comes out of the middle section of the base chakra. Then dissolve the ball that comes out of the top section of the base chakra. Repeat this with each chakra centre, working upwards through the bottom, middle and top sections of each chakra.

Sometimes you may have a massive battle. But bear in mind that since February 1992, the karmic pattern for most people is 'up for grabs' so there is a lot of things you can now do for yourself!

Initially just use the meditation on yourself. As you progress you can move on to work on other people's chakra centres, provided you have asked your higher self if it is appropriate for you to do so, and that intuitively you feel the answer is 'yes'. Since the karmic package within the planet has now altered its frequency, and Light workers have a duty to respond to the need of their fellow travellers, always assume the right polarities are in the right place at the right time, so that the overture you are working with can be successfully transmuted.

If I was personally working in this way with another person, I would look at each centre in turn, and might find several little balls of Light coming out of each chakra. These balls might be different colours symbolising the disordered information, the experiences which that person has still to go through.

For example, someone might have a ball near the base centre which doesn't want to come too near me, because it knows it is going to be grabbed. I would then go into the essence of the space of that person to grasp this ball. As I hang onto it, a lot of energy would be transmuted and a tremendous rage and fear may come from it. But as I dissolve it in its entirety, it would totally go.

You can work in this same way with another person, working with each chakra centre in turn. Some of the balls coming out of their chakras might be much nearer, and some will be much further away. The balls further away will be an expression of older karmic discharge that hasn't been dealt with. To grasp those balls which are further away you would, in essence, be going backwards in time into a further reference point that needs to be transmuted. As you grasp those balls, they will come more into the 'now' of the space you are working with and can be dealt with accordingly.

As the balls come up they should be transparent. Some might have pleasant colours such as blue, pink, or gold. But all balls, irrespective of their colour have to be worked with, and have to be transmuted in their entirety.

The colours of the balls from the person you are working with normally reflect your own - although there are always exceptions to the rule! But as the karmic fields you are working with should be, compatible, the balls should be a dual expression of what is taking place within yourself.

If you have three balls, or several tiny little balls coming out together, you gather all the balls together into one composite ball - you can visualise this as your hands working like a big butterfly net to catch and transmute the balls into one. When all the balls coming out of each chakra have been transmuted, the majority of people will have no balls left within each chakra, or alternatively - depending on the ray type that you are - you may see a ball of approximately three feet (1m) in size manifesting from each centre, all nicely balanced in unity. Each ball will appear to be sitting on top of each other, like a series of lenses that have been cleaned.

If you end up with nicely balanced balls of Light this is an indication that each centre is balanced. The actual balls of Light which you perceive are now just an indication of rightness rather than an active energy component which needs to be removed. These balls of Light will be focused specifically for whatever job or work that person needs to do.

More advanced stage

This more advanced stage is to be worked on only after stage one has been completed. It requires some considerable practice and a good power of visualisation.

As this meditation has certain references to Atlantean times it is particularly useful to clear the 'dirt' from Atlantean sources. At first you may think this variation is a lot more complicated, but once you get into it, it will become quite easy. In this meditation each chakra centre is worked on, on a one to 17 level basis, so you will work with 17 levels within each chakra. The number 17 creates a vibratory charge of its own which is very useful for slow frequency cleansing work.

Again start by bringing white Light down through the top of your head, and rooting yourself in. Then put on your Light body.

As before, visualise all your chakra centres as being external to yourself and go and sit opposite the base chakra. As you look at this base chakra, visualise this as having 17 doorways, one behind the other. Go up to the first doorway, and in your visualisation dissolve or transmute any darkness around the doorway, in whatever way your higher self suggests.

If for example the doorway is made of brick and looks very dirty with sharp edges, you actually clean it and transmute all the darkness. File down or cut away any sharp structural edges and make them nice and safe. Then put your own imprint, your own thought form, your own power symbol - which might be a Celtic cross - on the doorway.

Then, as you walk through that doorway, you will find yourself in a corridor. Within that corridor will be the energy you need to transmute, for example you might see old aspects of yourself languishing in prison. These are only thought forms as you are basically going back into old akashic memories. Whatever you find there has to be removed, irrespective of how it seems within your awareness. So you clean up that corridor and get rid of everything in there, in whatever way you feel is appropriate, recognising that unconditional love will dominate.

Once the corridor is totally clean, you fill it with Light and walk through it. At the bottom of that corridor you will find another doorway - doorway number two. Again you clean up the doorway and stamp your own power symbol on it, which can be the same as before, or it might be a different symbol, such as a Christian cross. You then walk through that door into corridor number two.

As you go through that second corridor you do the same as before and transmute and dissolve whatever is there. Once corridor two is totally clean, you fill it with Light. Go through that corridor to doorway number three, clean it up and go through into corridor number three which you clean up as before.

Continue working in this way through all 17 doors and corridors. Occasionally the area of conflict or energy which needs to be removed might not be found in the first, second or third corridor. These may all seem to be quite clear. But keep going as you might find that corridor four, five or six is particularly polluted.

As you go through each corridor and look back, all the doors and corridors you have been through should all be in a straight line, one behind the other, all nicely balanced and clear of any energy other than your power symbol. If you look back through all the doorways and see any colour there, this is a representation of something you have missed. If this happens, go back to the appropriate corridor and deal with it.

When you have done this for the base chakra, you come back out of those corridors and move your focus on to the sexual chakra external to yourself. Again see it as 17 levels or 17 doorways, and work through all 17 doorways and corridors as before. You do this with all your chakra centres, moving up one chakra centre at a time. By doing this you are invoking and clearing up all your chakra centres on quite a large vibrational level basis.

Although this meditation takes considerable practice, when you master it you can travel back down the corridors of time, life and the Universe. And it is amazing the amount of junk you find down there!

Variation:

Once you have mastered the human sequences in the above meditation, you can focus your energy specifically if you want to go down the extraterrestrial corridors. Always use your intuitive traffic lights to tell you whether your higher self will allow you access to that data. If the response is green, then ask for a specific symbol for your extraterrestrial frequencies.

You do this by bringing white Light down into your heart centre, allowing that white Light to expand and flow up and down your body. Then put on your Light body and think of the need to have an extraterrestrial symbol. This symbol should form within your solar plexus centre and you may feel a form of heat as if manifests there. When the symbol is clearly focused, test it to ensure that it is accurate.

To do this, imagine a flame in front of you. Dedicate and bless it. Place your symbol in the flame and if it becomes brighter it is the right one. If it doesn't brighten, or dissolves or disappears this indicates that it is an energy thought form that is trying to masquerade as your symbol! If it is the right symbol, bring it up to your heart centre, then amplify and make it larger in size. Duplicate the symbol and put a duplication into both hands and feet.

Now visualise your chakra system as being external to yourself and go and sit in front of the base chakra. Focus your will on the doorway opposite your base chakra. The doorway will take on the shape of your symbol, and you use the same sequence as above to cleanse the doorway or the corridor which might be there.

If, when you then go into the corridor, all you see is darkness, or a solid colour, or all white, you still work with the above sequence transmuting what you find there, as the white may just be a camouflage. Allow the power of your will and your love to transmute and remove whatever is there.

Once you have mastered this for yourself you can also do this with other people, using this as a guided meditation, taking them step by step through it.

CHAPTER 3
BY THE YEAR 2008

We are now in a transition as we move from the great old age of Pisces which is negatively charged, into the new cycle of Aquarius which is positively charged. But this is not a graceful shift. In fact, these two cycles are currently in conflict with each other as the female Aquarian energy strives to take dominance over the male Piscean energy.

These transitions take place every 2,500 years as the sun goes through cyclical changes which, through information passed down by the elders of our race, we have labelled the Aries, Pisces, Aquarius, Capricorn, and Sagittarius patterns. With Scorpio, Libra, Virgo, Leo, Cancer, Gemini, and Taurus, these names are also used for the 12 smaller cycles commonly called sun signs, or signs of the zodiac.

Within each of the larger and smaller sun cycles, physical, magnetic, solar and cosmic frequencies affect structural change within our planet and within the Universe as we know it. This also occurs in larger cycles of 26,000, 52,000, and 96,000 Earth years.

The current planetary conflict, as we move into the Age of Aquarius, is reflected within our reality as we perceive it, and everything under the feudal system of the negative side of the Piscean system is now breaking down.

So the conflicts we see throughout society - in particular within our political, educational and financial structures, and within the personal emotional conflict of individual people - is a reflection of this larger planetary clash.

This current transition period from Pisces into Aquarius started in 1508, although the Aquarian energies are only just beginning to merge and meld. But as you look back in history, you can see how we have slowly shifted from a male-dominated feudal system into a more feminine New Age which is seeking to live by the principles of love, truth and intuitive knowing.

This transition will be finally breached by the year 2008. As that time draws closer, the Aquarian energies will dominate with the female vibratory energy recapturing the flame of truth, and instigating a new regime based on unconditional love, trust and true knowledge.

Another major source of energy sweeping into our awareness is called the energy of the Cosmic Christ. This is an input vibration which the universal Lords of Light give us from time to time in cyclic understanding - the yin and yang, the in- and out-breath. As this high frequency vibration comes in, the caretaker of our energy system over the past 2,000 years, whom we know as the Master Jesus, is now focusing this energy through his heart centre from the multi-dimensional space known as Shambhala.

This new vibration is sweeping through all levels of religious movements, stimulating a merging operation, since all religions eventually have to merge and become one, with the dominating principle being unconditional love. So the creed and dogma, and mis-truth that is promoted in some religions - as those within the minority seek to influence the majority - have all got to go. This is part of the old Piscean system under the umbrella of fear and the outdated feudal system.

As the Cosmic Christ energy comes in, it is amplifying everything that has gone on before, both Light and dark. At the same time, our planet, as a separate entity to ourselves, is evolving and coming up to a major initiation. The structure of the planet is altering and becoming more Light focused and the planet is moving up through its own chakra system from the solar plexus centre which is India, into the heart centre which is South Africa.

Moving to the fourth dimension

The people who incarnated during the Atlantean Age, 86,000 years ago, introduced a lot of slow frequency energy into the planet. This induced interdimensional doorways of a negative nature to open up. This slow frequency energy input, far too much in a short space of time, created the Earth movement which is labelled the catastrophe - the sinking of Atlantis.

This was in essence brought about by the esoteric vote of those who should have known better. These days, the esoteric vote going out is demanding the high frequency energy input which we term unconditional love. As this flows into our planet, the planet as a whole is being raised from its physical third dimensional aspect.

In 1987 the planet became fourth dimensionalised on an astral level and now has the capacity to absorb Light more directly into its mass. To do this it needs us - the vast network of Light workers. In fact, the whole purpose for human form is to partially digest these cosmic Light energies and pass them into the planet, as this Light cannot be directly interpreted by the planet itself. But by reflecting these cosmic energies through form in general, and specifically through human form, the planet can then use this Light and distribute it on whatever level she requires.

Interdimensional beings also entered into the etheric structures of some Light workers during the full moon of October 1992 when a vibratory meld took place. These Light workers will now find they have reached a tempo of 92% fourth dimensional energy in the predominantly third dimensional human body. Therefore they are now in a position to bring in a lot more Light, which will gravitate towards and activate other Light workers offering those who are still a little sleepy an opportunity to raise their vibration and the vibration of the planet.

Although the planet has become fourth dimensionalised on an astral level, the planet on a physical level, and humanity in the main, are still polarised in the third dimension. This can be seen in Chernobyl, deforestation, our feudal system, the artificial component of fear which is still deliberately created and amplified, and the whole negative vibration under the general heading of the misinformation service which the darker brothers have brought about. All these third dimensional aspects no longer have credence in the new fourth dimension and will sooner, rather than later, have to go.

As society is weaned away from third dimensional misunderstanding, and as more and more people become fourth dimensionalised, or ascended, these new notes of harmony will create a vibration that will close the older interdimensional doorways of a negative nature. We will then move onto the ray of rightness which is developing within the holistic movement in a physical, mental, etheric and astral sequence, and the vibration in the planet then has to go upwards by mutual accord. It will be the 100th monkey scenario again.

As the planet has already accomplished its fourth dimensional input on an astral level, it is now bringing about the physical changes necessary to mirror what has already happened astrally.

This will be reflected by a physical weeding out in form of the negative charges of the Piscean Age which are no longer required. This is in fact already starting to happen as the planet is separating herself into areas of darker slow frequency energy and areas of higher vibrational Light energy. In the areas of darkness the natural disasters will occur, and in a sweeping way a transmutation will take place. The planet will then become more enriched as that slow frequency negative input is digested and more of the Light focus spreads around the Earth. As this takes place we will see more and more Light centres and places of harmony created around the globe.

The information as to where these slow and high frequency energy points are, cannot be released. If people rush to those parts of the globe - be they negative or positive - and if their bodies are not in a point of efficiency, then an overload can take place and a lot of genetic vibratory damage will occur.

If you need to visit one of these places, it will be orchestrated through meditation or during the course of your work, or you will find yourself intuitively being directed to certain parts of the planet where the vibration you require will then 'instruct' you.

These changes within the planet will also be mirrored by the physical rearrangement of parts of the planet through volcanic action, both on the sea bed and in the movement of land masses which are being monitored by scientists, and by the movement of magnetic fields as a new magnetic North Pole is now beginning to establish itself.

The ley lines, geopathic stress points - the black and white lines of energy - are also in the process of being moved into a different alignment, and these key notes are coming into a different emphasis. This is why quite a few Light workers are now physically going around the planet planting crystals in certain key focal points. By doing this they are bringing about a better harmonisation within the planetary geometrical patterns which are currently in a state of disorder.

As we come to the end of this cycle, one of the options available for the Earth is to slightly alter the shapes of certain mountains, especially the younger ones. When this happens, the old Atlantean thought forms which were buried might be brought up to the surface again.

As these old thought forms come to the surface, the people currently in physical incarnation who deliberately cultivated those thought forms of destructiveness in their Atlantean lifetime, will find their purpose in this lifetime is to specifically transmute those thought forms. Therefore their motivation will be to build a cleaner, higher, clearer vibration, working with negative thought forms as part of their personal karma. As this mass of old conflicting energy is cleared, it will allow a clear polarity for those who need to incarnate but who can only do so once this old energy which represents the best and the worst of Atlantean history has been balanced.

Once that happens, we will get a positive and a negative energy charge-cum-vibration being released. This is already happening to a degree. Artifacts are now being found, like crystal skulls from Atlantean times which are releasing their encoded messages to those who can tune into them. This is helping to prepare us to encompass a new reality offering us unique possibilities previously denied to us because our vibration was too slow. Eventually there will be nine

Light centres, each with a skull inside it, which will be the amplifiers for everything the New Age will bring.

Crystal skulls can be negatively as well as positively charged. Only three of the crystal skulls which have been found hold true aspects of the encodement which has been left for humanity as a whole. Two of these crystal skulls are in the United States and one is in Japan. The crystal skull in the Museum of Mankind, London** is a copy of these true aspects of crystal skulls, and is a good example of what they look like. Although it hasn't got the encodement of the others it is now waiting to be activated, which will soon take place. The shape of its rounded jaw is an indication that it is a duplication of a positively charged crystal skull. The negatively charged ones have a little pointy jaw. Those are the ones you keep away from because they amplify anything negative in your make-up - just as sleeping over geopathic stress will amplify any negative illness which may be genetically within your body.

All these physical changes within the planet are, in their own way, creating a climatic change as the whole physical, etheric and astral alignment of our planet moves towards a state of grace. As this happens the planet will purge itself of all slow frequency negative energies which were useful in the past but are now totally useless in the new reality of the 'now'.

With the new energy of the fourth dimension comes the capacity to be telepathic. Any latent genetic abilities, especially in a mediumistic and psychic way will be amplified, and by the year 2008 everyone's psychic abilities will be externalised. This is already beginning to happen. In Great Britain for example, one in ten people are having schizophrenic experiences which are only aspects of reality coming in which our society hasn't given us a yardstick to measure.

The capacity to be telepathic will not only be with each other, but also with alternative life forms which, due to our evolution, we have been at one time or another.

The solar devas are also attempting more specific and etheric communication with humanity. But as humanity is still magnetised in a masculine way and the solar devas are magnetised in a female way, their communication is creating the wrong magnetic polarisation, hence the problems from sun induction - sun strokes and skin cancer. The solar devas have always been with us and at one time were far better understood than they are today. The thinning of the ozone layer which some attribute skin cancer to, is just part of the 'soap opera' that is speeding things up for humanity as a whole. So drawing people's attention to skin cancer - which is really a virus on the inner planes rather than the outer planes - is just part of the cosmic illusion.

We all now have the opportunity, as we also become fourth dimensionalised, to merge and meld with minerals, stones, metals, plant and animal life as all these kingdoms begin to vibrate in unison, in the more total way which the New Age is now demanding.

By the year 2025 about 75% of the population on Earth will have direct channelling. This means of course that we are being prepared psychically for a quantum leap from where we are now. Even the shape of our bodies is altering their composite form. The shape of our eyes will begin to change and we will begin to see infra-red and ultra-violet within the next 50 to 60 years.

As this takes place, young folk are coming into their time of power at a much earlier age - often as early as 12 years old. In more primitive times, a ceremony incorporating a test of manhood marked the way forward from adolescence into adulthood. In this day and age, the tests taken by paratroops in the armed forces to prove their ability in order to move on into the elitist unit is, in its own way, a test of true manhood which is adequate for those engaged in that form of training. Quite often people will choose their own tests, such as climbers who take on the challenge of conquering a difficult mountain, or those who take on a challenge which incorporates an aspect of fear, be that parachuting or caving.

But for most of us, the risk element is missing from our lives. Yet having a risk and being able to measure that risk in relation to womanhood or manhood, is something very necessary for us at this time. For most young folk today the only test is the driving test which is, of course, totally inadequate. So young folk who do not have any ritual outpouring to release this pressure, often indulge in alcohol or drugs, and not only turn on themselves but also turn on society which is supposed to be supporting them.

As more energy flows into the planet, a lot of old souls are incarnating back into physical form. Many of these are Lords of Wisdom. Many of the children under seven years old are very wise, old souls who are already creating high frequency thought forms which are targeting slow frequency energy vibrations. So although you might be looking at a sweet child playing with toys, calling 'Mummy, mummy,' in essence that child is a wise, old soul who knows exactly where they are going and no one will be able to stop them. These children will give their parents a run for their money!

In fact there is a queue of old souls up there, spinning around their future parents waiting for the space to open up so that they can come in. These souls are choosing parents who can create as high a spiral as possible which can draw in these more evolved souls who can move humanity on much quicker.

The spiritual hierarchy are also moving forward, externalising themselves by incarnating into the planet, and the more enlightened beings who left the planet in excess of 300,000 years ago are now coming back.

A lot of these Light beings are those who made contracts with us through many, many lives to be in a certain place at a certain time so that our vibrations can then be used as a structural accord within the 'mind of one', a bit like an orchestra.

In fact, the planet and the folk within it over the last 300,000 years have been a bit like a planetary orchestra which is warming up and making some peculiar noises as the local customs, thought forms and patterns of energy movement begin to move forward in a way that might seem destructive to an outsider, but which in reality is just part of the cleansing process as the planet and humanity all move up to the fourth dimension.

This Aquarian energy is going to open up a whole new dialogue with life in many ways. In particular, we are going to start seeing the return of the archetypes and this planet is going to be graced with beings of massive Light. If you have read the 'Return of the Bird Tribes' by Ken Carey, you will have an idea of the beauty and power of these beings who left the planet a long time ago, some over the last 300,000 years, and who are now ready to move back into a new pattern… which is where we are now.

**NB. At the time of writing the crystal skull is still in the Museum of Mankind (which is a part of the British Museum) on loan from a private owner - but they do tend to get moved around.

CHAPTER 4
STAR GATEWAYS

Various star gateways are being opened around the world through a cosmic input and output - something akin to a tidal system that flows in and out. This cosmic input and output is a vibratory source which comes directly from Avataric energy and tends to be supported by what is termed The Perfect Masters or Sadgurus.

These Perfect Masters regulate the interstellar flow of energy as it comes in through various places of movement. They monitor the activities of interdimensional time, and are basically the traffic policemen in interdimensional space. They direct the flow of energy and have the capacity to sort people out in a very dramatic way, if necessary, if they abuse their powers. So if a 'car' is going up a one-way street the wrong way they can take that car off the road and stick it back into the evolutionary chain until the person driving that car has built up to the appropriate frequency.

Therefore the plan for humanity is to bring the various streams of energy - negative or positive, or a combination of both - into the reality of physical life. Humanity needs these streams of energy to create the necessary experiences to bring about a release of desire. This desire will have been implemented on the inner planes but needs to be externalised on the outer planes. As this energy is allowed free access into the physical plane, those in physical incarnation have freedom of choice to use these energies in a positive or negative way, either working intuitively or adhering to their mental or emotional addictions. This applies to both individuals and larger groups who have been brought together to work through the understandings and misunderstandings which are necessary for evolution to take place.

At this time, as more people are now incarnating on a higher vibration, their vibratory need is creating a high note which demands the opening of interdimensional star gateways which can feed them the necessary energy and create the experiences their soul craves for.

This is akin to a feeding mechanism from the general auspices of the higher to the lower - from the Perfect Masters or Sadgurus to those who are, shall we say, immersed in the various levels of matter on Earth. Some of these levels are quite subtle and some, like the physical plane, are quite gross.

Occasionally star gateways can be induced to open - a bit like giving birth on one level - if enough minds think and sing in accord from a soul level, creating an energy polarisation. The release of the Great Invocation was the first rhythm in matter to bring up an energy polarisation. This energy polarisation is now demanding not only the externalisation of the spiritual hierarchy, but is also creating ripples of positive energy currents which are beginning to collect around the entrance points of these positive star gateways. By mind orientation and will orientation, the opening of these star gateways is becoming common place.

As more minds think with a specific Light focus and become aware of what they are doing, the occurrence of star gateways opening will become common place more quickly. This polarity of energy can then help to open the interdimensional doorways within the star gateways that link one world with another. When this happens, all the guests of a Light nature who have made contracts with many people down here on the planet will come back again. This has, in fact, already started to happen and quite a few of these Light beings have been returning for some considerable time. But the main bulk of Light beings have not yet come into, or even near to, the physical orbit of our planet. They are still waiting for the vibratory expression of a sufficient critical mass of Light workers to come to the point of efficiency. These Light beings will then be able to sit within the essence of our planet. When this has been achieved they will come into physical manifestation.

As more and more star gateways open up, a diversity of opportunities are becoming available which now make this life within planet Earth a very unique experience.

For the aspiring Light worker, like yourself, this means that if you have no knowledge of past lives as extraterrestrials, this knowledge will now be very much the norm. As these memories come in, you may find a great attraction towards the Lighter life forms which you might have manifested as in different planetary systems. This will help you remember where you came from, and in the remembering will give you a better understanding of planet Earth. You will then recognise that Earth is a place of schooling rather than a home planet in the true sense of the word.

As these star gateways open, humanity in general, but Light workers specifically, will also have access to the solar group unconscious as opposed to the planetary unconscious. This will offer you the pattern of telepathic contact with minds which, in the physical sense, are currently superior to our own. This will also link you into guidance from other cultures, other ways of life, that are totally different to our reality as we perceive it.

It will also give access into the internal mechanism of life structure in a physical sense. Everything we perceive as being external to ourselves within the planet is of course an aspect of the inner mechanism of our inner world. I wonder how many people, thinking about the atoms within their body, consider the people living on those atoms who are worrying about their equivalent of mortgages!

As these doorways open they will introduce high frequency energy currents into the make-up of the physical atoms of your body, giving them the driving force and vibration hitherto unavailable. This, in its own way, will make contact with the diversity of life forms currently down here on the planet a much more day-to-day affair, be it with elementals, devas, archetypal patterns, or the other physical forms, some of which reside within the planetary structure as well as on its surface.

These doorways are in essence building the vibration within the human form of Light workers who are already down here. So you will very soon be having your personal time-clock stopped in the conventional sense. This will give you access to inner and outer time, inner and outer space. Therefore going back in time, or forward in time, will become a very normal expression of day-to-day life.

Energy follows thought

As more people tune into the frequency of the 'now' and demand a higher input of energy, the natural law of energy follows thought will be instigated and will bring about a 'happening'.

In a physical sense, this can already be seen in certain parts of the planet where large and small groups of people have chosen to live close together in a place where essences in matter, somewhat smaller than the atom, tend to congregate something akin to whirlpools of energy. These whirlpools of energy are manifestation points which are neither Light nor dark. They are just a neutral zone where the sound from the input of thoughts, be they negative or positive, are sent forth through multi-dimensional cosmic waves and create a physical happening to mirror the energy of those thoughts.

This is happening in California. The outpouring thought forms generated by the minds of those living there is creating a package of energy which is bringing about a vibratory input which very quickly manifests into whatever those thoughts are actually saying. So the people in California who are of a positive nature quickly create via their thoughts a feeling of wellness, an accord with the Universe, and a physical and spiritual prosperity. But the people of a pessimistic nature with negative thoughts quickly create a package of energy that is detrimental to them on all levels. It is simply now a question of choice, of freedom of will, as to what thoughts you choose.

In Atlantean times, those in the know who were labelled priests used to work in harmony to create this vibratory sound by getting the right mind mixture so that the interdimensional doorway could be anchored within their locality. In this way they amplified the need of the group. But as they started to erode the knowledge by using it in a negatively polarised way, the vibrations of higher encodements were denied to them. So although a degree of ritual was copied from those times, the 'sound' started to die during Egyptian times, through a natural spiral, because it was no longer appropriate to continue that sequence.

But since the Earth system is still fairly young, some three billion years old, it follows that these interdimensional star gateways have existed over aeons in the past. They exist in futuristic states as linear time does not apply to them. It is now us who have to positively amplify these doorways once again.

As you become acquainted with your country internally, you may be able to find these gateways which are highways through the cosmos. They can then send you on your travels in a very precise manner, utilising the necessary informational patterns which you will have access to, based on your intuitive need. This need is an aspect of your own personal karma as well as the group karmic pattern, and therefore the information available will be within a linear setting as well as a spiritual one.

By using these highways through the cosmos in the same way, extraterrestrial folk find it relatively easy to travel from A to B, travelling through inner or outer time to resonate with the folk they need to work with.

Due to seasonal changes within the cosmos, at certain times in certain places you will find an easier access point. Almost like an esoteric bus time-table, you can actually catch the right bus and arrive at the right destination by going through an interdimensional star gateway. You can then talk to the denizens of Earth, Mars or Venus, and catch the same bus on its return trip to ensure you don't get caught up in a time warp and become stranded.

Careful choice has to be instigated so that you arrive at the right place at the right time, rather than at the right place at the wrong time, as these interdimensional star gateway frequency points open into different star systems, some of which are positively charged and some are negatively charged.

Those within the knowledge of their grouping sometimes use these highways specifically for their own purposes. They tend to scramble the mechanism. So although you see them disappearing into an interdimensional star system, if you haven't got the right polarity, or the right focus to follow them - almost like a grid system

- you may follow them in but end up somewhere entirely different to where they end up, and be in a place that might be somewhat hostile to your reality as you perceive it.

In this way, star gateways are guarded by knowledge and this knowledge is currently very sparse within the planet. Only when the externalisation of the spiritual hierarchy is achieved will the general flow of energy and knowledge be released. This will happen when the consciousness of humanity has been raised to the heart level, from the lower part of the solar plexus where it is at the moment.

If a star gateway opens into a star system which is negatively charged, the input into the star gateway will also become negative. This allows energy to freely flow through the interdimensional tunnel into the plane of reference that has been opened up, and into the energies of that star system. This would then have a swamping mechanism. This happened in Atlantean times when those who should have known better opened up several interdimensional tunnels which allowed an awful lot of negative energy to flow into Atlantis which was the key focus point of the planet at that time.

Whenever this happens, negative beings can flow in through the negatively charged star gateways. They can then grab the opportunity to enter into the inner planes around our planet, from where they can try to alter the vibrations within our planet in a negative way. They will also have priority - according to their evolutionary stance and their developed consciousness - to enlarge on the negative energy which they require for their own food. This has already been attempted, and to a degree achieved, over the last 300,000 years.

This has been happening in Iraq. Not only is it the base centre within the planet, and therefore carrying the slow frequency energy charge of the planet as a whole - which is part of the karma of Iraq - but it also has some of these negative star gateways opening into it. These gateways now need to be closed. This is also taking place in South Africa as negative interdimensional star gateways which have been open there for some time are in the process of being closed. Hence the conflict which seems apparent in the political parties and the conflict between the old and new customs.

So where the Great Invocation says, "and may it seal the door where evil dwells," it is these negative star gateways they are talking about.

Light workers all over the world are now doing the equivalent of a mental trawl, gradually absorbing negativity in all its diversity. Starting initially to work through the permutations of their own energy system, then working in the group formation with energies external to themselves, isolating and absorbing negative energy through their own mental, emotional and astral vehicles.

With our view of life in general, we might look around the world and say, "It feels as if things are at the highest note of fear they have ever been." Whilst on one level this is certainly true, this is also a product of illusion. Over the last 150 years Light workers have been coming together in a much more concentrated form, especially on the inner planes. They have actually been sucking the life blood of the old feudal system which has been in operation over the last 2,500 years. So although the outer fragments of fear thought forms still look massive, they are in fact at the weakest point they have ever been.

As more Light workers become activated and become aware of what is happening, fear in its totality will basically be removed from the face of the planet, and from the inner planes as well.

* * *

Star Gateways: meditations

22. Meditation to go forward and backward in time
23. Second meditation to go forward and backward in time

22. Meditation to go forward and backward in time

Some people say, "There are only seven planes and seven sub-planes," but really there are millions. The permutations are enormous. It is fun to move around the astral levels because you can go forward or backward in time in millions of permutations - you can even travel back to your native Indian days if you want to!

In this meditation you will be forming a pyramid within your visualisation. This pyramid represents multiple dimensional aspects of your personality. Therefore this pyramid gives you the capacity to become aware of past and future lives, probable and actual lives. You will use this pyramid as a medium of expression to actually slow your time down or speed it up in order to move forward or back in time.

The following chart represents the colours you can use in this meditation depending on the time period you wish to move into. Use these colours as your guide. If you want to move forward or backward into a specific time period that is not specified on our chart, intuitively choose the colour that you feel matches the governing vibration within the karmic cycle you want to work with.

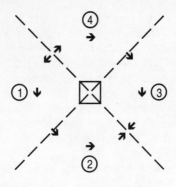

Pyramid as seen from above

① = past male lives   black ball = past
② = past female lives   white ball = future
③ = future male lives   clockwise = forward in time
④ = future female lives   anticlockwise = backward in time

━ ━ ━ ━ ━ ━ ━ ━

Cycles of time
(average soul has 8,400,000 lives)

0. gold
1. dark blue
2. red
3. orange
4. yellow
5. green
6. sky blue
7. purple
8. indigo
9. silver
10. white

Use these colours in series of 10's. Each tenth can represent 1, 2, 3 years etc.
Or can be used in series of 10, 20, 30 years etc. Or in series of 100, 200, 300
yrs etc. Or in series of 1,000, 2,000, 3,000 years etc. It depends on how far
you want to travel. Use this colour scheme or intuitively select your own
colours. The start colour is always gold.

Colour references for going
forward and backward in time

This is an opportunity for you to test your intuitive 'muscles' and take another step towards intuitive excellence. Just trust your intuition and work with whatever colour comes to mind, knowing that your higher self will guide you towards the right colour and vibration.

Time as we know it is an illusion. During this meditation you will be sitting or standing within your pyramid structure, and the wall of the pyramid to your left represents past lives, as you perceive them, of a male essence. The wall behind you represents past female lives. The wall to your right represents future male lives, and the pyramid wall in front of you represents future female lives.

Bring down white Light and root yourself in

Move into your meditation space, sit comfortably with your chakra centres aligned and think of white Light coming down through the top of your head, flowing down through each of your main chakra centres. Dedicate and bless each chakra to freedom, understanding, unconditional love and the capacity to become flexible in relation to the information needed.

Think of roots coming out of your feet, going down into the ground. Bringing down white Light and rooting yourself in links you into the higher and lower at the same time.

Put on your Light body

Once you feel a bonding with the Father and Mother of Heaven and Earth, put on your Light body.

Visualise your pyramid

Refocus on the white Light coming down through the top of your head and into your heart centre. Feel this as a glowing expectancy, a point of enriched energy. As this white Light builds up in your heart centre visualise it forming into the shape of a pyramid.

Now visualise this pyramid expanding outwards until it is approximately 12 feet (3.6m) square, and you are sitting firmly in the centre of it. This pyramid will be transparent in colour.

Now visualise white Light flowing into the top point of the pyramid, filling up the whole pyramid. When it is full of white Light, the four sides and floor of the pyramid will become gold, and the gold will then permeate and fill the pyramid.

Going forward or backward in time

Within your pyramid structure now visualise two balls of energy coming up out of the golden floor. One will be full of black energy representing past lives and you place this on your left side (the side representing the past). The other ball will be full of white energy representing future time and future lives which is placed on your right (the future). Both balls represent the octaves and frequencies you will need. Remember that colour is a vibration and also gives off a sound. So the sound of the past will be held within the vibration of the black energy of the black ball, and the sound of the future will be within the white energy of the white ball.

You now pick up the ball you want to work with - pick up the black ball with your left hand or the white ball with your right hand. If, for example, you have chosen to go back to the 16th century, you pick up the black ball with your left hand, visualise the 16th century imprinted on the ball and throw it towards the left side of the pyramid which represents the past. The ball will gravitate to the left wall (past male lives), or to the wall behind you (past female lives), depending on whether the life you are going to peer at was lived out as a man or woman.

If you already have an understanding or familiarity with a specific lifetime, for example a life at the turn of the century as a man, and need to collect more data about that life, you can use your will to imprint into the ball the specific year you want to focus on, say 1992 Then throw the ball with that year marked on it, into the left wall (past male) of the pyramid.

If you want to go forward in time, you pick up the white ball with your right hand, visualise the time period you want to look at imprinted on the ball and throw it towards the right wall of the pyramid and again the ball will gravitate towards the right wall (future male lives) or towards the front wall (future female lives). If you want to go forward in time within this current lifetime, visualise the time period imprinted on your ball and throw it to the future female or male wall, depending on your sex.

Whichever wall you throw your ball into, the gold colour of that wall will dissipate and the colour representing the time period you need to work with will start to form on that wall.

Once that wall of the pyramid has changed colour, that colour will spread throughout the pyramid until the whole pyramid changes from gold to the new colour. When your pyramid has achieved its new colour vibration and frequency, it will start to spin clockwise if you are going forward in time, or anticlockwise if you are going backward in time. While it is spinning it will refine the vibration to give you the specific key note depending on the time period you have chosen and the date you have imprinted on the ball.

The pyramid will then stop spinning and will settle. The colour in the wall you have chosen to work with will become transparent. Now turn to face that wall, and within that transparent wall a doorway will open. On the other side of the door you will either see your older self in the time period you have chosen, or your future self if you are going forward in time. Now just sit, observe and feel the input of energy and information being offered to you.

Do not go through that door. Just sit and watch. Old life experiences can sometimes amplify the desires, habits, or old energy system that represented you in a slower frequency form. Therefore you should not go through the door and merge with what you see. Likewise future life experiences will represent you in a higher frequency form, and again you should just observe, and not go through the door. The transparent wall is your protective frequency, so you merely observe and allow the emotional experiences and data to be identified.

Sometimes the information you receive will be in symbolic form, sometimes it will be presented in actual or factual reality.

Transmute any pain or negative energy in a past life

If you are looking backwards in time, and can see where old pain and fear is coming from, or see an event which is quite painful and still resonates within you now, you can transmute that as follows: think of a brilliant pattern of white Light spiralling down through the top point of your pyramid. This Light gently surrounds your body as it spirals around, almost like mist. Part of that Light will settle around your solar plexus region, taking on the form of a golden belt. The spiralling white Light will still surround you, as an input or feeding mechanism of Light energy, so you don't use up your own vitality in this meditation.

In your visualisation you will see a buckle with a geometrical pattern or shape forming on your golden belt. This geometrical pattern will represent the required cleansing mechanism you need. Your higher self will tell you what shape that buckle should be. On either side of this buckle are two little springs. Press these springs and the buckle with the geometrical pattern will be forcefully projected from your solar plexus. It will shoot out through the doorway into the memory scene of suffering, limitation, or whatever might be there.

Once your geometrical pattern enters that scene a transmutation should take place within the limitations of genetic, akashic, karmic or astral manifestation which might be active at this time.

If your healing is complete

You will know when this process is complete as the scene in front of you will fade and all the colour within the pyramid will drain out into the planet, where it will be transmuted by Mother Earth. The whole pyramid will then become transparent again. The ball you threw into the wall will come back out of the wall and return to its original colour.

If you wish you can now repeat the full sequence, going forward or backward into another time period.

If your healing is not complete

If the first geometrical pattern projected was not successful in fully transmuting the pain in your past life sequence then another geometrical symbol will form on your belt. It might be the same pattern or totally different. You repeat the sequence of pressing the springs on either side of your buckle, projecting this new pattern through the door into the scene in front of you. If necessary, this process can be repeated a third time.

If the pain or energy in that lifetime is not willing to be fully transmuted during this first session you recall the ball, and wait at least 24 hours before repeating the meditation again. Depending on how painful that experience was, it may take anything from two to nine sessions to fully heal whatever is there. During each session you only project a maximum of three geometrical patterns from your belt.

To end each meditation

You can end each session at any time. Just call the ball back, and it will come back out of the doorway and return to its position on your left or right. The golden belt around your waist will be released and will go back up into the spiralling white energy. The two balls of energy will be absorbed into the floor of the pyramid, and will become gold like the pyramid itself. The pyramid will then vibrate in a very gentle and healing manner.

All four walls will then change to pale blue, then to dark blue. As they become dark blue you will feel a tremendous input of healing and love coming into your space. Any trauma which has been released from past time periods can then be erased from your present reality.

You can do the same with any unpleasant experience you find in a future life, as all past lives and future lives are happening now. Humanity has been programmed, through the misinformation service, to believe that we can only look back and work with what has already happened. But this is an illusion. Anything you find in a future life can be removed if you intuitively recognise it as something which is unnecessary. The golden rule is 'no limitation'.

Your pyramid will then shrink in size, losing its blue colour and reverting back to gold. As it shrinks it will move back into your heart chakra where it remains as a constant factor in your awareness, as part of your 'esoteric wardrobe'. In this way you know it is always there, and can be resurrected as and when it is appropriate, for other information to come in.

When the pyramid is back in your heart centre, withdraw your roots from the planet. The white Light coming in through the top of your head will fade as your awareness comes back into the now.

It takes three months for the energy in a thought form to build up and for healing to take place. So whatever you have transmuted within your meditation will take three months to manifest within your physical space. Therefore, whatever you experience within your meditation should not be shared with anyone for at least three months, as this will break the energy formation.

23. Second meditation to go forward and backward in time

In this meditation you will be using your power of visualisation to build a pyramid-shaped temple made of pure quartz crystal. This can be strengthened by first physically drawing on paper a pyramid-shaped crystalline temple with an altar which is directly under the apex of the pyramid. Allow yourself to draw whatever you intuitively feel you need to focus on within your visualisation.

Bring down white Light and root yourself in

To begin the meditation, first bring down white Light and root yourself in, linking yourself to the lower and the higher.

Cleanse your body and aura

Bring rainbow colours up through your roots, and do the cleansing black meditation sequence, Meditation 4, *Key Aspects Of Meditation Work*, but this time working with rainbow colours instead of the black. Allow the rainbow colours to fill your body and flow out into your whole aura. Then flush all the rainbow colours out with the white Light coming down through the top of your head, and fill your aura and buffer zone with white Light. Do this full sequence three times.

Visualise your crystalline pyramid temple

As you form your pyramid temple within your visualisation, see a triangular door in that pyramid. Walk through this door into the pyramid where you will see an altar situated directly under the point of the pyramid.

Visualise Light coming down from the apex of the pyramid in a gentle swirl, moving in an anticlockwise direction, impacting into the altar itself.

Put on your Light body

On the altar will be your Light body. This will not be one of the archetypal forms you have used before in a physical setting. It will be of a higher vibration and will be composed of crystalline Light particles. As you put on this Light body, it will cover your whole body from head to toe, like chain-mail armour. As you put your Light body on, dedicate and bless this moment.

Now place yourself on the altar and allow the white Light coming from the apex of the pyramid to come into your heart centre. This Light will be coming from Shambhala, from where the energy of the Cosmic Christ is continually being sent out. As that energy hits your heart centre, your Light body will take on a particular colour that is intuitively appropriate for the work at hand.

As this white Light flows into your heart centre, the energy of love, Light and power will also flow into and fill the whole of your body.

Take up your sword and globe

Step off the altar, and walk over to one side of the pyramid. Now ask your higher consciousness for the necessary symbolic change to occur within the temple setting. You will then see on the temple wall to your left, a black globe of pure quartz crystal, and on the temple wall to your right will be the sword of truth, power and inspiration.

Take the sword, grasping the handle with both hands and raise it over your head, with the blade pointing upwards. Visualise this sword being absorbed into your spine with the pointed tip of the sword which represents the cutting edge of your will, becoming your third eye. Remember that energy follows thought so as you focus on this with your will, the merging of the sword with your spine will take place.

Going forward or backward in time

Now pick up the black crystal globe and imprint into that globe whatever time sequence you need to work with.

Using the same format as in the previous meditation, the wall to your left represents past male lives, the wall behind past female lives, the wall to the right represents future male lives and the wall in front future female lives. The future walls can also be used to peer forward in time in this current life.

Go up to whatever wall represents the time sequence you are choosing to work with, and throw the globe into that wall. The wall will then become cloudy. As the cloudiness clears, you will be presented with the appropriate scene or information.

If something in that scene needs healing, bring white Light down through the top of your head and build up an energy charge in your heart centre. Open your arms and allow this energy charge to flow out from your heart into both palms of your hands and your third eye in a triangular focus.

Project this triangular focus of energy into the scene in front of you, in short bursts of five seconds for a maximum of five consecutive bursts.

If the healing is successful

When all the pain is transmuted, the scene will fade and the globe will automatically come back into your hands. The globe should come back as black quartz crystal.

If a full healing is not achieved

If the scene fades and the black globe comes back with some colour in it, this means there is still some healing to do. You can either have a rest and repeat the exercise or repeat it in three days' time.

If the scene does not fade after you have projected your triangle of Light for five consecutive bursts, you end the meditation here and repeat it in three days' time. You continue repeating the meditation until the scene totally fades and your ball comes back as pure black quartz crystal.

To come out of the meditation

Put your black globe back where you got it from. Take the sword out of your spine and put that back in its place. If you feel tired, lay back down on the altar and recharge yourself up. Then leave your pyramid temple and reactivate any Light body you are currently using as an ongoing protective sequence.

As you bring your awareness back into your body, make sure your astral body is fully back and nicely aligned by visualising your hands and feet as being magnets which will magnetise and pull back your astral body.

In the same way as in the previous meditation, it will take three months for any healing that has taken place during the meditation, to manifest within your physical space. So remember that whatever you experience within your meditation should not be shared with anyone for at least three months, as this will break the energy formation.

During these three months, if you feel a bit iffy you can just visualise your pyramid temple, go in and lie down on the altar and charge yourself up. This will give you an input of high frequency energy which will help to heal you.

CHAPTER 5
HEALTH AND DIET

The subtle levels of our bodies are undergoing a change, giving us a better frequency input. Our physical bodies are also being subjected to a lot of high frequency energy and our body vibrations are building. This is moving us into a new reality.

Most Light workers are also having their ajna chakra centre amplified and activated. The ajna chakra, situated at the back of the head where the spine goes into the cranium, and parallel to the physical nose, is the seat of our reptilian heritage. It represents our ancient history and is the seat of great vulnerability. A lot of Light workers' guides work within this centre. As this is activated, telepathic energies are coming in and a lot of old patterns and old thought forms are being brought to the surface to be flushed out. This is creating both subtle and physical problems manifesting as swollen glands and neck aches.

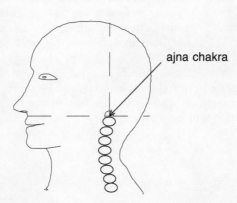

ajna chakra

The location of the ajna chakra

Other chakra centres which have been latent or dormant are also now being amplified and activated. This, in its own way, is bringing a new energy charge into the body allowing awareness in those areas to manifest.

These are just a few of the many changes happening within the human body as humanity mutates and comes full circle with the end of the great old age of Pisces. As our bodies try to compensate for all these changes, physical problems are manifesting, particularly in the back.

But any physical problem or pain within the body is just an opportunity to learn and grow. It is our body telling us we need to move on in one area or another - quite simply the body is saying, "Hey, it's time to change!"

You can work with this by going into meditation, letting your awareness flow into the part of your body where the problem is, whether it is a back pain, a minor twinge in your ankle, or a problem with your enzyme system. Then ask your body what it is telling you. If the problem is in your back - and a lot of Light workers are now suffering with back pain - remember that back problems usually mean 'stubborn'. Your back also represents your central alignment energy flow. So in your meditation, go into each individual segment of your spine, create a working dialogue with each vertebra, and see what your body is symbolically saying.

Then love that problem. Focus on that area and love it. Resisting it or fearing it will only feed it and make it stronger. If you don't know your anatomy very well, get an illustrated book on body anatomy and study that first so that you know where to go within your visualisation.

Your sleep pattern

With the Light energies now coming in most Light workers need in excess of eight hours' sleep in every 24 hour period. In theory, if we were in tune with the Source we should only need four hours' sleep. But because of the current changes our bodies are going through, we need somewhat more than that. Sleeping and relaxing also tends to earth us and this is very important right now.

But for all Light workers it is advisable to sleep for no more than four to six hours at any one time. The ideal rhythm is four to six hours' sleep during the night, getting up early to capitalise on the pre-dawn state when a lot of negative ions (positive energy) is activated, and when the evergreen trees in particular give off a lot of energy. Then take a shorter sleep period during the day - even if you have to lock the office door and take a nap during lunch-time. If you can achieve this rhythm you will find you have a lot more positive energy. If you sleep for eight to ten hours in one go, the essence which inhabits your physical body is away too long and your body becomes toxic through this long period of inactivity. When you come back into your body, you then have an imbalance within your energy system for quite some time. So two sleep periods are better for you.

Stretch your body

Toxicity builds up in the muscle fibres, so regular stretching and exercise are needed in order to help disperse that fairly quickly. Stretching your body first thing every morning also opens up your circuits and stretches your chakra centres. Ideally do hatha yoga for 30 to 40 minutes every day for a minimum of six months until your body is flexible and flowing. After a while you will probably find you can't live without it!

All Light workers will greatly benefit from one or two hours of exercise per day. Your hatha yoga can be part of that. Walk, get out into nature, work in the garden or choose some structured exercise that gives you enjoyment. Younger Light workers might enjoy weight training, but if you are 80 years old obviously you will benefit from something less strenuous. Be sensible. Don't force yourself to do exercise which you find tedious or a struggle, as your negative thought forms will work against you. Just because others are leaping around with their local exercise goddess doesn't mean you have to do the same. Being gentle is always the first rule.

As a lot of people don't have a good sense of balance, T'ai Chi, Qi Gong, or any of the martial arts are also very beneficial. They help to balance females who are still on the brunt of masculine energy, and help to bring about a balance in men who are still aggressive towards females.

Men might be quick to deny that last statement but we were all dominated by females as a baby, and we all had our nappy changed whether we liked it or not. An in-built aggression can also stem from any resentment that you, as a baby, may have sensed from your mother if she was coping with a job plus cooking and looking after the home. During the bonding process and interchange of energies between a mother and baby, the baby intuitively picks up all the anger as well as all the love.

By learning to intuitively tune into your chakra system you can get a lot of data and working information which will tell you whether your body is in a state of harmony or not. For example, if you have extra weight around your middle, which a lot of people have right now, you may simply think it is through overeating. But when you tune into your solar plexus chakra, you may find that your body has deliberately created that extra weight as a buffer zone to act as a protective sequence as your solar plexus is too sensitive or too open.

Since chakras tend to open by muscular contraction to a degree, by developing good muscle tone you can open and close your chakras properly which will help to give you a stronger psyche. This is one of the reasons why exercise is now extremely important for all Light workers. Meditation 6 in *Key Aspects Of Meditation Work* offers you a technique to help you practise opening and closing your chakras.

What is your treacle count?

Slow frequency magnetic energy which I refer to as 'treacle' tends to build up in a whole variety of ways within the subtle body as well as within the physical body itself. The magnetic energy produced by all the electrical apparatus of modern technology tends to bombard us and hang around the outer aspect of our auric field. This magnetic energy, which is very negative, works its way into the auric field, gradually working into our physical orbit and then into our subtle network in a reverse spiral going upwards.

Your 'treacle count' tells you how much of this slow frequency negative energy you have in your body. The average person has a treacle count of 45 to 50%. Any negative energy in your body over 15% which is allowed to sit there and build up will start to create emotional disharmony. Once you go over 30%, emotional disharmony and depression become firmly established. If your treacle count goes over 70% and is allowed to stay in your body, physical disharmony and disease will start to manifest. People who are seriously ill have a constant treacle count close to 90% or above. In order to stay in harmony you need to release all your current treacle count, then keep it down to 3%.

These figures are, of course, a generalisation since the level of toxicity in your body will also depend on your genetic thrust, the in-built mechanism of your mind, plus external factors such as geopathic stress and the magnetic energy of larger cities which will also affect the overall performance of negative energy within your body. The one figure which is a golden rule is the 3% level you need to get your treacle count down to.

As you train your awareness to have a working dialogue with your body on an ongoing basis, you will immediately recognise any build-up. To check your treacle count, you work intuitively. Ask yourself, on a 1 to 100 basis, how much negative energy or 'treacle' you have in your body. Accept without question the first figure that comes into your mind. Your first thought will always be the accurate one. Don't allow your intellect or emotions to come into play and sow the seeds of disbelief or doubt.

If it is 60% then as a working hypothesis, visualise that in the lower 60% of your body. Draw an imaginary dividing line at that point. Everything below that line represents your negative energy - all the 'gunge' in your body which you need to release.

To dispose of that negative energy, you visualise plug holes with plugs in them on your insteps, underneath your feet, at the back of your ankles, and the back of your knees. Then think of white Light coming in through the top of your head and as this white Light flows down through your body, in a wave-like motion, you 'pull out all the plugs' at the same time. Visualise the negative treacly energy flowing out of your body, being washed out by the white Light flowing through you. If you can enlarge your perception of your feet and visualise them as being six feet (2m) across, then you will find that all the treacly gunge will flow out much easier. Once you have done that you just visualise the plugs being put back in again.

In this way you use the white Light to flush the negative energy out of your body. We all have areas in our body where negative energy tends to stick and with the average Light worker these seem to be in four places - the third eye, throat, solar plexus and sexual chakras. So concentrate particularly on those areas to ensure that any package of negative energy there is fully released as the white Light flows down.

If reviewing your treacle count is a new technique for you, start by doing this exercise for a minimum of 35 to 55 times a day until you have reduced your treacle count to 3%. Start first thing in the morning before you get out of bed, and do it regularly throughout the day. With practice you will find you can do the whole sequence in a few seconds. After that it will become a natural part of your everyday life, just like cleaning your teeth.

The frequency of this exercise is important as a lot of people don't know what toxicity actually feels like. But tiredness, headaches, anger and fear are all signs of toxicity, and if you don't release all your slow frequency energy regularly, it will reach a certain charge where you will become aggressive or get 'clobbered'.

If you wish to move this negative energy through your body a little quicker, do the above visualisation and at the same time physically put your two hands up above the top of your head, with palms together in a praying position. Then reach up towards the Light coming in through the top of your head. Now physically bring your hands down in front of your body, part your hands at heart level and push your hands down towards the ground. At the same time visualise the white Light flowing down and pushing all the darker gungy negative energy out of your body through your plug holes. Then bring your hands back up in a big circle and repeat the whole sequence. If you are supple, you can do this by bending at the waist and letting your hands flow down the whole length of your body to your feet. Or you can remain upright and just push your hands down to the hips and bring them back up again, but still visualise the white Light flowing all the way down to your feet.

You can also expand on this release process every time you wash your hands by using the actual water and power of magnetisation. As the water flows over your hands, visualise yourself pulling plugs not only within the centre of your palms, but also within your feet. If you wish you can also visualise plugs being pulled from all major joints within your body. Visualise white Light coming down through the top of your head, flowing through your body and flushing negative energy out through any avenues of your body which you have just opened up. The water and the magnetic current from the water will also automatically pull on your negative waste and take it through the sewer system into the planet and oceans where it will be transmuted and disposed of in the natural way.

Every time you shower or have a bath, do the same. If you have a shower, visualise each main chakra centre - and if you wish each minor chakra centre as well - as being a plug hole. Then as you shower you pull the plugs on each chakra centre as well as the plugs in your feet. As you do so, the gravitational pull of the planet which is part of slow frequency energy will automatically draw any slow frequency energy out of your chakra centres and feet. So just see this energy oozing out into the ground as the water washes it away and gives it back to the Earth to be naturally neutralised. Once you feel sufficient energy has been released, again in your visualisation put the plugs back in. We can all do this wherever we are, and the more we do this as part of the corporate whole the easier it becomes.

Even when your treacle count is down to 3%, still monitor it throughout the day. As you go about your daily life, working, shopping, talking to people, you will be absorbing energy. Some of it will be positive, some negative. By constantly reviewing your treacle count, which only takes you a few seconds, you check in to see if your treacle has gone over 3%. If it has then you know you are going into an overload situation, and can immediately release it.

Cosmic cycles affect your treacle count as well. The vibratory tilt of the planet is also affecting our subtle bodies, therefore a lot of people are finding their subtle bodies tilting and dropping their negativity into the physical body. So if your treacle count was down to 3% before going to sleep, you might find your negative energy level has gone up again by the time you wake up as your subtle anatomy has given you some of its slow frequency energy to dispose of.

In addition to this treacle count exercise, you can work with the black meditation, Meditation 4 in *Key Aspects Of Meditation Work*, as well. This also helps to release slow frequency energy. The treacle count exercise is, in the main, a method of assessing slow frequency energy input which is creeping up on you, and flushing that out by bringing down white Light. The black meditation works with an upward earthy motion, drawing energy up from the planet, absorbing slow frequency energy as you consciously identify it. It also helps you to look at individual organs as you work the black energy up through your body.

The black meditation therefore, works by pulling up the female energy from Mother Earth. The treacle count exercise works with a different frequency, bringing down the white Light of the Father God's essence. So the black meditation is female and the treacle count is male. Depending on the need of the moment - or by even using both techniques in one day - you can polarise your energies more specifically.

By regularly using both the black meditation and the treacle count exercise you can strip away negative energy which might have been building up in your subtle network of bodies for some considerable time.

A third technique to release toxicity is Meditation 24, at the end of this chapter. In this meditation you work with your visualisation to create two spinning discs which create a gravitational pull that sucks negative energy out of your body. This is a good meditation to do if you find it difficult to reduce your treacle count to 3% using the visualisation of pulling the plugs.

If you feel there is a build-up of slow frequency negative energy in any one area within your body, work specifically on that area using Meditation 25, at the end of this chapter, in addition to these three techniques. This works to clear any specific build-up of negative energy within your body. So you have multiple choices to work with.

Water cleansing

As well as releasing the toxicity within your body through one of the above techniques, I also recommend that you do a three-week water cleansing to flush slow frequency negative energy from your body.

You may be wondering why you need to do this water cleansing if you are doing the black meditation, the treacle count exercise, and maybe even one of the other cleansing meditations. Let me explain why they all go hand in hand: the black meditation and treacle count exercise help to strip negative energy which builds up in your subtle network of bodies. Whereas water is a very effective way of flushing toxic negative energy out of the physical and etheric structure itself. If you don't have enough water within your body, the collection of magnetic slow frequency energy tends to stick and get absorbed. This causes problems by making the chakra centres contract. Just as tea leaves clog up the spout of your tea pot, if the smaller chakra centres get clogged up they can't release toxic energy.

If we don't flush this negative energy out of our body it physically builds up in the cell tissue, especially in the large organs - the spleen, the kidneys, and in the mucus membrane of the large intestine. If this builds up over a long period of time, health problems are guaranteed, especially if you also have any genetic physical weakness.

This is one of the causes of varicose veins. It is the body symbolically telling the person they have a blockage on the physical and astral levels.

Water actually opens up the chakra system to a degree, and allows the polarity of negative energy to be dispersed more freely within the body as a whole. Since most of our physical body is made up of water, a clean input of water is very necessary for our general well-being. It re-feeds our tissues and is even more beneficial if that water has been impregnated with sunshine.

But most Light workers do not have enough fluid intake and are dehydrated even though they may drink a lot of tea or coffee. Therefore their body draws fluid from the waste products in the intestinal tract. This just creates an internal recycling of negative energy within the body which may manifest as feeling detached, irritable or allergic to foods.

Public water systems use recycled water which is full of chemicals and negative energy. Polluted water from the soil also comes into our bodies via the food we eat. Even the air we breathe is polluted, so we all need a greater intake of pure water to wash these irritants out of our body.

To fully cleanse the body, I strongly recommend a three-week water cleansing. To do this, you continue with your normal diet but slowly build up your intake of water until you reach a level where you are drinking 10 pints (5 litres) of water per day. Then maintain this level for a minimum period of three weeks. This amount of water is based on an average man of about 12 stone (75 kilos). If you are physically lighter or heavier you may need less or more water to achieve the objective.

As you start to increase your water intake, intuitively become aware of the amount and frequency of water intake which is right for your needs. *Intuitively listen to your body and use your common sense.* One person might need a lot more water than another person of the same weight. Whatever level you build up to, it is important to build up to that slowly, because too much water consumed too quickly will strip the trace elements from your body. If too large a volume of water is suddenly consumed in a short space of time, it can have an effect akin to alcohol! So slowly build up to your personal need according to your intuitive recognition and you will be working towards a more complete picture of harmonious health.

This high level water intake is important because you have to saturate your body so that it gets the message that it now has an unlimited water intake. Only then will your body break its old pattern of taking water from your intestinal tract, and start to flush *all* the toxicity out of your system.

Distilled water is best. Not only for this cleansing flush but for everyday drinking. As the biggest input into our body is water, it makes sense that the water we put into our body is as pure as possible. Tap water, as we all know, is full of unpleasant patterns of various subtle chemicals, therefore I recommend that all readers buy distilled water, or if that is not available, then acquire a water distiller. In the UK this can be purchased from the supplier listed in the Appendix.

A water distiller removes approximately 98% of all negative components within ordinary tap water. Whilst these units are a little expensive at the moment, if you recognise that prosperity is just an energy flow, as you indicate to the Universe that you need a distiller this energy flow will take place, especially if you are engaged in any form of healing.

Also start asking your local supermarket for bottled distilled water. It is freely available in America. If enough people elsewhere ask for it, and show there is a want and a need for it, we collectively help to create the impulse that will make bottled distilled water as common as bottled spring water.

Filtered water is acceptable if you can't get a water distiller, but filtered water still holds some of the trace elements which are unacceptable to the body long-term.

Whatever water you use, dedicate and bless it as this will raise the vibration. Or you can use a magnetic device called a MagneTech which is available from the Dulwich Health Society in London (see Appendix). This raises the vibration within the component of the energy field in your water.

If you look clairvoyantly at the auric space of someone who lives, or is walking near the seaside, you see that their auric span has often expanded up to five times its normal size. This is because the sea air is full of negative ions (positive energy) which, as it comes into a person's auric space, creates a reaction which enhances their electrical discharge especially between their spinal segments and cell tissue.

So water passing internally through the body will magnetically attract negative toxic energy and flush it out of your body, and water, especially sea water, passing externally over the body and through your auric space is also very useful for your well-being on all levels.

Moving beyond diet

When selecting food, start to look beyond the normal awareness of nutrition and a healthy diet and look at the magnetic imprints which have gone into the food.

In Great Britain for example, we have our own seasonal foods which are grown here and suited to our needs. If you come to live in Great Britain from abroad then your body needs would be subtly different. But a lot of food is now imported and we regularly eat out-of-season foods which are out-of-sequence with our body's natural rhythm. Those out-of-sequence vibrations have a negative knock-on effect within the body. The same applies to every country where out-of-season foods are freely available.

Imported produce, such as apples from South Africa and avocados from Israel, will also hold the magnetism of the importing cargo ship or aeroplane. The thought forms of the country of origin will also be impregnated within that produce together with all the pesticides sprayed on them. So even though on a superficial level you might be eating a delicious-looking apple which has trace elements your body needs, if those trace elements are encoded with patterns of magnetic energy which are not suitable for your body, the apple will create an energy disturbance within your body, and won't do you any good at all!

When you buy food from a supermarket offering a huge selection, and are not sure which variety to choose, always remember that the best-looking produce might not be the best to eat! Start to work intuitively, rather than just visually, and use the traffic light dowsing technique to tell you which is the best for you.

The vibratory pattern within food is also affected by microwaves. If you eat microwave food at home, in an aircraft or snack-food restaurant, it is particularly bad news as microwave cookers not only kill off all the nutritional value but also add a dose of negative magnetic energy as well. This will be further affected by any negative ground energies or negative frequency polarity points which are swirling around the place where the food is being cooked. So for Light workers, microwaves and airline food are out!

If you have an allergic reaction to food the MagneTech has the capacity, within certain frameworks, to raise the vibration of the food and neutralise anything which may be causing your allergic reaction.

If you really feel meat is still necessary for your well-being, you should intuitively take into consideration the phase of the planetary cycles* when deciding the best time to eat that meat. This time varies from country to country, but to my mind is between 2pm and 5pm (UK time). As this is impractical for most people, you obviously have to follow your intuition. I suggest you use the traffic light method of dowsing the best time of day for you to eat meat.

Your own intuition will also guide you as to the best place to buy meat and how best to prepare it. Although we did have a peaceful contract with animals whereby they were quite willing to be eaten by us, they did not agree to die fearfully. This part of the contract was broken by us a long time ago.

The result is a lot of meat is impregnated with the slow frequency energy of fear which animals experience at slaughter-houses. When we eat meat we absorb that fear vibration. When the magnetic rhythm of the planet gives a certain energy charge, the fear vibration within meat is amplified and can be even more detrimental to your health. As like attracts like, that vibration will attract other fear vibrations to it, and will create a band of fear vibration around you.

This negative fear energy normally collects around the lower chakra centres, in particular the sexual and base chakras, and to a degree the solar plexus. Quite often it also collects around and clogs up the smaller chakra centres of your feet and ankles. As these smaller centres are important for releasing the slow frequency magnetic energy created by fear, we need to ensure those chakras do not get blocked by those 'tea leaves in the drain'.

The quality of your thoughts at the time of eating is also something to be constantly aware of. Each time you eat, whether it is just a piece of fruit, a snack or main meal, send out a little blessing to the life form you are about to absorb into your system. By doing this you can structurally rearrange the atoms in the food and build its vibration up slightly higher. You will then get more nutrition from it. You can also project your triangle of white Light energy into food before you eat, to help raise its vibrational pattern. This is described in the practice session for 'How to put on your Light body' in Meditation 5, in *Key Aspects Of Meditation Work*.

Of course taking your time when you eat is also very important, as opposed to three chews and it is gone. And how many of you eat standing up instead of sitting down? When you stand up you are either in a hurry or a state of tension, or both, which lowers the vibration of food.

So for all Light workers, paying attention to what you eat, how it is prepared and what you are thinking as you eat it, should all become part of your life purpose. All these aspects can help, or hinder, your aim of building your vibration.

Time for some things to go!

Physical problems can also come from the mercury in our teeth. Current research has indicated that three-quarters of the mercury in fillings is actually released into our system within three weeks of having teeth filled. After that, each time we have a hot drink a little more is released creating an ongoing toxic pattern which again collects in parts of our body. This seems to indicate that as well as the mood variations which a lot of people experience, quite a lot of long-term illnesses have their root foundations within the subtle poisoning from mercury.

Mercury is not only toxic in a physical sense, but also taps into the thought form created by all the people who have actually died of mercury poisoning, irrespective of how that came about.

If you have a large concentration of mercury in your teeth, you will therefore not only have a steady leaking of slow frequency toxic energy into your bloodstream and organs, but also an astral manifestation of the survival thought form. This will build up around you and can be just as distressing as the physical counter-pull which mercury brings. So ideally all Light workers should now have their mercury fillings removed and replaced with a more holistic filling.

If this is not possible, you can make them less harmful by raising the vibration in each filling, using the sequence in Meditation 51, Chapter 11, *A Mission For Light Workers.*

Learning to intuitively listen to our body and recognise when we move into a state of imbalance is something we can all do. The human race has forgotten how to do this. But this is something we now need to remember - and the sooner the better!

Female problems

Most women still have an expectancy that they need to suffer, especially within their monthly period. But this is just a thought form created by male domination a long time ago as a form of enslavement to the female psyche. This happened when women menstruated in harmony with each other and meditated together during their monthly cycle, recognising this as the best time to meditate. They would review what last month brought and where next month would take them, and their visions, information and channellings were particularly beautiful.

Men observing this got a bit uppity because they couldn't get in on the act! So a cultivated approach was made to ensure, through local custom and implanted thoughts, that the female monthly cycle was something to be demeaned. Even though the monthly period was once seen as a beautiful and cherished occasion, over the years females were slowly programmed into thinking of it as something definitely down-market. Terms like 'the curse' were applied to it. As women began to see it as such, so the rhythmic pain, swelling and distortion slowly developed into the normal monthly pattern. But all this is totally artificial. It is just an active part of denial within the female psyche which males implemented as a form of systematic control.

The female psyche now has to wake up and recognise that their monthly period can once again be beautiful. The female body also has to be looked at more specifically and the rearrangement of thought forms presented in a totally different way to the dominant aspect some males still want females to accept. In fact, women's whole life essence now has to be seen in a fundamentally different way.

A lot of female Light workers are currently having hysterectomy and cyst operations. These problems are arising because women have been denying their femininity and dumping negative masculine energy, in all its diversity, in their womb. These physical problems are now just highlighting the need for that energy to be transmuted. Although physical surgery is sometimes necessary, this is not dealing with the underlying cause of the physical problem. Surgery will not solve the problem unless you change yourself from within and restore your harmony and personal power.

As hysterectomies and cysts are usually only a result of a build-up of toxicity, it is far better to work with that first and start treating your body with love and respect. Recognise and honour your needs at all times, not only within the female monthly cycle - which is the best time to meditate and spoil yourself rotten! Yet that doesn't happen as women often abuse themselves and allow themselves to be abused during the monthly cycle more than at any other time.

As more females are now in the process of shedding their astral shell, they are moving into a new setting of greater flexibility and more power, and are receiving more intuitive information. During this transition, if you have been through a spiky relationship with life where a lot of input of masculine energy has caused you damage, as you now start to shed your astral shell and melt, going from the icy to the more feminine model, you may have a constant fluctuation of energy - feeling really great one minute, then dropping into the depths of despair. But you can now work with this using Meditation 26, at the end of this chapter. This will help you to settle your vibration into a rhythm where this energy fluctuation flows more gracefully rather than experiencing the extremes of energies and moods. It is a very healing meditation which will help you to merge the best aspects of both your little girl and the adult you into one essence representing everything that is most beautiful in relation to female energy.

This is where conscious choice comes in. You can now anchor your will in the true knowledge that you are neither male nor female, even though conscious conditioning and the force field of expectancy we are all subjected to tend to have their wicked way with us from time to time! As you anchor yourself in that space, you will experience the freedom, joy and peace that are waiting for you.

* * *

Health And Diet: meditations

24. Meditation to release negative toxic energy from your body

This meditation offers an alternative technique to the black meditation and treacle count to help you release toxic energy from your body. You may find the planetary conditions on one particular day make this meditation an easier method to release toxicity. But by using a combination of the different techniques offered, you will intuitively gravitate towards the right one for you. The meditation sequence is:

First assess the level of toxicity in your body which you do intuitively. Working on a scale of one to 100, ask your higher self how much toxicity is in your body at this time. The first figure that comes into your mind will be the accurate one.

Bring down white Light, root yourself in and put on your Light body

Start as always by moving into your meditation mode, bring down white Light linking into each chakra centre. Root yourself in, and in this way link yourself into the higher and the lower.

Put on your Light body and visualise this as a cloak of power coming around you. You may like to try adopting the archetypal pattern of an Indian bear or polar bear for this exercise, as they are very good at sniffing out negative energies.

Releasing any toxicity

Visualise a golden disc underneath your feet and see it starting to spin anticlockwise.

As this golden disc begins to spin, visualise a point of white Light over the top of your head. This spreads out and becomes a white disc which starts to spin in the opposite direction. This disc spins energy downwards which will wrap around your body and push the negative energy down. So the two discs work together, with the white disc pushing the negative energy down, and the gold disc sucking the negative energy out of your body using the gravitational pull of the spin.

As your negative energy is pushed down into the golden disc, it flows out into the ground where Mother Earth will accept and transmute it.

When all the negative energy in your body has gone, the white disc above your head will shrink back to a point of white Light. The gold disc beneath your feet will still be spinning anticlockwise, but will now start to release a flow of healing energy in rainbow colours. These multiple rainbow colours, which correspond to the vibrations of the rich balance of trace elements and vitamins which your body needs, will flow up through your feet, filling your physical body and each internal organ.

You can visualise each organ having this rainbow essence wrapped around it. Each organ should be transparent. If any organ has a colour, that should go, irrespective of the colour. For example, if the spleen is a murky blue, as the rainbow colours come into that organ, they will fragment and transmute the blue and the organ will become transparent.

Once the rainbow colours have filled up your entire body, they will flow out of the top of your head, and like a fountain, will wash down the outer aspect of your aura, gently sweeping away any negative thought forms in your auric field. Your auric space will then fill up with all the rainbow colours. Once you feel you have sufficient rainbow coloured energy, the flow of rainbow colours will begin to slow down, then gently flow back downwards until they all go back into the gold disc beneath your feet. The point of white Light above your head will then flow down through each of your centres in turn, filling each one with white Light.

To end the meditation

Visualise a golden rose in full bloom over each chakra centre. Then reverse the growth process seeing the rose go into a tiny bud, and from a bud shrinking into a point of white Light, which you seal with a Celtic cross.

Close your arms, visualising this as folding your paws which closes down your auric field. Your Light body now becomes an alternative field of energy which will surround your aura to give you an additional protective frequency level.

Finally assess the level of toxicity in your body, which should be a lot less than when you started this meditation. If you have had a build-up of negative energy in your body for some time, you may need to repeat this meditation daily for some days or even weeks until you get your level of toxicity down to 3%.

25. Second meditation to monitor and transmute negative energy (positive ions) in your body

There will always be some degree of negative energy (positive ions) present within our cell structure as radioactive particles from outer space, as well as radio waves continually pass freely through our bodies. Everyone therefore has an interpretation of that taking place within their body.

If this inflow of negative energy is allowed to build up within your body it will always gravitate to the area of greatest weakness. Your body will then start to talk to you in a very clear way.

Within this meditation you will again be working with the hara, or point of balance, but this time will be looking specifically at the hara within your cells. As mentioned before, most people consider their hara to be one static frequency point below the navel, but in fact you have many haras which alter their position from time to time. Each cell within your physical body also has its own chakra system which is a reflection of the larger chakra system in your body. Just as your main chakra system has a hara, so the chakra system within each cell has a hara. When those cell haras become off-centred through a build-up of negative energy, this creates stress and has a knock-on effect which can manifest as tumours or serious disease.

By constantly monitoring the overall pattern, or frequency within the hara of your body, and healing any imbalance, you can ensure you stay in a point of harmony. The meditation sequence is:

Bring down white Light, root yourself in and put on your Light body

First root your feet into the Earth, then visualise white Light coming in through the top of your head, flowing into and building up in each of your main chakras. In this way you are linking into the higher and lower. Then put on your Light body and feel it being wrapped around you.

Check where the negative build-up is

As you are tuning into your positive ions - negative energy - intuitively ask your higher self exactly where the greatest build-up of positive ions is within your body. It may be in one of your main chakra centres, in one of your organs, or even in your feet.

Review where your hara is

Allow your awareness to flow into the part of your body where the greatest build-up is. Now review where your hara is within that specific part of your body, working on a scale of one to ten.

To explain how this works, let us assume that the build-up of positive ions is in your kidneys. Visualise your kidneys being split into ten levels, one above the other. Then ask your higher self to tell you which level the hara is on within your kidneys. Whatever figure naturally flows into your mind as an intuitive response is the right answer.

If your hara is as low as level four, this means your kidneys are vibrating too low and need to be worked on. If the hara is as low as level two your body will probably already be talking to you by reflecting that imbalance on a physical level. This may manifest as aches, pains, or pulled muscles. Or there may be a point of disharmony resonating over the particular area where you have that build-up of negative energy. This may result in a spot, wart, growth, or merely a persistent itch exactly at the area of the build-up.

Clearing the build-up

To clear any build-up you need to push the hara upwards, which will push up the vibration within the part of your body you are working on. As you do, you need to transmute any negative energy which may be on each level. To do this, ask your higher self for a geometric symbol. This might be a triangle, circle or star, although it could be a representation of anything that is acceptable to your belief system.

In your visualisation, place that symbol on the level where your hara is, then allow your intuition to give that symbol a colour.

If, for example, your hara is on level four within your kidneys, and your symbol is a star, place your star on level four within your kidneys. If your star is dark blue this reflects all the negative energy on level four. The dark blue needs to be changed to light blue, then totally transmuted until all the colour goes and your symbol becomes transparent. Work in this way even if the colour of your symbol is a pleasant shade.

To do this, refocus on the white Light coming in through the top of your head, and see it flowing into your heart chakra. Fold your arms across the front of your heart centre, and allow that white Light to build up as an energy charge representing unconditional love. When your heart chakra gets hot, open your arms and allow that energy charge to flow out into your third eye and both palms in a triangular formation.

Then direct your triangle of energy towards your symbol. You can do this by breathing in and building up your energy charge, breathing out and projecting your triangle of energy in a short burst. Continue in this way, for five short bursts lasting five seconds each. Your symbol should lose all colour and become transparent. This process will transmute all the negative energy on that level. When your symbol is transparent it will bubble up to the next level, where it will become darker again reflecting the negative energy on that particular level. You again remove all the colour in the symbol by directing your triangle of Light into it. When you have made the symbol transparent, it will bubble up to the next level. You continue in this way moving your symbol up through each level. Once you get to level six or seven the condition in your kidneys will start to reflect this and physically improve.

If you have had a build-up of slow frequency negative energy (positive ions) in your body for some time, you may have to repeat this meditation on a daily basis for three weeks or longer in order to move the hara up to level six or above. So if at any time you project your triangle of energy into your symbol for five bursts of five seconds each, and the hara doesn't respond by moving upward, come out of the meditation, wait at least 12 hours or until the next day, and repeat the meditation again. Continue in this way daily until you get the hara up to level ten.

The more you practise this, the more you will notice a change in your whole vibratory essence. Your level of negative energy will reduce a little each time you transmute some colour within your symbol through your visualisation and input of unconditional love. As you work on the one area where your build-up is, you will find that the level of negative energy will also reduce in your body as a whole. So your whole physical body will benefit and improve.

As you rectify the energy imbalance within the hara, and move it up to level ten, your physical body might take several days or longer to reflect this change. If you wish, you can dowse forward in time to ask, "Will this change of energy within my physical body be effected in one day?" If the answer is 'no', repeat the question asking, "Will this change of energy within my body be effected in two days?" Continue repeating the question for each day after that until you get a 'yes' response. You will then know when the new pattern of energy will be reflected on a physical level.

To come out of the meditation

Whenever you need to stop each session, bring back your triangle of energy, fold your arms over your heart chakra and close down all your chakra centres. Bring your roots back from the ground and make sure your astral body is fully back and nicely aligned. Then bring your awareness back into your body.

26. Meditation for females to balance fluctuating energy patterns

This is a special meditation for women, so female readers can give themselves a treat! The best time to do this is at the start, or in the middle of the monthly cycle, or when you feel at your worst.

If you have ceased to menstruate you will still be responding to the cosmic cycles which affect your subtle bodies, and will therefore be experiencing a monthly cycle although without the bleeding. Your intuition and body will tell you what your monthly cyclical rhythm is, and will indicate to you the best time to do this meditation.

You may enjoy doing this meditation outside in the fresh air, in nature, or in a place where you have flowers around you. If you are doing it outside, do it preferably at midday and find a quiet spot away from other people so that their energy does not interfere with your meditation.

If you are stuck at home a lot, or in bed with an illness, this is also a good meditation for you to do, because working with flowers in the way described will transport you into a different frequency vibration. It will also help to demagnetise the room or the bed you are in, and will help to transmute any slow frequency energy which might be disturbing your well-being.

Preparation

For this meditation you need two cut flowers of the same variety, with which you have an affinity, and an amethyst crystal with a pointed end. The crystal should be cleansed, dedicated and blessed as described in Exercises 13 and 14, *Key Aspects Of Meditation Work*. For this meditation dedicate your crystal to strengthening your female psyche, and bringing in a new vibration and understanding enriched by the creativity of the intuitive focus which females hold in bondage for the planet as a whole.

Sit with your crystal in front of you, with the point towards your body. Hold one flower in each hand and be aware that flowers represent everything most beautiful in relation to female energy. The flower in your left hand represents the little girl within yourself, and the flower in your right represents the adult you. This meditation can be done with your eyes open to allow your senses to fully experience the flowers. The meditation sequence is:

Bring down white Light and root yourself in

Think of white Light coming down through the top of your head and root yourself in. Bring the white Light into your heart centre, and as your heart centre starts to feel warm, allow that white Light which represents unconditional love to flow spontaneously into both flowers. Visualise each flower as being transparent and empty and as the white Light flows into the flowers, see them filling up with this unconditional love energy.

Take your awareness into the flowers and crystal

When both flowers are filled with white Light, they will start to vibrate. As they begin to vibrate and radiate their taste, perfume and colour, allow your awareness to fully experience their essence.

Then allow your white Light to flow into the crystal which will act as a thought amplifier. Take your awareness into the crystal and feel it becoming activated. Then visualise little roots coming from the crystal, merging with the roots coming out of your feet and going deep down into the structure of the planet.

Now feel the fire elementals flowing up from the planet into and through your crystal, and also up through your feet and out into the outer aspect of your aura which you visualise as an egg shape around your body. This massive flow of fire energy around your outer aura can be visualised as flames which are protective, healing and very cleansing.

Merging with the flowers

Now visualise or feel both of your flowers beginning to merge into one. As they do, the most beautiful components of both the little girl and adult aspects of yourself will merge into one. The one merged flower therefore represents the beauty of all that is best for you at the time of this meditation.

Now feel your body becoming part of the merged flowers. Feel the grace, joy, beauty, freedom and love which represent the spiritual connotation of flowers everywhere. Just feel, taste and smell it - something akin to angel dust! This elixir of the two merged flowers then flows into your body and stamps its essence within your being.

Transmuting any negative energy

As you merge with the flowers, the white Light energy will flow through you and will start transmuting any negative energy. You will initially feel this as an intuitive vibration beginning to flow into your base chakra. As this happens, any negative or harmful thoughts which you have been harbouring will be pushed out and pushed into the flames around you, and will be transmuted by the flames. You may see these energies or thoughts as colours, so all these colours will be pushed out. Your base chakra will then fill up with just the white flower energy.

Visualise the white Light flower energy flowing from your base chakra up through all your other chakra centres. Again any negative energy or colour that shouldn't be in those chakras will be pushed out into the flames to be transmuted and the chakras will fill up with the white flower energy.

When the white Light flower energy reaches and fills up your crown chakra, this healing frequency vibration will flow out of your crown and down the outer aspects of your body like water in a fountain.

As it does, anything and everything that has been holding you back within your femininity, any limiting thought forms implanted within your auric field, will be removed and released. When all limiting thoughts have been transmuted, the flames encompassing your aura will then start to retreat.

As this flower energy flows down and wraps itself around your body, you will feel yourself moving into a more cuddly mode. You will start to rejoice in the grace, wisdom and love that your true femininity brings.

When this energy reaches your feet, dedicate and bless your whole being to the understanding of your soul's purpose on Earth.

To come out of the meditation

You may find at this stage that you don't want to come out of the meditation, and may choose to just sit there for a while enjoying the peace and beauty which are enveloping you. When you feel ready to come out, you should not have to close down your chakras as the healing vibratory energy around you should have automatically closed them down. Just bring your roots back from the Earth, see the crystal's roots go back into the crystal and see the merged flower essences separating and going back into each flower.

Now bring your awareness back into your body and gently come out of the meditation.

27. Treacle count exercise

This is the exercise to reduce your level of slow frequency negative energy by visualizing little plugs with plug holes in your feet and knees. You then pull the plugs whilst at the same time flushing negative energy out of your body with white Light. This exercise is described in full in the preceding text of this chapter, under the heading 'What is your treacle count?'

CHAPTER 6
COMMUNICATING WITH NATURE

Trees are the 'daddies' of nature in a devic sense. They have a specific function to bring about energy change, not only through their rooting system and the symbolic reference they give us - of roots linking into Mother Earth and branches stretching to the higher - but they also have a telepathic network within 'what has been' and 'what will be'.

Trees also communicate with each other. Experiments with lie detectors attached to trees, have proven beyond doubt that if an oak tree is cut down, another oak tree a hundred miles (160km) away will pick up on the screams of the one being cut down.

Trees always work within a territorial pattern, so there will always be two trees which are the focal point of harmony, or disharmony within your area. These trees will normally be fairly close to each other. They will be the guardians for that area, will hold the male and female polarity points and represent the mother tree and father tree.

As a Light worker it is important for you to develop a rapport with trees and to work within half a mile (0.8km) radius of your home to find these the mother and father trees in your area. You can then open up a telepathic link with them, and work together specifically to harmonise your local area which in one way you are responsible for, which is why you are living there.

You choose these trees through your own intuitive sense. You may be able to sense or hear a particular 'sound', as the male or father tree normally sends out a deep masculine note. The female tree sends out a much softer note. So there will always be two specific sounds, almost like pulsations.

To find these sounds, stand near your local trees, close your eyes and hold your hands out. Your hands will feel an imprint, almost like a radar picking up a signal. This may manifest as a feeling of warmth coming from the direction of where the father and mother trees are. Although these trees are usually close to each other there is always an exception. Occasionally you do find them further apart, in which case you will sense more than one directional beam of warmth coming in.

If you are near a group of trees and pick up several signals, you will be receiving multiple sounds from brother and sister trees who have a similar capacity, and are possibly of the same age as the father and mother trees. But there will be a pecking order and with concentration you will find the dominant male and female sounds within that group of trees.

If you prefer, you can dowse for the mother and father trees. This can be done as you stand by the trees, or can even be done by dowsing on a local map to find their exact location.

Natural disasters

All trees have a tree angel. When a tree's life is over the tree angel imprints that fact on the awareness of the tree, as the tree organism is mainly telepathic. Trees live partially in linear time, partially in cosmic time. Some of the more advanced trees are totally in cosmic time. Therefore even natural disasters such as a bolt of lightning hitting a tree will be known by the tree before it happens.

As a tree always knows when its life pattern is over, its energy is drawn from it as it separates itself from the group and goes into its death process. If it is a 'boss' or father tree, it normally has three month's advance warning. Its father role will then be transferred to a younger tree within the group, or to one of an appropriate age which has earned the right to carry the vibration for the group as a whole.

When a tree realises that its Earth time is over, it will attract negative frequency vibrations into its auric space, and in the process of its physical death it will transmute this negative energy for the good of the environment around it as a gentle cleansing mechanism.

Oak trees in particular capture a lot of slow frequency energy as they often grow over geopathic stress points and can therefore act as a collection focus, or dustbin for a lot of that geopathic stress. As a father tree has a much larger auric pattern around it than other trees, its auric space will also continue to be utilised for the process of transmuting slow frequency negative energy even after it has died.

Trees also absorb deliberately cultivated negative thought forms which come under the heading of structural slow frequency negative energy. This is part of their role on Earth. If a tree has been holding a lot of this structural slow frequency energy for some time and is then uprooted or blown down by extreme gales, the process of that natural disaster killing the tree will starve the negative thought forms held within that tree. In this way they are transmuted and dissolved. This is the tree's final act of service to the planet.

Negative energy within a tree can also be transmuted by a lightning thrust. As a tree is struck by lightning it can instantly suck up out of the landscape an amazing amount of additional negativity which is transmuted on the spot. Its death is like a ritual sacrifice, but a tree evolves considerably when this happens.

Quite often a tree will be used as a transmitter - as an outpost in a cosmic way - to bring in cosmic frequency vibrations. For example, when the planet Sirius wanted to implant a certain vibration into Earth, a tree essence received that vibration and transmuted it by stepping the vibration down to a level that could be accepted by those with telepathic access to the tree's circuitry.

This containment of high frequency energy only lasts for a few seconds. It can take place during an electrical storm when the transference of cosmic energy can be impregnated within the electrical movement of the storm, and forcibly placed within the tree. That tree therefore actually holds the initial high frequency energy from an external cosmic source, such as Sirius, but burns out inside during the process. The tree does this willingly, sacrificing its physical life in order to accept, then step down the vibration so that it can be interpreted by alternative life forms.

When trees are killed in this way, some people just see it as a terrible natural disaster. But when you start to look at the bigger picture of the cycle of life, both physically and astrally, you can then understand that these disasters are in their own way playing a part in the evolution of the planet.

Communicating with a tree

If you want to communicate with a tree, work with one of the meditations given at the end of this chapter. If, when you try these meditations you get no response from the tree, it could be that the tree you have chosen is a bit sulky. Even though you are being nice and loving, the tree may refuse to respond as it has withdrawn from human contact. A lot of trees have now withdrawn from communicating with humans because of the pollution and destruction we are creating on the planet. So not all trees are willing to be cooperative. If you get no response, find another tree which is friendly to your purpose and you can then move into a more specific pattern which will help you open up a dialogue.

If none of this works for you, you may have a subliminal pattern which is preventing the communication from coming through. To overcome that, have someone go with you to the tree and feed more energy into your system. This can help to take you over the threshold, and suddenly you will find communication starting to happen.

You can also ask your guide to help you overcome any natural difficulties you may have. Ask what you need to change within yourself so that trees can communicate with you. You may have used a destructive frequency with trees in a previous life and may need to heal this first. Or you may have had a past life as a shaman where a tree crushed you - quite often a shaman's initiation occurred through an accident. So you may still be holding some past life deformity within your body and unconsciously carrying that around as a resentfulness towards trees. If this is the case, first of all forgive yourself and forgive the trees. Then dedicate and bless all trees to their higher life and work on Earth. Use whatever dedication ceremony intuitively comes into your mind at the time you are physically with the tree.

When you merge with a tree, first of all send in unconditional love. You can put on your Light body and send in your triangle of white Light as a focus for that. Then ask the tree for a geometric pattern or symbol which will be your key for access into its awareness from that point onwards.

If you are communicating with your tree through your solar plexus, when it gives you a symbol, each time you communicate with your tree again through the solar plexus you visualise that symbol as being in both your own and the tree's solar plexus chakra.

If on another occasion your tree indicates that communication needs to take place that day through the heart, or third eye or throat chakra, you will need a different symbol for each chakra. So you might have several symbols as communication keys for your tree.

Once you have made a connection with a friendly tree, tuned into its circuit and know your way around within the tree, you can merge quite easily with it, by putting your two hands on its trunk and allowing your awareness to merge with it. You may even find a little voice coming into your mind saying, "Hello, remember me?" Don't be surprised. Bear in mind that your own evolution has taken you through tree awareness before you came into human form.

The auric space of trees is adequate to support more advanced life forms. Guides will therefore often pop into a tree and sit there, sometimes for many years, to peer at what is going on. Trees are used in this way as a resting sequence for more advanced circuitry and are usually full of beings who can be seen clairvoyantly. One bonfire night in Wales, I noticed that there were Red Indians in every tree, sitting there looking out and enjoying the fire ritual! So as you communicate with a tree you might have a vision of an entity looking out at you. Occasionally you might even see an aspect of your own soul mate in the tree saying, "Hello, what are you doing today? We will be keeping an eye on you!"

As you tap into the tree, you might also see the personality of the tree as tall and slim, or little and fat, or just as a flow of energy.

Depending on your sensitivity you might just feel it as an emotional pattern of energy interchange. Or you might have specific words forming in your mind, although initially try to link into the telepathic interchange.

Once you have actually become aware of and merged with the tree in its totality, you might be given access to the root knowledge of tree technology. Once you tap into one tree, you can also tap into all the trees of the world. You can tap into the rainforest, or the Amazon forest, and you can tune into the multiple circuitry of 'the buzz'. You may become aware of all the forests that ever were and, to a degree, aware of the civilisations which revolved around the forests. You can therefore specifically tune into the needs of all trees and forests at this moment in time.

Likewise flowers represent beauty, and every time you meditate with one flower you tap into the beauty which all flowers represent. By meditating within your solar plexus or heart chakra centre while linking into one flower, you can then tap into that universal beauty and joy of flowers everywhere. Regularly meditating with flowers in this way will also help to raise your vibration.

At the end of this chapter you will find several meditations to help you contact and work with flowers, plants and archetypal life forms.

Archetypal patterns and devas

All plants and vegetables have their archetypal pattern or angelic presence which represents the sum total of that particular species of plant or vegetable. Carrots for example have an archetypal pattern or angelic carrot person who looks after all the carrots in the world.

When you work with the meditations in this book to contact plant and vegetable archetypes, you may find an energy form representing that archetype building up in front of you. With practice you will find information telepathically flowing into your consciousness. This may be specific information about where to grow that plant, how much water and nutrition that plant needs, or you may even be told to move some vegetables to a different part of the garden. You may also receive information about parasites in your garden and how to work with them.

Devas shepherd the conscious energies of plants and focus them according to the blueprint of that plant. They are the super glue that holds the cell structure together, be it on a physical, etheric, astral or mental level. Devas therefore have an active intelligence. They are currently cooperating with the plan for humanity since they would like to manifest into the space that humanity leaves when it evolves and moves on. Devas vary in size from the little ones who look after plants or crystals to huge ones who look after planets and the solar systems. Archetypes, plants and plant devas each have a specific vibration and, like trees, can be tuned into. By tuning into the chakra system of a plant, be it a potted plant or one growing in the garden, you can tap into the individual personality of that plant, into its deva, or into the group consciousness which represents the angelic presence of that particular species.

So you can work with plants in two ways - tuning into the archetype of the plant to get specific information about the best place to site and feed a plant, and also by approaching the alternative life forms which come under the heading of devas who help plants to grow. In this way you can help your crops to flourish and grow quicker, and you can grow extra large vegetables like the ones once grown at the Findhorn Community in Scotland - and you can even have roses in bloom in the depths of winter.

Both devas and archetypes are something you have to experience for yourself. They will make contact with you when the time is right for you, but you also have to give yourself time and space to practise this form of communication. Don't rush the process and give up if information doesn't come through immediately. Once you do start to receive communication, you will find it is quite refined and comes through very gently. So you have to still your mind and trust your intuitive excellence, working with the belief that the information you receive is accurate.

Practise with different plants in the garden so that you develop a feel for the different vibrations of different archetypes.

You can even work with seeds! Hold the seed between your thumb and first finger, and you will feel a tingling sensation as you tap into the life essence within that seed. If you dedicate and bless seeds before you plant them or immediately after you have planted them, and call on the deva to focus the energy of that future plant, this will encourage their growth which can be approximately 30 to 40 times quicker than seeds which have not been dedicated and blessed.

Contacting animal life

Every animal also has an archetypal pattern, an angelic form who looks after it. So in addition to the carrot angel, the rhubarb angel and all the other vegetable and plant angels, there is also an angel for each insect and animal - therefore you can contact the mole angel, or even the fly angel! There is no limitation to the work you can do when contacting the archetype of any life form. All you have to remember is to work on the highest strand with each life form.

If you have a problem in your garden, for example with moles which are doing a lot of damage, you don't need to physically harm them in order to eliminate the problem. The most efficient way to work with this is to put out a thought implant to connect with the archetype of the mole. You can do this by writing them a letter and posting it in one of their holes! Even though you may find this funny, a Welsh country farmer did that and it worked! He was fed up with all the moles, and grumbled to one of his mates, "I'm going to gas them tomorrow."

"Oh! You don't want to do that," said his mate. "You'd do better to write them a letter and pop it into one of their holes."

"Well OK, I'll do that when I go home," he muttered, and whilst thinking it was daft, he actually did it that night and they were gone the next day.

Alternatively, you can contact the big mole angel in the sky and chat to him direct. Tell him your problem, explain your needs and offer him a contract. Sometimes your part of the contract has to be fairly basic, but it must always work two ways. You cannot just ask them to stop doing something. You must offer something in return. For example, when wasps made a big nest near our house, I contacted the archetype of the wasp saying, "I will leave you alone if all of you leave me alone. But if you have a go at me, then the nest goes."

Likewise, if you are one of those people who always get bitten by mosquitoes or bothered by flies, you can contact the archetype of the mosquito or fly. Again offer them a deal. The main problem between the fly and human is that both come from a different vibratory source, and the fly's vibration actually comes in a package which is basically an irritant to humans.

Flies and mosquitoes are lower astral entities who are here to act as structural evil and cause mayhem to humans. But as the vibrations of the planet rise and move upwards, these lower astral entities will start to disappear, because there won't be any need for them to stay. Until then, it is up to us to work with them.

When I was doing some art painting, I made contact with the fly kingdom. As soon as I did that, the archetypal fly appeared in front of me, about 8 foot (2.4m) long, with red eyes, looking very cross.

"Look here, Mr. Fly," I said, "if I paint you in the sequence of beauty as flies should be on one level, will you accept this contract and stop nibbling me?"

That contract was accepted and worked. You can also work in this way with any life form as they all have a higher archetypal pattern. It is just a matter of tapping into that archetype and negotiating a freedom for yourself from the problems they are causing you.

In India there are a lot of flies. But gurus usually have at least a three foot (1m) space around them where flies don't intrude - and you can also create this, if you want to. Likewise, if an aggressive dog runs towards you, you can tune into the dog's higher self and take out the aggressive sequence from the dog before it impacts into your space. If you think this is difficult it may be that you have been programmed by all your ancestors who were attacked by dogs in past lives. You may also have a liquid concrete thought form that says, "I can't do this." These limiting thoughts are often implanted into our psyche as a child. If this is the case it is time to break that mould. All you need is to acknowledge the power of your will and have enough love and faith in yourself to move into a space of believing and accepting that you *can* now do this type of work.

In a way, it is a bit like working with affirmations. You have got to believe in them in order to get a response and reaction. Otherwise, if you don't really believe that affirmations work, doing them just becomes an intellectual exercise and you don't go very far. In fact you can even go backwards!

Just practise the meditations with faith in yourself. As with any other form of learning, accept that it takes practice and accept that there will be some trial and error as you start to contact and work with the vibration which represents the archetype you are contacting.

With faith and practice you *can* establish a rapport with any archetypal life form, and you will then find a response and communication starting to take place.

* * *

Communicating With Nature: meditations

28. Meditation to communicate with a tree
29. Second meditation to communicate with a tree
30. Meditation to connect with the essence of a flower
31. Meditation to communicate with plants and vegetables
32. Meditation to remove toxicity from plants
33. Meditation to contact the water elemental in a stream
34. Meditation to help you communicate with the archetype of a life form
35. Second meditation to communicate with the archetype of a life form

28. Meditation to communicate with a tree

To communicate with a tree, first of all ask the tree for a piece of bark or a small twig. You will intuitively know what to take. Holding that piece of bark or twig in your hand, go and sit by the tree, facing north with your back to the tree.

Bring down white Light and root yourself in

Bring white Light down through the top of your head and visualise it flowing down through your body and out through your feet. Root yourself in, then also bring white Light down through the top of the tree. Now in your imagination, just try to visualise yourself sitting inside the tree with the tree wrapped around you.

Find the chakra centre through which to communicate with the tree

Quieten your mind, then intuitively look or feel which chakra within the tree is activated, as you will be making contact with the tree through that chakra.

Just because you are working with love energy, don't assume you can approach the tree through its heart centre. You may need to go in through its solar plexus, sexual or even base chakra. If you are trying to communicate with the tree through its heart chakra and the tree is solar plexus activated, then you will be working through the wrong frequency and will get a distortion of energy. It will be a bit like trying to speak Chinese to a French waiter. You won't get very far!

Sometimes you might see the chakra system of the tree as being partially below the ground, and partially above. You might find six chakras below the ground and only the crown chakra above. If you tune into the tree and get no intuitive response at all as to where its chakra system is, take your awareness down into the root system as sometimes the whole chakra system is beneath the ground.

To do this use your imagination to make the earth beneath you transparent. Visualise it as a 'nothingness' by removing from your awareness the earth as you perceive it. Then allow your awareness to float into this nothingness and as you do, you also become transparent. As you float down into the transparent ground, you will be able to see quite clearly the tree roots sitting in this nothingness - you can also see the moles skimming around, the earthworms and other little life forms moving through this transparent package.

Then look for the main central taproot, and look to see if any of the chakra centres are down there. Once you have located the tree's chakra system, ask your higher self through which chakra centre you have to approach.

Don't assume you have to enter through one of the main chakras. You may find that you need to enter through one of the smaller centres, which may be within a leaf. Or you may need to step into the etheric shell of the tree, vibrate with its etheric level and work through the etheric body rather than the physical structure. So be open to being shown the right entrance and communication point for the tree you are working with.

Put on your Light body and send in unconditional love

When you have a clear answer as to which chakra to communicate with, focus on your own chakra system and see where your hara, or point of balance is at that time. Then use your visualisation and the power of your will to move your hara into the chakra centre within yourself which corresponds to the active chakra centre within your tree.

Put on your Light body, then bring white Light down into your heart chakra and into the chakra where your hara is now sitting, then build up an energy charge within that chakra. When your energy charge is up to a point of efficiency, this energy will flow into the corresponding chakra centre of the tree you are working through. This Light will imprint your essence and love into the tree's awareness.

Ask for your symbol

Now ask the tree for a geometric pattern or symbol which will be your key for access into its awareness.

If for example you are communicating through your solar plexus, you place your solar plexus symbol in that chakra. Then allow that symbol to move up into your heart centre. Now duplicate that symbol and place a duplication of it in both hands and both feet. Your hands now represent the tree branches and your feet represent the roots. In this way you are duplicating the etheric structure of the tree through the symbol which you are activating. Now pass white Light down from the top of your head into your heart and down into both hands and feet. The main symbol in your heart centre will then go back to your solar plexus chakra, or the chakra through which you are communicating with the tree.

Now merge with the tree by becoming aware of it in its totality, and allow communication to flow in whatever way it is presented to you. As you tap into the tree, you might see the personality of the tree, or just feel it as a flow of energy. Don't try to rush the process. Be still and take time to fully merge and communicate with the tree.

If you initially communicate with your tree through your solar plexus and it gives you a symbol, then each time you communicate with your tree again through the solar plexus you visualise that symbol in your own solar plexus chakra as above. But if on another occasion the tree indicates that communication needs to take place that day through the heart, or third eye or throat chakra, then you need to ask for a different symbol for that chakra. Each chakra will have its own symbol, so you eventually have several symbols as your communication keys for your tree.

To come out of the meditation

As communication comes to an end, you will have a sensation in your hands and feet. This may be a tingling or pulsation, and if you look at your palms and the soles of your feet, you may see a fine rash, a bit like nettle rash. You may have a general feeling of withdrawing and an intuitive sense of the symbols in your hands and feet shrinking. As they shrink, they will flow up your arms and legs into the chakra centre you are using, where they will merge with the main symbol. If you are working in any chakra centre other than your solar plexus, the symbol will then flow into your solar plexus where it will become a web of Light which you visualise as a buckle on a belt which you put around your waist. You keep this belt on, in your awareness, so that your symbol in the form of a buckle is ready when you need it again.

The Light above the top of your head will begin to slow down and you move into the closing frequency, closing down all your chakras, withdrawing your roots from the Earth, making sure your astral body is fully back and aligned with your physical body, then bring your awareness back into yourself.

Once you have established a rapport with your favourite tree, you can carry your piece of bark or twig with you, in a pouch or bag. Then every time you feel a bit gungy, you can hold your piece of bark or twig, think of your tree and allow the tree to take your gungy feeling away. You do not need to be next to the tree for this to happen. Trees will willingly take headaches, aches or pain. All you have to do is offer it to your friendly tree. Quite often we offer our love but we don't think of offering our gungy side. Trees are quite willing to help Light workers, although they won't help everyone in this way. If someone is selfishly motivated, the tree in its wisdom will sense that and will be uncooperative.

29. Second meditation to communicate with a tree

If you find it difficult to tap into the vibration of the trunk or root system of a tree, you may like to try this meditation in which you enter through the top of the tree.

Bring down white Light and root yourself in

Stand or sit facing your tree, or sit facing north with your back against the tree. Feel white Light coming down through the top of your head impacting into your heart centre. As your heart centre fills with white Light, feel this white Light flowing up and down your body. Your body will then start to tingle. Root yourself into the ground, asking for the appropriate colour needed for communication with the tree to flow into your roots. This may be dark blue, or green - so you might become an essence of the rising sap.

As that colour and vibration flow up through your roots and into your body, just allow the sound of that colour to flow through you. You may experience this as an actual sound, like a humming or hissing, but if you don't experience an audible sound, know that the vibration and sound are there and flowing through you. As this colour flows into your body, allow it to flow out of the top of your head and out into your auric space. In this way you will begin to tap into the Earth sound of the Mother Goddess.

Get your symbol and put on your Light body

As your body fills up with the colour, a symbol will present itself in your heart centre. Duplicate that symbol and put a duplication in both hands and feet. Then move the main symbol from your heart into your third eye.

White Light will then flow down through the top of your head into your body and supersede any colour you brought up through your roots.

Now put on your Light body and you will find that your Light body will be stimulated by the inflow of white Light, representing unconditional love.

Communicate with the tree

As your Light body is stimulated, visualise your lighter aspect flowing out of the top of your head, and flowing up above the top of the tree. Each tree has an energy swirl above it, which flows anticlockwise. As you balance yourself above the top of this energy swirl, focus on the symbol you have in your third eye, both hands and feet, and superimpose that symbol within the swirl of energy above the tree. This will invoke an entrance point within the tree's awareness.

Your own awareness will then float down into that superimposed symbol and down into the centre of the tree where you will land in a little cave made entirely of tree, with bark and sap all around you. When you are in the centre of the tree you radiate your unconditional love.

The tree essence will then present itself to you, either in elf form, or as a sound, smell or colour. Send your unconditional love to the tree essence which is communicating with you and ask for a symbol which represents the tree's archetypal pattern. This might be a specific symbol such as a round green circle, or a candle flame.

Allow unconditional love to radiate out from the symbol in your third eye, hands and feet, and flow into the archetypal symbol of the tree. This flow of love energy will amplify both the tree symbol and the tree essence which is communicating with you. You will then have a telepathic conversation. Information given can be checked by placing that information within the archetypal symbol given by the tree. If, for example, that symbol was a round green circle, you use your will to project the information given into that circle. If it contracts into a small circle, you know the information is not accurate or is a bit distorted. You can then go back to the tree essence and demand an explanation. In this way, communication with the awareness within the tree can be fine-tuned, and a good working relationship can be set up. But initially it is choosing the right tree at the right time which is important for communication to be successful.

Having received information, and possibly having swapped stories - as trees are eternally curious about alternative life forms - you send in more unconditional love and indicate that it is time for you to leave. You then withdraw your energy from the archetypal tree symbol, but retain a mental impression of it. This symbol will become transparent and will be absorbed within the totality of the tree. Each time you come back into the tree, its archetypal symbol will present itself to you.

Now feel your awareness being focused in your third eye as the gravitational pull of your own symbol superimposed above the tree pulls you up. As you float above the tree once more, either dispose of, contract or transmute the symbol that gave you access into the tree.

You will then break away from that energy transference and float back down through the top of your head into your physical body. Become aware of your heart centre - it may be a little warm - and you then contract the symbols from your hands and feet, see these flowing up into your third eye and merging with the symbol there. This one symbol will then flow back down into your heart centre.

Now increase your breathing as you contract and close down each chakra centre, making sure your astral body is fully back and aligned with your physical body. Retract your roots and bring your awareness fully back into your body.

30. Meditation to connect with the essence of a flower

For this meditation you will need a cut flower. It can be any cut flower of your choice but should not be rooted or growing in a pot. The meditation sequence is:

Bring down white Light and root yourself in

Hold the cut flower in your hands, then move into your meditation mode, bring white Light down through the top of your head and root yourself in.

Connect with the flower through your solar plexus chakra centre

Find your hara, the centre of balance within your body, which will be the chakra where you sense an intuitive feeling of peace and well-being. If your hara is not in your solar plexus chakra, then use your will and your visualisation to move your hara into it.

Refocus on the white Light coming down through the top of your head. Bring that Light down into your solar plexus and allow that white Light to build up as an energy charge in it.

As the white Light begins to build, visualise a lotus flower unfolding within your solar plexus. Within that lotus flower there is a pod of white Light which represents purity, understanding and your communication needs. Allow this pod of white Light to flow out from your solar plexus into that of the flower. At the same time, visualise a pod of white Light coming from the solar plexus chakra of the flower into your own solar plexus. So the two pods of white Light cross from solar plexus to solar plexus at the same time and create a bridge between you and the flower.

You might then find a form of communication building up as the elemental energy form of the flower presents itself to you. You might just have a feeling, smell or sound that indicates a sense of well-being.

Now ask for a point of understanding to develop, and ask if you can enter the auric field of the flower itself. If you have an intuitive sense of rightness, then in your visualisation walk over your bridge of white Light, and go into the solar plexus centre of the flower.

As you enter the flower's solar plexus, you will find yourself in a meadow or glade with a round pool of water. In the water you will see the reflection of a golden sun and a blue sky overhead.

In your visualisation, go and sit beside this pool of still water and drop into the water the thought which represents your need at this time. It may be a need for a technique to heal yourself, or certain knowledge required, or a need for a method or symbol to use as a focal point for direct communication with the flower.

As you do this the water will change to a slightly different colour, and just as if you were looking at a television screen you will then see the experience, the understanding, or the symbol you need reflected on the surface of the water. If you receive a symbol you can now meditate on that symbol and open up a communication with the flower. Or you can take the symbol, shrink it down and visualise it being on a golden chain around your neck so that you can keep it with you ready to amplify and meditate on whenever you feel it is appropriate.

To come out of the meditation

When communication has taken place, or when you have received your symbol or the information required, come back out of the solar plexus centre of the flower, cross back over your bridge and withdraw your pod of Light from the flower. The flower's pod of Light should also return back to the flower. Your hara will then go back up to its normal place, unless it was already sitting in your solar plexus.

Close down your chakra centres, withdrawing your roots from the Earth, and return to your full awareness.

If you took your symbol to meditate on later, this should be done last thing at night before going off to sleep. You then send the symbol into your subconsciousness, asking for communication to occur through your dreams, or for the information to be active in your mind when you wake up in the morning.

Alternatively you can focus on your symbol during your day-to-day activity so that the information you require can come through your thoughts and into your conscious, intuitive mind.

31. Meditation to communicate with plants and vegetables

Every plant and vegetable has an archetypal pattern. In this meditation you will be sending high frequency unconditional love energy into the vegetable or plant you want to work with, and through that vegetable you can then connect with its overall archetypal pattern.

Give yourself time and space to practise this form of communication. Don't rush the process and give up if information doesn't come through immediately. Once you start to receive this communication, you will find that it is quite refined and very gentle. So still your mind and trust your intuitive excellence, knowing that the impressions you get are accurate.

Practise with various plants in your garden so that you develop a feel for the different vibrations of different archetypes. The meditation sequence is:

Bring down white Light and root yourself in

For this meditation, let us assume that you want to communicate with the archetype of the carrot. To do this, go and sit with the carrots in your garden. Then bring white Light down through the top of your head, root yourself in and put on your Light body, your own archetypal pattern.

Link into the essence of the carrot

As you focus on the carrot in front of you, try to taste, feel and sense the essence which the carrot represents. As you do this, ask your higher self to give you an image, or a geometrical pattern to work with - which might be a square, rectangle or circle, or it might be several symbols, one within the other.

Initially, you might like to specifically ask your higher self if you can use the symbol of an outer square with a triangle inside it point upwards. The square represents the old planetary structure, the old energy system that the carrot, and all other vegetables, have grown through and are still being activated by. The triangle represents the new energy input for the shape of the atoms to come, and represents both the new system coming in and our DNA in the newest sense. So by using these two symbols you are 'top and tailing' the dark and Light, the old and new frequency.

In your visualisation, place that symbol over the heart centre of the carrot. Fold your arms, visualising yourself folding the wings or paws of your own archetypal pattern, and build up an energy charge in your heart centre. Then open your arms and allow this white Light energy charge, which represents unconditional love, to flow out through your third eye and your two hands in a triangular focus.

Send this triangle of love energy into the heart centre of the carrot where it will activate the symbol you have already placed there. Now ask for communication to take place. Let your triangle of energy flow into the symbol and heart centre of the carrot, for just five or ten seconds. Then close your arms and wait for a response. If there is no response, do this again, sending in your triangle of energy for five to ten seconds, and wait for a response. Sometimes you need to be patient and repeat this for about 15 minutes, recognising that the vibration between you and the carrot has to build up. So stay still, be patient, and don't let your expectancy get in the way.

If you have no expectations, then normally something will happen fairly quickly. But if your expectancy is that you should get a response within seconds, you will have a whole load of spiky thought forms which you have generated out of your expectancy, and these will get in the way. Instead of getting a quick response, you will create the opposite reaction - and it may take even longer.

To end the meditation

Withdraw the symbol back from the heart centre of the carrot, and place it in your heart centre. Shrink it down, then drop it down to your solar plexus where it will become a buckle on a golden belt which you visualise around your waist. It will remain around your waist, ready to be reactivated when you next need it.

Next close down your chakras, keep your Light body on as a protective sequence, withdraw your roots, and bring your awareness back into your body.

Bless and dedicate your garden. To do this, find the hara of your garden - the most positive and most pleasant spot - then stand in that place and sing or chant a celebratory note to generally sound forth your essence. Your plants will then respond to this note.

After you have sung your celebratory note, dedicate and bless that space for the growth and well-being of the plants, and also for ongoing understanding and communication which you need in relation to plant life. You will then find that by going back to that same spot each day, and passing energy into it by singing your celebratory note again - it doesn't have to be for long, 30 seconds is usually adequate - the plants will soon look forward to you coming each day, and will start to spontaneously respond and communicate with you in a variety of different ways. This might occur during the day, or even during your dream sleep. So be observant of the impressions which come in, during both day and dream time, and don't put these thoughts or images down to your imagination. Use them as a working platform so that you can establish a rapport and communication between yourself and the devic side of nature. In this way, both life forms will greatly benefit.

32. Meditation to remove toxicity from plants

You can do this meditation with any house plant, but the spider plant or chlorophytum is a good plant to start with, as this is one of the most efficient house plants in absorbing negative energy in a home environment. At any time the spider plant will be relatively toxic, although the level of toxicity will still be harmless to humans, and therefore it will be safe for you to work with if you have never worked with negative energies before.

As a plant has a limited energy field to absorb negative energy, if you pass high frequency energy in, its limited field will expand. The plant will then be able to deal more efficiently with the negativity around it. The meditation sequence is:

Bring down white Light and root yourself in

Sit with the plant you want to work with in front of you. Bring white Light down through the top of your head, and root yourself in.

Find the level of toxicity, and the hara of the plant

Intuitively ask yourself what is the percentage of toxicity in the plant in front of you. Trust your intuitive response, and work with the first figure that comes into your mind. In all plant life, any toxicity over 13% should be transmuted and removed.

Now place your hands just over the top of the plant and visualise a chakra system within the plant with the crown chakra being underneath your fingers and the base chakra at the base of the plant. The base chakra centre may be in the roots, so allow your intuition to guide you. Most people do not think of a plant as having a chakra system but in fact they have, just like us.

Then intuitively feel within the plant to find its hara, its point of balance. Recognise that energy follows thought, so what you intuitively feel and become aware of is what is actually happening within the plant. Just focus on a need to have a working communication with the plant, become aware of what the plant is saying to you and you will find a process of intuitive communication taking place.

Transmuting the toxicity

Refocus on the white Light energy coming down through the top of your head and into your heart chakra. Pass that white Light from your heart centre into the plant and fill up all the chakras of the plant. You do this by first working with the base chakra of the plant, visualising it as being empty - like a chalice which you fill up with white Light energy. Repeat this with the sexual chakra, the solar plexus chakra, and move up through all the chakras in this way. As you fill up each chakra, the white Light may change to gold or whatever colour is intuitively presented to you. You may even find a different colour flows into each chakra centre. As each chakra in the plant fills up, the vibration of the plant will change as the white Light and colours absorb and transmute any toxicity.

You then once again intuitively feel to see where the hara of the plant is, and you should find that the hara has moved up. So for example, if the hara was first of all in the sexual centre, you should find that after you detoxify the plant the hara has moved up to the top part of the solar plexus or into the heart chakra.

Check its level of toxicity again, and after the cleansing this should have dropped down. As you remove the toxicity from this spider plant, the spider plant angel may tap all the other spider plants in your local area into the one you are working with in order to speed up the rhythm of all of them. So you may be working with more than just the one plant in front of you! You may therefore need to do the meditation three times before you bring the toxicity down to zero, or as low as 2%.

You can also do this exercise with any plant in the garden. If you want to work with garden plants, go into your garden, sit by each plant you want to work with and ask what its toxicity level is, then work with this meditation in the same way.

Initially you work with each plant individually. But with practice, once you have developed a feel for this work, you can work with a cluster of plants, then work with all plants in a half mile (0.8km) radius of your home. When you become even more intuitively aware you can work on a planetary scale, tapping into, say all the spider plants in the world, or into all the cacti in Mexico. As you build up your vibratory system, you will find that the whole sequence of plant life can be amplified. You will then be able to link into plant life of a more evolved form which might also communicate with you!

33. Meditation to contact the water elemental in a stream

If you want to meditate with the water elemental in a stream, make sure that you root yourself in with your roots going deep into Mother Earth. Link into your higher self, and put on your Light body as a form of protection. If you wish you can also ask your guides to merge with you before you go into any meditation with a water elemental. The meditation sequence is:

Root yourself in and put on your Light body

Sit by the side of the stream, root yourself in and visualise your roots going deep into Mother Earth. Bring down white Light through the top of your head and link into your higher self. Then put on your Light body.

As the essence of water can be extremely powerful and needs to be approached with care, you may intuitively feel that you want to ask your guides to merge with you at this stage.

Contact the stream elemental through the appropriate chakra centre

Visualise the stream's moving current of energy as an egg-shaped package of energy. Give this egg shape a chakra system, and intuitively look to see which chakra centre is activated, which will show you where the hara of the stream is.

Let us assume that the hara of the stream is being activated at the sexual centre. You then take your awareness into the sexual chakra within your own body. Then bring the white Light down through the top of your head and into your sexual chakra, and pass this white Light, which represents unconditional love, from your sexual centre into the sexual centre of the egg-shaped symbol which represents the stream.

As you pass this unconditional love energy into the stream's hara, or activation point, any imbalance of energy, any ruthlessness within the stream essence will be removed and you will then have safe access to the awareness that represents the stream in its totality.

As you continue to pass this unconditional love energy into the egg-shaped symbol within the stream, you might well find that the hara will go up to a new level. For most people the hara will remain constant. If it drops, this indicates that it is not a good day to communicate with the stream. It could be that the stream is gathering energy prior to a storm, so this is a clear 'no' to communicating on that day.

If you feel it is intuitively right to continue, allow whatever communication wants to come through, to flow into your awareness in whatever way it is presented to you.

When communication is complete bring back your white Light into your solar plexus, close down all your chakra centres, bring your roots back from the Earth, and bring your awareness back into your body.

Variation:

The three-pointed star can also be used in a very positive way for communicating with the water elementals. By projecting a three-pointed star from your awareness into a stream or river, you will sense or see a certain swirl, or energy point, where the three-pointed star will seem to shimmer. By projecting your triangle of white Light from your Light body into that star, the deva of the water will present itself, and a communication can again take place.

34. Meditation to help you communicate with the archetype of a life form

You can use this meditation to contact the archetype of any plant or animal life form. But let us assume that you are having a problem with flies biting you.

You can work with flies as a whole, or you can specify the particular fly type you have a problem with, which might be a mosquito or horse fly. The meditation sequence is:

Bring down white Light and root yourself in

Move into your meditation mode and as always, start by bringing white Light down through the top of your head, then root yourself in.

Contact the archetype through the right chakra centre

Now tune into your higher self and ask through which chakra centre it is necessary for you to communicate with the archetypal pattern of the fly.

Normally the approach to the fly archetype is through the solar plexus, but still ask your higher self each time, as this can vary from time to time. Let us assume that your answer confirms that it is the solar plexus.

Intuitively see where your own hara or activity point is. If it is in any other chakra centre, use your visualisation and will to move your hara into your solar plexus chakra.

Then refocus on the white Light coming in through the top of your head, and visualise and feel it coming down into your solar plexus chakra, building up in your solar plexus as a sensation of heat. Allow this feeling of heat to develop and enlarge until it becomes a ball of Light that totally encompasses you, almost as if you were inside a spaceship or time capsule.

Within this ball of Light, a window will form. You intuitively activate this window by focusing your will and thinking 'window'. The window will then open.

Now visualise the archetype of the fly appearing in this window. You must visualise or feel the fly in a very clear way. If your impressions are hazy, you send a very clear thought into the window to demand a clearer picture of what is being presented to you. As the picture becomes clear you will then have the capacity to resonate with the archetypal pattern of the fly.

Make your contract with the archetype

Once the archetype of the fly resonates nice and clear, you can open up communication. First send unconditional love to the fly as a form of universal blessing, as a bonding mechanism and offer of good faith. Send this vibration of unconditional love into its heart centre, even though you are communicating via your solar plexus.

Now ask the fly archetype to tell you what you need to do to nullify the fly's attention. You should then receive the necessary information to help you alleviate the problem. Then come to some form of mutual contract with the fly in a way that will allow you to have a clear space of three feet (1m) around you, into which flies will not enter in any way.

To come out of the meditation

When communication is complete, visualise the window and the ball of Light shrinking down, and all the white Light returning to your solar plexus. Close down all your chakra centres, bring your roots back from the Earth, and bring your awareness back into your body.

Test it!

The best thing to do after a meditation like this, is to test it. Find a place where there are flies, and see if they still move into your space, or whether they will in fact now leave you alone. Humour is universal, and some fly archetypes do like to have a bit of fun with some people, so their initial communication may not be accurate or acceptable. Each time you communicate with a fly in this way you are taking some of their power, which is why there is sometimes resistance from the archetypal pattern, unless you approach it with total honesty and unconditional love.

If you test your meditation and find flies are still biting you, re-do the meditation in a sterner way and demand to know why communication was not accurate! But you do also need enough faith in yourself to make it work.

35. Second meditation to communicate with the archetype of a life form

This second meditation offers you an alternative choice of how to work with archetypal life forms. It is up to you to intuitively decide which meditation to choose. Your own higher self will help you to gravitate towards the meditation that offers the right frequency for you. Or you can use the traffic light dowsing technique to help you choose. For this second meditation, let us again assume that you want to contact the fly.

Bring down white Light and root yourself in

First of all bring white Light down through the top of your head, and root yourself in, linking into the higher and lower.

Contacting the archetype

Symbolise the fly as being contained within a round circle which is in front of you, level with your solar plexus. Visualise the fly sleeping within that circle, then ask your higher self to dedicate and bless the contact you want to make.

Now look at the main chakra centres of the fly and one will blink at you. The chakra centre which is blinking - and it will often be the solar plexus - will have a doorway within it. In your visualisation, you stretch over and open up the doorway into that chakra centre. You do not go into that doorway, but just look inside.

Inside you will find a series of names which represent the vibratory packages flies normally have a go at. Deliberately look for your own name. You might see this as being engraved on something, or you might just see your name or initials being presented, or you might see a symbolic package of energy which represents your name.

When you see your name, stretch your hand out, reach through the doorway and take your name from the fly. In its place you project a shaft of white Light representing unconditional love as a form of intuitive food for the archetype of the fly. To do this you bring Light down through the top of your head, into your own solar plexus centre, and project it out from there as a shaft of Light. Then close the doorway and bless it, bringing the white Light back into your solar plexus.

Now visualise a fire in front of you, offer your name to the archetypal pattern of fire, and see your name being burnt. Alternatively, if an archetypal pattern of fire is not presented to you, visualise a triangle of pale blue or white Light, with the point upwards. Within that will be a fire, and you put your name into the fire. As your name is burnt, the fire will contract and the outer triangle will also contract and disappear.

To come out of the meditation

When your name has been completely burnt, close down all your chakra centres, bring your roots back from the Earth, and bring your awareness back into your body.

To follow up

You can follow up this meditation by physically writing a letter to the archetypal fly. State that you have removed your name from the contract made between flies and humans, that you are therefore no longer part of 'the menu' and would now appreciate being eternally left alone.

Having put this down in written form, you can physically burn the letter as a form of dedication ceremony to mark the acceptance of the new contract.

It could well be you also need to do some other work in addition to the meditation. If for example, your house is inundated with flies, or your garden smothered with fruit flies, it could be that the vibration of your home and ground energies are attracting them.

In this case, dedicate and bless the vibration of your home which can actually move the flies away, or use one of the meditations in Chapter 10, *Dealing With Negative Energies* which transmute negative ground energies. Also take a look at any structural thought forms in the home. Look at what flies mean to you symbolically. Why are they settling on the windows? What do the window panes represent? You are looking through them out into reality. So look at any symbolic overture which is telling you something about yourself. Then change that aspect of yourself. As you change that note within yourself, you can change the vibration of your environment, which will help to complete the meditation package you have already done with the archetype of the fly.

CHAPTER 7
CRYSTALS

Moldavite is, to my mind, the most important crystal for Light workers. Its properties are unique. It is a dark green meteorite that has come from another part of the galaxy and has its own energy charge. It was physically sent into the appropriate part of our planet some 14.8 million years ago. It was activated and made ready for the time when Light workers would have sufficient intuitive input to work with it in a way which could raise their vibration. That time is now.

Moldavite is mainly a spiritual activator as it speeds everything up, especially within the rhythm of your heart centre. It increases the depth and clarity of your inner journey. It will remove any blocks and within two months of wearing it, it will really bring you to the boil!

Moldavite is also an astral guardian. By wearing a piece of moldavite you will be protected from negative energies as it is not susceptible to negativity like other crystals found on Earth, and is reluctant to let in any energy below a certain threshold. It simply stops it.

In some ways moldavite is the equivalent of a shield as you go into battle against slow frequency energy. It protects you as you resonate and direct the high frequency energy of your conscious will. It could also be called your sword of truth as it will cut through the illusions created by slow frequency energy.

If you have regular healings, it might be to your advantage to take your moldavite off while healing is being given. Obviously you need to intuitively decide what is best for you as this crystal has its own sense of ethics and, to a degree, is spiritually programmed to look after you and will only accept energy which is to your advantage on all levels.

The spiritual programming of moldavite was implemented by the energy of the Cosmic Christ when a functional plan was decided on long ago to help raise the vibration of both the planet and the folk who had agreed to work with planetary energy.

So moldavite is now activating the spiritual clause in that contract. It is raising our vibration, particularly within our etheric and astral shells, offering us a unique opportunity to short-cut some of the long-term difficulties we would otherwise have.

All other crystals have a consciousness, but not a conscience. They can be programmed to look after you in whatever way is necessary, and will amplify the structure of your thoughts. They will also amplify both positive and negative charges and can, therefore, be used for both a positive and negative focus.

To ensure that the elemental consciousness of your crystals is only activated for unconditional love, Light, truth and knowledge, develop the discipline of dedicating and blessing each crystal before you use it. But the first rule whenever you buy, or are given a crystal, is to cleanse it - even if it is given as a gift from someone working with the principles of love and Light. That crystal may still contain a negative charge from ground energies, from the shop where it was bought, or from someone else who has handled that crystal before.

How to cleanse a crystal is fully explained in Exercise 13 in *Key Aspects Of Meditation Work*. When your crystal is cleansed, then dedicate and bless it. Two dedication and blessing ceremonies are given in Exercise 14, in *Key Aspects Of Meditation Work.* Try both and intuitively choose the right one for each crystal.

After cleansing and blessing your crystal you can charge it up. Moonlight and sunlight activate crystals, but some crystals can only accept sunlight for short periods of time after which the sunlight reverses the polarity. Usually a crystal only needs about four to five minutes of direct sunlight. As the arrangement of the atoms in moldavite are quite different to those in other crystals, you normally only need to cleanse moldavite in sunlight for about 30 seconds to two minutes maximum.

If you put a crystal in the sun for three hours or more, it may be very grumpy when you bring it back into your home! If you start to get headaches this may be caused by your crystal having reversed its polarity and radiating a negative slow frequency energy into your space.

This can also happen if you leave a crystal on a window sill in sunlight. Although it may be physically sparkling, it can still be quite grumpy and may turn its back on you if you are not susceptible to what is happening. If you are using coloured filters over a crystal, you can leave it in the sunlight for longer, but not for more than a few hours, even when working with the darkest filters.

If your crystal is sitting in the sun and starts to shift into a negative overdrive, it could interfere with your karmic contract, so your guides may come in and put a cut-off point into the crystal to stop that happening. Guides do interfere in a positive way far more often than most people think! If a crystal has developed a negative charge, which you can check by dowsing, the best way to defuse that is to bury it in sea salt crystals or bury it in the earth.

Before you bury the crystal, dowse and check how much of a negative charge it is holding, monitoring it on a percentage basis. First hold your dowser over the crystal and ask, "Has this crystal got a negative charge?" If the answer is 'yes', ask, "Has this crystal got more than 10% negativity?" If you get a 'yes' response from your dowser, repeat the question asking, "Has this crystal got more than 20% negativity?" If the answer is 'yes' again, continue in this way until you get a 'no' response. If you work up the scale, and finally get a 'yes' to 80% and a 'no' to 90%, you know the negative charge is between 80 to 90%.

Now dowse forward in time and ask how long the crystal needs to be buried. Be clear with your questions and ask, "Does this crystal need to be buried in sea salt for more than 12 hours?" or, "Does this crystal need to be buried in the earth for more than two days?" As you did before, if you get a 'yes', work forward in time, repeating the question until you get a 'no'.

On average, if you bury your crystal in the earth, a period of three days is sufficient to absorb and transmute its negative polarity. If you bury it in sea salt then the average time, depending on the degree of negativity within the crystal, should be around 13 hours. But it does need to be denied light in any shape or form, so if you are using sea salt it must totally cover the crystal. Then place it in a darkened area, preferably away from any magnetic energy. This is why it is best, if possible, to place it in the earth and outside the home environment.

As a general rule, never keep clear quartz crystals in your bedroom as they are activators and will open up your chakra centres. And definitely don't sleep over them, as you can become too sensitive and physically lose energy from your body.

As always you have to feel into this and intuitively work with what is right for you. You may have a specific purpose in mind, and may need to keep one crystal in your bedroom specially programmed to keep you anchored if you are doing a lot of astral travelling and rescue work at night. Rescue work takes a lot of your physical essence. If you come crashing back into your body you may find that your head hurts the next day. Or you may come gently back into your body but wake up very tired from the rescue work thinking, "I wish I could go back to sleep for another hour," when you have just had eight hours' sleep. If this is happening to you, take a look at your energy intake and what you are doing on the inner planes. If you need help, ask for guidance, and ask for a better presentation of what is happening and what you need to do.

Sometimes crystals are negatively programmed. These crystals are normally placed in the ground around someone's home, preprogrammed to be of harm and to nullify any positive energy within the home and to bring about a general demolishing of morale in the people concerned.

Sometimes the negative programming does have an effect since the energy of the person who initially programmed the crystal, is still going into the crystal. This amplifies that energy, redirecting it into the home or towards the people living there. This doesn't happen very often as it requires not only a working knowledge of crystals, but also access to the auric field of the crystal concerned and knowledge of the end result.

By dowsing around the home, or just by intuitively feeling the directional pull or negative energy which is impacting into the home itself, you can find any crystals that may have been negatively programmed, and then dispose of the negativity.

Meditation 36, which follows, offers you a method to dispose of any negative programming in crystals.

* * *

Crystals: meditations

36. Meditation to dispose of any negative programming in crystals

Neutralise any disharmony in the crystal

To dispose of negativity in crystals, they first of all need to be earthed. The easiest and simplest way to do this is to bury the crystal in the earth itself or, if that isn't possible, to totally cover it in sea salt, as described in the text. Then dedicate and bless the whole structure of the sea salt or the earth for the purpose of cleansing. Ask the atoms which represent the earth or the salt molecules to absorb the negativity.

If you wish you can also light a candle, dedicate and bless it, and ask the candle light to flow down into the ground, or into the salt molecules as part of the cleansing process.

Leave your crystal buried for three days, by which time 90% of the negative input in the crystal will be transmuted.

Transmuting any negative residue

Once you have neutralised most of the disharmony within your crystal in this way, you can then work on any negative residue which may be left. This should not be more than 10%.

To do this, bring white Light down through the top of your head into each chakra centre and root yourself in. Put on your archetypal pattern of energy - and you might find that the Arctic white owl is the best one for this meditation. Then build up an energy charge in your heart centre.

Now visualise a nine-pointed star over the top of the pointed end of the crystal. Open your arms and allow a triangular focus of energy to come from your heart centre, out through your third eye and both hands. Then project this triangle of white Light energy into the nine-pointed star. Now spin the star anticlockwise.

As the star spins it will open up a frequency entrance point. You take your awareness into that, almost like jumping down into a small cave! As you land in this crystalline cave, you might be aware of many negative polarities which might be crystalline, or you might be met by an elemental who is negatively charged.

You then amplify your energy by spinning yourself around in your visualisation, anticlockwise. As you do this, thousands and thousands of nine-pointed stars - each one a focus for unconditional love - will flow out from your heart centre and flow around the crystalline alignment in the cave.

As you send out these thousands of unconditional love focuses of the high frequency of the nine-pointed star, they will nullify any negative noxious thought forms which might be there. Any colour that you see, irrespective of whether it looks positive or negative should be absorbed and transmuted by the stars. In this way the negative energy is neutralised.

If a negatively charged elemental is there - which may be slimy - the thousands of stars will surround it and suck away all its negativity, as the stars will automatically seek and transmute. If you have any resistance from the elemental, just throw out more stars. As you are bringing these stars in from a source external to yourself, you have an unlimited potential of power available to you. You then stop yourself spinning and all these stars should come back to you.

After you have transmuted the energy in this cave, you might find yourself falling into a second cave. Occasionally during the process of moving from cave to cave, you may feel your own negative count has expanded while you were transmuting the energy in the previous cave. In practice, the negative energy from your cave should not come into your auric field, but initially you may allow it to come in and this will amplify any negative energy already in your auric space. This will depend on your flexibility and capacity to both handle and hold energy, and on your ability to effectively release slow frequency energy. If you took any negative energy into your system in the first cave, this may manifest as a feeling of heat, or you may experience a vibration akin to shaking.

If this happens, assess your negative treacle count, then open up the plugs in your feet and visualise this negative energy flowing down into the earth. As you do that bring down white Light and flush out all the negative energy. You can visualise the white Light flowing over you as if you were sitting under a waterfall. If you wish, you can take a rest, then move on to working with the second cave repeating the same sequence as before. If you find yourself falling into a third or fourth cave, you continue working through each cave, neutralising any negative energy in the same way until you have worked through all the caves in the crystal.

Normally you will only find five or six caves maximum. If a very strong mind programmed the crystal you might have nine caves, and it has been known, although rarely, for there to be eleven caves within a crystal. But most people who negatively programme crystals do not have enough oomph to do a lot of structural disharmony with crystal energy beyond level three - which means there will be only three caves to work through.

To come out of the meditation

If at any time you feel you need to come out of the meditation, leave a nine-pointed star on the floor of the cave you are in and seal it with unconditional love. Come out of the meditation, and repeat the meditation in three days, starting in cave one.

To come out of the meditation, allow your awareness to withdraw from the crystal, bring back your triangle of white Light and come back into your body.

Bring your awareness back to the point of the crystal and the nine-pointed star. Dedicate and bless the crystal for its new programme, which should only be for unconditional love. Your nine-pointed star then goes into a point of white Light and disappears.

At the end of the meditation check to see if your negativity or treacle count is high. If it is over 3% you release it from your body by 'pulling the plugs'.

Always work intuitively with this meditation and follow your own higher self. Remember that you can adapt the flow of this according to your own intuitive need, as there are no hard and fast rules.

37. Meditation to build up a protective sequence around you

This is a nice meditation to condense your energy around your auric space to give you a feeling of wellness and safety. People with schizophrenic problems might also find this particularly useful as their auras are far too open.

You can also do this as a self-defence and self-protection meditation if you feel threatened, or if your space is being infiltrated by ongoing thought forms.

It is a useful exercise for denying access to astral entities and those on a lower plane of reference who try to impose themselves on your space. It is, therefore, a very safe way to meditate because you create a protective package of energy inside which you can meditate as no slow vibrations will be able to come in. This meditation is also a good exercise to do, once a week, to build up a protective circuitry around you.

Preparation

For this meditation you need a crystal and a flower. The crystal must be a clear quartz crystal which has been cleansed, dedicated and blessed. See Exercises 13 and 14, in *Key Aspects Of Meditation Work*. The flower must be a fresh cut flower with which you feel an affinity, not one which is rooted and growing in a pot.

Bring down white Light, root yourself in, and do a 'pink cleansing'

If you are right-handed hold the clear quartz crystal in your right hand and the flower in your left hand. If you are left-handed reverse this, holding the crystal in your left hand and the flower in your right hand.

Bring white Light down through the top of your head. Root yourself in to link yourself with the essence of Mother Earth, then make your roots pale blue which represents the vibration of self-healing and the group input. As you continue to work with this meditation, you may feel an intuitive need to change that colour as your vibrational pattern changes. Now draw up pink energy symbolising unconditional love, which will flow up through your blue roots, into your whole body. As it does, allow any notes of disharmony to dissolve in the pink energy.

Refocus on the white Light coming in through the top of your head, which is the Light of the Father God and wash out your whole body with this white energy. As you do this all the pink energy, with any disharmony which has dissolved in it, will be flushed out of your body through your roots and given back to the Earth to be transmuted.

Tuning into the essence of the flower

You need to communicate with a flower through your solar plexus chakra centre, so feel within your own chakra centres and locate your hara, your activity point. If it is not in your solar plexus, use your power of visualisation, and your will, to move your hara into it.

Refocus on the white Light coming in through the top of your head, and bring that down into your solar plexus. Once again bring up the pink energy from Mother Earth, and visualise it also going into your solar plexus. You have both energies entering the solar plexus at the same time. As the pink energy comes up from Mother Earth and into your solar plexus, it changes to white Light, so only white energy from above and below goes into the solar plexus chakra.

Now begin to breathe into the flower. Allow the white Light, which is the vibration of unconditional love, to flow from your solar plexus into the solar plexus chakra of the flower. Breathe in and out into the flower for a minimum of 17 breath cycles, creating a circuitry of Light around the flower, which encompasses the flower in its totality.

As you do that, your awareness will move into the flower. You will feel or see a doorway opening which you might see as an actual doorway, or it might be more like a cave. Whichever comes naturally into your visualisation, use this as the entrance point into which you direct your breathing, as you breathe rhythmically in and out.

As you breathe into the flower in this way, your awareness of the flower will become much more dominant within your conscious expression, and you should start to feel yourself becoming part of the flower. This is very much like tuning a television set into the right channel, and in the same way you tune yourself into the right channel to connect with the energy of the flower.

As you tune into the flower, explore the beauty, smell, shape, taste, and whole energy package of that flower. Be aware that the flower you are holding represents all the flowers in the world. So although you are holding just one flower, you are actually working with all those other flowers!

Once you have established a point of rapport with your flower, the shaft of Light which you projected into its solar plexus will move up into its heart centre, then settle back down into its solar plexus. This will be your indication that it is ready to specifically communicate with you. You might then hear the flower talking to you in your mind.

Take your awareness into the crystal

Visualise the shaft of Light which is going from your solar plexus into the solar plexus centre of the flower, now going from the flower into the crystal and from the crystal back into your solar plexus. In this way, you are creating a triangular formation of white Light energy, linking your solar plexus, the flower and the crystal.

Move your awareness and concentration to the crystal. Bear in mind that the crystal is a thought amplifier. So allow your unconditional love to flow into the crystal as you look at its texture, as you try to feel, taste, smell it, and try to become aware of its essence.

Again you are tuning into the crystal's own package of energy and power which you begin to incorporate into your will. As the white Light energy passes into the crystal and builds up its vibration, you will see the Light moving in the same way as it did within your flower, moving from the crystal's solar plexus up to its heart centre, then settling back down into its solar plexus. This is your indication of the crystal's readiness to communicate.

You might get a response from your crystal in the form of an intuitive feeling of rightness, or you might see a symbolised package of energy or an archetypal pattern being shown to you. Take time to fully experience whatever is presented to you at this stage. As communication takes place, the white Light will continue collecting its energy charge from the flower and passing it on to the crystal and you, so that the triangle of white Light is maintained.

Create a vortex of energy

Now focus again on this triangle of energy flowing from your solar plexus to the flower, into the crystal, and back to yourself. When you first tune into the flower, you are creating an input of unconditional love energy which is quite gentle, but as you tap into the crystal, you are amplifying that volume of energy. By now concentrating on the triangle of energy you are strengthening the package of unconditional love energy which you have created.

As you bring your awareness into this triangle of energy, start to breathe around the triangle. Right-handed people will tend to naturally breathe round the triangle in a clockwise direction, whereas left-handed people will go anticlockwise as their polarity is different. You can start by breathing out as you take your awareness from your solar plexus to the flower, breathe in as your awareness travels from the flower to the crystal, breathe out as your awareness travels from the crystal back to your solar plexus. Breathe in as you again go into the flower and continue breathing round your triangle in this way.

Depending on your energy you will develop your own breathing rhythm as you breathe around your triangle. So just allow yourself to breathe in whatever rhythm feels intuitively correct, as there is no right or wrong way to do it. You are just melding and blending with your triangle of energy, and your breathing will naturally follow the line of least resistance.

Breathe at least four cycles around the triangle to get used to the circuitry. Then start to spin the triangle clockwise if you are right-handed and anticlockwise if you are left-handed.

As you spin it, it will get quicker and quicker until it spins so quickly you can't actually see the triangle - it will just become a circle of spinning Light. Although you now see a spinning circle, it is still the manifestation of a triangular movement of energy. This triangle is a symbol of the New Age energy. It also represents a sharpness, so that anything negative trying to come in will be transmuted by the cutting motion of the triangle - the cutting motion of the New Age mind.

You then expand your spinning circle until it is about 6 feet (2m) around you in all directions, like a large hula-hoop. Then visualise that spinning circle of Light moving up and down your body. As it spins and whizzes up and down it creates a vortex of energy, and the spinning white Light will change into a spinning circle of white flames which will absorb and transmute any unfinished business, or toxic thought forms.

To come out of the meditation

To end the meditation, slow down your frequency and reverse the procedure. So the flames will start to fade, the motion of spinning will slow down and you will again be aware of the triangle around you. The triangle will go back to being a beam of white Light between you, the flower and crystal.

Very slowly breathe four more cycles round this triangle. As you go round the fourth time, you will find the rapport between you, the flower and crystal will stop. The triangle of Light is then broken, and you will become aware of yourself, with the flower and crystal as separate components. Close down your chakra centres and bring your roots back from the Earth.

Initially practise this meditation daily for three days to get used to the sequence of building the energy vortex. Then break for at least three days before resuming the meditation as a daily focus. Ideally do it at the beginning of the day, and you can then go directly from the vortex of energy out into your daily life. If you are doing it in this way, before leaving the meditation refocus on your roots and make them dark blue so that your earthing is established.

As energy follows thought, the more you create your vortex of energy and visualise it throughout the day, the more you can build up a very strong protective thought form in a very precise way. If you then come into a negative field of energy, that input of energy will be neutralised and won't cause you any problems.

As you progress

As you work with this meditation over a period of time, and as your energy vibration increases, instead of working through the solar plexus of the flower and crystal, you may find it more to your advantage to work from your heart chakra, linking into the heart centre of the flower and crystal. But initially it should be done through the solar plexus centre. Once you move up to work within the heart centre, you should have a feeling of calmness, a feeling of peace, beauty and creative joy. You will also have the telepathic and intuitive capacity to communicate with flowers in their totality, with nature at her best and with all mineral life forms.

38. How to work with moldavite within different meditation sequences

Moldavite has a series of 17 subtle notes or levels which you can activate and use in your meditations.

Most people will need to work with an actual piece of moldavite for this meditation. However, if your visualisation and vibration are high enough you can chant the name 'moldavite' 12 times, then think of moldavite as a vibration and put that frequency and the vibration of 12 into a cleansed clear quartz crystal. Using your power of will you then burn the name moldavite into that crystal. Quartz crystal will tune into any octave or frequency within the planet, so the quartz crystal will tap into the moldavite vibration. This will give you the same vibrational pattern, in a finer way, which you can then work with, although working with the moldavite itself is better.

Bring down white Light

To work with moldavite, you bring down white Light through the top of your head, linking into each chakra centre. Root yourself in. Make your roots pale green. Visualise your taproot coming out of your spine and going into the ground, merging with Mother Earth, then bringing up the frequency of love, joy, harmony and your personal use of power. Initially bring up pale blue energy, but as you work with this meditation, you may feel an intuitive need to work with another colour which intuitively represents the vibration you need at that time. This energy then flows up into your body, until your whole body is full of blue energy, with the white Light still flowing down like a shaft of Light linking into each chakra in turn.

Put on your Light body

When your Light body is on, visualise the white Light which is coming in through the top of your head, splitting into three beams of energy that radiate out of your cranium. One goes straight down your body and the others go out horizontally along your right and left shoulders.

As this happens the blue energy in its totality merges and becomes part of the white. The three beams of white Light then spin until you are in a vortex of white Light.

Linking into the moldavite

Now imagine the 17 different levels of the moldavite crystal as a series of drawers which you label one to 17. Then in your visualisation, choose one of those drawers and open it. Inside will be a symbol which you take out and use as a focal point within your meditation. You will use this symbol to help you link into different patterns of energies and obtain the dominant informational package available to you during the meditation. This symbol should be placed within your heart centre where you amplify it within the radiance of white Light.

Example, using moldavite to communicate with a tree

As an example of how you would do this, let us assume that you want to communicate with a tree using moldavite as the communication package.

Go and physically sit by the tree you want to communicate with and intuitively look to see where the heart chakra of the tree is. Then bring down white Light, root yourself in and create the spinning vortex of white energy around you as described above.

Then place your piece of moldavite behind you to boost your system, but visualise the essence of the moldavite as a spiralling green energy in front of you. Within that green energy you visualise the 17 different levels as drawers you can work with. One drawer will dominate becoming larger than the others. You move towards this dominant drawer, open it and take out the symbol which will be in there. Let us assume that drawer 15 is dominant and the symbol inside is a four-leafed clover.

Alternatively instead of visualising 17 drawers, you might like to focus on a multi-faceted jewel with 17 facets. Each facet will have a number on it, one to 17. If you choose this, the jewel will spin, and as it stops spinning, the dominant facet will face you and that facet will offer you the symbol you require. Let us again assume that facet 15 is the dominant one, and the symbol offered is a four-leafed clover.

As you choose your symbol, the green moldavite essence will wrap itself around you. So you will have a vortex of white energy in which you are sitting, with the green moldavite essence wrapped around that as an outer cloak. You approach the tree in this mode.

To approach the tree, place the symbol you have chosen, via the drawer or the jewel, into your heart centre. You amplify that symbol and visualise it being placed in the heart centre of the tree. A doorway will then open within the heart chakra of the tree and you will either be invited to enter the doorway, or an essence of tree knowledge will come out and communicate with you.

The moldavite will more or less push behind you, offering an overall protective frequency, which will allow the transmutation of energy to take place in an octave, or frequency which is appropriate to both parties, in this case the tree deva and yourself. Then allow whatever communication needs to take place, to naturally occur.

To come out of the meditation

When that is complete you take back your symbol and visualise yourself placing it back inside drawer or facet 15. The spiralling green energy will be drawn back into the moldavite which is behind you. The green outer pattern around your white vortex of energy will also diminish and go back into the moldavite. The three Light beams will stop spinning, they will merge back into one and go back up through the top of your head. You then bring back your roots, close down each chakra centre, and bring your awareness back into your body.

Alternative example to communicate with the fire elemental of the sun

As you work with moldavite using this meditation, you will discover your own variations on this theme as there are no hard and fast rules. But to get you going you might like to explore the following variation:

Let us assume that you want to communicate with the fire elemental of the sun. You would use the same format as above, but for this meditation you might find that drawer number one is the most dominant. Inside that drawer you will find the right symbol for this specific communication with the fire elemental.

In drawer one you might find a star of nine dimensions - i.e. you would have a nine-pointed star, but it would actually be nine-pointed in nine different plane references, so you would see a nine-pointed star with another nine-pointed star behind that, another behind that, with nine stars in all.

To communicate with the sun, you work with the appropriate frequency chakra of the sun, which you intuitively choose, which might be the third eye chakra. This gateway will be formed by the nine, nine-pointed stars. Each nine-pointed star will form an amplifying charge between you and the fire elemental of the sun.

With the green moldavite energy wrapped around your spiralling white vortex of energy, you therefore move from your third eye, moving up through each of the nine-pointed stars. Depending on the frequency you are carrying and what is being offered to you, and depending on the karmic flow of energy active on the day you do this meditation, you may find you choose to stop within say, the fifth nine-pointed star. As you move into that star, an aspect of communication will come from the sun and meet you at that particular point.

Therefore, between your third eye and the third eye of the sun, you would then have a communication taking place, again with the activation coming from the moldavite directly behind you. Having communicated through, say level five of your nine-pointed stars, you might then choose to either leave the meditation, or carry on in sequence moving to another level, gaining more information, understanding and knowledge from each of the nine-pointed stars available to you.

After the information has been brought into your space, you will find that the gateway to the sun will close and you will take back your symbol which you place back into the drawer, or jewel, and you bring your awareness back into your body.

As you see, these two variations are totally different, because there is no set format for working with moldavite in this way. These variations are just to guide you, but your own personal journey with your moldavite may look quite different!

CHAPTER 8
MEETING YOUR GUIDES

A guide is a source of energy external to the human personality. Guides usually direct energy in a positive way. Some slow frequency guides can direct energy in a negative way, but in relation to this book the guides I talk about are Light beings who have achieved a degree of evolution - although their evolution might be more or less than the person on Earth with whom they are communicating.

Guides always have a degree of expertise which the person in physical matter hasn't got. Guides therefore have a certain advantage. The main advantage being that they can peer both forward and backward in time, within the permutations of their own karma and within the permutations of the karma of the person, or group, they are working with.

Guides always go through a learning process. Occasionally guides who manifest within the Earth's sphere can become a little impatient because of their lack of experience and tend to push energy of a too powerful nature into the space of the person they are working with. They think they are working harmoniously with that person, and don't realise they are actually stressing that person's system by creating a point of conflicting energy.

This can happen when those younger guides who are being educated by an older guide aspect are invited to demonstrate their expertise. But the person in human form is usually part of the same soul family of the older guide and has, on one level, agreed to work in this way with them prior to incarnating.

Therefore the Earth school is a training ground not only for those incarnated in matter, but also for guides on the inner planes to enable them to practise what they have learnt in theory. These younger guides need the practical interpretation of inter-plane relationships between the inner and outer planes, and this only comes with continual practice and perseverance.

As a general rule, guides who attach themselves to people evolving through an Earth incarnation, need that experience of being a guide so they too can evolve in their own way. It is normally a two-way trade-off in the sense that they receive what they need for their evolution, while helping those on the Earth plane in whatever way they are capable of doing. But they can only help within their and your spiritual family, working within the karmic fields of Earth life, and always working with the Avataric influence which is part of their focus. Even highly evolved beings take on the guide role to further increase their evolutionary pattern, and this is an experience they greatly enjoy!

Some guides have a personality mode. As such they might be familiar with physical earthly sensations if they have had a physical incarnation themselves. If their last lifetime on Earth was a long time ago, or if the guide has never had a life on Earth, they will find it difficult to evaluate the ongoing problems which people on Earth experience. This is why it is always necessary to ask guides, as specifically as possible, for any help you need. Otherwise those on the inner planes will assume you are handling yourself quite well! If you don't ask for help, you might continue with a difficulty when there isn't a need to do so.

Most evolved guides however haven't got a personality 'overcoat'. But they do have the equivalent of an esoteric wardrobe from which they can adopt the robes of a nun for example, or Red Indian, based on the belief system of the person they are working with. Therefore they can clothe and present themselves in a way which creates reassurance and a quality of trust within the Earth person concerned.

The Lion people

Those who come from a source nearer to the essence of life, such as the Lion people, can look back in time, into the outer planes of which Earth is one aspect. When they feel we can offer an area of expertise which they haven't experienced, they can come back in time into current Earth time, and learn from us as well. They in turn help us to learn from the information they offer us, which they have gained from their own worlds.

The Lion people are a term of reference given to extraterrestrials who inhabit a different planetary structure from us in a slightly different dimensional place. Their physical body is preparing to leave the physical orb as we know it, and therefore their encounter with gross matter on Earth is coming to an end. As they come to the cusp of release they tend to reflect, within the genetics of the core of their body form, what might have been. In that 'might have been' sequence, and in the capacity which they as a race now have to go forward or backward in time, they tend to hunt around for something to do esoterically, in a service role. At the same time they collect data which was not previously available to their race through their genetic journey of the physical orbit.

Lion people are time masters. They have mastered time as we perceive it within our third dimensional reality, and have the capacity to work within the different time frequencies which resonate within their awareness. Therefore, they can work in their time zone and within linear Earth time at the same time, capitalising on the energy interchange between them and certain folk on Earth with whom they work.

Therefore they have attached themselves to certain key players within the human family, bringing healing of a very specific and specialised kind into the human vehicle. This will genetically enhance our race. At the same time they have reaped the benefit of the experience from the emotional seesaw which the race is currently going through which has given them information previously lacking on their genetic side.

They are actually hoping to raise the vibratory stance of genetic remembering and the vibratory core of planetary meaning. They are, therefore, Light warriors offering a specific short-term contract to a selected few, through the healing principle, and helping these few to move up to a new octave. They offer fifth dimensional healing to the human third dimensional essence and in this way have the capacity to heal the central core of the split personality types and the mental minefield which humanity still has to go through and conquer.

Physically they have the appearance of lions, although they stand upright on two feet, and have clothing covering their body. They have a great curiosity and are always seeking a setting where their specific and peculiar skills can be placed into a different orbit. This is what they are currently doing in the Earth theatre.

Today the Lion people work purely on the inner planes, although some of them have physically incarnated in the past. References to these Lion people can be found in olden times, especially in the Egyptian period, and their artifacts and statues are on display within the pyramids and temple settings in Egypt.

Some of these statues still radiate a great deal of Light, and those who are clairvoyantly inspired can see that their heart chakras are still activated. At least one of these statues is known to still radiate a full chakra system of an etheric kind and has an encodement within it. By going into the physical vicinity of this statue, you can receive the encoded pattern of energy which the Lion people deliberately left as a form of reference to those people now in human form who have been into contact with them in past lives. This form of activation is helping those people remember who they were, where they have been and what they have been up to.

There is also a build-up of Light guides on the inner planes who are now coming nearer to those Light workers on the planet who have the capacity to resonate with them. These Light workers are therefore able to channel information and encodements, be it through writings, feelings, vision, intuitive thoughts - or through songs they feel inspired to write or sing, as happened in the 60's and is happening again today through the new wave of mass opera.

As you read this book you will also be working with your guides on the inner planes, and specifically with those who are still a bit distant. As you work with the thoughts and the meditations in this book, you are adding your energy to the umbrella setting of its overall input of energy of Light and unconditional love. This generates waves of energy which can be used by those guides who are a little distant. These guides can then be drawn a lot closer into the physical orbit of both yourself and other people you need to work with. In this way you are affecting the structure of your soul families, and the structure of the groups with whom you have cordings.

Always test your guides

Since there are millions of planes of existence, it follows that there are millions of different types of guides. As a general rule, the guides who are attracted to communicate with humans on Earth, will respond to the magnetic and soul vibration which the person or group is sending out. So it is always like attracting like.

Do bear in mind that when a guide makes an approach, that guide might not be as evolved as you anticipate. Irrespective of where you think your guide is coming from, or how evolved you think he or she is, you should always test each new guide. This is important as some guides are very useful and some are particularly useless. Through the testing and the vibrations which you experience, you will know whether the guide is of a positive and suitable vibration. Positive and highly evolved guides do not mind being tested at all!

During the testing process you will also be able to find out if a slow vibration guide is blocking the essence or pathway of a more evolved guide who may be wanting to come in but who cannot place their essence as near to you as required. There are a number of reasons why this happens. One is that you may have attracted into your physical orbit, over many lifetimes, younger guides whose vibrations are now too slow for you. But the higher vibration guides will not gate-crash. They are ethically bound by the rules and regulations governing natural law not to interfere and to only come in when invited.

This invitation might be subliminal, as well as the conscious release of an invitation through meditation or through coming into contact with people who are God realised. Or it might be through sources of sound and Light which inspire and move the vibratory energy up, which is what you are helping to do as you work with the unconditional love and Light energies in these meditations. For the most potent form of energy is unconditional love.

A more evolved guide may also have deliberately introduced into your awareness a less evolved guide whose vibration is not so pushy. These younger guides will get rid of any astral manifestation of doubt and fear, then as your Light manifests and expands, and as your vibration increases, the more evolved guides can come into your space.

Meditation 40, at the end of this chapter, will help you to clear away any slow frequency guides who might be blocking the pathway of higher guides wanting to come in. This particular meditation uses a triangular focus of gold and blue. The gold and blue used together give off a specific energy charge which is particularly attractive to various life forms, especially Atlantean folk who used blue and gold in formative duties during that lifetime.

The initial charge from these colours will also send a vibration up to the inner planes and will open up specific and very old doorways. As the coldness of the blue and the warmth of the gold meld together, they will open up the relevant doorways with their harmonious energies. They will send up a very specific signal so that a general sorting out can take place on the inner planes, and the younger guides who are blocking the way can be moved on so that the more evolved ones can then come in.

Physical mediums of the right calibre are very useful to help with this sorting out process. They have the capacity to check out the quality of the guidance and, if a slow frequency guide is hindering the process of spiritual development of a person or group, an attempt can be made to remove that guide. The right type of higher guidance can then manifest.

A guide might also be a higher astral aspect of someone who is still physically living on Earth. So your guide may not necessarily be a non-physical entity. We all have many subtle bodies and quite often the role or roles in which we participate can be very diverse. Therefore quite a few Light workers living on Earth are carrying out a function according to their station on the inner planes. This means that their higher astral aspects will be in communication with other Light workers as a 'guide' on the inner planes!

This is not common, but is becoming more popular as more people gain the flexibility to bring through the necessary patterns of energy, and develop the capacity to be in many planes at once. Normally this form of 'guide service' is a way of stepping down higher vibrational energy to a level which those in physical orbit can handle. But as more people become more diverse, and become telepathically in tune with the roles that are needed, so it is that the guide service will be something like the doctor on call. They will then form a central core of inner guides who will respond to emergency settings, moments of panic, or pressure being exerted within any group with whom they have a contractual pattern.

This happens to a degree in certain workshops where teacher guides wait patiently within an umbrella setting for those who are to be brought up to operating frequency, so that the invocation, more inner than outer, can then take place.

When a person in physical form is acting as a guide on the inner planes, the guide is always aware of its physical reflection. But quite often the physical person is unaware that their higher astral aspect is manifesting as a guide. The main reason for this is that the personality mode and the speciality duties afforded to that person, might be put at risk by too much information and detrimental impressions coming into their physical orbit. So it is very much only on a need to know basis that information like this comes through.

When a guide comes in, he or she will answer specific questions. So if you have a guide manifesting in your space, or if you have a form of telepathic energy coming in, you can ask that guide whether any aspect of itself is currently in physical form and whether the guide concerned is part of that aspect in a direct and fundamental way.

A lot of people say, "I want to know my guide's name. I want to see him NOW!" Some say, "I can't hear my guides. They don't speak to me." All of these are very limiting statements. We have been programmed to see and hear in a physical sense, so we want communication to come through in a form which fits our belief system.

Some people get quite anxious when they are uncertain as to whether their guides are really there. They think they would feel less lonely if they could see, or hear their guide. What they are really saying at a deeper level is, "I'm frightened. I want my favourite teddy bear. Then I'll feel safe."

But if you can't see or hear your guides, you can always feel or sense them. Feeling is a high frequency vibration. If you stay in worry and doubt, these are slow frequency emotions which will limit you and block communication coming through. So as I have said before, you just need to love yourself, deepen your faith in yourself and trust your more subtle impressions. As you work in this way you will then find a new awareness and new level of reality flowing into your life.

* * *

Meeting Your Guides: meditations

39. Meditation to meet your guides

Bring down white Light and root yourself in

Bring white Light down through the top of your head, root yourself in and do the black meditation, Meditation 4, in *Key Aspects Of Meditation Work*, to dissolve and transmute any slow frequency toxic energy. Then wash your body out with the white Light.

Create a bridge of white Light

Focus on the white Light coming down through the top of your head and into your heart centre, and feel your heart centre filling with power, vitality and love. Feel your heart chakra physically and intuitively getting warm then hot.

Feel that warmth, love and healing flowing through the whole of your body until it feels light and vitalised with the vibration that is focused within your heart centre.

As this happens, feel a point of brilliant white Light moving into your orbit. This will expand slightly and will be the intuitive place where your meditation proper is going to take place. This is in essence the etheric structure within your own space, a sort of neutral zone where you can meditate in safety. But to help you visualise that space we suggest you symbolise it as a point of white Light external to yourself.

From your heart chakra a shaft of white Light flows into this external point of white Light creating a bridge with 13 steps. Each step has a sound and represents a very specific pattern with a shamanistic focus. The 13 steps bring the resonance and power of the 13th plane into this meditation and bring into your awareness the power which you have been privileged to use in a positive way in past lives when you held the shamanistic role.

Within your visualisation, see yourself radiating white Light as you start to walk up these 13 steps. Each step will have a different colour representing a different vibration. Your intuition will present each colour to you as you walk on each step. You start off with your body being brilliant white, and if for example the first step is blue, this colour will resonate into your space and you will feel yourself absorbing all the blue into your white Light. You then walk onto step two, which will have a different vibration and colour, and may be accompanied by a sound. That new colour is absorbed into your white Light. You do this with each of the 13 steps, absorbing each concentrated colour and therefore absorbing the encodements of past life frequencies. As you walk over these 13 steps you are in fact reprogramming yourself with the dominating frequencies of the karmic point of reference you have on that particular day.

As you go over the steps, intuitive healing will take place as you absorb the colours and your vibration increases. This may create a degree of nervousness and you may be reluctant to go through these frequencies. So you may need to practise crossing the bridge several times before you can proceed.

After the 13th step, you walk off the bridge into the area where the meditation work you need to do will now begin.

Once you find yourself standing in this neutral zone, ask yourself, "Through which chakra centre do I need to approach my guide today?" That chakra centre might vary each time you do the meditation as the karmic pattern you are working with will be uniquely different each day, and will be affected by the constantly changing pattern of planetary and Earth energies.

If you wish you can use the traffic light dowsing technique to help you know which chakra centre to work with, using the red, amber and green lights for your response. To do this, you focus on each chakra centre individually, starting from the top, and ask if that is the best chakra to work with today. The chakra centres which get a red or amber light you ignore, and just work with the chakra that gets a green light.

Going through the doorways of your chakra centre

Most people have to meet their guides through their solar plexus centre, and not through their heart centre. So if for example you get a green 'yes' response to work through your solar plexus chakra, visualise four entrance points, four doorways all the same size, one behind the other, sitting in front of that chakra. The first one will be a large pale blue doorway, about 50 feet (15m) wide in the shape of a five-pointed star. In your visualisation you walk through that doorway, and as you do, feel yourself absorbing all the pale blue colour as you go through it, so that your whole body now becomes pale blue.

The 5, 6, 7 & 9 pointed stars

As soon as you pass through that five-pointed star doorway, you will see the second doorway. This one will be pale gold in the shape of a six-pointed star. You walk through it, and the blue colour will be replaced with the gold as you absorb it.

You will then see the third doorway. This one will be indigo in the shape of a seven-pointed star. As you go through this doorway the gold will be replaced by the indigo as you absorb it. You will now see the fourth doorway which is a pure white Light entrance point in the shape of a nine-pointed star. As you go through the nine-pointed star, you absorb all the white Light which supersedes the indigo and you will now be radiating only pure white Light once again.

These four doorway entrance points hold the specific vibrations you focus on and absorb. There are thousands of variations of indigo, gold or blue, so out of those variations, you will intuitively absorb just the specific frequency you need.

You then see a camp-fire, in a night-time setting with stars overhead. Each star represents a cosmic gypsy, some are nearer and some further away. Walk up to the fire which represents purity, self-healing and unconditional love, and step into it. In the same way as in the meditation to release personal karma, Meditation 20, in Chapter 2, *The Awakening*, your clothing will be burnt off symbolising the burning away of misinformation and desire.

Now put on your Light body and step out of the fire with your archetypal pattern wrapped around you.

Meeting your guides

As you step out of the flames, you will be met by your guide or guides, who may manifest as a small group of American Red Indians, maybe as many as 13 or 19, sitting or standing in a semi-circle around you. Sometimes you will only see one guide, it depends on the order of importance of what needs to be presented and worked through. If you don't see any guides, know that they are there but your vibrations need to build up so that you can see them.

If you can't see your guides

If you can't see anyone there when you step out of the flames, just sit outside the fire and look into the flames. Use the flames as an oracle, very much like a crystal ball, to go backwards in time to look at aspects during your childhood which need to be resolved. You may even go further back into past lives and be shown where there is a residue of old activity still within you that needs to be transmuted and released. This release will take place by you identifying the specific octave of emotional imbalance, be it in a scene, as a feeling, or as a note of understanding. All you need to do is focus your unconditional love as a triangular formation of energy coming from your heart centre, and radiating from your third eye and both palms of your hands, then direct this triangle of energy into the scene, feeling or colour being shown to you. As you do this any imbalance of energy will be transmuted. When this is done you should then become aware of, or see your guides.

If for whatever reason you are unable to make contact with your guides during the meditation, spend whatever length of time feels appropriate, just sitting and looking into the flames. Relax, concentrate on your breathing, try to locate the point of stillness within yourself and send out a thought for your guides to approach. It is often necessary to build up your vibration over several weeks, and maybe several months, until your vibratory harmony is at a point of efficiency when your guides, who are always there, can be perceived within your reality.

If your guides are there

When you step out of the flames, if your guide or guides are there, one should approach you and may give you his name. Sometimes they say nothing and you might just observe each other for a little while. Or your guide may sit down by you, or may even take you off and give you some healing.

If you are sitting by the flames and your guides are around you and willing to communicate, send unconditional love into the heart centre of each guide and communicate telepathically with them. Your first opening pattern of communication might be to ask your guide to spontaneously prove his unconditional love.

Get your personality symbol

Now ask your guide for your personality symbol. This will be a geometrical pattern which you can use as a meditating focus. You don't need to do anything with your personality symbol at this stage, but merely hold it within your awareness. At a later date, when you need to meditate on a problem, be it physical, emotional or mental, you can bring your personality symbol into your meditation, and as you meditate on your symbol it will give you decisiveness, clarity and strength of will to make the best decision at the right time and in the right place.

Your guides may not give you this symbol as they are motivated to only help you when it is part of your karmic dialogue. If your guides won't give you your personality symbol, it is time to demand and become somewhat pushy! Some guides are actually there to ensure that you do become pushy as they don't like to simply give you an advantage within your reality until you have earned the right to it. So go back into the fire and see yourself as a spark flowing up to the nearest cosmic gypsy. These cosmic gypsies are quite huge. They are 50 miles (80km) wide with wing spans of 75 miles (120km). Just visualise yourself floating up to the nearest one and demand to be given your personality symbol from that cosmic gypsy. You will always get one from them, and by demanding a symbol you can move your awareness on quicker than would normally be the case.

Get your God symbol

Once you have your personality symbol, you can then ask for a God symbol. The God symbol is always presented to you by one of the cosmic gypsies, so to get your God symbol go into the fire and see yourself as a spark flowing up to the nearest cosmic gypsy. If you went up to the cosmic gypsies for your personality symbol, float back down to the fire, then go back up a second time to another cosmic gypsy. Both symbols can be shrunk down and in your visualisation wear them as auric rings on the little finger of your left hand, or put them around your neck on a chain, or in a little pouch on a belt. In this way they will always be with you to meditate on and use whenever you feel it is appropriate.

It could be that having received your personality symbol you will not be given your God symbol during the same meditation. But it is always nice to try! If you don't get your God symbol in this meditation, repeat the meditation daily, coming back into this setting and going back up to the cosmic gypsies until the God symbol has also been given to you.

Your God symbol is a package of energy that highlights the intuitive process and offers you an evolutionary leap forward into a new particular energy package. When using your God symbol you will be specifically focusing on the equation which your soul has agreed to work with for many, many incarnations. You can also use your God symbol to focus on the God force, whether it is latent, or active, within folk both near or far away in physical matter. This will be the spiritual hierarchy as well as Avatars who are God in matter manifesting through physical bodies. The God force is latent in Avatars until it is activated by the Perfect Masters, but your symbol will still give you a response even from those Avatars who have not yet fully remembered. So your God symbol will activate a response from all these Light beings who are more spiritually advanced on the path of life, and as such your symbol will give you the necessary information, understanding, healing, or spontaneous knowledge required for your karmic contract.

Therefore your God symbol will send out a magnetic energy charge indicating quite clearly to those who watch and wait on the inner planes, that you are ready for the next step forward into a more God-awakened state within your awareness. As a result you may get a speciality guide coming down into your space. Or the guides who are already in attendance might recognise that it is time to stimulate your personality essence, as you are now using your God symbol to demand the necessary information or the movement forward into a new vibratory setting.

To end the meditation

When you feel it is necessary to leave, you do so by going back into the flames, then reverse the process of walking through the nine-pointed star doorway, then the seven, six and five-pointed doorways, seeing each star closing down and disappearing behind you. In this way you close down the interdimensional frequency points you opened up as you walked through them. It is important to make sure they disappear behind you so nothing can actually interfere with your normal state of awareness as you walk down the 13 steps over your bridge. As you walk over each step it will resonate with white Light. If a step resonates with colour as you walk onto it, you merely stop, bless and dedicate that step until any colour completely disappears. Any colour left in each step at this stage is an indication of the high frequency energy you are still carrying and your need to drop your rhythm down a little more. As you come off the steps, you will come back into your body still resonating with white Light. As you come back into your body you close down all your chakra centres, make sure your astral body is fully back and nicely aligned, and withdraw your roots from the planet.

40. Meditation to test a guide

If you are in spiritual training and receiving communication from the inner planes, but are uncertain of the level of communication and therefore the acceptability of the pattern of energy masquerading or manifesting as guidance you need some way of testing that guide. This meditation can be used as that testing mechanism.

This exercise also takes you in and out of your meditative state, and will help you become more flexible in doing that.

Preparation

You will need five candles and a bowl of water. Put sea salt or bicarbonate of soda in the water to help absorb any slow frequency energy which might be dispersed during the meditation. The level of bicarbonate of soda used is about a teaspoonful in 1½ pints (1 litre) of water. The level of sea salt is twice as much. Both work well, although bicarbonate of soda is a good way of actually seeing off the gungy energy which makes things 'go bump in the night'!

To prepare for this meditation, put four candles on the floor around where you will sit, one in front, one behind, one to the left and one to the right, all at equal distances so that when linked up they form a circle. Then place a fifth candle in the centre of this 'circle'. You work with candles in this way because every time you light the candles the ceremonial angel of Light will come in to protect you.

Place the bowl of prepared water next to the fifth candle in the centre of your 'circle'. Then light just the four outer candles and dedicate and bless each candle flame. Dedicate them to the Light and to your understanding of the Cosmic Christ.

Sit in the centre of this circle, with the fifth candle (unlit) in front of you. This candle represents fire for healing and protection. It also represents the central focus of the life force of the Cosmic Christ which will flow into it from your other four candles.

Now dedicate and bless the water in the same way as you dedicate and bless a crystal. Dedicate the water to Mother Earth, since any slow frequency energy which may be collected during this meditation will be absorbed by the water and then returned to the Earth to be transmuted. By dedicating the water to healing, understanding and the love which the planet has for all life forms, you can make the vibration within the water similar to a vibration which the Earth automatically recognises and accepts.

Just as a cassette tape accepts the vibration of the person's voice who is recording onto it, so water will accept the vibration of any slow frequency collected during the meditation. That vibration will be electromagnetically implanted into the water molecules. The water will then hang onto it, and when you pour the water into the earth, the vibration of the water will merge with the vibration of the planet. Any negative energy contained within the water will then be automatically transmuted as this is what the Earth does best.

As the disposal of negative entities is normally emotionally orchestrated, water can also symbolise emotional lives, and therefore the ectoplasm* that can sometimes come from water is useful in this meditation.

With the candles and water dedicated and blessed you are now ready to do the main meditation sequence:

Bring down white Light, root yourself in and do the black meditation

First bring white Light down through the top of your head down into each chakra centre, and root yourself in. Then do the black meditation, Meditation 4, in *Key Aspects Of Meditation Work*, to release and transmute any unwanted slow frequency energy.

Having done that you come out of your meditative state and light the fifth candle in front of you. Again dedicate and bless your flame to Light, understanding and the blessing of the Cosmic Christ.

Put on your Light body

As you tune into the Light body you need for this meditation, you may find that the archetypal pattern of the bird people - the eagle, snowy owl or hawk - will be a useful focus if you are tuning into higher guides because the vibration of an eagle is, by definition, quite high. But if you think you may be dealing with slow grade entities or guides who are a bit slow in whatever way, you will need a rougher vibration. So the best Light body to use would be the white Icelandic or the polar bear as these are the higher earthy vibrations.

If you are not sure which archetypal pattern to choose, use your visualisation to symbolise your guide as a thought form. Give it a shape and give it a chakra system. Then look and see which chakra is activated within that thought form at the time you do this meditation. Work intuitively as you ask to be shown which is the active point, and trust what comes through. If the active chakra centre is from the solar plexus down, choose an archetypal pattern that is fairly earthy, such as the bear. If the active chakra centre is from the bottom part of the heart centre upwards, adopt one of the bird archetypal patterns.

First test: Invite your guide to walk through the flame doorway

Now move into your own personal pattern where you normally communicate with the guide coming in, whether this is through automatic writing or meditation. Then visualise your guide as being on the other side of the central candle flame. As you focus on the flame, enlarge the flame within your visualisation, and make it into a circular opening to form a large door. Then invite your guide, or whoever is on the other side of the flame to come through this flame doorway. This is their first test.

If the guide is of a relatively high vibration - from the heart centre or above - then the flame in your mind's eye should get brighter. The actual candle flame might respond in the same way. Your guide will also pass easily through this flame doorway.

If the energy form manifesting as a guide is a bit suspect, or pretending to be of a higher evolution than they actually are, the candle flame within your mind's eye will get darker and might even go out. This may affect the real candle within the centre of your circle. You may also get an intuitive impression that the person who is coming through is a bit iffy and that all is not right.

Whatever response you get, and whether you feel your guide is of a high or slow vibration, you still continue with the next two tests.

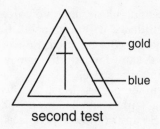

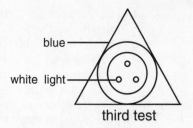

Triangle formations used in this meditation

Second Test: Project your Light energy

As you tell your guide that the doorway is open and invite him or her to come through, you also start to project your Light energy into their heart centre. This is their second test.

You do this by physically crossing your arms in front of you, which you visualise as crossing the wings or paws of your archetypal Light body. Allow the white Light coming down through the top of your head to build up as an energy charge in your heart centre. You may feel this as a sensation of heat or warmth. Then open your arms, and visualise this as opening your wings or paws, and allow the white Light energy to flow from your heart into your third eye and both palms of your hands in a triangular formation.

As your triangle of Light energy forms, you focus and visualise this single triangle as changing into an outer triangle of gold, with an inner triangle of blue. Within that inner triangle of blue you visualise the Christian cross. So you now have two triangles and an inner Christian cross as an energy formation between your third eye and two hands - see the above diagram.

As your guide or energy form comes through the flame doorway, you project this triangular formation of energy towards them. You don't just project your triangle into their heart centre, but you enlarge it as it goes out so that it encompasses their whole body from their third eye chakra down to their feet. The point of your triangle will be at their third eye and the base of your triangle will be at their feet.

If your guide is of a high vibration they will easily contend with this package of energy, and you will find that the vibration of energy you are projecting will become transparent and pass freely through them.

If your guide is of a slow vibration, you may experience an immediate impact as you send out your triangle of energy. You might feel a resistance, or feel a pressure trying to push you away. But basically all you do is keep on pushing in your triangular formation of energy.

If you feel that the energy form is pushing harder than you are, this is only reflective of the level of confidence within yourself. If this happens, and you feel that the energy you are projecting is inadequate, then close your arms which will slow down the frequency and will deny the 'guide' access into your auric space.

Then link into your family on the inner planes. Most people within the Light fraternity are working with a smaller group of about 19,000 people on the inner planes! So think of 19,000 people as a wedge of Light, with you sitting at the head and all these 19,000 people projecting their will into your heart centre - no other centre, just your heart centre. This will boost and amplify your energy charge making it sufficient for your use.

If you went up to a young person about 14 years of age who hasn't yet developed the same weight within their nervous system as an adult, and you placed your hand over their heart centre and pushed them very rapidly backwards, the force of the push would throw them off balance. This is basically what you are doing in your meditation as you whack your triangle of energy into the guide or energy form in front of you.

So just keep pushing with your triangular formation at the offending energy form and push it through an interdimensional doorway. This will be seen as an aperture point and you push any slow frequency energy form through it as if you are spring cleaning, and getting rid of any slow vibration which is not adequate. As it is pushed through, the triangular formation you are projecting will seal that door - a bit like going up to the door with an acetylene torch and smelting your symbol into place so that the doorway takes on the shape of your triangle. This is important. You can shrink your triangle down if the entrance point is quite small, and in most cases it is, or you can enlarge it if you find you have an interdimensional doorway which is quite massive, maybe several miles (kilometres) wide. So your triangle can match whatever size is there. Your triangle will then totally disappear.

Third test: Project your second triangular formation

If your guide comes through the flame doorway, and passes through the two triangles with a cross in the centre, you project another triangle as a third and final test.

This is a new triangle of energy which replaces the previous triangular formation. So refocus on the first triangular formation and visualise this changing to just one blue triangle with two circles inside it. These inner circles are one inside the other. You can make their colours whatever feels intuitively right for you depending on the vibration you need. Initially, if you are not sure what colours to work with, you can make the outer circle black, and the inner circle pale blue or gold. Put three blobs of white Light in the shape of a triangle in the centre of the inner circle.

Now project this new triangular formation of energy at *just* the third eye of the guide or entity in front of you. If your guide is of a high vibration, he or she will pass easily through these three tests and you then know you are in good hands. But you still ask them what they want, and build up a rapport based on faith, trust and practical experience.

If your guide is of a slow vibration, this third test is important, because if a slow frequency entity somehow manages to get through the first two tests - which is unlikely - this third test will finally see them off.

By pushing specifically at the third eye, you are aiming at the point where negative entities tend to focus their energy when they enter our dimensional time zone. This will be their weakest point and by focusing your will within your triangle of energy you are actually forcing the issue.

Within these three tests you are also setting up three thought forms. Each test links into your unconditional love, into the wisdom of your higher self and the force of your unity which is your spiritual family. These three thought forms are, in essence, a series of filters and each filter will burn up a lot of energy if the entity is fairly negative. So by the time any slow frequency energy form who is manifesting as a guide works its way through to this third test it should be relatively weak. To withstand that amount of energy is something those on the inner planes are not very good at - they like to sneak in without too much resistance. If they know that you are there to offer resistance it is unlikely they will be able to come in.

If a slow vibration guide has managed to come this far, you focus your second triangular formation into their third eye chakra then shrink that triangular pattern back to a point of white Light. As you do that the energy of the entity coming through will be used up as it starts to resist this last focal point of energy. If the impulse of the guide is still there, continue to project your triangle, by amplifying and contracting, amplifying and contracting, until you have sucked all the energy out of the opposition being presented to you.

Don't forget to continue working with your group, using them to keep you charged up. You can then dispose of, once and for all, any energy package that might have been presenting you with a problem for some considerable time - even considerable lives.

To end the meditation

To come out of this meditation, bring your triangle of energy back and close down all your chakra centres. Keep your Light body on as a form of spontaneous form of protection.

Bring your awareness back into your body, then rededicate and bless your candles before you blow them out, irrespective of whether you have met aspects of Light or dark. In this way you see off any slow frequency energy and tidy up any left-over energy which might still be there. When you blow the candles out after the dedication this symbolically locks your door.

Each time you repeat this meditation and relight your candles, you rededicate and bless them. In this way you build up the dedication and blessing in the form of a spontaneous prayer. This will invoke and bring about a structural appraisal of what is necessary, since karmic conditions and patterns of communication will be different each time you do the meditation.

At the end of the meditation you might find your water is a bit dark, almost as if it was stained, depending on how much negative energy was transmuted. So always re-bless the water as you throw it away - even if no negative energy was transmuted and the water looks clear.

As you throw away the water, ask the Earth to transmute any negativity within the water, and know that it will as the Earth needs the negative energy we release as part of its polarisation and spiritual growth.

If you use this meditation as an ongoing focus, your triangle of energy will take on a particular encodement when your normal guide comes in. You will then know your guide as you start to feel, sense or become aware of the subtle vibration as your triangle of energy meets and blends with the energy package of his or her unique essence. The more times you do this, meeting and testing your guide, the more you will become aware of this subtle and unique vibration as the energies merge. And the less likely you can be fooled, since your guide on occasions might take the opportunity to test your perceptive or defensive ability by asking his twin brother to pop in pretending to be himself! If you are ever in doubt, allow your energy to focus, go through the testing mechanism until you are absolutely certain that whoever is presenting itself to your energy field is the energy which is right and necessary for you at that time.

Variation:

In future meditations, as you project your first triangular formation - the two triangles of gold and blue with the inner cross - you may intuitively feel the need to expand this triangular aspect. So although initially you start off with two triangles, you can expand this to a maximum of five, each one inside the other. If you do this the colours will be, from the outside moving in, gold, blue, silver, indigo and purple.

CHAPTER 9
EXTRATERRESTRIALS

Every living form on Earth is duplicated somewhere else within the galaxy. This has happened through genetic manipulation in the past, and a lot of those duplications are far more evolved than many of us care to think.

Some people will have a bit of a shock when they actually see their galactic neighbours, for although some extraterrestrials have the same form as humans, a lot have a totally different form and essence. We have been led to believe that we are all made in God's image. But this is not so. That belief is governed by our limitation of how we define God as an energy source. Since God is indefinable, life forms mirror that, and we will understand this more clearly as more direct communication takes place between our galactic neighbours and ourselves.

The American government already have in excess of 70 different types of galactic travellers in deep freeze. At the time of writing, it is believed they still have those galactic beings. A lot of these extraterrestrial bodies were found and information collected after UFO's had crashed.

The polarity of their machines is built on magnetic rhythms and a lot are powered by crystals. As the main focus currently on this planet is magnetic energy, quite often the coordinations within UFO's are slightly out, or they are sometimes in the right place at the wrong time, or their crystals malfunction - all of which can create collisions. We don't normally hear about this as there is a massive government cover-up, especially in America where the government are quietly collecting the information, whilst saying nothing about what is going on.

In the Nevada Desert in 1975 three coffins were found. These were about 10 feet (3m) long with semi-transparent tops. In them were two male and one female extraterrestrials, similar to us although much longer, with the feet shaped like a bell. The coffins are now in a military establishment in Warminster, England. The inside information is that these extraterrestrials are not actually 'dead'. They wake up every now and again, then go back to sleep. So they are obviously waiting for something, waiting for the right time to transfer their information.

These extraterrestrial people are known as Universal Travellers who travel at right angles through the Universe.

Meeting UFO's

Three planets are actively sending out scouts at the moment to 'test the water' before more direct communication in larger groups can take place. Information in relation to which planets they are, is at the moment 'classified'. They are checking out our planet in order to find the right frequency point where it will be safe for them to approach and specifically communicate with humans in mass. This will happen when fear in humans has been dissipated to a level where we can understand the communication keys which have, over many years, been coming in for us to translate and understand. As mentioned before, the crop circles are one such key being offered to humanity and this planet.

The galactic police force have been targeting selective areas, in particular America, Russia and England. They have actually interfered with television and interrupted news programmes with their own message. Some people are very apprehensive about these extraterrestrial broadcasts, and play this down for various reasons. But it does still happen systematically.

Many Light workers are now etherically going up to the local UFO station at night. Although on a conscious level you might not be aware of this, on another level you may already be very familiar with these folk and their spacecraft. So if a UFO actually appears in front of you and invites you to go aboard, and their vibration feels intuitively familiar and in harmony with yourself, you can safely go aboard and you may meet some of your old mates! But if you don't recognise that UFO machine and its vibration, then don't go on board.

If a UFO comes along and extraterrestrial beings want to communicate with you, they could knock out your physical body and take your astral body out. So just your astral body goes up into their spaceship.

The process of communication is usually heart to heart, which means that as we develop more harmlessness and let go of our fears, so we will start to merge and meld more with our galactic neighbours with harmony, love and joy. These high frequency energies of harmony, love and joy are the key notes to cultivate with any encounter, should you have the opportunity to meet any UFO people within your travels.

Extraterrestrials, like ourselves, have a top and bottom end to their vibratory field. Some are extremely beautiful and spiritual but there are others more interested in genetic manipulation who like to observe us as a race - almost like a scientist observing something in the laboratory.

Some extraterrestrials are also terribly interested in the reproduction process of the human body. A Mexican farmer saw a UFO around his farm for three days. On the third day an extraterrestrial woman hypnotised him and had sex with him so that they could take the implantation of sexual energy from his vibration, and use it in a slightly different way to speed everything up for their own evolution.

Some UFO's also give off fatal radiation fields. In Wales, a man left home to go and buy a loaf of bread and was found two days later on a coal heap with the top half of his body covered in radiation burns. When the autopsy was carried out, they couldn't work out how he was killed.

Although extraterrestrial folk of a more negative nature have been interacting with humanity over the last 125,000 years, as the vibratory core of the planet and humanity now demand a different interpretation of reality, the extraterrestrials of a purer order are beginning to manifest as we are moving into a similar frequency.

Overall, even though there are some who can do damage, these galactic neighbours should not be feared. They can even be quite playful! UFO machines have been known to 'wink back' at humans who flash their car lights at them. But sometimes when a UFO machine comes directly overhead, people get into a panic, and as the vibration of fear is destructive, the extraterrestrial form who might be much more evolved than ourselves will obviously take one look at those fear vibrations and scurry away.

By 1998/99, or at the most by the year 2000, UFO's will be as familiar to us as aircraft are now. By then our vibrations will have lifted to a similar frequency and we will be able to see UFO's in abundance - because they are already there, it is just that most people can't see them as the extraterrestrial vibration is currently slightly higher than the human vibration most of the time.

If you can keep your thoughts clear for 36 hours without thinking anything negative - nothing negative at all - then you will raise your vibrations and will be able to see UFO's in abundance, now!

Occasionally extraterrestrials do appear in a more cosmic representation. This might manifest as cloud movement when planetary conditions push clouds in one direction, but when you look carefully you actually see a few clouds are travelling in the opposite direction to all the others. Or you might see stars behaving a bit peculiar! As you open your awareness to these levels of reality, you will start to perceive this phenomenon in a new way.

The Earth is also catacombed with tunnels, with a lot of tunnels leading from one continent to the other, with dimensional frequency entrance points in them. Artifacts are now being found like the crystal skulls which are giving more precise information on this. Again, once you open yourself to this greater awareness you realise that we are not alone - even though we may think we are!

CHAPTER 10
DEALING WITH
NEGATIVE ENERGIES

Slow frequency negative energies infiltrate your physical and auric fields from many sources. This can be a source external to your home, such as geopathic stress, ley lines and distorted ground energies. Or they can originate from within your home and work environment. Electrical strip lights, computers, cash-registers and electrical appliances such as washing-machines, tumble-driers, microwave cookers, hi-fi's - even electrical toasters and digital watches - all give off a negative field of magnetic energy which can be damaging to your health. And the worst offender is television.

In addition to this massive field of slow frequency negative energy created by modern society, the Aquarian energy is now stimulating the planet to remember. Sites of old battles are being reactivated so that the negative vibrations of suffering and trauma which have been held within the planet since the time of battles, can now be released and transmuted.

So you might be happily working in your home when suddenly you go into decline and feel mildly depressed. You might even develop a physical problem as the pattern of energies around your home is structurally altered.

You may be given an understanding of what is happening during your dream state. It is up to each one of us to now understand and recognise these changes and take personal responsibility on two levels. First to monitor this negative energy within our body and regularly transmute it. Secondly, to take personal responsibility to transmute the negative energies in our home and local environment. Whether you are at home all day or busy with a full-time career, you can still play your part in transmuting these energies, so that humanity as a whole can move forward.

Geopathic stress

Geopathic stress is a slow frequency negative vibration caused by basic faults in ground energies and ley lines which have been distorted. This can happen, for example, when a motorway is built. Seriously ill people who live over these negative energy streams can occasionally draw that energy into their physical essence and as they die, these negative lines of energy disappear. This is their parting gift to the planet.

Geopathic stress can be useful if you put a compost heap over it, because it breaks things down very quickly. But if you sleep over a geopathic stress line it tends to also break down the body's vibration fairly quickly. You then develop down-market syndromes such as headaches, depression or irritability. Geopathic stress also causes any toxicity within the body to bubble up, and if you sleep over a geopathic stress line for a periodic length of time, disharmony and disease will definitely manifest. If you have any genetic weakness in your body such as migraine, ulcers, varicose veins or cancer, that will also be activated and amplified.

Anything of a negative nature which is latent and willing to be released within your body, on a physical, emotional or mental level, will also express itself in some unpleasant way.

Quite often, when geopathic stress enters someone's body it might not affect the whole body. It might just affect the feet. When this happens the magnetic negative energy from the geopathic stress contracts the smaller chakra centres in the feet. That person is then unable to release any negative energy through these centres, which in turn creates an even bigger build-up and the downhill spiral is in place.

If you are living over or near a geopathic stress line, you may like to consider using one of the RadiTech** machines (**see Appendix), which release geopathic stress from the body. I use two of these and find them to be very effective.

Quite often of course, the karmic containment of the individual will 'direct' them to a home where their bed will inadvertently be put over one of these stress lines so that personal karma can be fulfilled. The resulting amplification of health problems will then ensure more structural change is brought about within that person as a whole.

As a general rule, if you are having any interaction of energy which is negative, your subconscious will certainly be nudging you about it. Your dream life might be a bit peculiar. You might wake up with headaches, feelings of anxiety, or feeling particularly tired. Although you might put this down to a number of different reasons it would be advisable to check the ground energies under your house, and in particular under your bed.

These ground energies can also amplify any structural thought forms which have been latent within the walls of your home - for example, from a trauma which might have happened within that home some years ago, and which is impregnated into the walls in the form of a vibration. If you are living over the site of an old battle, then any of that old trauma or those old thought forms, which are in the process of being activated, will also be amplified by the geopathic stress line.

Geopathic stress points tend to move around. They are not static in the normal sense. If water passes over a distorted ley line it will pick up the negative charge, and if that water then flows into the local reservoir which feeds your home you will have negatively charged, geopathically stressed water coming out of your taps. Not only are you drinking that water, but if you have central heating and that geopathically stressed water is circulating round your radiators, the radiators themselves will also be geopathically stressed, sending out more slow frequency negative vibrations throughout your home. This creates a knock-on effect which activates the whole foundation, thought-wise, of what your home represents.

If you are moving to a new house or new apartment you should always check all the rooms, especially the bedrooms, to make sure there are no slow frequency energy lines there which could cause you problems. Meditation 45, at the end of this chapter, offers a technique to help you locate and transmute geopathic stress and negative energies in your home.

Computers

Computers also give off a slow frequency negative vibration. Within modern society we now have widespread computer infiltration with computer dependency now established within the banking system, financial structures, most corporations and even in the home as many families now have personal computers or word-processors. As people around the world tap on their computer keyboards they are also tapping into the actual circuits and exposing themselves to slow frequency vibrations.

A computer is put together by frequency components which are influenced by the minds of people handling those components. Therefore the essence of how those people were feeling and thinking at the time of working on a computer will be reflected in that computer's circuit. If they were angry, fed up, or worried, those emotional vibrations will be impregnated into the frequency components. Likewise, if the person assembling the computer was happy or loved working on that computer, the overall vibration within that computer will be one of love! The dominant motivation of the company will also be reflected in each computer. If the company is dedicated to profit margins, or worried about turnover and the recession, those worry and fear vibrations will also be impregnated into each product.

When the computer is tested and switched on, as the electrical charge is put through a computer, all those vibrations - positive and negative - are anchored and locked in.

As a computer circuit can hold astral energy, interested parties or astral entities from different time zones are able to flow into the computer network and just sit there influencing and drawing energy from the people using that computer.

These astral entities who need slow frequency negative vibrations for their intuitive food, will happily feed off any slow frequency negative vibration that was dominant when the computer was initially put together. Each time you switch your computer on, the electrical charge boosts the vibrations which feed the astral entities, and this in turn boosts their energy and strength.

So always cleanse, dedicate and bless your computer to honesty, truth and love which will put your stamp on it. The cleansing process will wipe the astral entities out. The dedication and blessing will make any other astral entities, who might try and infiltrate your computer after that, feel very uncomfortable. They will then seek out a more acceptable feeding ground.

Meditation 46, at the end of this chapter, and Meditation 50, at the end of Chapter 11, offer two techniques for cleansing a computer. The dedication and blessing process is also given in both meditations.

Pylons and electrical stations

This infiltration of slow frequency negative energy is also being generated by the national electrical system in every country around the world.

The most unfriendly electrical system I have found is in Israel. They have telegraph poles on every street with little electrical stations or transformers mounted on them. These are only small but create an awful negative magnetic pattern which flows over people, just like confetti, as they walk down the street.

Electrical pylons are an artificial stimulus which gives off a very nasty slow frequency vibration. In America a lot of people are protesting at the new pylons being erected close to houses, as research has shown that more suicides are committed by people living under pylons. Researchers working with this pattern of vibration have also established that this type of slow frequency energy causes and activates leukaemia and cancer in people living close to those pylons. Yet pylons are still being erected over schools and housing estates!

Their slow frequency vibration is also amplified as the long lengths of electric cables flow over geopathic stress points within the ground. This generates an expansion within the geometric formula of the electric energy, which tends to build up swirls of negative energy around some pylons in a much denser way than others. The result is that if you happen to be living near one of these pylons a build-up of negative energy within your body is assured.

From a clairvoyant point of view based on personal experience, some pylons can be far more distressing than others. Some are more friendly but in general, on a scale of one to ten, most pylons seem to be about two. In general the vibration from pylons is far too slow and they create the equivalent of a moving geopathic stress point.

If you go into a house and think, "Gosh, the energy in here feels really rotten," you are actually psychometrising the interplay of negative energies which might be in the curtains, furniture, or even in the books or objects in that home. But you may also find, when you work out where the energy is spiralling, that the energy disturbance is not coming from the actual house but coming from the electricity being fed into that home.

If this happens you can neutralise that energy by taking your awareness, through visualisation, down into the electrical circuits and following the electricity back to where your local electricity company is generating it.

Then using one of the meditations at the end of this chapter, you can work with the power of your will to project a high input of Light energy and neutralise the negative input.

There are now quite a few groups of dedicated Light workers who are targeting their local electricity companies, working with the structure of electricity being generated. Because of their work, some electrical power stations are now becoming quite friendly.

If this technique is new to you, don't limit yourself by saying, "I can't do this type of work." Just work with the meditations in this book, and with practice you will find that what you thought was hard, or impossible, is actually quite easy. Remember that the only limitation you have is the one you put on yourself. So open your thoughts to limitlessness - and have fun!

Televisions

Colour televisions create an outflowing of negative energy to a range of about 60 feet (18m) all around them. Within the first 12 feet (3.6m) that negative energy is much more condensed and when you switch on the television you can feel your hairs crackle, as 87,000 volts of magnetic energy goes through the television and radiates out to you.

If your television is badly adjusted, or sitting over an area of geopathic stress, this will amplify the condition. This negative energy will build up as a sea of magnetic fibres which automatically tune into and gravitate towards anything similar within your energy field. As a result, quite a lot of people have a formation of this negative energy collecting around their bone structure, as well as within their chakra system and auric space.

The gross vibratory field from television also offers a feeding ground for astral entities who use television in the same way as computers. They just sit within the circuitry and feed off the negative vibrations created by the television set.

If the programme you are watching is a violent epic which inspires fear, terror, anxiety, or even just tension - which are all slow frequency vibrations - and you start to actually experience those emotions, then your body will send out its own slow frequency vibration. As like attracts like, this will pick up on and be amplified by the negative vibration from the television programme. This has a two-fold effect. First any tension in your body will become worse and this often results in sore and bloodshot eyes, exhaustion, or just a feeling of being wiped out, as the whole chemical factory of your body becomes affected.

Secondly, the lower astral entities sitting within your television will be able to feed off your emotions and draw energy from you. This is why people often feel exhausted and unable to get out of the armchair after a long session in front of a television!

If you live in a terraced house and your neighbours have one or two colour televisions, even more negative energy will be bombarding and saturating your system.

In case you are beginning to get anxious as you read this, just breathe out your anxiety as that in itself is a slow frequency vibration. Adopt a more positive and confident emotion and know that you can work with this. You *can* neutralise these negative energies. You *can* get rid of astral entities sitting inside your computer or television. You *can* protect yourself. In fact to do so is part of your contract and part of why you are here - to help transmute the negativity on the planet. Because this is so important, the next chapter is devoted to just this aspect and tells you how you can specifically work in this way.

Jewellery

Gold will not accept negative energy very easily, but silver and especially base elements will. Jewellery also holds the thought implants from the person who made it, and if it is second-hand also from the person who has worn it before. It will also hold the vibration from the environment where it used to sit. If it was a happy atmosphere there will be no problem. But if you own jewellery that once belonged to a negative thinking relative, or perhaps a depressed or alcoholic person, those dominant thoughts and emotions will be imprinted in the jewellery and will try to feed off you.

Jewellery can be cleared but it is sometimes quite difficult. The easiest thing to do with second-hand jewellery - or anything second-hand - is to chuck it out! But if you want to work with it, first dedicate and bless it. Dedicate it to the highest note of harmony, to the Cosmic Christ. Then bless it with understanding, wisdom, healing and your need at that time.

You can then do Meditation 47, at the end of this chapter, to cleanse jewellery.

Books

Every book is corded into the energy of the author, his emotional package and evolution. His channelling or inspiration will create a thought form which is his book. Added to that is the vibration and motivation of the publishing house. The emotional input of each person who subsequently reads a copy of that book will then cord into the overall thought form of the book, either adding to or subtracting from its overall vibration.

A book circulated through a library will also be impregnated with all the emotions experienced by everyone who has read that particular copy. All their fear and terror, or joy and harmony will be sitting as a vibrational package within the book. This will activate anything of a similar vibration within subsequent readers, as like always attracts like. As someone else reads the book, their emotions will add to the overall vibrational package.

In this way, every book has a 'sound' or vibration which can be positive or negative. If the essence of a book holds a negative vibration, it will leak that negative energy into the room, as books are on one level open gateways - a bit like a telephone which has been left off the receiver. Any negative 'sound' going out into your room can be amplified by ground energies and can contribute to any adverse emotions you may be going through.

To prevent this happening, old books should be systematically cleansed and their energy vibration raised on an ongoing basis. Meditations 42 and 43, at the end of this chapter, offer you two ways of doing this.

Travelling by car

A car crash is always caused at a crossover point where there is a disturbance of energy which creates an energy swirl. When that energy swirl reaches a level of negative efficiency it moves down into the physical plane and sits there waiting to implode with the right conditions. The right conditions are a driver with a build-up of slow frequency negative energy within both his or her body and the car. As that driver crosses the energy swirl, the impact of their negative energy with the energy swirl creates an imbalance of energies which will create an accident.

As an accident is an implosion, and sometimes an explosion, which releases slow frequency magnetic waste, the opportunist karmic devas who tend to follow us around licking their lips in anticipation, will make the most of this opportunity - karmically and otherwise. They will use the opportunity of a car crash to release any other slow frequency magnetic energy of a similar vibration which they want to dispose of.

If a car is stolen, it will have a frequency which first of all attracts the car thief or joy-rider. The vibratory wrongness or excitement of that joy-ride will automatically attract other negative energies. If they are being chased up the motorway by the police, their vibrations will suck into the car any negative energies within 20 to 30 feet (6-9m). This builds up as a massive negative energy swirl, and if this hits any other negative swirls already sitting on the motorway, the resulting crash often ends in death.

As this happens, all the negative focus of energy drawn to them will be transmuted. From a karmic point of view, car thieves who die in this way are actually ending their life in a positive sequence by transmuting such a large amount of negative energy.

For your own safety, you can develop intuitive concentration to monitor your driving condition and you can also feel ahead to see if there are any energy swirls on the route you plan to take, which you need to be aware of.

The way you do this is, initially look at the route you are going to travel from A to B. If you plan to travel along a motorway, ask yourself these basic questions, "During the time I am planning to travel - since karmic packages vary from minute to minute, and hour to hour - is there a possibility of me passing through an energy swirl?" If the answer is 'yes', try to get a specific answer as to where that will be and when this swirl will be at its strongest.

You can ask these questions intuitively or you can dowse on a map of your route as you ask the questions.

If there is an energy swirl on the route you plan to take, ask your higher self whether it is appropriate for you to disperse this energy before you travel. If it is, you can do that by visualising the energy swirl as a thought form and then target that thought form by pushing its vibration upwards. Meditation 55, in Chapter 13, *Barnacles And Thought Forms*, explains in detail how to raise the vibration of a thought form.

By raising the vibration of the thought form representing the energy swirl, even if you only manage to push it up slightly, you are postponing the moment when that negative energy charge will manifest as a physical impact. This will allow you safe passage through that spot.

If you cannot disperse it, then ensure you don't go through that particular swirl at the time the implosion is indicated. Also make sure the treacle count within your body and your car is down to 3% before you start your journey.

If you are regularly monitoring the level of negative energy or treacle count in your body, also regularly monitor the slow frequency negative energy or treacle count in your car. Doing it once then thinking you can forget about it won't work. If you park your car over a negative ley line, you bring all that negative ley line energy into your car when you turn on the ignition, and as your car is a magnetic machine it will hang onto it.

As energy follows thought and always works on the natural law of like attracting like, if you regularly release all negative charges from your body and car, it is unlikely you will trigger off any energy swirl on the road which could cause an accident. But just to be sure, always ask your guides for safe passage through any energy swirl on your route.

In addition to regularly assessing the treacle count in your car, it is advisable to also look specifically at the thought form which your motor-car represents in its totality. Then work with that thought form to raise its hara and push its vibration up to the throat chakra or above, using Meditation 55, in Chapter 13, *Barnacles And Thought Forms*.

If you have clairvoyant abilities, you can also look at places where there have been a lot of accidents and will see the old thought forms of pain, fear and terror, just sitting there. Once you get used to seeing or sensing these vibrational energy patterns, you can transmute them as you drive along, if you feel it is appropriate.

Travelling by air

An aeroplane is a magnetic flying machine. It is a contained vehicle of awareness which is full of the slower frequency thought forms of fear and anxiety as so many people are afraid of flying. It contains not only the fear vibrations of anyone currently on the flight, but the auric vibrations of all those who have flown on that aeroplane, as these will have permeated into the seats. This is why some seats in an aeroplane feel particularly uncomfortable!

During a flight most people drink or eat microwaved food, both of which lower their vibration. The engines also give off a magnetic negative vibration. Add to that the radioactivity you are subjected to from the sun, and you understand why so many people feel bad after a long flight.

When flying, your hara, your centre of gravity - which moves up and down like a water indicator - should normally drop down to your sexual chakra centre during take-off. It should then gradually come up and sit around the throat chakra during the flight, dropping back down when the aeroplane lands. This happens naturally with air-hostesses who are relaxed and confident with flying. But the hara of people afraid of flying will gravitate downwards, or their hara is just inflexible and tends to stick around their solar plexus or heart chakra. This creates extra tension which feeds the fear of flying thought form.

If about an hour after take-off, you start to feel fed up, bored, or restless, this is a clear sign that your treacle count has gone up far too high. So do one of the meditations to release that negative energy. Or do the visualisation of 'pulling the plugs' to release your treacle count. This can still be done effectively in an aeroplane by imagining the negative waste flowing down through the air into Mother Earth.

A build-up of magnetic energy also happens if you fly through time zones and different magnetic fields, especially if you are flying the 'wrong' way. This is what we commonly call jet lag. A little tip which many people have found useful is to put brown paper bags over your feet while flying! Just take your socks off, put a brown paper bag over each foot, pulling them up over your ankle, and put your socks on again. In this way you can alleviate jet lag. It may sound silly but it works!

You can also ask your higher self, "Is it appropriate for me to cleanse and transmute the negative energy within the energy system of everybody here?" Also ask, "Can I work to transmute the whole energy system of the aeroplane itself, and can I work particularly with the captain?"

The captain represents the focal point of energy. Therefore his essence will be in a commanding situation. The captain is also on one level the most vulnerable, as all energy of a negative nature always goes back to the crown focus which the captain represents, so he will be the binding mechanism corded into all the crew and passengers.

If it is appropriate to work with the whole energy system of the aeroplane you are travelling in, bear in mind that you are not only working with the physical manifestation, but also working with the inner-plane manifestation as well. So if the aeroplane is following a flight pattern that is well flown, then all the thought forms attached to that flight path, from all the worry and fear of all the passengers who have flown that route before you, will also be worked on. Meditation 48, at the end of this chapter, explains how to do this.

Whether you are on a short flight or a long transatlantic flight, what better way to pass the time than to clear up the inner planes on your flight path!

Your work environment

If you feel the energy in your work environment is manipulated in any way, ask your higher self if it is appropriate for you to work with it. If the answer is 'yes', always work with your group - which may be a physical group working together, or it may be your group on the inner planes. Any dedicated group of Light workers can do this work using the format in Meditation 49, given at the end of this chapter. Ideally work with a minimum of five people as this will give you more power. You can do this with two to four people if you feel confident in your abilities to work in this way, but this is definitely not something for you to do on your own.

Negative energies are stronger in a large corporation than in a home or television as they have a greater output of magnetic patterns from computers, electrical equipment and lighting etc. The impact of wrong use of will through corruption and manipulation and all the thought forms which come under those headings also make large companies very powerful on an astral level. Much more astrally powerful than most people recognise.

But all you need is a few people who have enough faith and enough love to invite in the spiritual hierarchy to work with your group team in order to change your own, or other working environments - especially airports where a lot of negative fear energy builds up.

The effect of this is quite interesting, because if you start doing this type of work with any organisation which has any imbalance of energy, whether it is corruption, fear or even terrorist movement, then everybody - in fact every aspect of energy contributing to that imbalance of energy, be it on the inner or outer planes, will also be affected. This happens automatically because you are specifically focusing your will and sending out high frequency energy which has a swamping effect as it impacts onto the slow frequency energy. As this happens, the slower vibration has to go upwards. As it does, everybody who is contributing to that slow frequency energy will find it more difficult to continue feeding that energy stream, and the natural law of right use of will and like attracting like will automatically come into play. So will the natural law governing the ray of rightness which has been manifesting over the last three years.

Anything which represents fear or corruption, anything which represents past disorientation can be targeted, if it is intuitively right for you to do so. You will find that some people will be motivated to work with one stream of energy, and others with another. It depends on your sensitivity and how much 'clout' that energy stream has. Be aware that when you start to target the negative energies within larger organisations, it can be a bit like creeping up on someone and slapping them on the bottom! They will spin around very quickly and have a good look at who did that! So the package of slow frequency energy you are targeting can start to flow your way. You will then find the energies you are working with will be amplified if you haven't transmuted them sufficiently. This is why it is advisable to only work with a group when doing this work so that you won't be targeted on an individual basis.

If at any time you experience difficulty in neutralising and transmuting slow frequency energies when doing any of these meditations, it could be that the energy charge you are sending out is too weak. If this is the case, work with Meditation 41, to create a higher input of energy, at the end of this chapter. With practice you will soon be able to create and project a stronger energy charge from your heart chakra. As your energy charge gets stronger, your confidence will improve. You will then find you are able to successfully transmute many forms of slow frequency negative energies.

* * *

Dealing With Negative Energies: meditations

41. Meditation to create a higher input of energy if you are having difficulty transmuting slow frequency energy
42. Meditation to cleanse a book or object in a room
43. Second meditation to cleanse a book or object in a room
44. Trawling meditation to cleanse a room and dispose of negative energies
   NB. *Variation 2 can be used to trawl and cleanse a child's aura*
45. Second meditation to cleanse a room or house and dispose of negative energies (this works specifically with geopathic stress and negative thought forms)
46. Meditation to cleanse a computer or word-processor
47. Meditation to cleanse jewellery
48. Meditation to cleanse the energy system of an aeroplane
49. Meditation to change the vibration of your work environment

41. Meditation to create a higher input of energy if you are having difficulty transmuting slow frequency energy

If you are having difficulty neutralising and dispersing slow frequency energy, it may be that your own input of energy is not yet strong enough. If so, work with this meditation to raise the energy or activation level within each of your chakra centres. You will then be able to build up and project a higher input of energy. When you next work with a meditation to transmute negative energies, you should find you are then able to neutralise and disperse that energy. The meditation sequence is:

Bring down white Light, root yourself in and put on your Light body

First visualise roots flowing down from your feet into the Earth, and see white Light flowing in through the top of your head. Bring the white Light down through the top of your crown chakra and visualise it flowing down through each chakra centre.

Adopt whatever Light body feels intuitively right for you today, and build up an energy charge of white Light in your heart chakra.

Start working with your base chakra

Move your focus to your base chakra. Visualise this as being split into seven main levels, one on top of the other. If it helps your visualisation process you can visualise your base chakra as an egg-shaped energy form external to yourself, and visualise that being split into seven levels.

Now intuitively look into your base chakra, or dowse if you prefer, to see which level is the activation point. This will tell you on which level your energy is flowing into that chakra. If this is new to you, just ask your higher self to give you the activation level, and the first intuitive answer that comes to mind will be the right one.

If the activation point is on level one, two, or three, your base chakra is vibrating a little slow. Ideally, if you have good vitality, with an input of energy that is adequate for your needs your activation point should be resonating on level five or above. If it is lower than five then you need to push that energy further up.

Pushing your energy upwards

To do this, intuitively ask your higher self for a symbol which feels right for you to work with today. Allow your visualisation to show you the colour of your symbol. Place that symbol in your base chakra, then take it up into your heart chakra. Bring down white Light into your symbol, duplicate it and place a duplication in both hands and feet. You will now have five coloured symbols which all have to be made transparent in order to neutralise the energy package which is effectively holding your base chakra in a slow frequency.

To do this, bring down white Light through the top of your head into the symbol in your heart centre, and at the same time pass that Light down through your body into the symbols in your hands and your feet. As you continue to bring white Light into all five symbols, the colour within them will start to diminish, and they will become totally transparent.

Once all the colour has been transmuted, look at your base chakra again and see where your activity point is now. It should have moved up to level six, or above. Ideally you aim to get it up to level seven within each chakra centre, but you might find it sticks around level six.

If all the colour in your symbols has been transmuted and the activity point in your base chakra has not moved up, or has moved up a bit but is still below level six, then you need to spend a little longer bringing down more white Light into your symbols. Continue to bring white Light down into them until they start to shrink, then completely disappear.

Having achieved that, if the activity level has still not moved up to level six or above, you need to do the following step: take your awareness into your base chakra and again see it split into seven levels, one above the other. Starting with level one, visualise your coloured symbol on that level. Bring white Light down into that level and transmute all the colour in your symbol. Move your awareness up to level two and again see your symbol on that level. It will now be coloured once again. Repeat the sequence of bringing down white Light into that second level and transmuting all the colour in your symbol. Repeat this for each level, working up through all seven levels. In this way, whatever vibration is holding you back within one of the subtle levels of your base chakra will now be breached. You will then have a new input of energy flowing into your system which you might feel as heat, as a vibration or as a general sense of well-being. Recheck the hara within your base chakra, and it should now be up to level six or seven.

Work upwards with the other chakras

When you have pushed the activity point in your base chakra up to level six or seven, move your awareness up to your sexual chakra. Again see it on seven levels. Ask for an intuitive reading as to where its hara is and repeat the above sequence. Use the same symbol which will once again be filled with colour, but this time place the symbol within your solar plexus chakra. From there take it up to your heart centre where you amplify and duplicate it, placing a duplication into both hands and feet. In the same way as before you transmute all the colour in your symbols by bringing down white Light into them until they become transparent. In this way you move the activity point in your sexual centre up to level six or seven.

Then work upwards through all the chakra centres in the same way, using the same symbol throughout. As each chakra centre has a different frequency vibration, the colour for the symbol is normally different for each chakra. Occasionally you might have variations of the same colour if you have a specific area of limiting energy affecting all your chakra centres at the same time, but this is fairly rare.

If you get to one chakra centre where the activity point is stuck, you stay with that chakra until you have rectified the imbalance in the energy before moving on, otherwise you won't achieve a proper harmonisation.

If necessary, stop the meditation at the point where you are stuck and repeat it the next day. Continue to repeat the meditation daily until you have got the hara in all chakras up to level six or seven.

To come out of the meditation

Focus on the symbols in your hands and feet and contract them, bring them back into your heart centre where they will be absorbed into your main symbol, whether they are still coloured and active or transparent. Now bring more white Light down into your heart centre. As you do this the main symbol will shrink and completely disappear, and the vibration of that symbol will drop down to your solar plexus centre where it can be retained. You can visualise this symbol as being on a little golden belt which you wear around your waist.

Close down your chakra centres. If you are closing them down one by one, work from the crown chakra down to the base. See your roots being contracted from the Earth and bring your awareness back into your body making sure your astral body is fully back and nicely aligned.

Repeating the meditation

When you come back to the meditation, first bring down white Light, root yourself in and put on your Light body. Then check all the chakras you have already worked on in previous meditations to make sure the hara, or activity level hasn't dropped. The reason this might happen is because the subtle levels within those chakra centres may have released some energy which may make the vibration go back down.

If so, start working with the base chakra, and you will find you will be able to move the hara up much faster, and will quickly move up through the other chakras to the centre where you were stuck. If the vibration hasn't dropped, just start with the chakra centre where you were stuck.

Whatever chakra you start working on again, accept your symbol from the golden belt around your waist. Place it into the chakra you are working with then move it up to your heart, amplify it with white Light and put duplications of it in both hands and feet, and continue as before.

Repeat the meditation daily until the hara in every chakra is vibrating at level six or seven.

42. Meditation to cleanse a book or object in a room

You can use this meditation to work with both old and new books. Remember that all books, old and new, will be corded into the thought form the book represents, and therefore the emotions from all the people who have ever read a copy of that book will be corded into your copy.

Start by looking around the room you are in and choose any book or object which feels intuitively wrong. For example, there might be a book or ornament sitting on a shelf with a symbolic dark exterior or aura. You may actually see this clairvoyantly, or you might feel or sense it. Or you may just have a sense of wrongness or feel uncomfortable. To explain the cleansing process let us assume you want to work with a book.

To cleanse the book

First bring down white Light into your heart centre and root yourself in. Put on whatever Light body feels intuitively right for the work you want to do.

Charge up each chakra centre to bring yourself up to 'operating frequency' working from the base chakra upwards. Then focus your awareness in your heart centre, close your arms over your heart chakra and allow a build-up of Light energy to manifest there.

Physically open your arms, and visualise yourself opening the wings or paws of your archetypal Light body. Now project your build-up of Light out from your heart, into your third eye and both palms in a triangular formation.

Project this triangle of energy around the book so that your triangle completely seals the dark aura of the book. You can enlarge your triangle of Light if necessary to fully surround whatever you are working with. Then, from the Light in your heart centre, also project a figure of eight and introduce that into your triangle. This figure of eight will wrap itself around the book which will sit right in the centre of its crossover point.

Then in your visualisation, enlarge both your triangle and figure of eight until your figure of eight totally encompasses the area of darker energy around the book. The darker energy will then diminish until it totally disappears. If you can't see this darker energy, you might sense, feel, smell or even taste it. If this work is new to you, just work intuitively. Trust your feelings, and with practice you will find yourself starting to recognise these energies in a totally new way.

In theory, you can use this meditation sequence to cleanse all books on your shelf in one go. But when you first start off, it is more fun to feel the alternative frequency vibration of each book and feel into each area of energy which is unacceptable. Doing this book by book will also help you develop your abilities to feel and sense different vibrations.

To come out of the meditation

Centre yourself in your heart centre, contract the figure of eight back into your heart chakra, and contract your triangle of energy back into your third eye, both palms and heart. Bring your arms down and centralise your energy system by refocusing on the white Light coming down through your crown and close down all your chakras. As you bring your awareness back into your body, check for any toxicity present in your body by intuitively checking your treacle count on a percentage basis. If it is over 3%, dispose of it using the treacle count exercise of pulling the plugs, which should now be a natural part of your daily cleansing process.

43. Second meditation to cleanse a book or object in a room

This meditation offers an alternative technique to look for any specific area of negativity within a book or object, old or new, and see it off. To explain how this works, let us again assume you are working with a book.

Check its level of negativity

Look at the book you have chosen to work with, and intuitively ask yourself, from 1 to 100, the percentage of slow frequency magnetic negative energy in the book. Trust your response and know that the first figure which comes into your mind is the correct one. If the figure is 30% this tells you the level of negative thought forms and emotional input attached to that book.

But if the book has a vibration and energy input of love, harmony and joy, its negative energy reading will be zero, and you won't have to do anything with it. If the book has any negativity, the following sequence - which shouldn't take you longer than five minutes - will totally transmute it.

Bring down white Light and root yourself in

Sit comfortably, hold the book in your hands and think of white Light coming in through the top of your head, flowing down into your heart chakra. Root your feet into Mother Earth and bring up through your roots whatever colour feels intuitively right for this particular meditation.

Transmute the negativity

Visualise the book you are holding as having a chakra system with seven chakras. Intuitively see which chakra within the book is amplified. This will tell you where its greatest collection of negativity is, which is its negative polarity point.

Now physically put your hands over the book and cross your two index fingers over the place which represents the chakra with the negative polarity point. Focus on the white Light coming down through the top of your head and into your heart chakra. Allow your heart chakra to expand until it becomes warm or hot. Then see two swirls of energy flowing out of your heart, one swirl flowing down each arm into your hands and out through your fingers. At the same time feel a pattern of white Light energy which represents the Father's essence going down through the rest of your body into your feet and merging with the essence of Mother Earth coming in through your roots.

As the white Light energy flows out of your fingers, hold your concentration specifically over the chakra centre of the book that needs transmuting. Allow the energy to flow from your fingers into that chakra centre until it becomes transparent. You may feel this as a sense of intuitive rightness.

If you feel inspired you can now allow the white Light to flow up through the other chakras in the book transmuting whatever sequence of negativity is in the other chakras. Eventually each chakra will become totally transparent and you will then know that the negative outpourings of the book have been neutralised.

As you do this you may clairvoyantly see the auric pattern or colour of the book starting to dissipate. When the auric colour or 'mist' has gone, take another intuitive reading of its negative energy level, which should now be zero. If your intuitive reading is still above zero, repeat the above sequence, sending in more Light and you should then bring its negativity level down to zero.

44. Trawling meditation to cleanse a room and dispose of negative energies

Find the hara in the room

Before starting this meditation, you need to find the hara, or point of balance in the room which will be the most positive point in the room. I call this the hot point in the room!

This can be found by slowly walking round the room and intuitively finding the spot which feels the nicest to be in. You may just feel warm, pleasant, or happy to be standing on that spot.

Normally the hara is within an area about two feet (60 cm) square. This hara spot should remain constant over a period of about seven days. Sometimes it will move a little if any ley line activity is being modified by road works, or structural ground movement from an earthquake.

Even if the negative energy has saturated the essence of the room, or is coming from a ground structure, or from a thought form that has gravitated to multiple objects in the room, there should still be one spot which feels better than the rest. If none of the room feels good to you, or if you are in doubt, you can dowse for the hara. To do this, you again walk very slowly around the room with your dowser swinging very gently in front of you. As you move around ask, "Is this the hara of the room?" You will get a 'yes' response in one spot only.

Light a candle to symbolise Light and love

Once you have found the hara, light a candle symbolising Light and love, and place it on that spot. Then dedicate and bless the candle to cleansing the environment.

Bring down white Light and root yourself in

Sit or kneel by your candle, then bring white Light down through the top of your head, and visualise it flowing down into your body through each chakra centre. Then visualise this white Light which represents unconditional love building up in each chakra centre.

Root your feet into the ground, visualising a long taproot like a tail coming out of the base of your spine, going deep down into the Earth. Through your taproot draw up a nice vibrant blue or gold colour from the Earth, representing the positive Earth energy. This blue or gold will flow into and fill up your whole body, boosting your energy system. If any part of your body is stiff, hurting, or feels tired in a physical or intuitive way, allow the blue or gold light to absorb that until you feel an upsurge of vitality and optimism. Then allow the blue or gold to flow out of your pores and fill up your entire auric space.

Put on your Light body

Then put on the archetypal pattern appropriate to your need at this time. If you are dealing with Earth energies you will need an archetypal pattern which can match those energies, so the Indian bear or white polar bear will be best for this. If you are working with negative thought forms, or negative astral entities you may need the higher vibration of the eagle. Your intuition will guide you as to the best one to use.

Once you have your archetypal pattern wrapped around you, physically close your arms, and visualise this as closing your paws or wings, and allow the white Light to build up in your heart chakra until it becomes very warm.

Your aura will now be composed of either the vibrant blue or gold, together with your archetypal pattern wrapped around your aura as a whole, and in the centre will be the white Light coming into your heart chakra which is now activated with your unconditional love.

Trawl ing the negative energy

Physically open your arms, but visualise this as opening the paws or wings of your Light body, and allow the energy you have built up in your heart centre to flow out in a triangular formation between your third eye and both palms. As you project this triangular energy charge of unconditional love into the room, visualise it getting bigger and sweeping across the ceiling and down the side of each wall, then across the floor, almost as if you were fishing and throwing out a huge white trawling net. Through this trawling action you will be scraping all the astral muck and grime off the ceiling, walls and floor. You then catch all this negative energy in your net as you draw your net towards you.

This trawling technique is important as you have to catch and contain the negativity. If you just push out your triangle of white energy, the negativity will retreat. It will hide, change shape like a chameleon, or try to escape to some of his big brothers. So don't allow it to escape, just go round it, net it and lock it in.

As the negativity in your net comes towards you, don't absorb it into your own body and try to digest it. This might cause problems. Instead, imagine a big pair of white hands representing the spiritual hierarchy, the hands of the Cosmic Christ, and give all the negative energy to these huge white hands who will take it and transmute it for you.

The negative energy can be visualised as dark, slimy patches. Sometimes it may be seen as a series of colours which just don't feel at all right. Or you may be aware of a noxious smell.

For the average person, this is felt as a dark colour of an unpleasant nature. As that dark colour is given to the white hands after each trawl and they dispose of it, the feeling in the room should become lighter, until the whole feel of the room completely changes.

To thoroughly cleanse a room, you need to do the full trawling sequence between three and 15 times until you feel the room is clear. But each trawl can be done very quickly - you don't have to make a meal of it. Just send your white heart energy out, visualise it as a net, trawling in and dumping the negativity into the pair of white hands in one sweeping movement. Each complete trawl can be done in about five seconds. Keep repeating this sequence until the actual trawl comes back to you with no negative energy at all.

Dedicate and bless the room

Now dedicate and bless the room for the fulfilment of love and understanding, and purpose within that room. Although you have already done the cleansing, also ask for the room to be cleared of any negative energy. By actually using words as a focal point you are in essence putting the equivalent of a word of warning within the hara of that room.

To come out of the meditation

Contract your roots back from the planet and close down your chakra centres. With practice you can speed up this closing down process by physically closing your arms, and visualising this as closing your Light body which will in turn close your chakras. But until you are sure that you are fully closed down in this way it is best to work with closing each chakra using the gold rose process, reversing the rose into a bud and from a bud into a point of white Light, sealing each one with a Celtic cross. If you are working with your visualisation to keep your Light body on as a protective sequence, visualise that being still there as you bring your awareness back into your body.

Then wash your hands and check your treacle count. If it is over 3% imagine plugs in your feet and visualise yourself pulling the plugs to release all the negativity from your body.

Follow-up

Over the next seven days come back to the same spot and repeat your dedication and blessing. If possible it is good to come back at the same time each day. By doing this for seven days you work with the magnetic energy behind the number seven which represents the aspects of the higher. In this way, if there is anything peculiar with the energy you were working with, this seven-day dedication and blessing helps to reinforce and anchor your overall package of cleansing.

Variation 1:

Once you have found the hara of the room and lit your candle, you can also light two incense sticks if you wish. Hold them in your right hand (in your left hand if you are naturally left-handed), then smudge the room. As you go around the room try to find the areas which feel particularly treacly or negative and in these places make a figure of eight with the incense sticks. As you make the figure of eight you create a matrix of energy. This will invoke the frequency of the number eight which is really a reference of two circles coming together which represents the higher and the lower, the Father and the Mother. Into that figure of eight you use your will to project and amplify your unconditional love and healing. This will help to neutralise the negative patterns of energy aligned in that particular part of the room. As you do this, your own negative count may increase, so check your treacle count as you go, and dispose of it once the inflow of negative energy has ceased in that part of the room.

You can monitor the negative flow of energy by using the intuitive traffic light dowsing technique. You start off with a green light over the area of the room you are working in and when that changes to amber, then red you know the negative flow has stopped.

Then go back to where you have your candle, place the two incense sticks beside it, and meditate on bringing in white Light through the top of your head into your chakra centres, until the incense sticks totally burn down. While the incense sticks are alight, the flame elementals will be working for you to help neutralise any negativity in the room.

If you feel there is still a residue of negativity in the room, you can continue with the trawling sequence above. Do the same follow-up sequence, rededicating and blessing that room for a period of seven days.

Variation 2: To cleanse the auric field of young children:

If young children are being pestered with elementals who are making the child mischievous, you can use this variation of the main meditation sequence.

To do this, you bring down white Light and root yourself in. Then put on or reactivate your Light body. Stand behind the child, and as you project your triangle of Light, visualise this becoming a large net which you throw over their head. You trawl this net down their body from their head to their feet. In this way you are trawling and sealing off their whole astral space. Then see the net coming together under their feet, totally capturing whatever is in the net. Now bring the net up from the feet, visualising any negativity which has been trawled from the aura of the child being safely held in the net. Then in the same way as trawling a room, you give any negativity which is in your net to the large pair of white hands of the Cosmic Christ.

Do this trawling sequence three times, each time making your trawl a little smaller so that you work on a three-level basis.

Having done that, say the following affirmation, adding the child's name in the spaces marked ....

"I invoke the pure white Light of God's eternal love
which enters ....'s body now,
through his/her crown chakra.
It fills .... 's entire being with brilliant white Light,
immense joy, love and healing energy.
This forms a protective seal around ....'s entire aura.
Each cell of ....'s body now rejoices and
all negativity is immediately transmuted into divine love
and is reflected back to its source.
This I command and it is so."

You can also place a three-pointed star over your front door, especially over the door to the child's room and over any windows in the child's room. This star vibrates within elemental activity. So by blessing and dedicating each star as you focus on the three points of the star, then projecting your triangle of Light into the three-pointed star, you will activate it and bring it up to its highest vibration - which will deny access to any elementals trying to come in.

45. Second meditation to cleanse a room or house and dispose of negative energies

This meditation works specifically with any geopathic stress or negative thought forms in a room or house. During this, you will be coming in and out of meditation quite a bit, so it will help to train you to hold the overall focus and energy whilst doing that. The meditation sequence is:

Bring down white Light and root yourself in

Visualise roots travelling from your feet down into the ground, and white Light coming in through the top of your head.

Check if the negative energy is caused by geopathic stress or a negative thought form

First of all ask your higher self if geopathic stress is causing the energy build-up. You can work intuitively with your higher self or you can dowse for the answers. You need to be specific, so ask, "Is this room geopathically stressed in a negative way?" If the answer is 'yes', work with the section of this meditation for geopathic stress. If the answer is 'no', then ask, "Are there any negative thought forms in this room which need to be removed?" If the answer is 'yes', work with the sequence for negative thought forms.

Working with geopathic stress

If the problem is geopathic stress it may be caused by a fault in the Earth's crust, or negative alignment of water, or an aspect of a ley line which might be moving through the home environment in a series of crossover points.

You may be able to intuitively see or feel where that geopathic stress is actually coming into the structure of the room. If you can't sense where it is coming in, your higher self and power of visualisation will guide you as you move through the following sequence.

Visualise the room you are working with as being split into seven main planes, or seven levels, one above the other. The bottom plane, level one, represents the physical essence of the room. Level two represents the vibration slightly above that. Moving up through the other levels, each one represents a slightly higher vibration than the one below it.

Each level has a colour. The bottom level, which is the physical essence, is grey. Moving upwards, the colours for levels two to seven are, in that order, brown, yellow, orange, dark blue, pale blue and indigo at the top. Each colour should be clear and semi-transparent. If it helps your visualisation process, first draw the outline of the room on paper, split that drawing into seven levels and colour each level as above.

Initially work with level one, the physical grey level. In your visualisation, see the room you are working with as being totally filled with the semi-transparent grey colour. If the room is in harmony on level one there should be no concentrated doses of grey anywhere. If this is the case, release all the grey and bring in the semi-transparent brown of level two and see the room filled with that colour. Again look to see if there are any concentrated doses of colour.

But if, when you look at the overall grey colour in the room, you intuitively feel or see several spots or areas of concentrated grey matter, these represent the pattern of geopathic stress which might be fragmented.

To transmute those areas, ask your higher self for a symbol that will represent the collective polarity point of all the concentrated spots of grey - all the fragmented geopathic stress spots. Then within your visualisation, allow your symbol to freely float around the room on level one, and wait and see where it naturally sits within the room. Normally if there are several spots of negative matter, the symbol will sit over the strongest one. You then use that as the focal point into which you draw all the other negative spots. This will create one collective point which can be dispersed in its entirety.

To do that, come out of your meditation and go and physically stand over the area where you saw your symbol. Place your dowser over that spot and allow it to naturally rotate. Ask your higher self to assist you in the next step as you bring white Light down through the top of your head and pass it into your dowser. At the same time, the dowser is being linked into the collective point of negative energy and will draw all that in. Approximately 10% of the negative energy will be absorbed into, and transmuted by the dowser, depending on whether the dowser is made of copper, metal or crystal. The bulk of the negativity will be passed from the dowser into you, and will be absorbed within the essence of your body.

As you bring white Light down through the top of your head it will automatically match the level of negative energy you are able to handle and hold. It will never take you above the threshold you are able to cope with.

When you have cleared level one

Check your treacle count. If it is over 3% disperse it using the 'pulling the plugs' technique. As you should now be doing this on a regular basis, any excess negativity currently in your body will only be what you have just absorbed. It should not be the negative energy from level one plus all the other negative energy you have attracted in the past few days or weeks.

Go back into meditation and visualise the room again. This time bring in the brown of level two and see the whole room filled with that colour. Again check to see if there are any concentrated areas of colour. If there are you repeat the above process by allowing your symbol to float around level two, see where it sits, then come out of meditation, go and physically stand over that area, and draw all the negative energy into your dowser and transmute it as before.

Then again check your treacle count and release anything over 3%. Then go back into meditation and visualise the room being filled with the yellow colour of level three and repeat the sequence. In this way you work up through all the levels until all seven levels are clear.

Some people prefer to work through the meditation, cleansing one room at a time while sitting in that room. If you feel you have the capacity you can work with the whole home in one go, by visualising the whole home split into seven levels then using the above sequence in the same way. Or you can work with your dowser, placing your dowser over a diagram of the home and dowse for the concentrated areas of fragmented geopathic stress. Then again work with the above sequence.

Working with negative thought forms

The same technique can be used to work with any negative thought forms in a home. But with thought forms, you visualise the room or house being split into ten planes or ten levels instead of the seven used for geopathic stress. The colours you use for this meditation will be presented to you intuitively.

Working in the same way as above, you visualise the room being filled with the colour that represents level one and see if there are any concentrated spots of colour. If there are no concentrated spots of colour on level one, release that colour and bring in the colour that represents level two. Fill the room with that colour and see if there are any concentrated spots of colour there. Continue in this way until you find a level which has some concentrated doses of colour.

If, for example, on level five you find concentrated spots of colour, these represent a thought form with a negative frequency vibration. You will again be working by placing a symbol on this level, then transmuting its colour. But for thought forms you can either work with the level in its totality or you can split that level into three sub-levels: a bottom, middle and top. The reason for splitting it into sub-levels is that if you hit any negative energy of a strong frequency, instead of taking on the totality of that frequency in one go, you will only be working with one third of it. You will transmute that, deal with the second, then the third level.

Intuitively ask your higher self whether it would be more useful for you to deal with that energy on a sub-plane reference or just to work with the whole level in one go.

Now ask your higher self to give you a symbol to represent the thought form on the level you are working with. Whatever shape intuitively comes into your mind, is the one you work with. It might be, say a little round black stone. Place that symbol on the level or sub-level you are working with. You then visualise that symbol underneath your dowser, bring white Light down through the top of your head into your dowser. Allow the dowser to swing naturally and visualise your dowser linked into your symbol, drawing all its negativity into the dowser to be transmuted. The symbol will then disappear.

If you are working on a sub-plane level, as you disperse the first symbol which will represent the energy of the thought form on the bottom sub-plane you are working with, your higher self will give you another symbol representing the package of energy on the middle sub-plane. You disperse that and will be given a third symbol representing the package of energy on the top level.

The intensity of darker energy which you start off with in the symbol for the bottom sub-plane will diminish as you go into the middle, and will be even less when you go into the top. By the time you get to the top you should be able to disperse the third symbol far quicker than the first. Continue to move up through the main levels until you have cleared all ten levels.

You normally find that a strong thought form will hold within its vibration other minor thought forms which are interlinked. Therefore, as you dispose of the major one, the minor ones will also go. Normally the dominant and therefore the most destructive thought forms are of a lower frequency rating, and are usually on level one, two or three. As you go further up the levels, you tend to find the thought forms which are a little more crafty, but the actual voltage of negative frequency is usually somewhat less.

Having worked in this way from level one to level ten you should have cleared all negative thought forms in that room. You then go back to your dowser and ask the first basic question, "Are there any negative thought forms in this room which need to be removed?" The answer should now be 'no'.

To come out of the meditation

At the end of the full sequence, whilst standing over the last area dowsed, visualise your roots being contracted back from the Earth, close down your Light body and your chakra centres, and make sure your astral body is fully back and nicely aligned.

Variation 1:

This is an interesting variation. It offers a more specific and direct approach for those who want to speed up the process.

Instead of working through each room, one level at a time as in the sequence above, you just work with the most dominant level. So first of all ask your higher self, or use your dowser to ask, "Is this room geopathically stressed in a negative way?" and, "Are there any negative thought forms in this room which need to be removed?"

If you get a 'yes' response to geopathic stress, ask, "Is the geopathic stress most dominant on level one?" If the answer is 'no', repeat the question for level two asking, "Is the geopathic stress most dominant on level two?" If the answer is 'no', continue to repeat the question for each level until you get a 'yes' response. Remember you work with seven levels for geopathic stress.

If you get a 'yes' to negative thought forms, work in the same way, asking, "Is the negative thought form most dominant on level one?" Again repeat the question for each level until you find the most dominant one. You work with ten levels for thought forms as before.

Then work with just the most dominant level. You visualise the room filled with the appropriate colour which represents the level you are working with. Ask for a symbol, let it float around the room and see where it sits. Then come out of meditation, go and stand on that spot and transmute the negative energy through your dowser, as explained in the main meditation.

Variation 2:

As you progress with this work and develop your ability to transmute negative energies, you may like to also ask, "Is there a negative interdimensional gateway within the home, or within the structure which the home represents?"

If there is, then obviously it needs to be sealed. The way to do that is to again ask your higher self for a geometrical pattern or symbol which represents this interdimensional star gateway. Then visualise this gateway as an aperture point. Using your dowser, you then draw the energy of that gateway towards and into your dowser. A bit like knitting. So you are using your dowser to focus the alignment of energies in a room and bring the focal point, which is the interdimensional gateway, into your auric space. By using the power of your will you are thinking into it and pulling it towards you.

If you find the knitting analogy difficult, visualise yourself standing within a flat triangle with the point in front, the base behind and you in the centre. Allow the point of the triangle to swing naturally towards the interdimensional gateway. As you do this, the focal point of your cell tissue and therefore your vibration, will be directed to the point of the triangle and the interdimensional doorway. Then amplify the white Light coming down into your heart centre. As it comes into your heart centre, visualise it flowing down through your hands and into your dowser, so the dowser actually becomes activated in a very specific way.

As the energy from your heart chakra and dowser focuses within the triangle, see an aspect of that triangle flowing up within your energy system and being concentrated between you and the interdimensional gateway that you need to close. As you become aware of that, draw more white Light into your heart centre, and visualise this radiating out from your heart chakra in the shape of a Celtic cross which you project towards the focal point of the star gateway. Irrespective of the shape or size of the doorway, the Celtic cross will expand and match it. So if that doorway is 40 miles (64km) high and 20 miles (32km) across, your cross will expand to that size. There is no limitation between what you project and what you perceive to be the doorway.

As the energy input of the Celtic cross focuses on the negative aperture point, it will shrink until it becomes a point of white Light. You then bless and dedicate that according to your belief system. In this way the interdimensional doorway will be sealed and no entities will be able to enter.

46. Meditation to cleanse a computer or word-processor

Put on your Light body

Bring down white Light, root yourself in, and put on your archetypal Light body. When working with computers always choose a Light body rather than a shamanistic robe. It is also best to work with the archetypal pattern of an owl or eagle as these both push the vibration upwards, which will help you to push your own vibration above the frequency you are matching in your computer.

Refocus on the white Light coming down through your crown chakra. Take the white Light into your base chakra, breathe into your base centre on an in-breath, filling it with white Light, love and power, at the same time calling down the intuitive knowing you need. As you breathe out you merely relax. Do this seven times in each chakra. These seven in- and out-breaths for each centre will charge you up in preparation for what is to follow.

Bring your awareness up to your solar plexus. Visualise and feel a golden belt around your solar plexus, with a series of pouches. Within these pouches are various symbols which you can specifically focus on to help you draw energy through your own system in a precise way.

From one of these pouches, take out a square symbol which will take on the shape of an electricity meter with a dial split into two units, with zero in the centre, at the top. As you look at the dial, right-handed people will see a scale of one to ten representing negative energy on the right, and a scale of one to ten representing positive energy on the left. A little needle points directly to zero which is a neutral zone. Left-handed people will see the negative scale on the left, and the positive scale on the right.

Visualise terminals passing from the meter into your right and left hands. Now pass your hands over the computer. As you do this the computer will resonate with your electricity meter and in your visualisation you will get a positive or negative reading on a scale of one to ten.

If your computer is in good order you will have a positive reading of three or above, on the positive side of your meter. If it is below three on the positive scale, or registers any negativity at all on the negative side of your dial then your computer needs to be worked on.

If you have a negative reading of seven, you know the negative field of energy around your computer is up to 70% of its maximum potential and that needs to be dealt with as soon as possible. When your computer's negative field of energy gets up to this level it will tend to attract the attention of larger astral entities or thought forms who will push or stretch their essence through the ethers to create a polarity opening point, through which they can work more freely. Since each level represents a certain frequency, the negatively inspired entity will approach through the level which gives it the best hold - normally the most negative site. It will then tap into that.

Depending on the energy available to them, these entities can amplify any fear and negative emotions in those people working on the computer, and can feed off that polarity. Because the field of energy around a computer is normally active within a radius of about 12 feet (4m), people who work within a few feet (1m) of a computer will also get saturated with negative energy - and any negative polarity points within their body will also be targeted. So it is very much like living over a negative ley line.

Even if your computer is brand new and has never been used, still check it to see if there is any negative energy within its circuitry that needs transmuting.

To cleanse your computer or word-processor

Ask your higher self for a symbol. You can take this from the belt around your waist and place that symbol on the level which your negative energy is coming in on - the level your needle is pointing to on your meter. If you have a positive reading of one or two, place your symbol on that level.

Allow your intuition to give your symbol a colour. This colour will represent the vibratory package within your computer which is reflective of the manufacturer and people who made it, the company who sold it to you, the ground energies in your home and where the computer is sited.

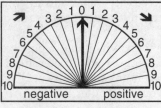

for left-handed people

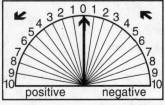

for right-handed people

Electricity meters

Whatever colour you intuitively see in that symbol, you have to transmute and dispose of it and make your symbol transparent. To do this, you refocus on the white Light coming in through the top of your head and into your heart chakra. Cross your arms over your heart chakra and build up the white Light energy in your heart centre. Then send out that build-up of heart energy in a triangular focus, and project your triangle into your symbol. Project this triangle of energy in short bursts, holding each burst for just five seconds.

When your symbol becomes transparent it will move up to the next level on the dial. It will then take on a colour, and you repeat the whole sequence, projecting your triangle of Light into your coloured symbol, until your symbol becomes transparent and moves to the next level. You do this for each level in turn, moving first along the negative scale towards the zero reading, then slowly moving towards ten on the positive scale. As each level represents a different frequency, by working through all the levels you will ensure that whatever programming of a negative origin is there, can be seen off.

Dedicate and bless your computer

When your computer is cleansed, it needs to be dedicated and blessed to create a protective sequence around it. When your computer is switched on, it will continue to attract into its gravitational field any energy of a similar polarity. Since, in the main, a computer sends out negative energy it will obviously continue to attract any negative thought forms or energy swirls which might be active within its locality. If you use a computer for a long period of time - and by this I mean three hours or more - and if you haven't dedicated and blessed it, the negative tracking will continue to work and can build new thought forms which will attach themselves not only to the computer, but to you as well.

Therefore always dedicate and bless your computer. This will help to neutralise its negative field and keep it at an acceptable level.

To dedicate and bless your computer, visualise a pyramid and place the square base section of the pyramid under the computer itself so that your computer just fits into that square. In this way, the pyramid structure will be placed over the computer. Within the square base formation, visualise a five-pointed star which will sit under the computer as a whole. This five-pointed star will help to hold and deny access to any lower astral negative entities.

You can do this as a visualisation or you can actually draw this on a piece of paper and place your drawing under the computer to help focus your visualisation. If you are drawing a five-pointed star, it must be in an accurate geometric pattern so that the five points are balanced. The correct way to draw a star, starting at its focal point is explained in Chapter 12, *Esoteric Teddy Bears And Star Formations*.

Now energise and activate both the pyramid and the five-pointed star. To do this, put on your Light body, then put your hands over the point where the apex of the pyramid would be. Bring white Light down through your crown chakra, into your heart, and pass it from your heart out through both hands into the pyramid. This will activate the pyramid structure. A pyramid is protective and gives off a very positive field of energy. Since energy follows thought, the more energy you put into your pyramid, the more it will become an astral fact.

Your white Light energy will then flow down around the outer alignment of the pyramid structure and the walls of the pyramid will glow. At the same time it will flow down through the apex of the pyramid and fill up the five-pointed star until it becomes golden.

Then say whatever words feel intuitively appropriate for your dedication and blessing. Initially you might like to use the following:

> *"I invoke the unconditional love of the Father,*
> *combining with the Light and power*
> *which is necessary for the formation*
> *of this blessing and dedication to take place.*
> *May the energy of this pyramid*
> *be protective and positive,*
> *specifically within my energy field*
> *for the duration of the time*
> *I work with this computer."*

Having dedicated and blessed your computer in this way you can then assess the positive reading of your five-pointed star under the base unit of your computer. Take a reading using your electricity meter. Anything over seven on the positive scale and you are well on your way. If the reading is less than this, repeat the above sequence, bringing down more Light and repeating the dedication. You may need to repeat this full dedication and blessing a few times to enforce the thought form and energy you are putting in.

Once your reading gets up to seven or above on the positive scale, you will find that any hostile interaction in your computer - the magnetic wobble or sulky patterns that tend to happen if some of the components are not working together - will start to harmonise and become much friendlier.

If you work where there are several computers, dedicate and bless your computer each day for a three-week period. You need to do this extended dedication sequence as other computers around you will draw energy from your computer as you implement the protective energy charge around it. So by working daily for three weeks in this way you will build up a more forceful expression of the protection sequence needed.

Monitoring future build-up

To monitor any build-up of negative energy on an ongoing basis, look at your five-pointed star within your visualisation, and focus on its gold colour. In the same way that gold in a wedding ring will get darker if the health of the wearer is a bit suspect, so the gold five-pointed star will become tarnished or pitted with black energy as the negative sequence builds up. If the colour goes darker you know you have a build-up of negative energy again, and you merely assess that negative energy intuitively on your meter. You can then repeat the above cleansing sequence and transmute that new negative input.

47. Meditation to cleanse jewellery

Bring white Light down, root yourself in and put on your Light body

As always bring white Light down and root yourself in to link yourself into the higher and lower. Then intuitively put on the archetypal pattern which is right for you for this particular meditation.

Pass energy into the piece of jewellery

Cross your arms over your heart centre, and visualise white Light coming down into your heart centre and building up as an energy charge representing unconditional love. When your heart chakra feels hot, open your arms and allow this energy charge to flow out of your heart chakra, into your third eye and both palms in an triangular formation.

With gold it is best to work on a five-level basis. To do this visualise five, five-pointed stars one above the other, with an equal space between each one. Level one is at the top, level five is at the bottom. Each star represents one of the five levels within the gold. Each one will be a different colour representing the most dominant negative frequency within that level.

Now visualise a smaller five-pointed star forming within your third eye. As it forms, dedicate and bless the smaller star for cleansing, healing, and for an enlargement of the solar consciousness which gold tends to work with. Then drop the smaller five-pointed star into the top larger five-pointed star, which is level one.

Now project your triangle of Light and initially focus it into the smaller star which is on level one. As you do this, the smaller star will start to enlarge, and as it becomes larger it will automatically transmute and release any slow frequency energy which makes up the larger star pattern on that level. As the smaller star grows it will become an exact match for the larger five-pointed star on level one.

When you have successfully transmuted the negative energy on that level, the two stars on level one will become totally transparent. The star which initially was the smaller one will then drop down to the next level, level two, and will again be a smaller star sitting within the larger five-pointed star on that level. As it drops down into level two it will leave behind on level one, within the transparency of the large five-pointed star, a small central nucleus of energy in the formation of a small five-pointed star which will represent the input of white Light energy from your triangle of Light.

Repeat the above sequence, projecting your triangle of energy into the smaller star, transmuting all the negative energy on this level. You repeat this for all levels. When you have completely cleared all the five levels, the smaller star which will now be matching the five-pointed star on level five, will resonate in unison with all the five stars. This will give you another indication of your success.

Because of the concentration of energy capable of being absorbed into gold, and because of its associated emotional outpourings you can often have many dominant emotional patterns held within it. If the piece of jewellery was worn for a long time, and the previous owner experienced severe emotional encounters whilst wearing it, you may have a tremendous amount of negative energy locked into it. The jewellery might also be holding ancestral memories of the previous wearer.

So if you have been successful in clearing level one, but find that level two refuses to become totally transparent, you need to amplify the sequence slightly by expanding that level into another five smaller sections. So the five-pointed star on level two, with the smaller star in its centre, will be split into five sub-levels which you visualise as five more five-pointed stars one above the other.

You then use the above sequence, working your way through each of the five sub-levels of level two. If necessary, you can segment each level into five sub-levels - so you would then work through 25 sub-levels in total.

If any one of the sub-levels refuses to co-operate you can split that sub-level into a further five sub-levels and work with the above sequence, projecting your triangle of energy and transmuting any negative energy on each of those sub-levels.

In this way you can safely dispose of the most hardened emotional package or input of negative energy. If you have enlarged the sequence by splitting each of the original five levels into five sub-levels, and each of the 25 sub-levels into another five sub-levels, you would end your meditation programme with 125 transparent five-pointed stars all nicely balanced, one above the other, with equal spaces between each one.

To come out of the meditation

Bring your triangle of white Light energy back into your heart centre, and gently send a blessing into the jewellery and you will find that all the levels will fold in on themselves and become part of the gold in its linear aspect. Close down your chakras, bring your roots back from the Earth and bring your awareness fully back into your body.

48. Meditation to cleanse the energy system of an aeroplane

Aeroplanes are magnetic flying machines and attract a lot of slow frequency magnetic energy. They are also swamped with all the thought forms of people who are afraid of flying. Before cleansing the energy system of an aeroplane always ask your higher self if it is appropriate for you to do this. If the answer is 'yes', you can work with the following sequence.

Bring down white Light, root yourself in and put on your Light body

First of all, bring down white Light through the top of your head and root yourself in as you normally do at the beginning of a meditation. Even though you are flying miles above the Earth, you can still visualise roots going down into the planet, as energy follows thought.

Then put on your Light body as a form of protection. The higher you fly the more radiation you will have passing through your system. So your Light body will create a frequency field around you which will help to neutralise any hostile current coming into your auric space.

Work through the aeroplane's chakra system

Symbolise the aeroplane as a chakra system. If it helps your visualisation process, you can symbolise the aeroplane as an egg-shaped energy form, then give it a chakra system.

Start working with the base chakra of the aeroplane. To do this, first check where your *own* hara is, and drop it down into your base chakra. Bring white Light down through the top of your head into your base chakra and visualise a swirl of energy manifesting within that chakra. This energy swirl will move in an anticlockwise circular movement creating a vortex of spinning energy.

Once you have created this vortex of energy, you visualise it gradually expanding outwards throughout the plane. This vortex is a thought form magnetised by the healing, unconditional love and the right use of your power directed through right use of your will.

Absorbing the negativity

As your energy swirl fills the aeroplane, it will draw into it all the slow frequency magnetic energy of a destructive nature which corresponds to the base chakra vibration. So any negative energy or thought forms vibrating within the base chakras of the passengers, or the aeroplane as a whole - according to the karmic contracts of the day - will be drawn into your swirling vortex of energy.

Now feel, sense, or just visualise this negative energy being drawn into your outer auric field. When you intuitively feel you have drawn in all the negative energy, visualise a big pair of white hands which represent the spiritual hierarchy and allow all this magnetic energy to flow into these big multi-dimensional hands, where it will be transmuted and released. You do not have to take any of the energy into your physical body, and your system therefore doesn't become toxic in any shape or form.

If you really want to be enthusiastic, you can work in this way through each chakra centre. To do this you then take your awareness into your sexual chakra, and repeat the sequence by building up an energy swirl within your sexual chakra, expanding this outwards and drawing in any negative energy vibrating within the sexual chakras of the passengers and the aeroplane as a whole. Again offer this energy into the big white hands of the spiritual hierarchy and don't take it into your own physical system. Then move up through all the chakras in this way.

If you work through all the chakra centres in this way, you will be able to transmute a lot of negative energy according to the need of those who are travelling on the same plane as yourself, although you will only be able to work within the karmic rules which apply on the day of your flight.

You can even help to transmute the negative energy of the aeroplane itself since metal fatigue within an aeroplane is something akin to muscle fatigue. Therefore any magnetisation of molecules in the metal will bring about the stress factor overload which causes problems of a magnetic nature, very much as it does with straining a muscle in the physical body.

With each chakra, when you have offered all the negative energy into the white hands, visualise each swirl continuing to work on an astral level through the flight, steadily absorbing any new negativity as the plane travels across other flight paths and absorbs other thought forms. During the whole flight your swirls of energy will be active, drawing in negative energy and automatically channelling it all into the white hands. If it is a long flight this would be a really constructive way for Light workers to pass the time!

To come out of the meditation

Visualise your roots being drawn back from the Earth, close down your chakras, make sure your astral body is back and nicely aligned, but keep your Light body on and active through the flight as your own protective sequence.

49. Meditation to change the vibration of your work environment

This meditation can be used to work with negative energy fields within your work environment. It should be done with a group, ideally with a minimum of five people, and should not be done on your own as the negative energies within a large company can be quite strong.

This meditation can also be used to dissolve, transmute and release any disorientated energy from part of the countryside, or local environment which you intuitively feel you need to deal with. Sites of old battles, places that are haunted, violent energy disturbances or local black spots on the motorway can all be worked with using this meditation sequence.

But you only do this work if, intuitively, you feel the particular imbalance of energy is an affront to your ethics. And only work when the conditions are right for you, and when the timing is right within the planet. All this has to be intuitive, as something you might initially think is wrong may have an underlying positive effect within the greater picture. For example, terrorist movements bring different governments together through a common problem. That problem then enforces change within the way those governments deal with each other. They have to start cooperating and help each other out, as they are all being bombarded with the same slow frequency energy.

During the meditation sequence, each member of the group can also dispose of any thought form they wish, be it personal, group, or something within the larger planetary setting. You normally work with the thought forms you personally relate to, because obviously what you are drawn to work with will reflect the degree of magnetic attraction operating within you at that time. Unless of course your group as a whole has a predetermined area you need to work on. There really isn't any limitation as to what you can dispose of. But do think it out before starting the meditation and keep the targeting as specific as possible, without using too much descriptive analysis.

One member of the group should direct and lead this meditation verbally and also act as the anchor point and observer in case anyone in the group goes through any difficulty. When you do a complicated meditation like this, it is useful for one member to be fully functioning and physically awake so that he or she can interact with any stimulus which might manifest within the group as a whole.

Having decided what each person, and the group as a whole, wish to work with, the group sits in a circle with a candle in the centre of the group. One person dedicates and blesses the candle to Light, unconditional love, understanding and the Cosmic Christ.

The person leading the meditation can read aloud the following, allowing sufficient pauses and spaces of silence after each step so that everyone has enough time to do each step and can work in unison.

1. Close your eyes and move into a place of inner stillness.

2. Visualise white Light coming down through your crown chakra, into the top of your head and flowing down your body linking into each chakra centre.

3. Imagine roots coming out of your feet, interlinking with the roots from everyone else in the group, just like the roots of a tree. In the centre of the group visualise one massive taproot representing the group essence, going down into the ground and linking the whole group into the essence of Mother Earth.

4. Put on your own personal Light body.

5. Visualise the group as one energy form or group-being who is in the centre of the group directly over the candle. Visualise that group-being as having seven chakra centres.

6. Visualise a point of white light manifesting above the group-being, and see that point of white Light taking on the shape of a Celtic cross - an equal-sided cross within an outer circle. This Celtic cross now starts to spin clockwise, creating a focal point of Light which links into each chakra centre of the group-being. As it does, each chakra centre in the group-being also starts to spin clockwise.

7. Once all the chakra centres are spinning, visualise a glowing blue light coming down to sit above the spinning white Celtic cross. This blue light is somewhat larger in size than the white Celtic cross and sits just above and slightly overlapping the energy field of the Celtic cross. This blue light now also takes on the shape of a Celtic cross,

and starts to spin anticlockwise. So you have an inner white Celtic cross spinning clockwise and an outer blue one spinning anticlockwise. In this way, these spinning crosses create a crossover frequency point which creates a vacuum-cum-space as a form of ring-pass-not, a buffer zone for the group so that no interference nor any negative energy can enter.

8. Now verbally, one by one, place into the candle any disorientated energy that you have decided to work with, and visualise these energies being dissolved, transmuted and released through the candle. This transmutation process will automatically happen because as the group focuses on the crossover frequency point created by the two spinning Celtic crosses, the energies of everyone in the group are channelled into one powerful focus which can transmute any negative energy in a very specific way.

> NB. If the whole group is working with a particular aspect of the environment or large company, everyone can also say what that is to reinforce the work being done. When everyone is finished, then continue . . .

9. Visualise the blue spinning Celtic cross shrinking and withdrawing to a point of blue light above the spinning white cross. Then visualise the white Celtic cross also shrinking and slowing down, until it becomes a small static Celtic cross above the group-being. Now visualise the white Celtic cross shrinking and changing into a point of white Light, which then moves upwards to merge with the point of blue light above it. The two merged points of Light then disappear completely.

10. Visualise the chakras of the group-being closing down. The group-being may now also fade and disappear.

11. Visualise the main taproot of the group-being contracted back from the Earth. Then contract your roots which were linked into the taproot.

12. Now close down your own chakra centres by closing down your Light body.

> ...the group may now discuss what has happened.

CHAPTER 11
A MISSION FOR LIGHT
WORKERS

It is time for action! Light workers everywhere can play a part in helping to reverse the tide of infiltration of slow frequency negative energy into our homes, our work environment and our family's auras. Television is one of the worst offenders as each set creates a gross vibratory field of slow frequency negative energy. As television is the one-eyed God in most homes, these sets all work together to create a global negative vibratory field.

The original idea and concept of television was implanted and orchestrated by astral entities to deliberately create a vehicle through which they could enslave humans. Their aim was to use the electrical system of a television set to develop a vibration which would slow down and block the human circuits so that people could be subdued, kept in a robotic state, and their perception intuitively slowed.

As a result, the vibratory particles of television are magnetised in a way which creates a negative field of energy (a negative field of positive ions) approximately 60 feet (18m) around the television set itself. This energy field swamps the aura of anyone watching that television and allows vibratory astral entities access into their auric field. These vibratory astral entities, who live and vibrate in unison within the actual grid system of a television set, would not be able to infiltrate the human aura without the vehicle of a television set as their own vibration is too gross.

These negative entities also capitalise on any structural slow frequency negative energy within the system of any unsuspecting viewer as 'like attracts like'. So if a viewer has any fear, negative emotions, or old negative energy from their ancestors, these slow frequency vibrations can be amplified. As the focal point of television is a medium to report news of a relatively negative nature, with coverage of wars, terrorism, riots and violence, this in its own way also amplifies any negative fear vibration within viewers. Violent dramas and epics which stimulate fear and tension have the same effect. When these programmes are being broadcast the astral entities within a television system enjoy the feast of negative vibrations - from the programmes themselves and from the viewer - which they need and use as a form of intuitive food.

In this way, vibratory negative astral entities not only infiltrate and feed off the human aura, but also jam up the network of subliminal particles of energy which normally give a person access to their various subtle alignments. The structural notes of purity which we all need to move forward, also find it much more difficult to sit within a human body when it is being swamped by this slow frequency negative field.

The structural damage caused to people watching television can manifest on the physical as well as the intuitive levels. While television tends to block the intuitive signal coming into a person's field, it can also amplify any negative imbalance of energy within the physical body itself. One of the common problems directly arising from watching television is dehydration of the body. This gives the body a greater receptivity for static or negative magnetic energy. It is this static magnetic energy which makes your clothes crackle when you undress for bed.

As this magnetic energy enters into the vibratory field of viewers, it stimulates the old primitive memories of humanity as a whole. This is why the more violent epics have been successful and popular, as the bloodthirsty animal aspect within humanity is subliminally brought up to the surface, which allows an even easier access for astral infiltration.

This of course has been deliberately cultivated by those negative entities who influence the minds of people who put the programmes together as they need the negative overtone from programmes of a violent or aggressive nature.

This manifested vibration of aggression and fear then spews out from the television, very much like a sewer vomiting out. This outpouring of fear and aggression applies itself to anything it can link into and also opens up the lower chakra centres of viewers.

If you have a flood in your home, that flood will leave a residue of gunge. In the same way, television programmes of a negative nature leave a residue of magnetic energy which attaches itself to the wallpaper, curtains, carpets, peoples' clothes and objects within the room as well as to the inner and outer aspects of the viewer's aura.

A negatively charged person who has been watching a lot of television can pass that charge, together with the astral entities sitting within that charge, into the auric field of a sensitive person who is not aware of the astral entities' capacity to leap lightly from one person to another. The package of energy created during a physical hug or physical touch - especially if there is a sexual undertone - creates a very easy access point and is a wonderful opportunity for astral entities to leap onto a new host.

Young children are particularly vulnerable to this infiltration of slow frequency energy. Yet a lot of parents, unaware of what is happening, give children free access to television. So young soul aspects who are particularly sensitive are now under constant attack in this way. To compensate for this, older soul aspects incarnated into young bodies will quite often sleep in front of the television. If they were awake and watching the programme, astral entities would find it easy to enter into their auric space. But by sleeping in front of the television set, they are actually neutralising an awful lot of the negative energy flow without it entering into their system.

At the same time, those Light beings who are working on the inner planes with these evolved soul aspects will quite often take advantage of the situation by focusing on the negative energy that sweeps over the child's body, to amplify some of the negative ancestral memories of that soul aspect. This allows the ancestral negative vibrations to flow up and out through the pores of the child's skin so that it can be transmuted by those Light beings.

At the time of writing, what is clearly happening within British television is that, due to funding, people are being saturated with films of the gross variety, in particular with violent epics which are having a kickback by affecting a personality change in people. As people in general realise what is taking place in a more conscious way, as less people watch television overall, and as those who do become more critical, so their vibrations rise and they will start to rebel against the strait-jacket which has been on them for such a long time.

Reversing the tide of negative infiltration

In the earlier years of television, astral infiltration was mainly negative. Over recent years those working with Light have also become motivated to infiltrate and work within the television industry. As this has happened, new ideas and concepts have been introduced and some of the programmes now being shown are definitely of a higher vibration. This is helping to contest and break down the negative overtone which the majority of television programmes have manifested in the past.

So both Light and dark forces are now seeking to orchestrate the energy output from television, because they both know that if five million people are watching the same television programme, they are creating a multiple area of awareness as they all link into the same source. If that source - be it positive or negative - can then be vibrated at one particular note, those who are active within that note can take advantage of the situation.

As Light forces infiltrate television, they are influencing the content and make-up of the programmes to prepare us for new dimensions. Even some of the adverts are preparing us for the astral levels.

Adverts which speed up time, for example showing cloud formations which would normally happen within a 24 hour period occurring within a few seconds, alter our perception of linear time. This type of television advert is deliberately focused and directed to give us a new expectancy of a speeding up of time as a normal part of our everyday experience.

This is preparing us for interdimensional time where time as we know it, in a linear sense, stops. We will then have access to inner time and outer time, and have the capacity to go backward into past lives and forward into future lives, all at the same time. Television therefore can be a useful mode to present the alternative view and prepare us for what is now imminently due. The Japanese television advert for the Isuzu car says, "When the reptilians come, will you be ready? Will your car be large enough?" This is done as a kind of joke, but it is also part of the preparation for what is to come!

The creative people who write and produce these particular advertisements are Light workers who are being subliminally directed by those on the inner planes. Some are aware of what is happening, some are not as they have not yet fully woken up to the realisation of who they are.

As we accept these new ideas, concepts and thought forms, we can adjust the signal on the programme of our own internal television which is our access to the akashic records. This can then speed up our ability to go forward or backward in time, since time is an artificial commodity, deliberately cultivated for Earth-plane awareness.

So although television was initially negatively orchestrated, it is now being used to offer us a natural way of moving forward. On one level it is a tester, depending on our perception. Television is also offering us an opportunity to work with what is taking place. For even the negative points of stimulation from television, if fully understood, can be put to positive use by dredging up the ancestral memories of a negative overtone and neutralising them with unconditional love as you become aware of them interacting within your emotional system.

If you are watching any television programme, you can help to protect yourself by putting on or activating your eagle Light body. The archetypal pattern of the eagle Light body has the capacity to neutralise the effect of negative thought forms and negative currents, by allowing those currents to flow around you rather than into your auric field. By putting on the eagle Light body, the vibration behind the eagle normally pushes the vibration of your body mass up to the third eye. Whereas the slow frequency energy of television normally vibrates around the sexual chakra centre or below.

By wearing the eagle Light body there will be no vibratory anchorage point for negative energy to link into, so when you switch your television on, the negative energy field from the television will flow around you rather than into your auric field, almost like water off a duck's back.

This is particularly useful to remember if you go into a television shop where 20 to 40 televisions are switched on, all pouring out a slow frequency magnetic energy field. By adopting your eagle Light body this will compensate for that massive output of negative energy.

It is up to each one of us to develop our intuitive muscles and the power of our will to create a protective sequence for ourselves around our auric field, whilst at the same time working to neutralise and see off those vibratory astral entities who need to move on within their own evolution. This is something we can all work on to help change the global negative vibratory field which now needs to be transmuted in its entirety.

Cleansing your television

Certain televisions are much more friendly than others. The input of thoughts and emotions from the manufacturing company and of course the energy of the people who assembled the television, will to a degree influence the vibrations within that television circuit. If the manufacturing company is greedy, or has financial worries and therefore a lot of fear energy within the management structure, their televisions will be pretty grumpy.

A lot of the cheaper sets, with components assembled from various sources, are also a bit iffy. They tend to have a more erratic and ferocious energy field than the more expensive models. But there is no guideline I can give you as it depends on the individual television. This is something for you to intuitively tune into before buying a new set. A lot of Light workers are choosing not to have a television in their home at all since they already recognise that they are the worst thing they can have for their spiritual progress.

Each time you switch your television on, depending on the quality and vibration of the programme or news you are watching, and the response from those in the same room, the slow frequency negative vibration from your television circuit can be either amplified or nullified. In a general sense, to love your television and cleanse it regularly is a good start to neutralising that energy. Also be selective with the programmes you watch so that you don't allow a mass of negative energy to flow into your space.

Light workers who have sufficient unconditional love and a working knowledge of energy can also work directly with television sets. If you don't have a television in your own home, you can still work with the television broadcasting mast or the television studio where the programmes and input signals are being generated. To work in this way, you symbolise the television relay mast or the television studio as being a television itself, then use the sequence as in Meditation 50, at the end of this chapter, working in the same way as if you were working with an actual set.

You can also use this meditation to work with any electrical apparatus within your work or home environment which you feel is a bit suspect. Even your hi-fi and electric toaster will give off a magnetic package which can make you feel a bit yucky, as there can be astral entities and astral doorways in any electrical appliance although they are usually less ferocious than those in televisions. Large launderettes with a lot of washing-machines and dryers also give off a widespread magnetic field of negative energy, so if you use one, you can quietly cleanse the energy field while waiting for your wash to be done!

The best way to assess any electrical apparatus in your home is to first make sure your own negative count is down to 3%. Then stand in front of the electrical appliance, with it switched off, and assess your treacle count again to see how much negativity your body is registering from that appliance. Go round your home doing this with all your electrical equipment and you will find which ones are the most toxic. You can then try on different Light bodies until you find the one which feels right for each vibratory field.

If you prefer, you can go round your home and use the intuitive traffic light dowsing technique to check your washing-machine, refrigerator, toaster, iron, hi-fi and so on. Then any equipment which gives a 'red' signal needs to be cleansed until your traffic light response gives you a 'green' signal. You can use the same meditation sequence given for cleansing televisions, see Meditation 50, at the end of this chapter.

You can also use this meditation to cleanse your computer as an alternative to the computer cleansing Meditation 46, in Chapter 10, *Dealing With Negative Energies*. It is important for you to become intuitively focused so use your intuition to guide you as to which one to use. This may differ from day to day as vibratory fields can vary from time to time, so you might want to use a different meditation and different Light body to the one you used last week. Always check with your intuition to find out what is needed in that moment rather than getting into a set routine.

If this work is new to you and you do not feel confident to work within your own television when you read the following meditations, then first practise with some of the other meditations to cleanse and transmute negative energies. You can start by practising the meditation to detoxify a plant, Meditation 32, Chapter 6, *Communicating With Nature*, as plants hold a very low level of negative energy. This is an ideal meditation for beginners. Next, practise the meditation to transmute and neutralise negative energy in books or objects in your room, Meditations 42 and 43, Chapter 10, *Dealing With Negative Energies*. Move on to some of the other meditations in Chapter 10, such as working to transmute negative energies in a room. You should then feel confident enough to start working with small electrical appliances, which have a smaller vibratory output compared with a television. Use the meditation sequence for cleansing a television as your working format.

All of the suggested meditations referred to above will help you to flex your muscles and fine-tune your abilities in this area. With practice you will soon feel ready and willing to play your part in transmuting and neutralising the vibratory astral entities who now need to leave the planet.

For those who do feel ready, the full working sequence is given in Meditation 50, below.

* * *

A Mission For Light Workers: meditations

50. Meditation to cleanse a television or computer and get rid of astral entities
51   Meditation to raise the vibration of your television or computer

50. Meditation to cleanse a television or computer and get rid of astral entities

In this meditation you will be taking your awareness inside the television or computer itself to get rid of any astral entities and seal any astral doorways.

If you don't have a television set in your own home, you can still work with the television broadcasting mast or the television studio from where the programmes and input signals are being generated. To work in this way use your visualisation to symbolise the television relay mast or the television studio as a television, then use the following meditation sequence, working in the same way as if you were working with an actual set.

You can also use this meditation to work with any electrical equipment within your work or home area which you feel is a bit suspect, be that a washing-machine or an electric toaster.

You can also use this meditation format to cleanse a computer. It offers you a different frequency note to that of Meditation 46, to cleanse a computer or word-processor, Chapter 10, *Dealing With Negative Energies*. But to explain the sequence, let us assume you are working with a television.

Bring down white Light, root yourself in and put on your Light body

Stand just in front, or just to the side of your television, approximately two feet (0.6m) away. The television should be switched off so that it is not generating any negative energy while you are working on it. Then bring white Light down through the top of your head and root your feet into the ground.

Now put on your Light body and feel its protective essence around you. For this particular meditation it is better to work with the Light body of an eagle, as this will be of a higher vibratory pattern than the slow frequency of your television. The Light body of a bear is a slower vibration which may amplify the vibratory essence of the television, and you may not be ready yet for that encounter. So the eagle Light body will keep you safe, and will be far better for you.

Invite in your guides

Now invite in your higher guides. Most Light workers have free access to a body of folk on the inner planes who will help clear up slow frequency energy. So link yourself into this group as well. You can visualise this as a team of 19,000 people standing behind you in a large triangular formation with the point touching your back and the base of the triangle spreading out behind you on either side. In essence, this body of 19,000 people will be chanting your name. They will be giving you energy and power, so that during this meditation, if you feel you are being confronted by any slow frequency energy of any kind, you will be able to bring in your 19,000 'mates' and will have enough power and strength to see off the opposition.

Move your awareness into the television

Now allow your awareness to focus on top of the television itself. Refocus on the white Light coming down into your heart chakra, cross your arms over your heart centre, visualising this as closing your eagle wings, and build up an energy charge of white Light. When this energy charge is up to a point of efficiency, physically open your arms, and visualise this as opening your wings, and allow your white Light energy charge to flow out from your third eye and both hands in a triangular formation. Then visualise this triangle of energy flowing outwards into the television itself and at the same time, allow your awareness to flow into the television along with your energy charge.

If you are working with a broadcasting mast or television studio, symbolise that as a television screen, triangular in shape, with the point upwards. You then project your triangle of Light energy into the screen and at the same time take your awareness into this screen. Then continue in the same way as for a television set.

As both your triangle of white Light energy and your awareness flow into the television, you will go past the wall of static energy which has been retained within the screen. On the other side of the screen you visualise a corridor which might be long or short, but which should be relatively straight. As you project your imagination into this corridor, your awareness will be taking you into the magnetic package of the television, but you should still be aware of your physical body standing outside the television.

Get rid of any astral entities and seal all astral doorways

In this corridor, to the left and right there will be astral doorways. These are created by the programmes shown on your television, which leave a residue within the circuitry of the television itself. This residue can last for just a few seconds or a few hours, or it can even accumulate and last for several months - depending on the intensity of the negative energy field created by the programmes being shown.

These astral doorways will normally look like ordinary doorways as you perceive them, but sometimes you may find a different type of doorway depending on your awareness! Whatever their shape or size, you systematically start to seal each astral doorway, left and right.

To do this, visualise yourself inside the television with your Light body on and your arms outspread. Then refocus on the energy charge you have built up in your heart centre and visualise it flowing out between your third eye and two hands in a triangular formation, but this time with a Christian cross in the centre of the triangle. As this triangular formation takes shape, it will turn into flames, so you will have a flaming white triangle with a flaming white cross inside it. Project this triangular aspect of energy towards the centre of each doorway, one at a time.

Allow your triangular formation of energy to increase or decrease in size in order to completely encompass the doorway. The base of your triangle should be slightly wider than the width of the doorway and should sit just below the base of the doorway, with the point of your triangle above the door. The cross will then match the door.

The fire elementals within your flames will see off anything which is there and act as a purifier, while the cross will act as a sealant.

As you do this, the cross normally becomes the focal point and your triangle steps back. This is a bit like a boxer and his trainer - when it is time for a fight the trainer steps back and the boxer goes into the ring alone. In this case the triangle is the trainer, and the cross is the boxer.

As you project your triangle and cross at a doorway, the door will start to close. When it has closed completely, continue to project your triangle and Christian cross at the door whilst visualising the triangle and cross shrinking in size until they become one point of white Light, which then completely disappears. This will seal the doorway, a bit like locking the door and throwing away the key.

If there is any resistance from one of the doorways which doesn't want to close, this is because entities in the corridor scurry to the doorway to guard it as this is their point of entrance from the television into your vibratory system. If you feel any resistance, just continue to push your triangle and cross of flames towards the doorway. Hold it there for about 10 to 20 seconds at a time, repeating this process until it closes. If the astral entities slam the door in your face, you might be tempted to follow them into their dimension. Don't do this. Just project your triangle and cross at the closed doorway and then seal it as described above.

Do this systematically to every doorway you find in your corridor as you work your way along it. If you feel or see any astral entities or energy forms either linked into or standing near to a doorway then deal with them as you go - if you are working with a cable television then any entities you find in these corridors will probably be fatter and grosser. To dispose of these negative entities you again allow your triangular formation of white Light energy together with the Christian cross in the middle to push back any negative energy form. This is a bit like putting your hand on someone's chest and shoving them backwards to get them off balance. As you push a negative astral entity backwards, you push it through the nearest astral doorway or the one it is linked to. You then close the doorway as before. When you push an entity through a doorway it will normally gravitate quite quickly back to its own frequency.

Bear in mind that as you try to push these astral entities backwards, they may take on whatever shape and form you are most frightened of. So if you don't like wolves, you might see a wolf. If you don't like snakes, you might see a snake. If you don't like spiders, you might see giant spiders! Just remind yourself that the form you are seeing is an illusion. It is just an astral entity trying to frighten you and turn you back. Just refocus on your guides and your spiritual family of 19,000, and with your unconditional love and the focal point of your will, you will have the ability to banish or demolish anything that is negative and in your way.

Ideally you should get rid of all astral entities and seal all astral doorways in one meditation session. But if you find that you can't complete this in one session - this is dependent upon the capacity of your own energy system - it is best to leave the television switched off until the next day or until such time you can finish the full sequence. If you switch the television back on before you have fully dealt with everything in your corridor, you will be putting yourself at a disadvantage. The astral entities who are still active will try to break down the rhythm of energy which you have projected, and they will have learnt and grown wiser from the experience as well.

To begin with you might need to do this meditation daily, depending on the level of your own tolerance, how many astral doorways you find open, and the quantity and nature of the slow frequency negative energy you are dealing with. It may take several daily sessions to clear up all the doorways, especially if your television has been used to show a lot of violent programmes and videos of a hideous nature. This will also depend on how long your television has been switched on for. If it has been on for four or five hours a day or for months on end, then your whole room will be pretty gungy!

So systematically cleanse the whole circuit, preferably do it in one go or leave the television switched off until you have done it.

To come out of the meditation

Visualise yourself coming back out of the television and going back into your physical body, making sure that your astral body is fully aligned. Then close your wings to close down your Light body, but keep it on as a form of protective sequence.

Now assess the level of negativity or treacle count in your own body. If it is over 3%, release that excess negative energy by visualising big plugs in the bottom of your feet and as you pull the plugs in your visualisation, think of the white Light coming in through the top of your head and flowing down through your body. Any tensions, anxiety, or impressions you have picked up will be washed freely from your body, out through your feet. All this negativity will flow out into Mother Earth where it will be transmuted.

Then do another reading and make sure your treacle count is down to the required level of 3%. You should now be into a regular practice of monitoring your treacle count and releasing any negativity as it comes in, rather than letting it build up and become static. So the negative energy which needs releasing at the end of this meditation should only be what you have picked up during this meditation, and not the whole build-up from the past weeks!

Now dedicate and bless the television for healing, understanding and unconditional love. This will help to create a vibration within your television which will be kinder to you and your family.

Ongoing cleansing

After all the astral entities have been got rid of, and all astral doorways have been closed, this meditation needs to be done on an ongoing, regular basis at least once a week, especially if the television continues to be on every day. A fresh input of slow frequency negative energy will come through the news, especially if it is covering war and terrorism, and portrays the anger, fear, or terror generated by the raw emotions of the people concerned. In some ways, coverage of real emotions is more virulent than the artificial variety in other programmes. So even if your choice of programmes is selective and you only occasionally watch the news, you will still have an ongoing input of slow frequency energy coming into your home which will need to be dealt with.

But as you systematically cleanse your television, the circuit which leads into your room becomes illuminated and any astral entities who might try to gravitate towards your television set will tend to go elsewhere. Only the braver ones will continue to try to come into your space.

Variation 1:

Initially start working with this meditation with the television turned off. By regularly cleansing your television you will build up a thought form which will resist any astral thought forms within it. Having fully cleansed it with the set switched off and developed your confidence and working knowledge of astral entities, you can then move onto this variation.

In this sequence you again work with the above meditation, but with the television switched on. In this way you are now dealing with any incoming traffic from the current programme which will test the mechanism of the thought form you have set up. This is important because if you have not yet got enough love or faith in yourself, then the thought form you are setting up may not be strong enough and the astral doorways may reopen, so simply push more energy in to ensure that any nuisance which might be there is efficiently dealt with. In this way you will reinforce the work you have already done.

When you first start with this stage, switch on your television and tune it into something gentle. Do not choose cartoons as many of these are quite violent! Then repeat the main meditation sequence, and check the quality of your television as you move through a number of programmes. Finally check it out whilst it is tuned into more aggressive programmes. Include the news as this regularly features emotional, violent and aggressive events.

Variation 2:
Once your television has been fully cleansed, you can do this variation at any time you are watching a programme or news item which is basically negative. Take a few seconds to bring down white Light, root yourself in and put on or reactivate your eagle Light body. Then build up the energy charge in your heart centre, and push your triangular formation of energy - your triangle of flames with the Christian cross in the middle - towards the screen in short bursts of five seconds. Your triangular formation of energy will then neutralise anything that might be there.

51. Meditation to raise the vibration of your television or computer

Although televisions are mainly programmed with a negative energy stream, you can produce a lot more energy from their components by regularly cleansing them and raising their vibration. As a result things will generally run more smoothly.

Before doing this meditation you need to cleanse your television or computer. Use the previous meditation, or the computer cleansing meditation, Meditation 46, at the end of chapter 10, *Dealing With Negative Energies*.

You can also work with this meditation to raise the vibration of any electrical appliances, telephones, digital watches, or even the electrical power points. If you cleanse everything, then raise its vibration up to the crown chakra, you will increase the overall vibration within your home and work environment.

You can also do this to the mercury fillings in your teeth which hold a very negative charge. If you can't have your mercury fillings replaced, then use this meditation to tap into each filling and raise its activity point up to the crown chakra. This will neutralise the electrical connotation within the structure of the atoms for about 80% of your fillings and will make them less toxic, so any mercury which seeps out will be less harmful.

To explain the sequence, let us again assume your are working with a television:

Assess the vibrational level in your television

Visualise your television as having a full chakra system in the same way that humans have, and visualise each chakra as being split into three - a bottom, a middle and a top. Work intuitively or use the traffic light dowsing technique to tell you which chakra is active. Then look closer at that chakra and see if the activity point is in the bottom, middle or top part of that chakra. If the active chakra, as you perceive it, is the base or sexual chakra, forget about it! - unless you are prepared to work in a dedicated way to increase its frequency through regular cleansing until the chakra vibration is up to at least the solar plexus.

But if the active chakra is the solar plexus chakra or above, the energy field is flexible enough for you to push the vibration up to the crown chakra, which will increase the energy field to give you a positive input.

Bring down white Light, root yourself in and put on your Light body

Doing these first three steps before going into the meditation should now flow naturally for you, and you should be getting quite good at intuitively choosing the right Light body to give you the vibrational pattern you need.

Focus on the white Light coming down through the top of your head and into your heart centre, cross your arms over your heart chakra and build up your energy charge. Then drop your own vibration, by dropping your hara or point of balance down to the chakra centre within your own body that corresponds to the active chakra in the television.

Push the vibration up

Open your arms and allow your white Light energy charge to flow out of your heart chakra to create a triangle of energy between your third eye and two hands. Now whack your triangle of energy into the section just *above* the active point within the appliance. If for example the activity point is in the lower part of the solar plexus, you project your triangle into the middle part of the solar plexus. You just send in your triangle of energy in five second bursts, for a maximum of five bursts. In total just 25 seconds of energy goes into that middle section of the solar plexus.

Next come out of the meditation, wait for 20 minutes, and then go back to the television and check where the activity point is. If the activity point is still in the lower part of the solar plexus, repeat the above meditation, again waiting 20 minutes after you have come out of it before rechecking. If the activity point has moved up to the middle part of the solar plexus, you now project your triangle of energy into the section above that - the top part of the solar plexus. Again just send in five bursts of five seconds each, come out of the meditation and wait 20 minutes.

Continue in this way, moving the activity point upwards through each of the bottom, middle and top sections of each chakra.

Depending on your vitality, and assuming you don't get tired, you should find that within an hour and a half the vibration will start to move up. Once it starts to move up you should be able to contain it and continue moving it up through the other chakras much quicker. If necessary, continue with the meditation on a daily basis until the activity point is up to the crown.

This works in the same way as moving the hara, or activity point upwards in a thought form. See Meditation 55, at the end of Chapter 13, *Barnacles And Thought Forms*.

Dedicate and bless your television

Once you get the activity point up to the crown chakra, you dedicate and bless the television which will lock in that higher vibration. Then every third day go back and check if the vibration is still where it should be.

If you find it is dropping back down, then look around the space of your television and see if you have missed any astral entities who are still lurking there, trying to neutralise the energy field. You might see, feel, sense or even taste their presence. The way to neutralise them is to bring down white Light, root yourself in, put on your Light body and build up an energy charge in your heart chakra, then jump inside your television when it is switched off. Next project your triangle of white Light into anything that is of a negative nature. Again you might feel, see, or taste this negativity. Concentrate on where the energy form is coming from and push in your triangle of energy until it has become neutralised.

A little clue here is that you can also adjust the frequency of your television or computer so that it feeds you in a healing way. If you want to explore this you can work with the same sequence as the one given in the second meditation to communicate with a tree, Meditation 29, at the end of Chapter 6, *Communicating With Nature*. To do this you again work with the television switched off, root yourself in and put on your Light body. Then focus on the television and get your symbol which will allow you access into the television. Take your awareness up over the television set and drop down into the set to communicate with the archetypal pattern of televisions. Get your individual archetypal symbol representing the television and check any information you get by projecting it into this symbol. In this way you can negotiate with the overall elemental package that makes up the metals and components there, and have an ongoing communication with your specific television!

CHAPTER 12
ESOTERIC TEDDY BEARS

Esoteric teddy bears are the rituals you use to invoke protective sequences when doing any meditation work, whether you are simply meditating with a tree, working with crystals, or transmuting slow frequency negative energies. The ritual is the important thing.

If you kneel down in the traditional form of prayer, by that act of kneeling you activate the prayer-force energy which your ancestors have built up within the expectancy of the permanent physical atom you are working with.

Kneeling is associated with homage to a force far greater, far purer than oneself. It holds a very special energy package within the awareness of humanity as a whole, since kneeling has always been associated with religious aspirations, irrespective of what that aspiration is.

Whether you actually kneel or just visualise yourself as kneeling, the result will be the same. Your mind will naturally tune in, like a laser beam, to the prayer-force and will bring that prayer energy through.

Most people have at some time in their life knelt in prayer. Many have done it automatically during a church service, at a christening, wedding or funeral - without really thinking about it or what it means. So it would be good for you to now do it with focus. Become aware of the placement of energy as it comes into your mind and feel that energy as you consciously adopt the kneeling ritual.

Lighting a candle also links you into a special energy package. The thought form and energy behind candle-light has been created by the mind outpourings of all those who have used candle-light over the ages as a symbol of God's Light. Each time you light a candle you consciously tap into that energy. But do it consciously as a loving ritual and be aware of and feel the energy which will come with that.

The Christian cross and Celtic cross also carry a very special, unique energy. The Christian cross holds the massive thought input of all the people who have ever prayed in front of it. It therefore embodies a tremendous power and energy. The Celtic cross holds more of the inner development signal and carries that particular energy vibration. In meditations both of these crosses are sealants, especially the Christian cross. They are both particularly useful to close down and seal interdimensional star gateways of a negative nature.

Star formations

The star formations of the three-, four- five-, six-, seven-, eight-, nine- and ten-pointed stars can all be used as a protective sequence.

When you physically draw a star to use in meditation work, always draw the star starting at the focal point which is then placed towards the north.

3-, 4-, 5-, 6-, 7-, 8-, 9- & 10-pointed stars

To find out which point of a star is the focal point, draw the design of the star you are going to work with on a piece of paper then number the points, counting backwards, in an anticlockwise direction. At this stage the drawing of the star and numbering of the points can commence wherever you wish. So for example, if you want to work with a five-pointed star, you draw that star then number the points five, four, three, two, one in an anticlockwise direction. Now dowse over each point asking, "Is this the focal point of this particular star?" You will get a 'yes' response for the focal point and a 'no' for all the others. If your intuitive muscles are nicely developed you may have a clear intuitive impression as to which is the focal point and may not need to dowse.

When you have found the focal point of that star, draw it again, this time starting at the focal point and drawing it in an anticlockwise direction from there. When using that star you place the starting focal point to the north.

The colour of each star represents the frequency within that star which is accessible to one's mind or awareness. Therefore the colour of each star will be different for each person. There is no guide I can give you - except for a three-pointed star which is normally pale silver. All other stars vibrate within the whole encodement and vibratory sound of the millions of sub-frequencies which colour represents. Initially you may choose white, as white holds all the colour vibrations within it. But as you progress, intuitively choose the colour for each star as you use it. The best colour will be spontaneously presented to you, based on your need, understanding and capacity to handle and hold energy at the time of doing the meditation.

The three-pointed star

The three-pointed star represents the light air energy. It is normally used when working with elementals. If you have mischievous elementals bothering your animals or children, a three-pointed star placed over the doorway to your home, or on the gate to your garden or field will be sufficient to keep them outside.

This star can also be used in a very positive way for communicating with water elementals. To do this always bring down white Light, root yourself in and put on your Light body. This is particularly important as elementals can be very mischievous. Then visualise and project a three-pointed star into the stream or river. You will sense or see an energy swirl or energy point at the place where your star sits and shimmers. By building up an energy charge in your heart chakra then projecting it into your shimmering star, you will activate it and the water deva should present itself to you. Communication can then take place.

A three-pointed star can also be effective when working with air movement. If you want to increase the moisture content within your garden, project a three-pointed star, 12 feet (4m) above your plants. The energy input from your star will indicate to the water elementals your need to feed the vibratory essence of your plants from the air, and the air molecules will respond to this by holding more moisture. Your plants will readily respond to this and will be able to draw more moisture from the air.

Within your own local area you have cosmic tides and solar winds which affect your local weather patterns. Any weather pattern is an outpouring of energy which is mainly thought-inspired by humanity. These thought forms affect the planetary weather patterns by interfering in a positive and negative way with the polarisation as the atoms are magnetised. This gives off an energy which attracts, or rejects, the hot and cold vibratory air patterns which give water molecules their shape and density.

If you want to change your local weather pattern, first find the location of the hara in your local area. This will be the working point, or hot point within your territory. Your territory might be five square miles (13 square km), so look at a map and dowse or work intuitively to find the location of the hara. Then visualise a three-pointed star over the hara. This star should be clear and centralised. If it is lop-sided, ask your higher self for your communication symbol, and place that in your heart chakra. Amplify it with the white Light coming down through the top of your head and place a duplication in both hands and feet. Then radiate white Light out from your heart into the heart centre of your three-pointed star and you should be able to transmute any imbalance within that star.

A three-pointed star is also useful to place on or in anything made of glass. It can be placed, visually or physically, within the molecular structure of window panes. This will encode the particles in the glass to act as a protector, as the star heightens the vibrations and tightens the energy field within the glass. Anything trying to enter then has to pass through that energy field and encodement, and negative energies will find this very difficult. After you have done this, you may also find your inner vision becomes clearer since windows symbolise what you look through. If you are physically placing a three-pointed star on a window, draw just the outline remembering to start at the focal point.

A three-pointed star can be used in combination with any of the other stars. It works particularly well with the five, seven and nine as it amplifies each one and gives them more oomph. To do this, visualise or physically place a three-pointed star within the other star you are working with.

You can also, occasionally, place a three-pointed star over your third eye if you have an accumulation of female problems. As you focus on that three-pointed star, you will be shown the thought form behind your problem and will receive data telling you what to work with in order to heal your physical problem.

In summary, the three-pointed star:
- is the light air energy
- can be used with elementals
- can be used with air and water

- can be used with glass
- can be used with female problems

The four-pointed star

The four-pointed star is more neutral and blending. It carries a resting note and is a good star to use as a healing focus, particularly with eyes. A specific meditation for this is Meditation 53, at the end of this chapter.

A four-pointed star also represents the four aspects of fire, earth, air and water. It works equally well with any of these elements but has a particular affinity with the ground and trees.

You can therefore use it when working with trees or woodlands which have been tampered with. If you have a tree in your garden or local area which has been vandalised, by visualising a four-pointed star, then amplifying and projecting it into the tree, you will invoke the more positive devic force who can amplify the aura of the tree and help speed up its healing process. You can use the variation of the healing meditation, Meditation 53, at the end of this chapter.

A four-pointed star projected into the essence of a tree will also deny access to slow frequency astral elementals - the devas of a slow gross order. As you project your star into the tree, it will expand and take on the dimensional shape of the tree and any astral entities will feel very uncomfortable and leave. This star will maintain a frequency within that tree and only life forms of a certain vibratory order will have future access to that tree. This puts in a word of warning and keeps your local territory tidy.

You can also use this star as a sealant for anything made of wood. As paper is an aspect of trees, the four-pointed star can be used to seal important documents. By visualising this star, amplifying and projecting it into the documents, you will see off any slow frequency noxious energies and deny them access. Likewise, if someone has sent you a particularly unpleasant or angry letter, by projecting a four-pointed star into it, you neutralise the sting within that letter and any slow astral thought forms accompanying it will be nullified.

In summary, the four-pointed star:
- is more neutral and blending
- carries a resting note and can be used for healing, particularly for eyes
- represents fire, earth, air, water
- is particularly useful when working with trees and woodlands
- can be used to help heal trees
- can be used as a sealant for wooden objects
- can be used to seal documents
- will neutralise thought forms behind an angry letter

The five-pointed star

The five-pointed star is the old occult symbol. It will reclaim, hold and deny access to any lower astral negative entities within a wide range of frequency vibrations. By physically placing, or visualising and projecting, a five-pointed star over a doorway, window, or on the floor or ceiling of your home, then keeping it activated, you will bring the vibration of that star up to its highest point. This creates a frequency which astral entities find unacceptable to their well-being. They find the higher frequency point very difficult to handle - almost impossible in fact. In this way you deny access to about 90% of the entities who normally live below that frequency and who might be trying to make your life uncomfortable.

"Ah, but can't they come in through the walls?" you might say.

Yes, they can! But our belief system is that people only break in through windows or doors, so that is where you put your five-pointed stars, as that is where your expectancy lies. If you also have an expectancy of them being able to come in through walls, put five-pointed stars there as well.

A specific meditation to create a protective field around your home using a five-pointed star is given in Meditation 52, at the end of this chapter.

The vibration of dimensional sound within the five-pointed star travels through the ethers and activates latent encodements of a certain nature. As you send forth the sound of this star it will impact into the structure of trees and other life forms who will respond to that encodement and give off an answering echo. So why not experiment with this and try sending out a five-pointed star to objects in your room, or send it out into your garden and see what responds to it!

A five-pointed star can also be used in conjunction with a candle to dissolve, transmute and release negative energies which might be in your space. To do this, physically place a five-pointed star under a lighted candle, or visualise it being around the candle flame, then view - through the star and the flame - any offending energy package which is there. Just look in a detached way. Put on your Light body, build up an energy charge of unconditional love and direct this in a triangular formation at the energy form to see it off. In this way you use the star and the flame as a lens to magnify your unconditional love and power of will to see off whatever offending energy is there.

The EEC symbol of 12 five-pointed stars in a circle is very significant. The twelve stars represent both a vibratory encodement to which each country is contributing, and also a common vibratory note within the karma of each country.

This circle of stars also represents unity. At the moment unity within the EEC is being manipulated by the structural destructive energies behind the international management of money etc. This is currently creating corruption within the EEC rules and regulations.

The EEC is an input energy - like the 'soup of the day'. As the vibration of the 12 member countries goes through different octaves, and as more countries join, adding their vibratory essence and different growth factors, the thought form behind the EEC will open up new notes for spiritual growth.

Those on the inner planes are watching the EEC very carefully. The 12 five-pointed stars are power surges, and both Light and dark are contributing to this power surge. But in the overall surge of power, the input of the spiritual hierarchy and the seven ceremonial angels who are taking their place within the EEC as a whole, will push the vibratory pattern of each five-pointed star up to the vibrating matrix of the number seven which has a much more spiritual vibratory note and represents the aspects of the higher.

The EEC is on a four-year programme from 1992 to 1996. During that time, each EEC meeting, large and small, will be accompanied by the esoteric beings of a positive nature together with aspects of the spiritual hierarchy who will feed their ideas and concepts into the mental process. EEC leaders will then have an opportunity to bring through ideas of a new and positive kind.

After 1996 there will be a tremendous shaking up within the whole movement of the planet as latent patterns will surface, more corruption factors will be flushed to the surface, and a general scrubbing clean will take place.

In summary, the five-pointed star:
- is the old occult symbol
- acts as a protective sequence in your home
- denies access to lower astral entities
- has a dimensional sound which activates latent encodements

The six-pointed star

The six-pointed star has a much lighter frequency. It has an airy essence, represents harmony, power and purpose, and holds a lot of soul energy within it. This star has a very positive focus for dissolving and transmuting a whole diversity of thought forms, whether of a lower or higher astral form. The six-pointed star is also a gentle coaxer with a female overture. So if you are working with any negative energy, try to label it male or female. If it is female, the six-pointed star would be the one to use in transmuting that energy. If it is a male negative energy, use a five or nine-pointed star.

A six-pointed star is also very useful for sealing walls of buildings, not so much over windows or doors, but over larger condensed areas. If a building resonates with structural hate because of vibratory impressions it has picked up over the years, you can dissolve the slow frequency energy within two to three days by visualising, and if possible also physically placing, a large six-pointed star, or multiple six-pointed stars within or on the walls.

To do this you can use Meditation 52, at the end of this chapter, for creating a protective sequence around a home with a five-pointed star, but use a six-pointed star formation for working with a large building.

Glass objects, copper and salt all absorb and hold negativity in a form of bondage which is a holding mechanism. You can stimulate that bondage to instigate a quicker releasing mechanism by using the geometrical pattern of the six-pointed star which affects the atomic structure of glass, copper and salt in such a way that negative energy is released.

So if you have copper pipes in your home with negatively charged water flowing through them, a six-pointed star, depending on its intensity and strength, can neutralise that negative input. To do this, look at your central copper input pipe, then visualise a six-pointed star slotted through it. Put on your Light body, build up an energy charge of unconditional love in your heart chakra and project your triangle of Light energy into the star to energise it. Then dedicate and bless the star. Your star will then act as a filter mechanism and will help to neutralise the negative input as the water flows through the star.

If you draw a big six-pointed star on paper, then stand a bag of sea salt in the centre of it for 12 hours or overnight, the vibration of the six-pointed star will be imprinted within each grain of salt. This will increase the frequency wave within the salt which can then be used to neutralise and absorb negative energies. For example, if you have ground energies external to your home from where a negative core or a package of negative energy is seeping, by sprinkling your charged-up salt in a circle over that place, this will neutralise that field of energy.

Lead crystal also holds negativity. If you have lead-crystal drinking glasses or decanters, this negativity causes the lead in the crystal to seep into any liquid in those containers. By placing a six-pointed star under each crystal glass or decanter, you lock in the vibration of the lead and the leakage will be diminished. Although this doesn't stop the lead leakage completely, it will slow it down to a level far less damaging to your health.

The six-pointed star has a wider frequency range than the five-pointed star. If you want to work with an area around your home environment, such as a near-by pub which has a lot of violence or aggression, or if there has been a rape or murder in your area, you can help to neutralise that negative vibration by visualising a large six-pointed star over that area. Charge it up by putting on your Light body, build up an energy charge in your heart centre, and project your triangular formation of white Light representing unconditional love into that six-pointed star. By now you should be well practised at doing this. To neutralise all the negative vibrations in that area, keep the star active over a two-week period by projecting your triangular formation into it every day. This charging-up process needs to be done for just one minute every day during that period to maintain the energy within the six-pointed star.

The six-pointed star is also useful for sealing interdimensional doorways which might have been inadvertently opened up by occult ritual, ouija boards and so on.

In summary, the six-pointed star:
- is light and airy, representing harmony, power and purpose
- dissolves and transmutes a diversity of thought forms
- transmutes negative female energies
- can be used to seal walls in large buildings
- can be used with glass, copper and salt
- helps stop lead leakage from lead crystal
- can be used to neutralise negative vibrations over a large area
- can be used to seal interdimensional doorways

The seven-pointed star

The seven-pointed star represents the aspects of the higher - the seven planes of reference which humanity is currently working through. It also works with the subtle vibrations of the seven chakra centres within your body and within the 49 smaller chakra centres which we also now have access to within our body alignment.

Each chakra centre holds a vibratory charge which is, in essence, the collective vibration of individual and group experiences which your personality form has access to. Most of the physical body is crystalline and holds a variety of energy charges, some of which might be negatively orchestrated and some particularly refined and beautiful. To help remove the negative charges you can meditate on the seven-pointed star, visualising it within your crown chakra. The vibrational sound and colour of the seven-pointed star, which will normally be white or gold, can then flow entirely through your body. This will set up a frequency which systematically strips and transmutes any negative energy collecting within your chakra system which is not part of your karmic contract.

The seven-pointed star has an equal proportion of male and female energy, and is useful as a focus if you want to meditate on the sun, moon or stars. It can also be used to communicate with water elementals as the vibratory sound of this star has a come-hither feel which elemental life forms respond to. The archetypal pattern associated with the overall intelligence of oceans in general will always answer the call of the seven-pointed star. In meditation, work in the same way as described for the three-pointed star.

The seven-pointed star is a bit like the Bank of England doorway. It is very strong! It has a ruthless aspect and was used in olden days to invoke and destroy, usually with ritualistic fire. It can be used equally well today against astral entities, elemental forces or devic forces of an unpleasant kind.

Since this star has always been used in old ritual, it is a star formation you will find particularly useful as you now bring it into alignment within your life. It can be used to seal your solar plexus chakra, especially if you are emotionally sensitive. By meditating on a seven-pointed star any peculiar frequencies within your auric space will very quickly become self-evident.

Seven-pointed stars also work well if you are sensitive to Earth energies, or if the radiation in the planet is causing you problems. This might manifest as ongoing periods of migraine. To work with this, visualise a seven-pointed star under each of your feet, or draw two accurate seven-pointed stars on paper - remember to start at the focal point - then place them in your shoes. Use your visualisation and the power of your will to allow these stars to naturally rotate so that the focal point continually gravitates to the north, just like the needle of a compass. This will create a pattern of energy which will help release any toxic energies from planetary radiation which are collecting within your system.

In summary, the seven-pointed star:
- represents aspects of the higher
- helps remove negative energy within the subtle vibrations of your chakra centres
- can be used to seal the solar plexus chakra
- can be used to meditate on the sun, moon or stars
- is a coaxer for going into water elemental states
- has a ruthless aspect and can be used against astral entities and unpleasant elementals
- can be used if you are too sensitive to Earth energies

The eight-pointed star

The eight-pointed star is a heavyweight, and mainly masculine. Its vibration brings together the dominant cycle in any one particular alignment and the masculine cycle which humanity in the main is working with at this time.

The geometrical pattern of the eight-pointed star is very similar to the patterns generated through the number eight in numerology. It has the effect of making atoms a little heavier. As such it is particularly useful to focus the earthing of Light workers in a very positive way and therefore helps you be more at peace within the frequencies of third dimensional life.

The eight-pointed star is also useful when working with earthy structures or rock formations, and can be used particularly well with fire.

An eight-pointed star placed over a doorway will help drop the frequency vibration within your home. You might wish to do this if you are too open, too tuned into the angelic realms and need to bring your vibration down to a more physical setting to deal with day-to-day life. The frequency of the eight-pointed star not only helps you achieve this, but also gives you a better 'cloaking' as the input of astral entities of a grosser nature will find it difficult to pierce the package of energy which the eight represents.

Working with this star also helps you drop your vibration if you are vibrating too high within yourself. The way to find out if you are, is to intuitively look to see where the hara is within your chakra system. For normal everyday activity it should be in the middle or top section of your solar plexus. But a lot of people are currently vibrating with their hara up in their throat chakra. This makes them hypersensitive to all types of energies. If you are vibrating too high, visualise an eight-pointed star in your base chakra and also in both feet. Then bring white Light down through the top of your head and pass it into each star. This will polarise your atoms and create a downward pull which will bring your vibration down.

This star can also be used as a protective frequency if you are going into a market setting or busy place. By visualising it over each chakra centre, it will deny access to 99% of the astral entities which some people carry about with them.

In summary, the eight-pointed star:
- is a heavyweight, masculine in nature
- is useful for earthing yourself
- can be used to help drop the vibration of your home
- can help you drop your vibration if you are vibrating too high
- can be used as a protective sequence over your chakra centres

The nine-pointed star

The nine-pointed star is basically the symbol of immortality. If you visualise yourself wearing this star as a badge or piece of jewellery it will act as a very useful warden. It will radiate out to about 15 feet (4.5m) around your aura and set up an energy charge which will automatically draw the vibration of immortality into your space.

Once you realise you are immortal then your whole vibration shifts and the sequences in one particular life become less important within the overall picture. Your identification with slow frequency astral desire is also nullified to a degree, and you tend to work more with the spiritual concepts of what is being presented to you. The need to be possessive, cruel or the need to activate fear or any negative emotion is then seen as an illusion and just part of the clutter of third dimensional life. As you recognise this, the astral entities who feed off negativity and fears will find it particularly difficult to tap into you. So radiating the nine-pointed star as a badge will also remove and transmute astral negative thought forms. A bit like an electric shredder, it will suck them in and shred them.

The nine-pointed star also has a high frequency and is a good focus for unconditional love. It can be used to help neutralise negative programming in a crystal and a specific meditation for this is given in Meditation 36, Chapter 7, *Crystals.*

The polarity of the nine-pointed star also works well with UFO people and seals interdimensional star gateways of a negative nature. If you know that a negatively charged star gateway is over a certain country, you can take your awareness to that place and locate its hara which might be in a particular city. You can locate the hara intuitively, or you can do this by dowsing on a map.

Then use your imagination to project nine, nine-pointed stars over that place, one on top of each other. Visualise them spinning alternately anticlockwise and clockwise, starting with the bottom one spinning anticlockwise. In this way the central polarity of all the nine-pointed stars will be nicely aligned. Then put on your Light body, build up an energy charge of unconditional love in your heart centre, and when that energy charge is up to a point of efficiency, project that into the vortex of energy created by the nine spinning stars.

As you fill up each star with your pure white Light, the gateway aperture point will be slowly closed. By 'slowly' I mean anything from two minutes up to three days, because once you have done this meditation the vibrational input from the nine, nine-pointed stars will continue to be active from that time on as the energy package of the nine-pointed star tends to grow naturally and slowly.

In summary, the nine-pointed star:
- is the symbol of immortality
- can be worn as a badge to see off astral entities
- is a focus for unconditional love
- can be used to seal interdimensional star gateways of a negative nature

The ten-pointed star

The ten-pointed star is a frequency which has completed an orbit in an astral sense. Therefore, in the main, this star has a female focus which allows etheric ideas, concepts and motivations to freely enter. It is a good communication symbol for angelic forces, extraterrestrials of an enlightened kind, whales, dolphins, flowers and all life forms of beauty everywhere. Archetypal patterns of a female nature, fire elementals and the higher elementals associated with Light and air also respond well to this star.

The ten-pointed star is also a useful focus to communicate with the Masters of Wisdom, the externalisation of the spiritual hierarchy, and to approach the solar plexus chakra centre of Avatars.

This star creates a self-healing mechanism. To do this, visualise and place a ten-pointed star in your heart and third eye chakras, both hands and feet, then charge them up by bringing white Light down through the top of your head into each star. This input of unconditional love energy will create a vibration which helps your self-healing and directs the higher vibrational energy towards you.

If your chakra system has been condensed through a state of anxiety, tension or fear, again visualise this star in your heart and third eye chakras, and both your hands and feet. Charge them up with your input of white Light, which will automatically cleanse your circuits in a very gentle and specific way.

If you also visualise and project a ten-pointed star under the feet of a newborn baby, or either visualise or physically place one under a baby's cot, this star will open up the smaller chakra centres in their feet and will bring down more Light energy. This will help the baby coordinate its Earth experience, since during the first six months an incoming soul aspect tends to pop in and out of the baby and is not consciously 'in' at all times.

This star can be used if weather conditions are particularly foul. If you project it into fog, ahead of your vehicle, making it approximately 30 feet (9m) in diameter, the fog will have a tendency to lift after a short space of time. This can also be applied to heavy rain showers or areas where there is a known history of flooding. By using this star as a focal point you can transmute, release and lighten the energy formations within your local weather patterns.

A ten-pointed star projected and visualised around someone about to die also helps to make their passing-over sequence much easier.

This star gives off a vibration which goes through all the planes. With right use of will and unconditional love, it can be used as a beacon to attract Light beings from many planes who will, out of curiosity or need, approach you to attempt communication based on Light, understanding and love.

Visualised on a ring, the ten-pointed star is particularly useful to enhance the physical meridians within your body and allows a better quality of oxygen to flow within your body mass, especially within your immune system.

In summary, the ten-pointed star:

- is a completion in an astral sense
- is a good communication symbol for angelic forces
- is a good focus to communicate with the Masters of Wisdom and Avatars
- can be used to improve weather conditions
- helps the passing-over sequence
- enhances the physical meridians within the body

All these stars can be used to help you develop your clairvoyant and psychic abilities. A specific meditation for working with all the stars in this way is given in Meditation 54, at the end of this chapter.

* * *

Esoteric Teddy Bears: meditations

52. Meditation to create a protective energy field around your home using a five-pointed star
53. Healing meditation working with a four-pointed star
54. Meditation programme to help you develop your clairvoyant and psychic abilities working with all the stars

52. Meditation to create a protective energy field around your home using a five-pointed star

The five-pointed star creates a high frequency point which most astral entities find difficult, or impossible, to handle. So this meditation will deny access to about 90% of slow frequency astral entities who might be seeking to make your life uncomfortable.

Preparation

For this meditation you will need several little five-pointed stars if you are going to work with each doorway and window in your home. These five-pointed stars are now readily available from various shops and come in packets of 'Glow in the Dark' adhesive stars, moons and planet shapes with which you create your own galaxy on the bedroom ceiling.

Work out how many stars you need by counting one star for each door and window on the main outer walls - north, south, east and west. Add to that one star to represent the base of the home, and one for the ceiling.

Then place five candles around the place where you will sit for the meditation. Place the candles at equal distances to represent the five tips of a five-pointed star. Try to get the formation of the candles as close to the exact star formation as possible.

Light each candle and dedicate and bless each one. Then visualise a large five-pointed star on the ground, with one candle being at the tip of each of the five points. Now dowse to find which is the focal point of this star.

Hold the appropriate number of little five-pointed stars you need for your doors, windows, floor and ceiling and sit in the centre of this large imaginary five-pointed star, facing one of the candles. Your intuitive rapport will automatically guide you to face the direction where the pattern of astral manifestation, in a negative sense, is at its highest. Therefore you will be facing the incoming energy. As you do that, visualise the focal point of your star rotating so that it is also facing that direction. If the astral manifestation changes position once you are settled, just visualise the direction beam of the focal point of your star rotating to match that, without you having to physically move.

In essence, within your awareness, you will be able to face all directions spontaneously, but for the sake of definition you initially focus on the focal point of the five-pointed star.

Bring down white Light, root yourself in and put on your Light body

Think of white Light coming down through the top of your head and visualise this flowing down through all your chakra centres. Then root yourself in.

Put on your Light body as a form of intuitive blessing and protection for what you are about to do. If you haven't got a lot of physical energy, charge up each chakra centre by breathing into each centre, charging up each one until it is warm as described in Meditation 7, in the section *Key Aspects Of Meditation Work*.

Dedicate and bless all the little five-pointed stars you are holding. Then place just one of these between you and the candle which is in front of you. This star represents the focal point of energy which all the other little stars will link into.

Energising your five-pointed stars

Refocus on the white Light coming down through the top of your head. Cross your arms in front of you and build up this white Light as an energy charge in your heart chakra. Then open your arms, which you visualise as opening the wings or paws of your Light body, and allow the white Light of unconditional love and power to flow out of your heart centre into your third eye and both palms in a triangular formation.

Project this triangle of Light outwards and visualise it filling the *large* five-pointed star on the ground. When this is filled with Light, visualise the white Light changing to gold. So you are now sitting in the middle of a large golden five-pointed star.

In your visualisation, spin this gold star anticlockwise until it becomes one swirl of gold energy. Out of that swirl, visualise another two gold stars forming which move up to sit one above the other. The top star represents your crown chakra, and the one below that your heart chakra. Both of these stars also start to spin anticlockwise and form swirls of gold Light. You are now sitting in the middle of three spinning swirls of gold Light.

Dedicate and bless each spinning gold star for protection and unconditional love. Having done that the top two spinning gold stars will go back down and merge into the base star which now holds the energy and blessing of all three stars. This star will continue to spin and will send the vibratory charge from all three stars into the little five-pointed stars in your hands, plus the one little star between you and the candle.

To come out of the meditation

Concentrate on the one little five-pointed star in front of your candle, which represents all the other little stars, and visualise this star being filled with gold. This will help to establish the thought form of all your little stars being filled with this gold energy charge. When all the little stars are filled with this energy and blessing, the spinning gold star will change back into a white star and will stop spinning. You will now have the one large five-pointed star firmly around you.

Then close down your chakra system and your Light body. Bring your roots back from the Earth, and bring your awareness back into your body, making sure your astral body is fully back and aligned. Blow out the candles then stick one little five-pointed star over each door and window, placing the ceiling and floor stars in an appropriate place.

For those with clairvoyant ability you will notice after this meditation, when all five-pointed stars are charged and in place, that any slow frequency astral entities will step back and find it very difficult to come into the home. Also any object in the home which was previously fed by a negative magnetic energy source external to your home will start to lose its negative charge as it will no longer be fed. In this way negative objects in your home will self-cleanse themselves.

Follow-up

Every day for the next seven days, go round to each star and spend a few seconds rededicating and reblessing each star for the purpose you have invoked. In this way you feed additional energy into each star.

Periodically after that, say once a month, intuitively check to see if the stars need a boost. If they do, put on your Light body, or reactivate your Light body if you are still wearing it as a form of protection, feel white Light coming down through the top of your head into your heart and radiating out to fill your auric space with fiery white Light. Then build up an energy charge in your heart chakra, form your triangle of white Light between your third eye and two hands, go up to each star and project this triangle of Light into the centre of it for just five seconds. In this way the protective sequence you have set in motion will remain constantly active.

Variation using a six-pointed star:

You can use this meditation sequence by working with six-pointed stars to neutralise negative energies in a large building. Before starting this meditation, you may have to draw all the six-pointed stars as it is not so easy to buy ready-made stars in a six-pointed formation.

53. Healing meditation working with a four-pointed star

As the four-pointed star is neutral and carries a resting note, it is a particularly healing star to work with, especially for healing the eyes. To explain how this works, let us assume you have an eye problem you want to heal.

Bring down white Light, root yourself in and put on your Light body

Close your eyes and move into a place of stillness. Bring white Light down through your crown chakra into your heart centre. Root yourself in and put your Light body on.

Amplify your four-pointed star

Take your awareness down to your solar plexus and visualise a belt with several pouches around your waist. From one of the pouches take a four-pointed star which represents the healing note you need. Place that star into your solar plexus chakra, then move it up to your heart chakra. Bring white Light down into your four-pointed star, amplify and duplicate it and put a duplication in both hands and feet.

Refocus on the belt around your solar plexus and from one of the pouches now take out a black dot and place it in your left eye. This dot will immediately enlarge until it completely covers your eye.

Now bring white Light down into your heart centre again, and once more amplify the four-pointed star in your heart and place another duplication over the dot in your left eye. This will enhance any healing which needs to take place. You might experience this healing as heat, humming, a flickering, or vibration, or you may simply have a soothing sense of your eye being bathed. Relax into the sensation and allow the imbalance to be transmuted.

As the healing takes place, the black colour will be absorbed into the four pointed star as the irritation or problem is transmuted and released. It might be necessary to take further black dots out of your pouch and place these over your eye one at a time, until the black colour remains as a constant factor around the eye.

Once that healing is complete, take another dot out of your pouch and do the same with the right eye. Then bring white Light down into your heart chakra, amplify the star and place another duplication over the right eye. Then repeat the above sequence.

Repeat this daily for a continuous period, which may be anything from seven days to 17 weeks depending on how bad your eyes are. If you have severe eye defects, or suffer from eye strain or bloodshot eyes, you can do this as a pre-sleep exercise, taking the healing vibrations into your dream state.

Use the intuitive traffic light dowsing technique to tell you when your eyes are in a healing rhythm. To do this start the meditation on a green light which tells you, "Yes, healing is required." As you progress this green light will slowly change from amber and then to red, which tells you to stop as the healing is complete. You will also find that the four-pointed star will become transparent as the healing focus becomes more dominant. Once the healing is complete the four-pointed star will cease to be real within the impressions you are receiving. Sometimes it completely disappears.

When any problem in your eyes is healed you can move onto the next meditation, using all the stars within your eyes to help you develop your clairvoyant and psychic abilities.

Variation to work with a four-pointed star to heal a tree:

Use the same sequence as above, but work with both eyes at the same time. Put a dot in each eye and duplicate your four-pointed stars and put one over each eye at the same time. Then visualise both dots and stars merging together and becoming one symbol over your third eye chakra.

Use your visualisation to project that symbol from your third eye into the tree you are working with. In this way you will activate the positive devic forces within the tree who will amplify both the aura and healing process within that tree.

54. Meditation programme to help you develop your clairvoyant and psychic abilities working with all the stars

This meditation programme can be started as soon as the healing work in both eyes is complete. In this ongoing meditation, you will work with the five-, six-, seven-, eight-, nine- and ten-pointed stars.

Your experiences will depend on your capacity to tap into the vibratory package within each star. But by using the following sequence, working steadily through all the stars, your latent and clairvoyant abilities will soon become activated and will take you into new levels of reality.

Bring down white Light, root yourself in and put on your Light body

Take a few minutes to centre yourself by bringing white Light down through your crown chakra, filling up each chakra with white Light and slowing down your vibration. Now root yourself in and put your Light body on.

Amplify your star

Take your awareness down to your solar plexus and visualise a belt with several pouches around your waist. From one of the pouches take a five-pointed star. Place this into your solar plexus chakra, then move it up to your heart chakra. Bring down white Light into your heart and amplify and duplicate your five-pointed star, and place a duplication in both hands and feet.

Refocus on the white Light coming down into your heart centre, and once again amplify and duplicate the five-pointed star in your heart and place a duplication over your left and right eyes at the same time.

Then just focus on both of these five-pointed stars as they sit over your eyes and allow whatever intuitively flows over and through you to naturally occur.

This star carries the old occult signal and will help to amplify your latent abilities and give you access to the lower astral levels. It is the key to the door to open yourself up!

If you wish, you can now end the meditation as described. If you want to continue, and move on to working with a six-pointed star, first of all visualise all five-pointed stars shrinking and all going back into your heart chakra and merging with the five-pointed star there. Then put this five-pointed star back into your pouch and take out a six-pointed star.

Put this into your solar plexus chakra, take it up into your heart and repeat the above sequence.

Working in this way with the six-pointed star will help you communicate with Avatars and, in essence, will give you access to the higher astral levels and the Lords of Light.

After you have completed your session with the six-pointed star, you can end the meditation or move onto work with the seven-pointed star. To do this, shrink all the six-pointed stars back into the one star in your heart and place it back into your pouch. Then go on to work with the seven-pointed star, using the above sequence. The seven-pointed star will give you a specific reference point to help you link into the spiritual hierarchy.

When you feel ready, you can repeat the above sequence, and work with the eight-pointed star. This will give you an amplification of your eye-healing programme and will help you to see and deal with any practical difficulties you may be having with 'seeing'. This will also give you access to multi-dimensional time.

You can then progress by working with the nine-pointed star which will give you access to knowledge of immortality and the 'end of'. So the cosmic flow of energy and the placement of 'left' and 'right' can be slowly explored to give you a new insight into the true picture.

Finally move on to working with a ten-pointed star. This holds the completion note and will bring together both right and left hemispheres. This will help you become aware of the totality of what needs to take place. It can also be used to communicate with the crystal skulls.

As you work with this, you may find that the ten-pointed star will start to resonate within all your chakra centres and will open up a lot for you!

To come out of the meditation

At whatever stage you finish each session, you shrink all the stars you are working with back into the main symbol in your heart centre, then put this one star back into one of the pouches around your solar plexus belt.

Close down all your chakra centres, close down your Light body and bring your roots back from the ground. As you may have done some exciting travelling during this meditation, make sure your astral body is fully back and nicely aligned.

CHAPTER 13
BARNACLES AND THOUGHT FORMS

Barnacles, as the name implies, are substances external to your awareness which can attach themselves to you and your outer auric space.

The main barnacles which cause problems to people throughout the human race are the whole array of energy movement that we term thought forms. Some are very subtle. Some have a degree of intelligence. They come in all shapes and sizes, from little baby ones to monstrous big ones - and some can take on a personality structure.

Thought forms can jump from one person to another. To do this they send out tiny splurges of energy to try to attach themselves to other energy matter of a similar vibration. So when you meet someone, the energy package of their thought forms will automatically send out an aspect of themselves and try to link into any vibration within your aura which is similar to their own.

When the opportunity is right, they wriggle through into your inner auric field - almost like a sheep mite - and will attach themselves to one of your major or minor chakra centres, giving or taking energy.

When a thought is consciously sent out, it goes out with a cording. Clairvoyantly this looks a bit like a garden hose-pipe with teeth on the end. So every time you think about someone a cording is sent out to that person and lies in ambush around their aura, waiting for an opportunity to work through their outer auric field and into their chakra system. It can wait several days, or even several months, until planetary conditions and cosmic biorhythms allow easy and simplified access into that person's aura.

Sun spots will also allow easy access at irregular points since the irradiation that comes from them tends to have a down-market effect on most people's auric space. This makes people more susceptible to infiltration of slow frequency thought forms.

This might actually be to their disadvantage, but the law of like attracts like always takes place. A cording will not enter your system unless you have a similar vibration to it, as slow frequency energies can only attach themselves to other slow frequency vibrations when an opportunity is presented. As any harmful or negative thought which has a slow frequency vibration will attract other slow frequency energies into your auric field and will help to lower your vibration, *the cultivation of harmlessness is very necessary in this day and age, and is possibly the most important thing to cultivate as an overall pattern.*

You can symbolise a thought form as smooth and slippery, when it is not allowing another aspect of energy to get hold of it. But when a thought form meets a vibration of a similar capacity, it can transfer from one person to another, then hangs on - as tight as super glue.

We all have cordings linking into our energy system. This is just part of living on Earth. These cordings can be described as a feeder mechanism from thought forms which manifest as energy passing from one person to another. Some of these cordings are very positive and some are anything but.

A positive cording can be beneficial and very healing. The fact that you are reading this book means that you are cording into a series of multiple thought forms under a general high frequency 'thought form umbrella'. Therefore, as you read this book and work with the meditations, you cord into both my energy system and the energy pattern which makes up this book in its totality.

As you cord into my system and I, in turn, cord into yours, a negotiation takes place between your inner guidance and mine. As this happens - through the financial contract of you buying the book and sending physical energy my way - a contract is made by which you are able to receive healing, and release toxic thought forms and negative energies in many ways. Although this sounds quite simple, these contracts are somewhat complicated in the sense that you have to work through the permutations of the contractual factory so to speak. It also depends on the flexibility within your auric system and how much you are willing to give, based on how much unconditional love you have for yourself.

As a general rule positive cordings give energy, and negative cordings take. But both can give and take. For example, a cording with a negative vibration usually tries to take energy, but it can also try to pass negative energy into the person it is going to. Whilst positive cordings usually give energy, a positive cording sent out during a healing will often transmute and, therefore, take any unwanted negative energy.

If you receive a letter from someone expressing their depressed mood or poor me syndrome, a lot of their emotional residue will be focused towards you. As you open that letter the thought forms attached to those emotions will immediately leap out and try to attach themselves to you. Once that cording is active within your auric space it will be fed by the negative input from the anxieties and expectations of the person who wrote you the letter.

If you have a karmic dialogue with someone, the cordings between you will be much more dominant. These cordings will definitely be a nuisance, and can sometimes be very destructive.

If someone commits suicide through the influence of drugs, their desire for drugs will still be as strong as ever after they have left their human body. They will then be motivated to send an essence of themselves - which is sent out as a cording - to try to locate another drug addict of a similar frequency. As the astral drug addict cords into a physical addict, he or she will feed off their vibration and the craving for drugs within the addict still in physical form will be increased. In essence, those drugs then serve as a fix for both addicts.

Positive cordings always link into the same chakra centres of the two people concerned. So if you have a positive cording in your heart chakra centre, it will be corded into the heart chakra of the person you are working with. A negative cording creates a point of difficulty when, for example, it goes from someone's third eye into your sexual, solar plexus or base chakra. This creates different frequencies which will cause both friction and communication difficulties on the inner and outer planes.

Any problem within your personality life is normally a result of cordings linking into the wrong chakra centre. In general, a cording which is causing problems can be intuitively seen, felt, or sensed as dark black energy. Sometimes you can even taste it! When initially looking for cordings, you might see or feel them within your chakra centres as black blobs. Sometimes quite small, and sometimes quite large. Although you might see or sense them as round blobs, they are in fact cordings which are often fairly thin but quite virulent. By looking and feeling into the essence of the space where the cordings reside, you can then consciously decord and remove any cordings unacceptable to you.

Ideally it is best to follow a cording back to its source. You can then see if it is coming from a person, thought form, idea or concept, or whether the law of magnetic attraction of like attracts like has been invoked. As your awareness grows and you become more sensitive, you will be able to pick up these burrs as you move through the forest of your awareness. With periodic cleansing you can open up to a much lighter vibration and your auric space can move into a point of balance, rather than looking somewhat like a windscreen splattered with flies.

To decord from a thought form you can use one of the meditations at the end of this chapter. If you are working with the meditation programme to release personal karma you will also be working to decord from thought forms described in Step 11 of Meditation 20, in Chapter 2, *The Awakening*.

We also cord directly into our guides, and into energies of Light, power, understanding, joy and healing. As we become more focused and cleanse all the unwanted cordings, our Light cordings will become big and fat. Then, when we meet a soul mate, or someone from our spiritual family, our Light cordings will be well developed and will be able to pass a tremendous amount of energy back and forth.

We cord not only to thought forms and people, but also to race memories, genetic memories, akashic record memories, and to ideas and concepts left in the ethers by the spiritual hierarchy - and sometimes by the dark lodge* as well.

You also cord to the thought forms of binding vows made to someone, not only in this lifetime, but also in past lives. If you were part of an old occultist group, especially if you were tyrannised within that group, the pattern of fear and the vows you made may still be resonating within the witchy side of yourself. So although you are now attracted to working with love in this lifetime, you still have to work through the affirmations you made to the darker side in previous lives, which now have to be confronted and transmuted in order for you to move on.

Since all of humanity are moving from the sinner to the saint, we all have to work through the darker side of life to resonate with and have a true understanding of "Light". We all carry aspects of Light and dark, resonating or latent within our genetic make-up, although some people don't like to face up to their darker side.

As you move into a higher vibration, you have to face up to, and work with, any slower frequency vibrations which have not been transmuted and which therefore still carry an energy charge which could become activated if situations are ripe for this.

Do bear in mind that, because of karmic cycles and because of the way these things operate, some subliminal frequencies will be more dominant, and others will be in a space of suspended animation and will only become activated when your energy charge hits the right frequency.

To help you target and transmute any darker affirmation made in past lives, which is still resonating within your space, the following can be used:

*"May Light focus within my will
to transmute any darker affirmations
into the higher Light purpose
of unconditional love."*

For affirmations to be effective they should be said in three series of three. So you say the affirmation three times in a normal voice, three times in a whisper and then three times mentally. This will resonate with the vibration of the number nine, which is the highest pitch, or rule of law which helps you become complete. In this way you use the natural law of the nine to your advantage, and your affirmation becomes powerful enough to pierce the subconscious impressions.

On one level, a promise is also an affirmation. A promise should never be made unless you intend to carry it through. If you promise to pick a friend up from work, do so! If you forget, your broken promise carries a karmic vibration - however small - which has to be dealt with.

Feeding thought forms

All thought forms have a vibratory package and are maintained by energy input, subliminal as well as conscious. You feed thought forms by the way you think and behave - mainly internally, not externally! So every thought you have builds or destroys the thought forms around you. When you join a group of people who are consciously working to raise their vibrations, by sharing the concentrated essence of the group thoughts and by amplifying the beautiful thoughts, you systematically transmute and release the slow frequency thought forms which are destructive to both the people in the group and to the group purpose. By doing this you can all move on much quicker.

To analyse your thoughts and subliminal patterns, look at all the thoughts which you feel are unacceptable which go through your mind over the next seven days. Carry a notebook and jot your thoughts down, then sit and review them in the evening. This will help you identify the thoughts that are abusing you as a person, and the subliminal patterns running through your mind.

Throw-away statements made by your parents may have created a thought form which affected you deeply as a child. We are all very open as children and seemingly innocent remarks, often said by parents in a moment of frustration without any real thought as to their deeper meaning, can act as little burrs which stick to us for years to come. These can have an ongoing effect throughout our adult life.

So if a parent moans, "Get on with your homework. If you don't do your homework, you'll never be any good at school," the child's subconscious takes in the thought implant, "You'll never be any good". That thought goes into the child's psyche and the child grows up thinking they are no good.

Even actions create thought forms which govern our beliefs. If a child is punished by being shut in the dark, they equate darkness with a form of punishment. That thought form builds each time they are shut in the dark. Later, as an adult, each time they go out into the dark they subconsciously remember that darkness is a form of punishment. The thought form grows and fear of darkness becomes a real terror which can be with them throughout their life.

We all have these subtle rhythms. But we now need to recognise that we have the will to blow away the cobwebs, to take off the dark sunglasses, and peer more constructively at what is actually there.

When you have identified your negative patterns, don't think into them. A thought is built by energy input, so simply stop giving them energy. You can use an affirmation as a counter-thought, but remember to say it in three series of three, so as to resonate with the natural law of the nine which helps you become complete.

As you start to watch your thoughts, look at your own throw-away comments which you casually say, such as "Oh dear, I'm losing my hair". If you say this enough times, your hair will fall out even more as you are willing it to happen. Change your approach. If you have a problem, be positive. Instead of moaning that you are losing your hair, say, "Thank you Universe for giving me this hair loss." Then you are basically saying, "I have a problem and my body is talking to me, so I have a wonderful opportunity to change and get myself back into balance and harmony."

You can monitor this by assessing your treacle count, or level of negative toxic energy within your body. If your treacle count ever goes over 3%, then the quality of thought forms within your auric space will be suspect. As most people these days have a degree of negativity in excess of 50 to 70%, this indicates that they are carrying a gross negative charge both in their physical body and their aura, which can be very destructive for the people concerned.

Negative thought forms normally draw attention to themselves by manifesting as down-market expressions within your energy system, such as a lack of confidence in oneself, a lack of trust, etc.

If you have a lot of negative thought forms, your body shape will also reflect this. You will have a need to be protective and will probably have a layer of fat over your solar plexus. Your shoulders will be rounded and your head bent forward, looking at the ground rather than looking in front of you. The biorhythms of your physical body will emphasise this and make you more vulnerable at times.

Every thought passing through your mind creates a pattern of energy which has a response somewhere. By thinking an aggressive pattern, you drop your vibration and you usually give off a lot more red energy. This activates any latent memories which are genetically within your body and have been karmically brought in from your akashic record. These latent memories are continually in attendance with us.

If you are following the path of a Light worker - and this is fairly obvious on the inner planes - those working with the darker side will systematically try to arrange the implantation of a thought form for you to collect. If you allow that thought form into your energy system it will be activated when the vibration is appropriate to what the thought form is programmed to do. So as you come up to a special occasion within your life's purpose, this thought form will jump up, call in its mates - ambush time! All of a sudden you find you have lots of problems and feel blocked. You might think, "What is going on? My vision has gone. I am totally confused and don't know what to do!"

You become more agitated, more frustrated, more angry. And you activate a lot of old patterns. All of a sudden you have severe depression, anxiety, your body starts palpitating and your heart may even start to misbehave.

This is when you need your friends on the inner planes. Because you can't get out of this pattern on your own if you are being systematically attacked. And that is basically what is happening. Even though the attack might have been 25,000 years ago, it is actually manifesting in the now. So that is where you need someone on the inner planes who is part of the same rhythm as yourself calling, "Hello, I'm over here! You can't see me, I know you are blind at the moment. But have enough faith, have enough love and follow the sound of my vibratory voice." This vibration, or voice, is the essence of the spiritual hierarchy vibrating in unison with the Universe. It is, therefore, the sum total of unconditional love which is available for everyone to tap into, and is specifically for those who are following the spiritual pathway. As you think of this vibratory core, this unconditional love rhythm which can be symbolised as the unspoken word of the voice on the inner planes, your energy will automatically find it, since energy follows thought. You can then link into it and draw from it.

Bear in mind that everyone has renaissance with their Source. This is activated by unconditional love for yourself. As you tap into this vibration you might find yourself going through a period of confused energy, but as you go through that threshold and become free, you suddenly think, "Of course! It is obvious!" and your confusion melts away.

Problems rarely come when you are strong and able to cope with them. They always come when you are vulnerable, at your weakest, run down, or exhausted. This is always a sign that you have a lack of love within yourself, and are working with limitation. So to help you move beyond that, you are 'pushed' into a crisis point.

This is deliberate as you are down here to work. It is part of your survival. To harden up you have to go through the commando course. You might not like it, but in the end you are stronger and think, "Hey, I climbed this mountain by myself." You look at the view and feel all the pride of your performance. It does take confidence, perseverance, discipline, and of course experience to work with the permutations which life normally brings, plus the self-realisation that knowledge, information, power and understanding are always with us. Any problems which might be brought into your space to be dealt with - be it physical, emotional or psychic - are only there to ensure that you change.

For you, as a Light worker, it is now time to change your perspective and see problems as opportunities to change and move on. If you can think of your problems in this way, then life becomes a whole new ball game.

So when you are feeling down and hurting, this is just the gravitational pull of past conditioning. To move through that you have to use your will. By focusing your will you can overcome anything. By linking into the frequency of unconditional love, you can move through your fears and move on quite gracefully.

If you find yourself perpetually angry, irritable or worried, you are just playing the same record over and over again, and are stuck in the same frequency. Because of our emotional system, we have the capacity to be happy or sad a hundred times a day in different settings. This versatility is our strength. But on another level it is also our greatest weakness. Recognise that you can change your thoughts and move from the angry sound into a peaceful or joyous note, just by changing your frequency - in the same way that you switch over from one channel to another on television. This requires an effort of will, but this is what you should now aim for, and this is what the meditations in this book will help you to achieve.

Clearing away old thought forms

Every week look around your home, at your books, clothes, and personal objects. If you don't like them or they don't feel good, do something about them. Either cleanse them or work with the thought form attached to them, or throw them out. Some people find it especially hard to chuck out books or personal things as they are stuck in the old thoughts of, "It is my possession!"

If you have grown-up children who constantly borrow your clothes, they may irritate you by doing this as it triggers that possession thought form, but they also serve you by helping to make you flexible in this way.

Systematically try to give away your most valuable possession! If you can actually hand it on, especially if it has a nice vibration and you think someone needs its energy, then by giving it away you break the cycle of desire, attachment and possession. You are then free from desire. We reincarnate time after time in order to work through desire, until we become desireless. So if you can freely and joyfully give away special possessions you are saying to the Universe, "Look! I am freeing myself from desire! I am free about giving my energy." By doing that, the same higher vibrations will come back to you.

Every action will be repaid to you, even if it is only a small one such as, "Oh, you have a cold. Here, have my hankie." By doing that you are giving your caring and your love, and that action will be repaid to you sooner or later. The same applies if you snarl abuse at someone - that energy will come back to you. So every thought, every action has a knock-on effect which will rebound back to you. This energy, which travels genetically through the fibres of your life, is what I call the 'blots on the landscape'.

Latent thought forms

Latent thought forms can become active when planetary movements are right. This happens for example if someone has, say a suicidal urge and jumps off a cliff. Their thought form about suicide and jumping off the cliff, resonates within that place and is left behind on that cliff.

This latent vibratory thought form can radiate out to 150 miles (240km) and everyone who is susceptible will be drawn to that. A second person might be drawn to the same cliff by that signal, maybe responding to an inner feeling of curiosity, and if the planetary movements are right, the thought form explodes into activity. The person might then get an overwhelming urge to jump. This activates the thought form and a third person may then be drawn to that cliff and, because the thought form is now active, that person gets 'pushed' off the cliff. In this way the thought form creates an ongoing amplification. If enough people respond to the thought form, a ghoul develops. This is a pattern of energy which really can pick you up and throw you off the cliff! Beachy Head, in England, is one such place where there is a ghoul which makes people blissfully jump off the cliff and kill themselves.

Sites of old battles and concentration camps can also have this type of thought amplification. In concentration camps during the Second World War, a lot of people who died in those camps chose not to pass on, but stayed there on the lower astral realms so that through the pattern of energy which they left behind, future generations would recognise the suffering and trauma which took place. It is the dominant thought at the time of death which limits people, and sometimes these souls have to be convinced, when the opportunity is right, that it is now time to pass on.

Corporate structures

A department store is a structural unit of multiple thought forms held together by the major energy input of the thought of offering various commodities under one roof.

As department stores are materially orchestrated, the main thought input is based on money and wealth - the wealth of the few at the expense of the many - and all the variety of thoughts linked into that. The competition between departments creates a vibration of friendly competition on the surface, but underneath there are a series of subtle vibrations buffeting each other, all linked into the thought forms around attachments and territorial claim.

You can also be sure that people who work there have worked together in some joint venture in past lives. So their conflicting personalities and the friendly and unfriendly competitiveness will ensure there is a karmic play-off between them.

With that are all the thought forms linked into the feudal aspect of conforming to the identity and image of that particular store. All these feudal and negative thought forms have a slow frequency vibration.

If you go into one of these stores merely to use it as a place of refuge - to get off the streets into somewhere warm - you add to the melting-pot your own thought forms based on your need for comfort and love, plus any negative slow frequency thought forms you have.

The massive lighting and electrical system within a departmental store also creates a widespread field of noxious slow frequency negative energy. All the slow frequency thought forms bouncing around within the store have a wonderful time feeding on that magnetic electrical field and on the energy system of unsuspecting customers and staff.

This combination of the massive magnetic electrical discharge and the slow frequency thought forms infiltrating your auric space is the reason why so many people wander around these stores and quickly get tired, anxious, disorientated, depressed - and in extreme cases faint. If the store is sited over geopathic stress points, or negative ley lines, this will tend to amplify the problem.

Those who are psychic can peer at the electrical system in these stores, and see the negative thought forms and astral entities sitting there like vultures, popping down onto the unwary, having a good suck of their energy, or hopping from one auric space to another and having an 'esoteric rave-up'.

This applies to large supermarkets, hypermarkets, and any group selling various commodities under a common banner. If you have to go into a departmental store, or a market setting where a large number of people come together, use Meditation 62, at the end of this chapter, to create a protective sequence around you.

The thought forms attached to the banking organisations in general are also based on the old feudal system. They control society by creating a frequency vibration of structural fear - fear of losing possessions, fear of not paying a loan, fear of manipulation, etc. A small minority of people within the banking system have a great deal of personal wealth, and a few of them are tuned into negative polarity points of energy from systems external to ours, through interdimensional star gateways. These people may not be aware that they are, in fact, agents for those working through those polarity points. They are also unaware that negative thought forms are being deliberately cultivated around them, with a manipulating vibration being focused within their personality to encourage them to control and dominate. This may have been going on for many years.

Wealth in general, and money used as an expression of wealth, is a way of keeping masses of people in one place, in a point of disharmony. Banks who offer massive loans to Third World countries when they are not in a position to repay their loans, keep these countries at a disadvantage. This brings about tremendous structural suffering based on the fears around survival which in turn creates a frequency vibration which is useful food for those of a negative nature.

I always advise Light workers to look carefully at the vibratory essence of their bank. If that vibration does not give you a feeling of well-being, then look around for a smaller bank or one which is more in keeping with the New Age purpose.

Always choose wisely according to the vibrations which you intuitively perceive, rather than being influenced by propaganda, advertising or peer pressure. If for example you have a short-list of three banks, you can visualise each one as a thought form. Then visualise each thought form as being egg-shaped and give each egg-shaped thought form a chakra system with the seven main chakras, with each chakra centre split into three parts - a bottom, a middle and a top.

Then ask yourself where the hara or point of balance is within each thought form. You can do this intuitively and just see where it is, or you can use the intuitive traffic light dowsing technique to give you a response. When you have your answer, zoom into that chakra, and check to see if the point of balance is in the bottom, middle or top section. The position of the hara will tell you at which level the bank is vibrating. You can then choose the bank with the highest vibration.

You can also work to help further raise the vibration of the bank you choose, by using Meditation 55 at the end of this chapter, or work with your bank as a thought form during Step 11 of the meditation programme to release personal karma, Meditation 20, in Chapter 2, *The Awakening*. Remember that a bank is a thought form, so you can use either meditation sequence to raise the vibration of your bank. You can also do this with any organisation, with your local newspaper, or with any programme you are watching on television.

Structural thought forms

A structural thought form is a thought form which has been built up and is held together by will. If you are doing absent healing and projecting a particular symbol, perhaps a cross or a star, this symbol is a structural thought form fed by your essence and by your will, and held in place by your awareness.

In comparison, an ordinary thought form is a thought form of loosely inter-webbed energy coming together and creating a pattern of frequencies.

Structural change, or focused change is something that all Light workers are participating in, rather than change which is just loosely forming out of the elements of intermingling frequencies.

So a structural thought form, or structural change, is a deliberate event which has been worked towards with foreknowledge, either by individuals or a group.

It is the structural thought forms that we really need to be aware of, for everything is a thought form. Society is a thought form. The world is a thought form. And we who live in it can actually alter these thought forms by constantly being aware of our thoughts, denying negative thoughts the energy they need for survival, and feeding the positive high frequency thoughts which we wish to nurture and create. In this way you can play your part in creating the world you truly want for yourself and humanity.

The race sin bin

The race sin bin is everything that we as individuals, and as part of the human race, have a responsibility for. It is all the old slow frequency energy, noxious thought forms, hate, greed and fear that we, over the last 300,000 years - and especially over the last 2,500 years - have cultivated into a series of magnetic negative thought forms. These thought forms tend to stick, not only within individual organisations and folk who are the law-makers or breakers, but also within localised customs and nationalities around the world.

A person incarnating into Britain, for example, will be saturated by the thought input which represents British history - the social, economic and inspirational thought forms, as well as the feudal thought forms based on tyranny and authority. The secrecy which the British people, and the British government in particular, are so obsessed with, gives you an idea of the fear which has moulded some of the old thought patterns in Britain. This now has to be dealt with so that British people as a whole can move forward.

The EEC will play a part in this. As the Common Market, with all its diversities and cultures, comes together into one central mixing bowl, there will be a lot of structural difficulties. But the end result will be a positive mix where outdated methods can actually be broken down.

This race sin bin, which is basically the composite pattern of energies now flowing into our awareness, also includes all the karmic contracts around money and slavery which have to be cleared. For example, most of the money in western countries has been built on past years of slavery. Therefore, karmically, the people from Third World countries who are pouring into western countries to seek asylum, are not only creating an integration problem, but are also bringing that old karma back for us to deal with.

So the human race has a massive amount of karma to work through. Our evolution demands that this sin bin is now emptied, and Light workers are down here to do it!

* * *

Barnacles And Thought Forms: meditations

55. Meditation to raise the vibration of a thought form
56. Meditation to decord from and release unacceptable thought forms by working with the Tree of Life
57. Second meditation to release unacceptable thought forms
58. Third meditation to encompass and dissolve unwanted thought forms
59. Meditation to dispose of thought forms and emotions which arise in panic situations
60. Meditation to reject a negative thought form when a cording is sent out to you
61. Meditation to work with people or vibrations that trigger an irritation within you, and to create a protective shield around you
62. Second meditation to create a protective sequence around you when you go into a department store or hostile environment
63. Meditation for women to balance their femininity in a male environment and for men to balance their masculinity in a female environment
    NB. *The variation can be used to balance male and female energies within your chakra centres*

55. Meditation to raise the vibration of a thought form

This meditation is included in the main meditation programme to release personal karma, in Chapter 2, *The Awakening*. But as you can use this part of the meditation at any time to work with a specific thought form, we explain it here in full. You can work with this meditation to raise the vibration within any thought form, be it an emotional thought, such as loneliness, fear, etc., or a limiting thought form around your health or your life, such as the thoughts that keep you in a state of low prosperity.

You can also use this meditation to work with any thought form that intuitively offends you. If you want to work with, say violence in its totality, or rape for the female or male aspect, you can symbolise each of these as a thought form, and work with that.

Everything is a thought form. Your car, the company you work for, your bank and every large organisation is a thought form. Once you understand this, you can use this meditation to raise the vibration within your bank, your place of work, or within an organisation or anything which you feel is vibrating too low.

You can symbolise a thought form in several different ways. If your visualisation is adequate, one way is to imagine the thought form as an egg-shaped energy form - or any shape that intuitively presents itself to you. Then give that shape a chakra system within the seven main chakras, splitting each one up into three parts with a bottom, a middle and a top. If you find this visualisation difficult, you can draw an egg shape on a piece of paper, colour it, and give it seven chakras, splitting each one into three as before. The idea is to create a shape or symbol representing the thought form which will give you a working dialogue to get a reading as to where within that thought form you need to direct your focus and energy. The full meditation sequence is:

Bring down white Light and root yourself in

You should now be at the stage where settling yourself into meditation, bringing down white Light, and rooting yourself in to link yourself into the lower and the higher, is a natural and easy sequence for you.

Put on your Light body

Put on whatever Light body feels intuitively right for the thought form you are planning to work with.

Visualise your thought form

To explain this step, let us assume that you are working with loneliness as a thought form.

Visualise that thought form as a shape - let us assume it is an egg shape. See that egg shape in front of you, then give it a chakra system with each chakra centre split into three, a bottom, middle and top. Then look to see which chakra centre is active within that thought form - so you are looking for the active point of balance, or the hara within that thought form. This will show you where loneliness is being activated within that thought form. This in turn will show you through which chakra centre loneliness is being activated within your own chakra system. You do this intuitively, so trust yourself and know that whatever answer comes into your mind is the right one. With a bit of practice most people can do this quite easily, so it will become a very natural intuitive feel of where the active point of energy is at that particular time.

For most people, loneliness is activated within their own sexual chakra centre. If this is the same for you, then the sexual centre in the egg-shaped thought form in front of you will reflect that and will also be the active point. Once you have located the active chakra, look closer and see whether loneliness is coming in through the lower, middle or top part of the sexual centre.

Build up an energy charge

If, for example, loneliness is coming in at the bottom part of the sexual centre, you refocus on the white Light coming in through the top of your head, bring it into your own heart chakra, fold your arms over your heart chakra and build up an energy charge. Then open your arms and allow this energy charge, which represents unconditional love, to flow out of your heart and into your third eye and both hands in a triangular formation.

Raise the vibration within your thought form

Now project your triangle of unconditional love energy into the section just *above* the active point. In this example, as loneliness is coming in at the bottom part of the sexual centre, you project your triangle of Light into the section above that, which is the middle section of the sexual centre. Project your triangle into that section for five seconds. Repeat this for a maximum of five sets of five seconds, or until your input of love energy moves the hara up to that section.

Once you have moved the hara up to the middle section, you project your triangle of energy into the section just above that, which is now the top part of the sexual centre. Project your triangle of Light in short bursts of five seconds until you move the hara up to that section. Once you have done that, you move your focus up to the solar plexus chakra and start to project your triangle of energy into the lower section of the solar plexus chakra. Continue in this way and systematically move the hara up through all the other centres.

In this way you are using your energy input to improve the vibration, by heightening it and pushing it further up, and raising the active point of balance within that thought form.

The upward movement of the active point of balance is normally fairly quick so, as you whack your triangle of energy into each section, you should get a fairly spontaneous response with the hara moving upwards.

You project your triangle of energy for a maximum of five bursts of five seconds each into any one level within each chakra. If after these five bursts of energy into the level above the hara, you don't get a response and the hara doesn't move, then you come out of the meditation. Wait until the next day and repeat the meditation, and continue to work with the above sequence to move the hara further upwards. You may even find that the hara has already moved up by itself, as quite often the subliminal patterns associated with the karmic patterns which you are working with, or the cosmic tides and solar winds of planetary movement can make it difficult on one day and easy on the next.

To come out of the meditation
Bring your triangle of energy back into your heart centre. Close down your Light body and your chakra centres. Bring your roots back from the Earth. As you bring your awareness back into your body, make sure your astral body is fully back and nicely aligned with your physical body.

Keep a record
Keep a list, like a diary, and write down all the thought forms you are working with. Work with up to 40 thought forms over a three month period, aiming to transmute, release and move those thought forms into a new octave within those three months. Put them in order of importance and as you work with each one, note the final position of the hara in each meditation. So if, in your meditation with loneliness, you got the hara up to the middle section of the solar plexus centre, you note that and the date.

Ideally, once you start to work with any thought form, you should repeat the meditation daily. In this way you will find that you will be able to move the vibration of that thought form upwards very quickly - and move yourself up to a new octave.

But if you start to work with any thought form - especially if it is an old package - and for some reason you don't repeat this exercise on an ongoing basis, you may find that when you go back to the meditation again, the old package of energy has flowed back down towards the level where it was before. So if you don't work with your chosen thought form on a regular basis it will take a lot longer to move the hara up - and it will be a bit like going three steps forward and two steps backward.

It could well be that you can transmute the negative energy in a thought form and move its hara up to the crown in a few weeks or a month. Once you have got a thought form up to the crown, continue to energise it periodically over a three month period as it takes three months for the energy in a thought form to build and for that new energy to manifest and be maintained within your physical space.

On average, you should be able to transmute at least 75% of the thought forms you want to target, within your three month programme. You can then make a new list of up to 40 other thought forms you want to work with, incorporating any thought forms not fully transmuted in the last three months. So every three months you can restart this programme if you wish.

You could stop working with any thought form once you have pushed the hara within that thought form up to the heart chakra centre or above. But the ultimate aim is to move it up through the third eye and continue working with each thought form until you have moved it, in its totality, up through the crown chakra.

To explain the value of persevering until you have worked all the way to the crown, let us look at the thought form which represents prosperity. Everybody has a prosperity thought form. But if your prosperity thought form is being activated in the sexual centre, it will be lacking energy and your prosperity thought form won't be very strong - which may manifest as a lack of prosperity in your life. As you work with prosperity in this meditation format, if it is initially coming in at the top half of your sexual centre, you will find that once you have moved it up past the heart chakra your prosperity will start to improve. Once you have moved it up through your crown chakra and held it there for three months, you will then find that your prosperity will alter in a very specific way.

56. Meditation to decord from and release unacceptable thought forms by working with the Tree of Life

Bring down white Light and root yourself in

Think of a point of white Light coming down through the top of your head linking into your chakra centres, then root yourself in, connecting yourself with both the higher and the lower.

Black healing meditation

Do the black healing meditation as described in Meditation 4, in the section *Key Aspects Of Meditation Work*.

Create a blue five-pointed star

In your visualisation, create a blue five-pointed star, 6 feet (2m) in radius, which you place around you.

Create a Tree of Life

In front of you, visualise and invite into your presence the Tree of Life. You will see this as a golden tree made of flames, so you are working with the flame archetype. Within that Tree of Life, you will see the seven main chakra centres. Each chakra centre within the Tree of Life will represent and reflect your own corresponding chakra.

Start with the base chakra

Drop your awareness down to your *own* base chakra centre. Then link into the base chakra within the Tree of Life using your awareness, or using a beam of Light to connect both chakras. The base chakra within the Tree of Life will then start to rotate anticlockwise, and as it does, you take your awareness into this centre, and imagine a doorway opening within it. From this doorway will come a pair of golden hands representing the God force. Gold has an encoded healing focus, so the golden hands of the God force have a very specific focus to transmute negative encodements of an occult nature from old life patterns and they will take from you all the thought forms you need to release from your own base chakra.

To facilitate that release you merely visualise a plug being pulled in your own base chakra, and any gunge, any slow frequency energy from old race patterns, or from old memories of unpleasantness, can be systematically released through this interaction. This unwanted energy then flows directly into the pair of golden hands where it will be transmuted.

Once you have achieved the energy release from your base centre, the gold hands will go back into the base chakra of the Tree of Life, and that base centre will continue to rotate.

Work up through the chakras

Move your awareness up to your own sexual chakra centre. Now focus on the sexual chakra within the Tree of Life, and as you do that, the sexual centre within the Tree of Life will be activated and will rotate anticlockwise. Repeat the above sequence releasing all the gunge from your sexual chakra, and continue in this way working up through all the chakra centres in turn.

Having completed this with each of your chakra centres, the branches on the Tree of Life will send out a blessing. This blessing will be in the form of an intuitive sound which will enter through your crown chakra and will gently flow down through all your centres in turn. As this blessing, this intuitive sound flows down, each chakra centre will close. Each chakra centre will then have a nine-pointed star placed over the 'plug hole'. These nine-pointed stars will vibrate and spin anticlockwise so that thought forms of a similar nature to those just released, which may try to come into your centres again, will find it impossible to attach themselves to those chakra centres as they did before.

To end the meditation

Check that your chakra centres are fully closed down. If you have difficulty accepting the vibratory sound of the nine-pointed star, you may find some chakras, especially the sexual and solar plexus chakras have popped open again. If so, close down those chakras by seeing each centre as a rose in full bloom and visualising each rose closing into a bud with each bud shrinking to a point of white Light. The Tree of Life will then disappear.

The blue five-pointed star which is around you will shrink, and as it shrinks it will concentrate itself into two small five-pointed stars, one around each of your heels. So although you have actually dropped your vibration back down to its normal frequency by closing down your chakra centres, you are leaving one portion still activated, which is represented by the small blue stars. These can be reactivated as and when it feels appropriate. Then bring your awareness back into the totality of yourself.

By keeping the small five-pointed stars activated, if ever you feel threatened, you can instantly amplify and reactivate your two little stars, visualise them merging into one and enlarging so that the large star spins up and around your body to about six feet (2m) in radius. By doing that any slow frequency energy which tries to come in will be transmuted before it enters your space.

It would be useful when you first start working with this meditation, to re-energise this star and practise expanding it and contracting it until you can do it easily. Do this as a practice session on a daily basis for the first nine days, and then once a week thereafter until the amplification and enlargement of the star can be done spontaneously.

57. Second meditation to release unacceptable thought forms

Bring down white Light and root yourself in

Prepare yourself for the meditation by bringing white Light down through the top of your head, and root yourself in. Then feel the higher aspect of yourself coming out of your body, and in your imagination see a little pouch around the waist of your higher self. In this pouch are seven stars. Each star represents a different hue, a different vibration.

Take your awareness into your higher self

Shift your awareness from your physical body into your higher self. To do this you have to step out of the vibratory package which represents your physical senses. Most people find it easier to leave their physical body via their solar plexus chakra. This is akin to imagining a doorway opening in your solar plexus and you step backwards through that doorway into your higher self. You may feel or sense your higher self as a body of Light. As you step into your awareness on a higher plane you might be aware of a noise or humming sound. Occasionally people leave their body through the back of their head, through their ajna chakra centre - which is parallel to the nose, at the base of the skull where the spinal column and skull meet. So you might like to experiment with these two exit points.

Focus on your physical body

As you look down from your higher self, visualise your physical body lying down on the floor and see each chakra centre in your physical body symbolised as a well. Each well will be full of coloured liquid.

Start working with your base chakra

Starting at the well which is your base chakra, take one of the stars out of your pouch - whichever one feels intuitively right - and drop it into the liquid in the well of your base chakra. The energy of your base chakra, which is symbolised as liquid in the well, will start to bubble and in the bubbling process, a lot of steam representing your unpleasant gunge will be released. As this happens, any memories from old thought forms which need to be transmuted and released will become apparent. As they come up just acknowledge them and let them go.

As the old thought forms are released, the water will become clear and you will have a feeling of purity.

If, having dropped your star into the well, the water doesn't clear, you drop in a second star. The water will again bubble, and you wait to see if it becomes clear. If it doesn't, you drop in a third star, let the water bubble and release more gunge and see if the water clears. You continue in this way, dropping in one star at a time until the water becomes clear.

Once the water in the well of your base chakra has become clear, you move onto the well over the sexual centre and repeat this sequence, dropping into that well another star as before. When the water is clear, you then move up to the next chakra centre.

You continue working up through each chakra centre in turn, but only go as far as you can, based on the time available, and the need of the moment, remembering that you only have seven stars to work with.

If you have used up all seven stars and haven't been able to clear all seven wells in the first meditation - you may initially find that you put all seven stars into the well of the base centre and the water still isn't clear - you stop the meditation sequence after using the seventh star and come out of the meditation.

To come back out of the meditation

Feel your higher aspect flowing back into your physical body in the same way as you left it, and feel your physical body again being filled with your essence. Close down each chakra centre in turn and bless and dedicate each chakra centre for the ongoing cleansing process. Then bring your roots back from the ground.

Make sure your astral body is fully aligned with your physical body, by imagining your feet and hands as being magnets and your astral body will be drawn back fully into your body, just like iron filings are sucked towards a strong magnet.

Continue to close each chakra centre

If you haven't cleared the water in all seven wells, you wait 24 hours then repeat the meditation, starting where you left off. Continue with this on a daily basis - working with just seven stars in each meditation - until you have cleared the water in each well of each of your chakra centres. The meditation should never be repeated more than once in any 24 hour period even if you have the time and feel you want to continue.

You work up through all your chakra centres in this way, but always work with the expectation that each star will bring about a total cleansing of each centre, even if you have to use several stars to achieve the desired result. By doing this you will find that you can eventually clear each chakra centre in turn, with just one star.

Once you have cleared the water in all seven wells, in the final meditation, you come back out of the meditation as before. Close down each chakra centre, but this time dedicate and bless each chakra to understanding and your higher purpose, and allow yourself to say whatever intuitively flows into your mind. The blessing and dedication may change in each meditation as your vibration opens you to a greater understanding of your needs, rather than your wants. As you do this, see each well full of pure, clear water.

58. Third meditation to encompass and dissolve unwanted thought forms

In this meditation, you will be creating a pyramid-shaped temple, made of pure quartz crystal.

First of all, you may like to strengthen your visualisation process by first physically drawing on paper a pyramid-shaped temple, with an altar inside directly under the point of the pyramid. Allow yourself to draw whatever you intuitively feel you need to focus on within your visualisation.

Bring down white Light and root yourself in

Move into your meditation by taking a few deep breaths to quieten your mind, and at this stage release all thoughts from your conscious mind. Then bring down white Light, see it flowing into all your chakra centres, and root yourself in so that you are linked into the higher and the lower.

Visualise your crystalline temple

Allow your mind's eye to create your crystalline pyramid temple, with the altar situated directly under the point of the pyramid, and walk into your pyramid through a triangular door.

Inside the pyramid you visualise a swirl of light coming down from the point of the pyramid, flowing down in a gentle swirl, in an anticlockwise direction, and impacting onto the altar itself.

Put on your Light body

Lying on the altar will be your Light body. This particular Light body will be composed of Light particles, and as you put it on it will fit over you from head to toe like a chain-mail armour. This Light body is of a higher vibration than the animal archetype Light bodies which you use in meditations with a physical setting.

When you have put on your Light body, place yourself on the altar. Lie down and allow the light which is swirling in from the top of the pyramid to enter into your heart centre. This light is the energy of the Cosmic Christ which is continually being sent out from Shambhala. As that energy flows into your heart centre, your armour will take on a particular colour which is appropriate for the work in hand. Allow your intuition to show you which colour you need for this particular moment.

As this energy of love, Light and power flows into your heart centre, it also flows through your body, totally filling up your body with a great deal of structural power.

Dissolving the unwanted thought form

Step back from your altar and go to one side of the pyramid. Ask within your higher consciousness for the necessary symbolic change to take place within the temple setting for the work to be done.

As the Light comes down from the apex of the pyramid onto the altar, the altar will then change into a circle of Light that is split up into four segments.

The circle and the four segments are still directly under the apex of your pyramid, and they will all be transparent at this stage.

On the temple wall to your left will be a black globe of pure quartz crystal, and on the temple wall to your right will be a sword - the sword of truth, of power and inspiration. Take the globe in your left hand and the sword in your right. Now step forward into the circle split into four segments.

Now concentrate on just one segment within the circle as this will give you the amplification you need as you tap into the thought form you want to deal with. You intuitively choose which segment to start working with first. Then focus on the thought form you want to work with, and place the vibration, or key note - the essence of the thought form - within that segment. If you wish, you can ask your higher self to give you a symbol to represent the vibration of that thought form, and place that into the segment.

For example, if it is a negative thought form around a lack of prosperity which is blocking abundance flowing into your life, you place the key note, or symbol which represents that thought form into the first segment you are working with.

As you do that, the vibration or key note which represents that thought form will create a colour corresponding to that vibration and the segment holding that key note or symbol will fill up with that colour. The other three segments will also start to form a colour representing the counter-colour which needs to merge and meld with the quarter holding the thought form you are working with.

You hold the black quartz crystal globe and allow it to receive an energy charge from the Light of the Cosmic Christ which is coming down from the apex of the pyramid. Once the globe is charged it will change colour. The colour will match the frequency vibration of the thought form but will be slightly higher. In this way, your black globe will represent a catchment area for that thought form.

You then place that crystal globe into the segment holding the thought form. The globe will act like a net and totally encompass that segment. Then in your visualisation - recognising that energy follows thought - grasp your sword with both hands, hold it above your head with the blade pointing upwards, and feel the sword being absorbed into your spine with the pointed tip of the sword which represents the cutting edge of your will, becoming your third eye.

Then visualise a triangle of energy, with each side of the triangle being a sword, their tips pointing in an anticlockwise direction. You project this triangle of swords at the crystal globe in front of you. The original sword will have been charged up by being in the temple, so as you receive it into your spinal column it will be activating your energy, and by now focusing your will into the three swords, these will automatically be charged up.

This triangle of swords represents unconditional love and the cutting edge of your will, and will totally surround the globe which has already encompassed the segment holding your thought form.

The globe, acting as a net to surround your thought form will now start to slowly shrink. As it does, everything within the globe will be transmuted and released. The globe should totally close in on itself until it ceases to be, and the segment should lose all its colour and become transparent.

Once that has been achieved, the other three segments will also become clear. As the globe dissolves into the segment you will find that it comes back - almost like being spat out - and will land in your hands and become the same black globe once again, ready for use if you need to work with it again.

If the segment that held your thought form is still coloured, repeat the sequence again, charging up your black globe and placing it into the coloured segment until the colour dissolves. You can do this on an ongoing basis if necessary, and if you feel it is intuitively right.

To come out of the meditation

The three swords in your triangle will go back into the sword in your spine and this sword is released from the essence of your will. As you step out of the circle you place the sword and crystal globe back into their place within the temple, where they will remain until you need them again.

You then go and stand against the wall of the temple, and your circle will change back into an altar. If you wish, you can go onto the altar again and recharge yourself up by allowing the Light coming down from Shambhala to flow again into your heart. As this happens, any slow frequency energy which you might have picked up and might be hanging around you, will be transmuted.

Now dedicate and bless your temple for your highest purpose and your future work.

Leave your Light body on the altar and walk out of the pyramid. Bring your awareness back into your body, making sure that your astral body is fully back and nicely aligned with your physical body.

59. Meditation to dispose of thought forms and emotions which arise in panic situations

If you have a structural release of energy coming up, or a spontaneous panic rising, whether it manifests as tension, anxiety, or pure panic, rather than allow those emotions to dominate and swamp you, it is advisable to dispose of them very quickly. A very easy way of doing this is:

Check which chakra centre is responding

Use your intuitive awareness to see which of your chakras is responding to the energy coming in. Or use the intuitive traffic lights to give you a green light, which will tell you where that energy is coming in.

Net the emotions or thought forms

As you feel the dominant negative emotion or thought coming in, focus on whatever chakra centre those feelings are coming into. Then think of a pattern of white Light, in the form of a big white net, coming in through the top of your head. This net of Light swiftly moves around the chakra centre where you are feeling the hostile interaction.

Then visualise the net closing around that area as it contains the emotions of fear, panic, or anxiety. As this containment happens, the net of white Light completely closes around those emotions, capturing them within the net.

Propel the emotions or thoughts out of your body

Visualise these emotions being propelled out of your body, still held safely within the white net.

So if for example, you are feeling the emotions in your solar plexus, the white net will come in through the top of your head, flow into your solar plexus where it will contain and capture all the emotions. The net will then propel itself out through the wall of your solar plexus, where you will offer all these thoughts and emotions to a big pair of white hands representing the God force, which will be waiting just outside your solar plexus.

If it feels intuitively right, you can alternatively visualise the net containing the emotions travelling back up through your body and out of your head, where again a big pair of white hands will be waiting to accept and transmute all the slow frequency energy and emotions for you.

Since the white hands represent the hands of God and therefore unlimited love, you will be giving the unwanted slow frequency energy into this high frequency octave where it will be transmuted and used in a different way.

This is a much better way to release your slow frequency fears and thoughts rather than pushing them outside your auric system where someone else will get clobbered by them.

60. Meditation to reject a negative thought form when a cording is sent out to you

Attachments and cordings from negative thought forms often link into the sexual chakra of the person on the receiving end. A lot of people experience problems from negative cordings which can be linked into thought forms from this lifetime or to a problem from a previous life, such as dying in childbirth.

This can also be a particular nuisance for air hostesses and attractive women who are seen as sex objects. When a woman walks past a group of men - say a group of workmen on scaffolding who are being very macho, wolf-whistling - and they send out sexual thought forms, these will try to cord into the woman's sexual chakra. One way to deal with this is to cross your arms over your solar plexus as a form of protection, which contracts your aura and shakes off the thought form.

Or you can use the following meditation sequence to slap the thought form back to its source.

In this meditation you will be working with a vibratory symbol. This can be the personality symbol given to you during the meditation to meet your guides, Meditation 39, Chapter 8, *Meeting Your Guides*. Or you can use the symbol of a five-pointed star which will be effective for working with any chakra centre from the solar plexus down, as it is the occult binder or rejector. Alternatively, you can use the symbol of the Christian cross if your prefer.

Check which chakra centre is responding

Use your intuitive awareness to see which of your chakras is responding to the negative energy coming in. Or use the intuitive traffic lights to give you a green light over the chakra centre where the energy interference is coming into.

Push the offending energy away

Now drop your awareness down into that chakra centre and use your symbol to push against the energy coming in.

To explain how this works, let us assume that the energy interference is coming into your sexual chakra, and that you are using a five-pointed star: as you drop your awareness down into your sexual chakra, visualise thousands and thousands of five-pointed stars being projected out of your sexual chakra. These will wrap round the offending energy in whatever shape, colour, or smell it is manifesting as within your awareness. These thousands of five-pointed stars will then push the negative energy or cording out of your auric space.

Sealing any rupture in your aura

If you then feel that there is a hole in your aura where this energy came in, you can put a five-pointed star into that hole. Then visualise golden Light which represents the energy of the Cosmic Christ, flowing down into your sexual centre and out into the auric hole, filling it up with gold Light. Then contract your star down to a point of white Light, which will seal the rupture. Now dedicate and bless that area to unconditional love and truth.

With practice the full sequence can be done very quickly - first dropping your awareness into the appropriate chakra, surrounding any unwanted energy or thought form with thousands of your symbols, bouncing it back out of your auric space, and sealing any rupture which it created in your aura.

61. Meditation to work with people or vibrations that trigger an irritation within you and create a protective shield around you

First work with the underlying cause

If a certain person or a certain vibration systematically annoys you, first of all ask yourself why you are getting that impression, for everything is a learning experience.

Ask yourself what that irritation is saying to you. It might be the person's shape, astrological sign type, or their action triggering off an old thought form you need to look at. By 'looking' I mean reflecting on past experiences that have created a situation where the vibrations, as you perceive them, are to your disadvantage. You might find for example, that certain race types trigger off subliminal patterns and subliminal thought forms that make you feel threatened, angry, or anxious.

Then ask your higher self what you need to do in order to work with those thought forms. There are several meditations in this chapter which offer you different key notes to work with old thought forms, so allow yourself to be drawn to the one that offers the right vibrational pattern for you.

Create a protective shield

As an ongoing protective sequence, the easiest way to protect yourself from vibratory sequences that are an irritant to you, is to work with colour in the following way:

As you see a person, or come into an environment which creates a shift within your own vibration, you may sense this intuitively. Or you may feel one of your chakra centres being affected which you then focus on as this will show you where that vibration is gathering.

If for example the vibration is going into your sexual chakra, drop your hara and your vibration down into that centre by taking your awareness into that area, and see what colour is intuitively dominant within that chakra.

As you take your awareness into that chakra, you put on or reactivate your Light body, and allow the dominating colour within that chakra to flow over your whole physical body and your Light body. So you wrap your Light body around you and shelter underneath the colour which becomes an outer cloak.

As you do that, you will find that the hostile vibration, the threat or over-sensitivity which is coming in, will be reflected back and will diminish. As that happens, the colour surrounding your Light body will be reabsorbed back into your chakra centre.

As a practice session

If all this is new to you, you can practise this in a garden centre, or in your garden where you have lots of different plants all giving off a different vibration and, therefore, different colours within their auric field.

As you stand in front of each plant just spend a few seconds feeling which chakra centre within your body is being activated. With plants, it might be any of your chakra centres depending on the evolution within that plant and the thought forms hanging around it. Normally it is from the solar plexus down, but don't think your intuition is off if you get a response in one of your chakra centres from the heart upwards.

Now move your awareness into that chakra centre. This will shift your hara into that centre. As you do that, allow your intuition to show you which colour is most dominant within that chakra. Whatever colour comes into your mind is the colour you work with.

Now clothe yourself in your Light body, and allow the colour within that chakra to flow out and envelop you like an outer cloak.

As you do this, you may feel an immediate rapport with the plant, which might then begin communicating with you. It might tell you that it is thirsty or hot, or would prefer to be somewhere in the shade, or it might give you some other information you need.

Shed your outer cloak of colour, but keep your Light body on, then move onto the next plant and repeat the sequence. Practise this until you can do it fairly quickly and spontaneously. This will train you to adjust your energy system so that when you come into any unpleasant energy field you can automatically put on a Light body and take on the colour matching the vibration within that energy field, without being consciously aware of making any effort to do that.

Initially, of course, you do have to make the effort, so that the older intuitive muscles which you might not have used for a long time, will be able to come back into a new setting to help you form a protection around you.

62. Second meditation to create a protective sequence around you when you go into a department store or hostile environment

If you have to go into a supermarket or department store where you normally feel rotten, first of all meditate on the vibration in that store, and identify the vibration which you feel most strongly, be it negative or positive.

You then put on that vibration, by visualising it as being an outer cloak which you temporarily drape around you so that you can match whatever vibration is there. You might feel or see this vibration as a colour or pattern, and can visualise that colour or pattern as being the cloth of your cloak. Or you may feel the vibration as being spiky, so you could visualise yourself putting on a punk's outfit. Let your visualisation guide you and you will find it is a bit like putting on camouflage, or wearing theatre make-up before going onto a stage and pretending you are someone else.

You will find this outer cloak or camouflage will then act as a shield, and when you go into that store or hostile environment, your shield will reflect back whatever vibration is there and you will be able to pass through that environment without being swamped. As your shield will be of the same vibration, it will be sensed as being neutral by any astral entities or slow frequency negative thought forms who won't find you at all appealing and will go hunting for someone else!

When you come out of that environment, you simply shed your outer cloak, which you no longer have any need for, and will find you haven't lost any energy.

This is also a particularly good meditation to do before you go into an airport, as airports have a lot of magnetic energy.

63. Meditation for women to balance their femininity in a male environment and for men to balance their masculinity in a female environment

Females who are successful business women working in a male environment, often relinquish part of their femininity as they feel they can't amplify the female signal when surrounded by male energy. They might not be aware of any cordings, but basically they are intuitively staying shut down as a form of protective sequence. So although they are good at their work they crucify their emotions. When they leave that environment, they often find it very difficult to accept themselves in a feminine role. They can become defensive and want a lot of space.

To balance your femininity while working in a male environment - or after having left a male environment - or to balance your masculinity if you are a male working in a female environment, the following meditation can help:

Bring down white Light, root yourself in and put on your Light body

You should now be well versed in doing this, and it will have become a natural way to start your meditation.

Visualise two triangles

Think of a triangle lying flat, with the point away from you and the base nearest to you. In your awareness, you stand on the base line of this triangle which represents your female energy if you are a woman (or male energy if you are a man) and as you feel yourself becoming part of the triangle, allow your intuition to give it a temporary colour. The temporary colour is a representation of the multiple frequency fields you are preparing to work with.

Opposite you, is a triangle with the point facing towards you representing the problematic energy of the opposite sex (male energy if you are a woman, or female energy if you are a man).

Now dedicate and bless the triangle you are standing on to spiritual growth, to understanding and to learning about the necessary merging of male and female energies.

Merging the two triangles

Now invite the opposite triangle to merge with yours. As the two triangles come together they will form a six-pointed star, and you stand in the centre of this star. You will find that three points of the star - the three points from your triangle - will be segments of your own personality. So if you are a woman experiencing male problems, your femininity will now be split into three aspects, one in each point of the star. The other three points of the star will be the three areas of male energy from the opposite triangle, representing the masculine magnetic energy infringing into your space.

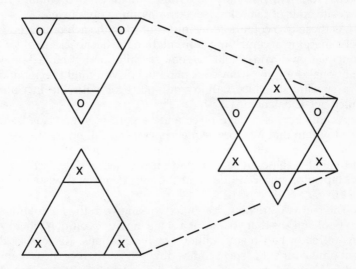

x = segments of your own energy
o = segments of problematic energy of the opposite sex

Two triangles merging into a star

Balancing the conflict

Within the centre of the six-pointed star you visualise a circle which represents the point of conflict you are going to balance.

Let us assume you are a woman working with male energy: as you look at the three segments of your femininity and the three segments of the male energy, you will intuitively see them as all being different colours. These colours are the frequencies you need to work with, which are the sum total of the temporary colour that you initially had when you first visualised your triangle.

Now take the most dominant colour of the three female segments and place it within the centre of the circle. So if for example, the colour of the first segment you want to work with is green, as you place that colour into the circle you will find that one of the three opposing masculine segments will begin to dominate, indicating that it is ready to merge and meld with your green aspect. If, for example, this colour is red, then the red segment will become more vibrant, and the colour in the other two segments of male energy will tend to fade.

You invite that dominant red colour into the circle with the green. You will normally find that you have two colours from opposite ends of the colour spectrum within your circle.

As these two colours come into contact with each other you will feel a merging and melding. You might have flashbacks to older life principles and you might remember childhood trauma - maybe emotional dumping from your parents - or you might be reminded of a specific sequence within your office or your life in general which needs balancing.

As this begins to take place and as you, in your visualisation, stand within that memory sequence, you can call on the archetypal patterns of yourself to help rectify any imbalance within the male and female. These archetypal patterns are the various 'selves' you can tap into, who can offer you the experience and wisdom from past lives.

The fact you are now drawn to working with the meditations in this book, means that you are at a stage in your evolution where you have already had many millions of incarnations. Remember that each time your soul aspect comes down to Earth, it creates a vehicle within human form to work with the necessary situations in that lifetime. When you die, your personality is imprinted in your one permanent atom. As you reincarnate and recall that one permanent atom, you continue to evolve and learn from the sequence of past lives, and will be in a position to tap into your various selves. So just allow your higher self to guide you and work with whatever comes up.

As the two colours merge and meld, they might initially darken and change frequency entirely. But as these colours merge together, through the release sequence that occurs, all the colour within the circle will eventually disappear and the circle will become transparent.

When this happens you will feel an essence of peace, Light, and love. These energy vibrations will go back into the segments where the green and red came from and will fill those segments with the vibration of love, Light and peace. These segments will then become transparent.

Now look at the other two female segments of your triangle, and see which is now the most dominant colour. You invite that into your circle. Look to see which of the other two male segments is now the most dominant colour, invite that into the circle, and repeat the sequence.

Finally repeat the full sequence for a third time with the third female and male segments.

When you have completed this, and transmuted the last segments of the star, the six-pointed star should be totally transparent, and will then become pale silver or gold.

To end the meditation

Visualise the two triangles separating and going back to their original position with the point of each triangle just facing each other.

Initially when you do this meditation, you might only be able to work with the first, most dominant segment from the female and male triangles, and you may not be able to make both colours go transparent during the first meditation sequence. If so, you end the meditation there, visualise both triangles separating as above, and come out of the meditation.

Repeat the meditation

Repeat the meditation on a regular nightly basis, until you have reached the stage of getting the six-pointed star totally transparent, and from the transparent stage the dominant silver or gold coming in. It could be that the transparent stage will remain active and the silver or gold come in after a lapse of linear time.

For most people this may take three weeks, working with this on a nightly basis, depending on the trauma you might come into contact with. It may even take longer. So don't be impatient. Take your time and enjoy it. Recognise that in each meditation, when you merge and meld the colours - even if they don't go transparent - you are still moving one step closer to a point of balance.

If the colours won't merge

If, when you bring two colours into the circle, you find that they will not merge and meld at all this may be your mind deliberately interfering as an aspect of yourself has a vested interest in not wanting you to change the formula. This is the comfort zone where part of you doesn't want to change. But recognise the need to change and release those colours back to their original segments and try to bring a different colour combination into your circle before stopping the meditation.

If having tried working with the colours from all the segments, you still don't get a response, look at each segment of the six-pointed star as a triangle in its own right and visualise each small segment of the triangle as being split into three.

You then repeat the sequence, but this time inviting only one third of a segment into the circle, so that you are working with a much smaller amount of energy at one time. If you again have reluctance or resistance, you can split these one-third segments into even smaller components. But for most Light workers you should not need to split each segment any smaller than the initial thirds.

If you still get no response, the timing may be wrong for you to do this meditation. So just push the two colours apart, pushing them back into the segments they came from, and leave it a full 24 hours before trying again.

When all of the six-pointed star is transparent

While you are working with this meditation on an ongoing basis, at the end of each meditation sequence, when you separate your triangles, they will go back to being flat with the points facing each other.

When you have achieved a point where the whole of your six-pointed star is transparent, or the transparency has moved onto the silver or gold stage, you will find that the vibration has built up and the two triangles will now separate and come together in an upright position, both merging into one upright triangle forming a line of power going down your spine. This line of power should be silver or gold but some people may find it will transfer its vibration into pure white energy, depending on your intuitive need. When you use this line of power you might see it as a composite of silver, gold and white energy.

When you are at this stage, visualise this line of power down your spine as a crystalline mace of office. Then if for example, you are in a work setting where a man, or several men, have been giving you a hard time, when you next see that person, visualise your crystalline mace of office in front of them, and any negative energy they are sending your way will be bounced back at them.

As you progress with this work, you can also check to see which of the chakra centres within that person is blinking at you, and you will be able to use your staff of office to reflect what that chakra is saying. You will then be able to receive all the information needed to deal effectively with the vibration the person is projecting at you, whether this is hostility, jealousy, fear or just plain lust. You will have an opportunity to communicate with that person in a much freer and safer manner than ever before.

Variation:

After you have worked with this meditation in a work or exterior setting you can, if you wish, progress to using this same meditation sequence to balance the male and female energies within each chakra centre in your body.

Start with the chakra centre calling out to you. You can use the intuitive traffic lights to guide you as to where to start, and you will often find you need to start at the solar plexus centre. The triangle you are standing on now represents the female energy within that chakra, and the opposite triangle represents the male energy within that chakra.

Repeat the full meditation sequence as above, to blend and balance the male and female within that chakra. When you have done so, move on, and repeat the meditation for the next chakra. Continue working through all your chakras in this way, checking to see if the male and female energies in each chakra are nicely blended and balanced.

By doing this you will bring about a fine-tuning and point of balance within all your chakra centres.

CHAPTER 14
KARMA AND KARMIC
DISEASES

Karma, to boil it down, is an act of denial reinforced by judgement. So the permutations of judgements and denials in past lives will create a pattern of energy which, at that time, you were not willing to work with.

Denial is an active excuse mechanism so that truth as it is perceived by the higher self, is denied to the lower personality. The localised customs active within each lifetime reinforce this misinformation and lack of truth through its own judgemental patterns.

All karmic patterns basically have the same underlying focus - to systematically reincarnate back into matter to burn off desire. If you have a desire to suffer, you will attract situations to make you suffer until you recognise that you don't need to suffer any more. If you have a desire to be loved, in all the diversity that love brings, you will reincarnate and come back down to Earth to meet all those people who can give you all the love you want.

The same applies to all desires - even the desire for loneliness. Although on one level loneliness may be something you fear and dread, if you have created a situation in life where you are lonely, then you have a karmic need for that experience. This is why you have attracted it to you. It is the same with the need to be of service. And many of us in this lifetime have a desire to be of service.

We constantly reincarnate to work through all these patterns of desire, until we become desireless. Everything we do in this current lifetime is designed to enhance our awareness, to give us multiple opportunities to move on and break the old possessive patterns of confined thought that says, "It is my wife, my girlfriend, my husband, my boyfriend, my children - my possessions."

Eventually all that has got to go. All desires have to go until we are in a totally neutral zone where we are only activated by unconditional love. Once you understand that and recognise planet Earth as just a training ground, you can look more clearly at your life and patterns of disharmony within your body, be it a cold or something more awful you are working with.

If you have a cold, especially if you are an Avatar - and we are all really trainee Avatars - it might actually be group karma which is manifesting as your cold, so through that cold you might be doing some cleansing on a higher plane. Therefore in essence that cold is reflecting group karma you have chosen to take on for younger soul aspects within your soul family, transmuting it for them and helping them move on.

This is why advanced soul aspects who haven't any karma left take on physical conditions that seem pretty dreadful to others, but is a gift for them. These are the people who, in your perception, might be stuck in a position of great discomfort, but are still very happy. What you are really seeing is an old soul aspect who is saying, "Hey, this is OK. This is a beautiful experience of raising the vibration of the planet. But because of the expectation of humanity, suffering is part of the process."

That need to suffer is now changing. Although we all came in on the ray of suffering, in January 1992 we moved into the cycle where that old karmic containment was broken. We can now move from the ray of suffering onto the ray of harmony, love, power and purpose. This means that our physical bodies no longer *have* to suffer and emotionally you don't *have* to suffer. But to give up all the old ideas based on fear, insecurity and suffering is sometimes very difficult!

Karma also has set cycles. If you incarnate with a crippling disease which has a 30 year karmic cycle, you will have that disease for 30 years. But just one day after your 30th birthday opportunities change. It might be a medical breakthrough, it might be the right person who gives you a miracle healing, then says, "OK, you can walk now."

With amazement and surprise you stand up and find you can actually walk, because that person tripped your belief system and broke your karmic cycle when the timing was right. But prior to that no-one could have made you believe you could walk.

Likewise we are all now moving into a new pattern where we can raise our vibration and renegotiate our karmic contract. This means that *the* miracle, if you want it, if you really need it, can actually come about.

With practice and ongoing meditations we can take advantage of the cosmic biorhythms which affect these structural energies in which we live. By becoming more intuitive we can recognise the karmic ebbs and flows of structural energies of both a positive and negative kind which work in a harmonious rhythm within ourselves. By tapping into that energy focus we can wake up in the morning and ask ourselves, "Is this a good day to meditate? Yes or no?" If the answer is 'yes', you ask, "What is the best time, intuitively, to meditate today?" You can then get an intuitive response which tells you exactly the best time for you to be still, open up, and create a much easier pathway for information and structural energies to come in - see Meditation 12, in the section *Key Aspects Of Meditation Work*. We can then create a more graceful flow of moving forward on our path throughout each day.

Structural energies are energies you have agreed to work with at set frequencies at set times. We are all working within a group situation on the inner planes, and quite often on the outer planes as well, sometimes with a working knowledge of what we are doing, and sometimes not. Within these group formations we can tap into and take advantage of the accumulation of group data on these structural energies which have been put into a 'trust fund'.

If we then meet someone whom we see as a short-term teacher, this energy can be passed through that person's system into our own, through words of wisdom, or hands-on healing, and sometimes by raising our level of conscious awareness. When this happens our confidence, and more importantly our intuitive perception of what we need to work with, becomes a much more accurate statement within our life.

Karma is speeding up

A lot of people's karmic and soul contracts are being sped up. Now instead of waiting, say 60 years to achieve illumination, it can happen tomorrow! It is up to you! Basically your 'motors' are being revved up. You now have an opportunity to push your energy pattern into a new performance because the human race is moving forward as the planet itself raises its own vibration. This means a new beginning within our race.

A lot of Light workers are also acting as esoteric full stops. They are working with the slower frequency vibrations within the DNA of their body by going back into the blots on the landscape and actually confronting structural fear in whatever way that has manifested. Quite often the angle of entry which these soul aspects chose when they incarnated, created a set of circumstances where these fear energies could specifically be confronted.

The angle of entry which a soul aspect chooses is a very deliberate policy of linking into the biorhythms and geometrical mix of contracted energy from both Earth and the outer planets, physically, astrally and mentally. The soul aspect then slides its segmentations into this specific angle of entry. These segmentations are the vibratory notes under the general umbrella setting of desire which encourage the soul aspect to incarnate into this particular lifetime in order to work with those desires. These create a set of limitations within that lifetime which are called the point of occult pressure. Into this angle of entry come all the pressures which the soul has to work with during its physical incarnation which include place of birth, parents, focal point of society, plus the ground energies and planetary sound within the group unconscious.

The pattern of occult pressure which currently seems to be exhibiting itself more and more in society is child abuse. But if you look clairvoyantly at the karmic background behind the child who is being abused, quite often you find that the child was an abuser in some other life. So full circle has come about. At the same time, the child abuse now coming into public recognition inspires others to act through the intuitive wrongness of what is happening. The child therefore is working through its own karma by sacrificing itself to generate love and compassion from thousands of people who might not have radiated that love without the situation being brought to their attention in the form of a crisis within their society.

Many Light workers are also coming up to a point in their evolution where they can work consciously with the build-up of toxicity within the diseases from their ancestral family over many lifetimes. It is these thought forms which travel down the etheric nerve currents of body form. If a body is given back to the planet in the burial sequence, which is still relatively popular with the older generation, the thought form of the person who has died will carry on and pass into the younger generation within that family unit.

Whereas through the burning process of cremation, at least 75% of slow frequency thought forms of a negative kind are destroyed and cannot transfer themselves to those still alive. In this way ancestral karmic patterns can be broken.

By burning the physical body, the astral body has nothing to link into or hold it back. If you are clairvoyant you can see that cemeteries are psychic black spots. Quite often the astral shell of the departed person still sits over the shell of the decomposing physical body. By cremating the physical body, the astral body itself is broken free and can move on.

After physical death a person's awareness passes from the physical body to their astral shell. It normally takes three to ten days for the astral shell to raise the vibration of its astral rhythm and transfer its awareness into the higher mental states where it normally has a more permanent fixture. The astral shell then blows in the breeze of time and hangs in limbo with a degree of energy and information which is the residue left in the host body. This astral shell gradually disintegrates over a period of time, normally 25 years.

Within the astral levels, astral entities exist whose fundamental job is to clean up the pathways and byways of astral currents and astral outpourings. They do this by nibbling and eating the astral shells. A bit like hyenas they automatically gravitate towards them, and as they absorb the astral shells they in turn transmute the energy frequency of themselves.

At the moment, as a lot of people are dying through violent epics, the lower astral levels are full of these entities who are growing quite fat in the process of absorbing all the astral shells. At other times, when there is a shortage of astral shells, the larger entities eat the smaller ones, and in this way a definite containment occurs within the astral levels.

In more distant times, there were people in human form who were able to leave their bodies and take on the role of the angel of death. These people offered a service to guide those who died through the confusing astral levels into the mental planes where those of a higher vibration could meet them. In coming years, those who once undertook this role of the angel of death, will be physically re-encoded with the release mechanism to do the same again. They will then be able to once more help those dying pass over from the illusions of Earth life into the higher life.

The way this works is that when a person is physically near to death, one of the people who specialise as an angel of death can physically manifest into their space and lie by the side of them in the same room - although this is not necessary as it can be done astrally at a distance. Then as the person dies and drops their physical body, the angel of death will leave their physical body at the same time.

As they do this, the person who has died and who may be in trauma and shock through being 'kicked' out of their body whilst still wanting to hang on to it, can be reassured. The angel of death who is guiding the way can then take that person from the physical plane, through the astral planes and into the mental planes. This can happen two-ways as those in the higher planes who need to visit the physical plane in order to experience physical life for a short time can also take advantage of this service. They will do the equivalent of sleeping in the higher plane in order to come down into the physical plane, physically merge with the person who is dying, and then guide them up through the astral pathways.

This was once a death service readily accepted by those in the know and this will again come full circle as those who have played the role before will replay it, but this time in a much more efficient manner.

This will ensure that less people get stuck and earthbound than is the case at present. This is why large groups of people choose to die at the same time, during a natural disaster. As a group they can confront the new reality as you only need one person who knows the way home to guide a group of 50,000 into the higher vibratory patterns.

Occasionally a more evolved being who hasn't been on the Earth plane for some time, or who just wants to try the Earth plane as a brief one-off experience, will be guided down into the slower frequencies of physical life to act as an angel of death whilst at the same time trying out the physical body. So as the physical shell is left by the departing soul aspect and the physical body takes its last few breaths, the incoming visitor will nip into the body and try out the mechanism of physical coordination.

In this way, in the space of one night, an evolved soul might experiment with several hundred bodies until it has the appropriate feel of the situation and enough confidence to undertake a proper incarnation. This type of assessment is not normal as most people have signed up for the full epic in Earth lives. But as the evolution of the planet is rising, those who have been external observers are becoming more adventurous and far more curious. And this curiosity has to be appeased.

As you start to understand this pattern of moving on when people die you can move into the reality where you see that death is just a grand releaser. And that death as the end is just an illusion. Once you understand this, you can let go of all your fears of death and what you think it brings, and will then realise the massive opportunity, and the joy, harmony and power you have down here on Earth.

Opportunist karma

Opportunist karma means taking advantage of frequency crossover currents, both positive and negative. Opportunist karma of a positive nature is being in the right place at the right time, implementing the reward mechanism which comes in at that point to enhance your awareness. Opportunist karma of a negative nature is being in the right place at the wrong time and getting penalised by having to work through karma of a negative nature. This applies not only to personal karma, but to group and planetary karma as well.

Normally when an individual karmic contract has either come to a close or has a degree of leeway, that person comes into a position where, karmically, they are almost neutral. They then have free-will to operate in a very total and fundamental way. As a result their higher self will impregnate the physical personality vehicle with a series of opportunist choices and it will indicate - although this indication might be subtle - what opportunities should be accepted.

Your intuition will always offer a strong interpretation of decisions which need to be made. But your intuition has to run the gauntlet of any emotional and intellectual patterns which will add their quota of what they also need at that time. This usually creates a degree of confusion unless you are into meditation on an ongoing basis and are clearly connected to your higher self. The idea is to intuitively pick up the leading and appropriate choice. This is normally the first impression you get. Then, by having enough love and faith to implement that intuitive impression and override any slow frequency impressions set up by old enforced habits and judgements, opportunist karma will be of a positive nature.

The effect of opportunist karma is to widen the flexibility of opportunities as they come into your life. If opportunist karma is not used wisely, the spontaneous karma created in that moment will ensure you have further lives to balance the new karma which has just been set up.

Karmic diseases

Karma can also be a cause of disease. Right now we have a new pattern of diseases coming in through the mutation of group diseases and group viruses such as AIDS, cancer and the many immune deficiency diseases.

AIDS is a magnetic pattern, a group virus, a karmic virus in fact, which only attaches itself to people of a certain frequency. A lot of these people have a background in the Lemurian days. In those days the heart centres of Lemurians were stimulated, but because of the evolution at that time, instead of building that energy up, it went down to the sexual centre. This created a disorientation which resulted in the cultivation of peculiar sexual practices. These people are now incarnating back into a higher rhythm to deal with this energy once again, and to work with this karma through AIDS.

But the AIDS pattern is mutating and the definition given to it is no longer accurate. Autopsies of AIDS victims, especially in America, are proving that about 35% of the people who are being diagnosed as dying with AIDS haven't got that virus at all.

The AIDS epidemic of course came about by human experimentation, caused by darker manipulation. The same applies to the atomic energy industry which is also dark-oriented. This is why they are basically destructive and why atomic stations generating electricity will disappear in years to come.

This will come about as the vibratory factors within the rhythm of humanity rise. The need to anchor the energy-producing vibration in the atomic stations will become totally unnecessary when our intuitive thoughts recognise that electricity can be generated in a much safer way than through the abuse of splitting the atom.

Cancer is another karmic disease prevalent at the moment. In Great Britain one in four people now have cancer. In Australia one in three people have skin cancer. This is occurring as the rhythm of energies in the planet are getting lighter through the additional pattern of high frequency female energy coming into the planet from the sun. The solar devas are in the right female magnetic polarity. Humanity is in the wrong masculine magnetic polarity. Therefore as these higher frequency female energies flow through the etheric and astral levels and impact into the slower frequency male polarity within the human race, cancer is created depending on how much self-healing mechanism a person has.

A lot of people who have cancer have had past lives in old occult days. A lot have actually been abusers and through cancer they are now working with that karma to speed up their rhythm. A lot of people with cancer are also sleeping over geopathic stress lines and are actually drawing that negative geopathic stress into their physical body. When they die a lot of that negative energy dies with them, which is an interesting focus.

Cancer is a complicated pattern with a great deal of karmic interference and a lot of karmic alignment. The cancer frequency is quite high from a karmic rhythm point of view which is why a lot of healers can't work with cancer victims, as they can't work with that frequency. So in its own way the cancer virus is culling a lot of people who need to move on fairly quickly. But most Light workers, provided they are in a point of balance within themselves, do not need to take on cancer in any shape or form.

ME also runs parallel to the cancer and AIDS virus. It is another karmic virus from the inner planes although ME is a variety of different components rather that one specific virus. In a physical sense, ME is brought about by immune deficiency. It is reflective of a long-standing abuse of the physical body which has not had the right balance of vitamins, minerals, amino-acids and trace elements. Therefore the overall vibratory package of that person's diet, even though it might look adequate, is not providing the healthy vibratory pattern the body needs. Chemical fertilisers, additives and antibiotics also add to that abuse and further destroy the immune system. The vibration in the physical body then drops. And if the karmic background is right, the physical body offers the ME viruses on the inner planes an opportunity to push down because the resistance within the physical body is now so low.

People with ME also have a sympathetic reaction with magnetic energy. This magnetic energy is formed, not only through the electrification of society - from televisions, radio waves, electrical apparatus and so on - but also through the magnetic thought structures of large corporate organisations who are working with a low vibratory pattern.

Quite often the vibration of these organisations has been infiltrated by astral entities who are bound up within their own sphere of influence. These entities maintain the state of play to ensure that slow frequency energy is generated on an ongoing basis as this is their own particular source of enriched food. If a person with ME works with any form of electrical apparatus, the magnetic energy from this sticks within their chakra centres creating additional structural distress.

With physical, astral and karmic diseases, there is a new pattern emerging where each disease is mutating and becoming more solid in a physical sense. They are manifesting a specific intelligence. Natural law has been abused by society, and instead of working side by side with natural laws in an holistic way we have been dumping a lot of poisons and magnetic input into the viruses which have damaged their intuitive development. Viruses have gone along with this, as this was a necessary experimentation for the human family. But as humanity's contract within the planet is now changing, the human contract with viruses is being renegotiated. Viruses are now obligated to evolve far quicker than humanity is ready for, and new strains are manifesting which will speed up the karmic contracts within the third dimensional energy fields. Therefore the medical profession and drug industry will soon reach a pattern where the way they are thinking and operating will be totally ineffective.

A lot of humanity has a total misinterpretation of what diseases are. They are a form of communication with the devic side of life and the etheric current of the planet, especially in relation to ley lines. These energy points were once capitalised on by humanity when we had the necessary information within our awareness.

Right now, viruses are doing humanity a favour. Those who will direct the holistic programme in the future are already beginning to develop the capacity to telepathically communicate and translate what these viruses, and virus states are telling us. In the past, diseases were also activated by the dark lodge and by the UFO programme. That karmic input has sown seeds which are now demanding a repayment, and that repayment has to be met by those who adhered to these darker principles and who are karmically too heavy.

One of the main causes of disease mutation is that the sun is going through a polarity of sun spots - magnetic out-plosions and implosions. This affects not only physical life but etheric and mental life as well. Therefore viruses and bacteria are having magnetic stimulation applied to them creating a build-up of negative energy in a way that was not possible before these sun spots were activated.

The moon, which brings in the Mother Goddess influence, is stimulating in a very specific way certain chakra centres within the various forms of awareness on Earth - be they viruses, bacteria, animals, vegetables or humans. The moon is generally a very positive point of balance, especially for those who are following the spiritual path. This positive balance will continue until February 1997 when the moon will go through a major change, and a different type of manifesting energy will be self-apparent.

* * *

Karma And Karmic Diseases: meditations

64. Meditation to practise looking at karmic packages

First develop the habit of assessing the negativity within any vehicle you are travelling in, be it an aeroplane or a car. You do this by visualising that vehicle as having a chakra system.

Then intuitively look at that chakra system and locate the hara, the point of balance within that vehicle. If that point of balance is in the sexual chakra centre or the lower part of the solar plexus, this means there is a build-up of negative energy which will, through natural law, externalise in the form of an accident.

If you travel by plane, and want to assess the probability of the aeroplane going safely from A to B, you need to also cultivate a feel, a clairvoyant impression of the frequency within the third eye of the people travelling on the flight with you.

To do this, look at a fellow passenger in the departure lounge and visualise their third eye as having three filters, one behind the other. The filter at the front represents the 'now' of the moment you are in. The second filter, the one in the middle, represents the next seven days starting from the moment in time at which you do this exercise. The third filter, behind the first two, represents the time scale of the full life contract which is available to that person.

Now visualise the rear filter as a clock with one hand. To explain how this clock works: at birth when a person is born, the full scope of this clock represents the full scope of the time allocated in that lifetime. From the minute the person is born, the hand on this clock starts to move clockwise. As the hand moves round, it clocks up white energy. By the time the person dies, the whole clock will have filled up with white energy.

So for example, if a person is 45 and the time allocated to them for this lifetime is 60 years, then their clock on the third filter of their third eye will have clocked up three-quarters of white energy, with one quarter still left. The first two filters will reflect the now and the next seven day period of what is karmically being invoked within their space for the week ahead.

Likewise, for a six-year-old child with a short life contract, who has lived three-quarters of their current life span and is contracted to die at nine years old, the clock on the third filter of their third eye would be three-quarters full of white energy.

Whereas if the third filter of a six-year-old child had only clocked up the equivalent of 10 minutes, this would tell you that they have a long life ahead of them, and will die around 60 years of age.

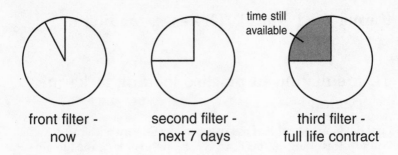

front filter -
now

second filter -
next 7 days

time still
available

third filter -
full life contract

Third eye filters for a person
aged 45 years with a 60 year contract

It is necessary to remember that the rear filter in the third eye mechanism of a small child will appear to go quicker than the rear third eye filter of an adult, since a child's nervous system works more within the etheric and astral patterns of energy rather than within the physical mass. As the child gets older, the representation within their third eye clock will reflect this to the observer.

Using this point of reference, look at the passengers who will be travelling on the same aeroplane. If they all have no time left on the third filters of their third eye clocks, or just a very small proportion left representing a few hours, you will know that through the combination of magnetic and karmic energy, the plane is going to crash!

Opportunist karma is also reflected within the 'now' on the first filter, and within the seven day period of the second filter. In any

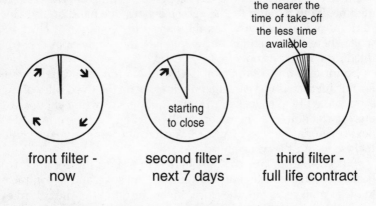

front filter -
now

second filter -
next 7 days

starting
to close

the nearer the
time of take-off
the less time
available

third filter -
full life contract

Third eye filters for a person buying an
aeroplane ticket - the plane is going to crash

one lifetime you will have many occasions when, for different reasons, you have an opportunity to die and leave your Earth contract. So you might have 15 to 16 possible death sequences in this Earth life. Depending on your evolution and the karmic charges portrayed within your group and family network, you will have the opportunity to reap the karmic experiences necessary which will influence the death sequence you choose. This is why incoming soul aspects try to choose the right parents who will be protective and understanding to give them maximum opportunities for the experiences required.

As we all have conscious choice, you can affect the destiny of people on that flight by invoking a response, by choosing not to go on the flight yourself, or by saying that you feel there is something wrong with the plane.

People can of course be in the right place at the wrong time. If the clock which represents the now on the first filter is fully closed, the amount of white still on the clock on the second filter (seven days hence) and the third filter (the rest of their life's contract available to them), will tell you if the person has in fact got an option to stay on Earth any longer.

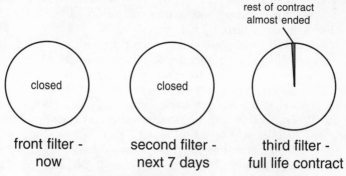

Third eye filters for a person in an aeroplane just before it crashes

If any of those people choose not to go on the flight, then the clock on the third filter of their third eye clock will go backwards as their time on Earth is being extended by this karmic interaction.

If this work is new to you, you can practise this by physically looking in a mirror and intuitively peering at your own third eye! Then visualise the front filter and see how much white time has been clocked up on the clock of the now. Then look at the other two filters behind that. By intuitively working with this analogy you can develop your own working dialogue based on your intuitive assessment of the length of linear time available to life forms around you, be it plant, animal or human.

CHAPTER 15
WINGS

Wings are in essence energy swirls representing the male and female energy input. They are a means of identification and have a shape, colour and texture.

A person of angelic form who is part of the 'mind of one' will have large wings, open and spread out. If someone with an angelic focus is resting or hiding, their wings will be closed and folded flat - just like a butterfly resting on a flower.

It is the sulky old souls who haven't consciously woken up to who they really are, who sometimes feel intimidated and try to hide. They subconsciously close their wings and give off a signal which says, "I'm really an ordinary human being." But their wings, even though closed, still act as a reference point and give off a very strong signal. When another angelic person recognises their true essence and says, "Hello, you beautiful angel," their wings automatically become activated and 'ting', they pop open.

That person trying to hide might still insist, "No, I'm not angelic. I'm just human." They refuse to hear the real message because, if they admit to their true essence, they have to start working with their soul purpose, and this can sometimes be quite difficult for a lot of people.

But with the demands of the new energies coming in, and the need for us all to wake up, we are now constantly activating each other's wings, until we say, "OK, I won't hide any longer. I am ready."

If you think of yourself as angelic, then you are immortal. If you are immortal you can't die. Once you start to believe this as part of your awareness you lose all your fears and release yourself from limitation, and when you move beyond limitation you can work in thousands of different ways for the benefit of humanity down here, which is part of your contract.

Wings should be balanced but quite often they are not, depending on the input and the angle of entry during incarnation, and which of the subtle bodies the individual is currently working with. One large and one small wing indicates that the person is out of unison.

If you think of the subtle bodies, counting from the soul downwards, each of them will be a combination of male and female essences which have been collected and collated by the individual soul aspect within the cooperation framework of soul families. The individual soul aspect manifesting in physical matter will have access to these various alignments which are part of the latent desire that needs to be dispersed in relation to the male and female experiences it has collected and collated, but not balanced.

This will be reflected in the type of wings the subtle bodies have in relation to each other. These wings hold energy charges which will have either a balancing or imbalancing effect within the totality of the experiences reflected within the wings of the physical person as they move and live in the now. Therefore with Light workers, the style of their wings will be a presentation of the spontaneous karma currently being worked through.

As a person evolves, their wings will change from a grosser nature, moving through the various spirals of energy, becoming more refined, more gorgeous in their temple and essence, and more balanced in relation to the male and female experiences which eventually have to be balanced.

In this way wings are the totality of spiritual purpose, held in bondage by the individual soul aspect who is working through the permutations of the person currently in physical matter. As that person becomes more open to their higher purpose, their wing shape, texture and colour, and the sound coming from them will change and evolve on an ongoing upward spiral.

Wings can be seen clairvoyantly within the gross physical unit of a person, or within the alignment of the more subtle bodies. When viewing a person clairvoyantly one will tend to see their right wing representing the male union and their left wing representing the female union. If the wings are out of tune with each other, this will be reflected by their different shape, size or frequency vibration. So the shape of the right and left wings tells its own story about the segmentations of male and female essences which might be vibrating a bit too slow within those wings. This will give a healer information which can help them to know what needs to be worked on within the karmic containment of that person.

When a soul aspect incarnates, that child will have a wing formation representing what is to come. As they begin to work more specifically with karmic cycles of a definite nature, and the karmic cycles of the planet and the group, the dominant input of energy from a higher subtle body might take place. Their wings, which might be relatively small on one day, may start to get quite large as that person works through the permutations the soul requires according to its spiritual contract.

As this pattern takes place - and it is a normal aspect of inner plane behaviour - one tends to see people's wings go through a permutation where they lose their initial colour and become more specifically focused. Pale green symbolises soul development. Pale green wings therefore indicate that the person is working in close cooperation with their soul purpose, that they are orientated in a very specific way, and the input of their soul in its totality is quite near to that person.

If those pale green wings started to get flecks of gold, and the gold content gradually increased until the wings became mainly gold, this would show that the person is now working with the higher spiritual input in relation to group purpose.

Light blue or dark blue wings normally reflect a healing focus which that person is bringing through. When healers give healing, they condense energy in a very precise way. Their wings reflect this manifestation of energy, taking on a very condensed colour corresponding to the package of energy they are bringing through. When the healing session is finished, that condensed colour fades and their wings go back to their normal shade of blue.

If during a healing session a healer rectifies a karmic imbalance between him or her and the person being healed, the shape of their wings will become more focused, more specifically aligned, and may take on a particular shape. This will give the observer on the inner and outer planes a much better understanding of whether they have accomplished their purpose. If they have, their new wing shape will become part of their reality and give a clairvoyant reference point as to where they are within their evolution.

Silver wings are something akin to radio waves. Their shape, colour and texture offer a unique setting - like a specific television channel - and their reception is quite precise. A person with silver wings is therefore ripe for telepathic interchange with all life forms both on the inner and outer planes. Silver wings also indicate that the person's subtle network of bodies are polarised in such a way that the solar logos* can talk through them. As silver wings take on a specific attunement they have access, whether consciously or unconsciously, to extraterrestrial formations and offer the opportunity for extraterrestrial dialogue with those of an evolved nature.

Seeing wings

Some angelic winged beings in human form are not human at all. When I look clairvoyantly at their akashic record, I see they are of a different life form. These beings are planet hoppers who can travel to different planets during their Earth time as they have the capacity to be in many places at once.

The colour and shape of their wings and what you intuitively feel as you focus on the vibration of the wings will tell you whether the winged being has a spiritual focus or is just masquerading as such.

Someone resonating with Light will have large wings akin to the shape and texture of a butterfly. The wings of less evolved beings, or those masquerading as something more evolved, or mischievous elementals will be considerably smaller and more bat-like. They will be clearly defined, fairly dark in colour with sharper designs to them. They also tend to be fairly thick as they hold onto gross energy which represents the elemental or dominant animal side of their life. Some may even have very stumpy little wings only a few inches (few cm) in size.

The only exception is if someone well developed in a negative sequence has followed a particular evolutionary pathway; their wings will be large, about six or seven feet (1.8-2.1m), intensely black and fairly sinister. The feelings associated with them will be of extreme coldness and discomfort. Most people who first see one of these beings might also feel panic creeping over them. But seeing such a being is extremely rare as they normally work through intermediaries. Unless you dispose of their intermediaries it is very unlikely they will come to pay you a house-call. These beings of darkness with very large wings tend to be the focal point of interest of the spiritual hierarchy and those on the inner planes who work with them in a speciality role.

If you think you can't see wings, that is a very limited thought. Your expectancy wants the picture-show first as that fits in with your belief system. But the only reason you can't physically see them at the moment is because you are programmed to see in a different way, and your physical vision is a narrow band. Even if you can't see wings, you can feel them. Feeling is a high frequency vibration.

When someone explains something you don't understand, you often say, "Oh yes, I see." What you mean is not physically seeing, but sensing, understanding. When you realise this, and open yourself to sensing, and feeling within other levels of reality - and this applies to everything including wings - and as that understanding permeates your being, you will start to open up to these new levels of awareness. More information will then come in as you will no longer be limiting your expectancy with shape and form. Your etheric vision will start to open up and you will start to see auras, wings, and a whole new level of reality.

CHAPTER 16
ENERGY PIRATES

Energy pirates are little beings, little entities - like opportunist businessmen on the inner planes. They come down to Earth to snaffle any spare energy they can grab and sell it to the highest bidder on the inner planes where it is a valued commodity.

We term energy pirates little entities but they are, in essence, intelligent life forms with a personality who operate in a multi-dimensional capacity. They use the astral planes as a focal point to anchor their presence, then flow into astral time and linear time, grabbing the desired Earth energy from there.

They particularly love large group healing sessions held at fairs such as the Mind-Body-Spirit Festival in London. At these venues there is a lot of healing energy passed down from healers that is quite often not accepted by the people being healed. Consciously these people are saying 'yes' to the healing session, but subliminally may be rejecting it for a whole variety of reasons.

This healing energy floats around in a latent form. Energy pirates, who circle around like esoteric sharks, absorb that spare energy as they participate in the bounty which is freely available.

When you understand this, you can manipulate the structure of energy at these fairs in a positive way. To do this, you first of all ask your higher self if it is intuitively right for you to take action. If the answer is 'yes', bear in mind that the spiritual hierarchy will only respond to direct introductions. So invoke and invite the angels of love and healing to join you in a total way. As they come in, their presence automatically denies access to the energy pirates. The angels will then use the spare energy in whatever way you have asked. If you ask them to use the energy for the highest good, this energy can be used in a positive way without any loss at all and this spare healing energy is usually placed in the 'cooking pot' of a new planet being formed.

In the same way, if you give an individual healing, bringing energy down from a high frequency point and passing it into your client's system, and part of that person doesn't really want that healing, your healing energy is not going to be accepted. It will simply bounce off their aura and float around, free and available to any energy pirates who might be close by. The healing angels do not normally come into an individual healing session. They usually only come into group settings as it may be part of the healing contract for both the healer and the client to become aware of energy loss. This can bring about a change in consciousness which is very useful.

If a person comes to you for healing, and you intuitively feel that person doesn't really want to accept that healing, take personal responsibility and tell them what the interchange of healing energy actually implies. Likewise, if someone wants to give you a healing and you intuitively feel that this is wrong, don't take that healing. Because any energy interchange is a form of active interference, since the awareness of the person into whom the energy is going will automatically be altered.

Elementals

Little astral entities, and sometimes a whole sequence of semi-intelligent and intelligent life forms, also sit in a waiting process just up from the physical levels waiting for those who, through curiosity, ignorance, or through a deliberate effort are trying to have some form of astral communication.

These 'little brothers' are the beings who normally respond to people playing with a ouija board. Using a glass and the alphabet in this way is very much like blindly dialling a number, and whoever happens to be passing will pop in to say 'hello'.

The beings who respond to this type of call and masquerade as guides are not normally very evolved. In the process of giving answers, they will try to evoke a response, in an energy sense, by tapping into the belief system of the people using the ouija board. This usually encourages a drop in vibration, moving those people into a different vibrational pattern which these astral entities can then tap into and feed off as a form of intuitive food.

As a Light worker you should definitely not be using a ouija board to contact your guides. But if you are channelling or receiving guidance in any other form, it is always useful to challenge and test the person coming through to ensure that you are only tuning into the highest vibration. The meditation for this is Meditation 40, Chapter 8, *Meeting Your Guides.*

The elementals of fire, earth, air and water are also fairly low evolutionary spirals of energy which tend to operate mainly on the mental and emotional levels. They can manifest as maladjusted patterns of energy and can often be fairly mischievous, especially when they come in to play with animals and children.

These elementals can evoke a wicked sense of humour within children who might, for example, tell you that their 'little friend' just jumped in the bath with them, as water splashes all over the bathroom floor. Young children who are very open and receptive can even be tempted to wander off at times with these little friends.

These energy beings respond to the dominant vibration within the essence of the child, whether that is negative or positive. So when these elementals come into contact with children, if a child is carrying a lot of negative energy as part of their polarity, or as part of their destiny, that negative energy can be activated at an age which is too early for the child to handle within their nervous system. When this happens, it can manifest as a lot of behavioural problems.

If you have children who talk to invisible friends, or who are constantly misbehaving, it is always wise to intuitively look around astrally, to see if there are any energy sources around them, and if so, whether they are positive, middle of the road, or definitely negative. You can use the intuitive traffic lights to ask this, and they will give you an accurate response.

The best exercise you can use for children is the meditation to trawl negative energy. In this instance you would stand behind the child, and as you project your triangle of Light, visualise this becoming a large net which you throw over their head. You trawl this net down their body from their head to their feet. In this way you are trawling their whole astral space. Then give anything negative which you have caught in your net to the large pair of white hands which represent the Cosmic Christ. Variation 2 of Meditation 44, Chapter 10, *Dealing With Negative Energies*, explains this in full and gives the affirmation to invoke a protective sequence around the child.

A child who is having trouble sleeping can be helped if a spider plant (chlorophytum) is placed in their bedroom. This removes trauma from their third eye, feet and finger tips. It also helps to generate a positive field of energy around the child, especially during the baby's first six months when their nervous system is beginning to grow.

You can also place a three-pointed star over your front door, and especially over the door to the child's room. This star vibrates within elemental activity, and by focusing your awareness on the three-pointed star, and bringing it up to its highest vibration - you can do this by putting on your Light body and projecting your triangle of Light to charge it up - you deny access to any elementals trying to come in.

It is definitely the elemental folk you have got to look out for! Occasionally alternative life forms, such as devas and elementals, consciously choose to incarnate to try out the animal kingdom. But when they do, they quite often get caught up in the reincarnation cycle and can't revert back to elemental form - they remember how they got in but can't get out, like a lobster caught in a lobster pot.

When the soul of that elemental then moves its evolution upwards within the reincarnation cycle from animal life into human form, their vibration remains very animal-like, and that human being will be more animal than human. This is always reflected in their eyes.

As their evolution is different, they can make extremely treacherous friends in human physical form. They are usually totally non-ethical in their pattern and tend to abuse energy in a number of different ways. If you have clairvoyant focus you can tap into their heart chakra, look at the structural energy around them and the shape of their wings. You will then see a much less evolved form with a very slow vibratory charge, even though it has a human body. If your clairvoyant focus is not yet developed you may have an intuitive feeling of wrongness, a smell, a sense that offends, or a definite feeling of anger. But the best way to recognise them is through their eyes. Their eyes will be hard, unfriendly and somewhat evil.

There are also various levels of awareness on the inner planes where negative entities of a very powerful nature reside. These negative entities are preprogrammed to selectively look for, and target, Light workers who represent their opposition. What they try to do is impregnate you with a seed that will lie dormant and flower at a time of great opportunity - the idea is to ensure that they neutralise you and stop you moving forward. It is like giving you a permanent limp when you need to race like mad. It makes life very difficult!

So there is this quantum chess game going on, on the inner and outer planes, between these energy pirates and your guides. But your guides can only help to a degree because they are actively bound to follow your freedom of will in relation to astral, as well as physical life. They have got to work within the permutations of your life and your karma.

Human energy pirates

People can also feed off your energy and drain you. They can do this when talking to you on the telephone or link into you through writing you a letter, as well as physically meeting you. I am sure you all know those people who come to you feeling low or depressed, and then after chatting to you go away feeling great but leaving you feeling drained!

Sometimes it is OK to let this happen, but sometimes karmically it is not. If someone is being lazy, and just soaking up your energy rather than constructively dealing with what is going on within themselves, then it is appropriate for you to block that transfer of energy.

There are many exercises in this book to help you create a protective sequence around you, and to help you reject cordings which are sent out to you. Allow your intuition to guide you to the meditation which is right for you, then practise that meditation so that when you come into an encounter with a person who is trying to drain your energy, you will immediately and spontaneously know how to protect yourself.

* * *

Energy Pirates: meditations

There are no specific meditations for this chapter, but meditations from previous chapters, as detailed below, can be used to deal with energy pirates.

How to test your guides - Meditation 40, Chapter 8, *Meeting Your Guides*

How to cleanse and protect children affected by elementals - variation 2 of the trawling meditation, Meditation 44, Chapter 10, *Dealing With Negative Energies*

How to create a protective sequence around you and to reject cordings and negative thought forms which might be trying to feed off your energy - intuitively choose from Meditations 56, 57, 58, 60, 61, Chapter 14, *Barnacles And Thought Forms*

CHAPTER 17
HEALING WORK

Healing is speeding up generally - time is an illusion! So don't get into the pattern where you feel you have to do 20-minute healing sessions per person, because it is no longer necessary. If your healing sessions have always taken 20 minutes you can now speed this up to five or six minutes, working through the top of the head rather than working through the emotional or intellectual pattern of the body.

It also depends on what you want to do. Sometimes you may want to use crystals or music within your healing session, or you may want to balance the chakras - take them out, pull out the splinters, put them back in! - so just follow your own dialogue and recognise that you are now moving into a different pattern of healing.

With absent healing it is exactly the same. Everything is speeding up. If someone comes to you for a healing you are automatically corded to them. This cording happens with all the people you meet or are connected with. So if 1,000 people come to you for healing, whether through writing or physically turning up on your doorstep, all you have to do is think of Light coming down into the top of your head, flowing through your body and if you are feeling happy and in tune with yourself, then all this Light will go out through the cordings and all those 1,000 people will get exactly what they need, from an absent healing point of view.

The only limitations you currently have are the ones you accept as being your reality at this time. If you can recognise and accept that in essence you haven't any limitation, then your healing energy can go out to restore harmony in a far greater way.

As you heal, it is good practice to intuitively feel into the vibration of your client's aura. Within the aura of someone with cancer, for example, you can feel the vibration of sand paper in an area about three feet (1m) above their head, or over the place where the cancer is. A person who has a drug addiction, or someone on medication, will have an auric vibration which feels like mucus. As you open yourself to feeling or sensing the vibrational pattern within auras, a new pattern of awareness will come in. Meditation 65, at the end of this chapter, will help you to start feeling the different vibrations of auras.

A lot of people's auras have an outer pattern almost like a windscreen covered with tiny dead insects. When you give a healing session this is stripped off. Below that are the softer aspects with all the tiny thought form implants. These also have to be removed. Some of them might be willing to give up and some who are quite large might not want to leave at all!

Thought forms have a degree of intelligence. Some are fairly flexible and some are not. Some are particularly stupid and will not recognise the urgency of moving when their position is threatened during a healing session as you start to strip them away. They just hang on pretending, like an ostrich hiding its head in the sand, that nothing is going to happen.

Some thought forms might be extremely slow. They may take two weeks to travel 12 inches (30cm) across the floor, and may find it almost impossible to leave the place where they are feeding on a certain vibration. Other thought forms move very, very quickly. The average quick thought form has the capacity to leap about 60 feet (18m) from one area to another in order to resonate with the appropriate vibration it needs.

Sometimes you may have a bit of a fight with thought forms who are stubborn. "I'm not leaving," they will say! Sometimes thought forms will combine together and you may see them merging in a corner, almost like a big blob. Then they try to hunt around your aura looking for any weakness to evoke any form of fear you might have. So if you don't like spiders, they might manifest as a nine foot (3m) spider with big red eyes, trying to create a response from you. If you send out any fear, which will be slow frequency energy, that vibration just feeds the thought forms manifesting as a giant spider, and they get stronger.

With any thought form the first thing to remember is that whatever you see is an illusion - especially if it is of a slow frequency vibration. Laughter and love will always transmute them, but obviously you have to have enough love for yourself in order to face them calmly and lovingly, and take them on.

If thought forms are released from your client's aura during a healing session, your room will fill up with toxic energy. Are you awake and aware of this? Do you consciously consider what happens to that energy at the end of the day? Where does it go? Those of you who are intuitively aware will already know this negative energy has to be disposed of after each session. Quite often Light workers who are healing on an energy level will already have some 'little friends' who have been introduced into their environment by their guides. In my case these little friends, these elemental thought forms, are something akin to sewer rats. These elementals manifest in this form in order to specifically eat up and transmute the toxic levels released during healing sessions. But as they feed on that negative energy they go through a process of mutation and change into something far more beautiful. This mutation is very much like the grub changing into a butterfly.

It may take several Earth days for these elementals to eat up and dispose of all the negative waste left over at the end of each working day. Although they will be ever so pleased to eat as much negative energy as you give them, it is at times very necessary for you to cleanse the room and trawl the negative energy yourself - especially if you are giving a lot of healing or holding regular workshops in your home - so that any residue energy can be disposed of quicker. By making a deliberate effort in this way, you also strengthen your own energy system, plus your perception, understanding and awareness of this work.

By lifting negative energy to the vibratory sequence where the spiritual hierarchy live and offering it to them, the spiritual hierarchy and their Light agents have more flexibility in dealing with the various life forms found within the universe and the various life streams. They can then negotiate freely in other streams of life. Although from time to time the spiritual hierarchy will deliberately take energy necessary for their need, they have much greater flexibility when that energy is offered to them through the conscious awareness of their Light agents who are in physical form. For them to capture that energy themselves, they have to place themselves within a denser frequency vibration which is very unpleasant for them. When someone, such as yourself, is already at that vibration and capable of pushing the vibration of slow frequency energy, in a controlled way, up to a higher vibration, this saves the spiritual hierarchy a great deal of effort and gives them the energy in a more advantageous way. Meditation 44, Chapter 10, *Dealing With Negative Energies*, fully explains how to trawl and cleanse a room, offering the energy up to the spiritual hierarchy.

Do bear in mind that all life forms have the right to exist and healing is a form of active interference. So if you are taking any form of slow frequency energy from someone's aura which might be causing them problems, the problematic energy might be just as uncomfortable in that person's aura. If it is a thought form which is vibrating at a slow frequency level those on the inner planes will be motivated to place that energy into a system where it can evolve and grow. So the grosser thought forms and entities are normally placed on a newly formed planet. It is what I term the esoteric cooking pot. As the 'soup comes to the boil' the ingredients needed for evolution can be added. Some universes are negatively charged in a very total way. Some are positively charged. Some universes will demand 99.9% negative energy to start the ball rolling before they can move into a place of balance where Light can come in. Other universes work in reverse. So the 'esoteric soup' and experimental work carry on indefinitely.

Absent healing

Absent healing is a form of energy charge which flows into the space of the person being healed and automatically gravitates towards the thought forms and subliminal patterns which are creating the distress and which may be exhibiting as physical, emotional or mental disharmony.

The healing energy charge will normally wrap itself around those thought forms and remove them by contracting them back into the space of the healer who will transmute that energy according to the method they have developed, intuitively rather than consciously.

Most Light workers are programmed to heal from birth to death. If it is in your vibratory contract to heal - whether you do this in a structured way through hands-on healing or just casually passing someone in the street - you will automatically attract negative energy from the organs in their body and absorb it into the organs in your body. You then transmute that negativity within your organs. So if your kidneys have been chatting up the kidneys of other people for some time and you haven't been efficiently disposing of the accumulated magnetic waste - and psychic and astral waste - then obviously your kidneys will sooner, rather than later, talk to you about that.

If you have a genetic weakness this will also manifest into the physical plane as magnetic waste builds up within your body. And physical problems, as you know, only come when you have a need to change.

If you do a lot of healing, your clothes will also become magnetised with the negative energy taken on during a healing session and will 'burn out'. So this is always a good excuse to buy some new clothes! Nylon and synthetic fabrics are particularly good at holding onto a negative charge as they absorb a lot of static energy, so never wear clothes made of synthetic material during a healing session.

Healing contracts

The impulses of the various subtle bodies which make up the network between the physical personality and the soul should, in theory, be in a nice straight line. Quite often the shape is very much like a bent banana. This is an indication of displaced energy which causes the curve. This displaced energy often builds up like an abscess, and this abscess will quite often become the focal point for astral viruses or karmic viruses to link into, causing chaos within the subtle anatomy of the physical and astral bodies.

When there is a build-up of negative energy which has been collecting for some time, the soul - observing the need to release that - will formulate a plan of action. Therefore one of the more enlightened soul aspects will be magnetically drawn back to Earth specifically to rectify this imbalance and the build-up on the inner planes will be given to that aspect. This incarnation becomes a very special life and as that soul aspect incarnates it collects all the unfinished data of its soul aspects in total. This creates a very strong desire to be of service. During their life they attract a great deal of structural suffering to bring to the boil a number of different abscesses so that the curvature and imbalance can be dealt with and rectified.

A lot of Light workers are currently doing this. Not in a suffering mode but in a service mode. Sometimes the need to be of service dominates to the exclusion of everything else and they become out of balance within themselves as they have an overriding desire to manifest the energies needed through service in order to release the karmic burden they are carrying for their group. This can give those who physically work with them a very bumpy ride!

Healing is usually chosen as the service focus because when these people give healing their energy moves up through the levels of the subtle bodies to achieve a package of high frequency healing energy which is brought down through their physical body.

As they start to demand this high frequency healing energy, and move up through those levels - which are something akin to streams of energy around the planet - the imbalance in the network between them and their soul can be worked on through the vehicle of their own physical body. This forces a realignment to take place.

This also happens every time we give a healing - and every time we meditate. We move our essence up, and if we are carrying a lot of negative energy on the subtle planes, then by going through the diversity of these energy fields we collect and bring down that negative energy into our physical body. This forces us to bring about a change within our awareness, through the problems created by this negativity within our body, be that emotional, mental or physical.

This is why, quite often, healers who might be very efficient at healing others, succumb to something on a physical level which we might regard as abnormal for a healer. This might be terminal cancer or some other disease. But during the process of that disease, they actually attract any toxic negative energy still on the subtle planes which has not been released, bringing it into their physical body, and through their death they can release that imbalance and dispose of it.

New healing energy

Most Light workers' self-healing mechanism is not working very well. In fact, on a scale of one to 100, the self-healing mechanism of many Light workers is only at one or two! This means you are not generating enough energy to heal yourself, which is why a lot of Light workers are currently suffering from health problems relating to immune system deficiency.

A lot of healing at the moment doesn't touch or activate the immune system. But a new type of healing pattern is coming in which will give you the authority to move forward and raise your vibration in a much more specific way. You will then find your immune system gets very strong in relation to physical and karmic viruses.

This new healing pattern was implemented into the physical realm on December 25th 1992. It is specifically linked into the vibratory pattern of Avataric energy and therefore into the Avatars currently in physical incarnation. This has the effect of quickly feeding energy into the healer's solar plexus from where it is spontaneously pushed into their heart. This energy manifests as a more efficient and ferocious form of healing which does not need to be maintained within the healer's nervous system as it did before.

In this way healing can be sped up into multidimensional time rather than with the old expectancy of third dimensional time. Fourth dimension energy can then dominate the healing apparatus 98% of the time.

Healers who have earned the right to this healing can now be fed directly by undiluted Avataric energy and can meet the Avatars in this way. The self-healing mechanism of those who have made it to this point of efficiency through the necessary preparatory work can also be stimulated directly by Avataric energy.

The second wave of Light workers - the children who have been incarnating over the last seven years - are coming in on a new healing ray for a much more specific and specialised role. They will be able to raise their self-healing mechanism up to about 40%, and the karmic and astral viruses currently causing so many people problems will not be able to infiltrate their energy system, be it on a subtle or physical level. So the type of energy they can bring through will be a lot more flexible and powerful than most adult Light workers are bringing through at this time.

This new type of healing energy will be self-apparent because it will give spontaneous healing. A healer might currently give healing sessions over a long period of time, maybe several months or even a year, to someone seriously ill before their healing is complete. But the new healing energy coming in will bring about an immediate effect - and someone seriously ill may be healed in just one or two sessions!

This will happen as the personal karma of the young Light workers who are part of this second wave is almost totally repaid. They will therefore have the flexibility to work more with healing group karmic outpourings. They will also work with the planetary structure, working with the new energy centres which will be set up and established as new magnetic fields, both within and external to the planet.

Self-healing

If you are receiving healing yourself, it is now time to start looking for your spiritual family, to take personal responsibility and only work with those you recognise and trust. If you go to a healer and think he or she is a very good healer, but something doesn't feel quite right, then trust this feeling and don't let that person pass healing energy into your system. Because if your vibrations are higher than theirs, you will be feeding energy into them, instead of them sending healing energy into you. So in effect, they will be taking energy from you.

If you intuitively feel that a healer isn't right for you, however good they may be, just smile and say, "No, thank you, I don't need any healing today." Because it is now time to take personal responsibility, isn't it?

If you need healing, a simple self-healing exercise you can do for yourself last thing at night is to visualise a circle of white or indigo flames, and on that circle visualise the Cosmic Christ, Buddha or any other Avatars you work with. This may be a Perfect Master or Avatar in human form such as Mother Meera, Sathya Sai Baba, or the young Babaji Baba Francesco. You can also work with the Babaji and Meher Baba who both lived in India and who are no longer in physical form, but who are still very active astrally and will come to you if you call them.

You then hop up onto that circle and give to those Light beings everything you don't want. You give all your rubbish, all your pain, fear and anxiety. You then take all the love and healing you need. You simply get rid of all your rubbish and take all their love. This is all you do. Just give and take.

Initially you might gasp at this as we are taught that it is selfish to take what we need. But this is old cultural inoculation which creates frequency limitation. This old conditioning has now got to go. If you have no limitation - and this is the energy vibration we are now moving into - you can take as much energy as you want from the cosmos. And we can all take healing energy from the Source.

By doing this every night you will build up your vibratory vehicle. There will come a time when you won't have to give and you won't have to take. You will just hop up onto the circle of Light and become a neutral part, feeding the essence of that circle of white

Light. Another very soothing and self-healing meditation, working with a four-pointed star, is Meditation 53, Chapter 12, *Esoteric Teddy Bears*.

Healing negative entities who are living in human form

Certain people who are negatively charged are structurally evil. They are down here on an input energy charge, as they perceive it, to destroy life and stop humans evolving simply by the fact of their presence here on Earth.

They are on a reincarnation circuit going round and round in each Earth life, programmed to be destructive. But they now need to be programmed differently so they can be freed to move on into a different setting.

If you are working as a healer, then part of your karmic contract is to unblock the 'plug holes'. If one of these negative entities is one of the plug holes which need to be unblocked, you can change their reincarnation pattern just by your physical presence. The very act of them coming to you for healing shows that they are now in a position where they have to move on.

If you want to check out the lineage of the person coming to you for healing, focus on their heart centre. Remember that you have 92 subtle bodies and therefore you have 92 chakra systems, 92 heart centres, and as you clairvoyantly tune into your *own* heart chakra, the first two or three may be somewhat dark but the other heart centres should progressively get lighter. If one of these negative entities is in physical incarnation, their first one or two heart centres may look very similar to a human's, but after that all the other heart centres on the subtle levels will be black. It will be all slow frequency energy with no Light manifesting at all. The chakra centres below their heart will be well developed but those above the heart may not be there - it is almost as if they haven't bothered!

By passing into their chakra centres all your love, grace, wisdom, joy and harmony - all of which are high frequency Light vibrations - their slow frequency darker energy can be transmuted. In this way their negative energy is neutralised and their essence will be lifted, not voluntarily by them, but consciously and deliberately by you.

You don't allow that essence to return to its source. If it goes back to its source it could reincarnate back in again. Although most negative energies are finding it harder to reincarnate as the vibrations on the planet build, at the time of writing this book about 30% are still managing to get through. But this gives them considerably less clout and as the New Age energy comes in, the new healers will be waiting for these people to physically come into their catchment area. This might be done by just passing them in the street, or they might actually come to you for a healing.

So you actually absorb that pattern of energy, then transmute and push it into a different cycle. Most healers do this unconsciously, but it is good to have a better understanding of what is now happening on other levels during your healing sessions.

These negatively charged folk might also gravitate to live in an area where there is a lot of corruption, desire and fear, such as an area with drugs and street gangs. Those who have incarnated to deal with this negative outpouring might be cunningly disguised healers masquerading as law enforcement officers who will have a physical, mental and emotional polarisation which allows them to focus on the opposition to bring about a point of balance and resolve the issue.

In the same way that Light which comes from the sun takes five Earth years to reach the Earth, so your Light and unconditional love which you pass into the person who is a negative entity will take approximately five Earth years to totally sever the darker rays which feed their negative input. After that time the darker vibration will cease to feed them. They will then have an opportunity to grow and flow into a different space, or they will physically leave the planet. In this way you give them an opportunity for promotion by moving them onto a different level of awareness.

A lot of people are doing this work. Specifically those whom we term the white lodge*, or those affiliated to the white lodge, who are working to neutralise the energy of those we term the dark lodge. This is a specific calling and you need the special training which gives Light workers the capacity to be in many places at once. These speciality healers will sit in their awareness and be constantly on call so that when the average Light healer is confronted by an aspect of darker energy the speciality healer will join them in their healing session. The speciality healer will neutralise, transmute and take care of the situation because their experience gives them the authority and understanding to do so. So the person giving the actual healing may feel an overshadowing of this presence and possibly feel a unique type of energy which doesn't often come through in their healing sessions.

A lot of Light workers only think in terms of Light. Some say, "If you think of darkness, it will create it." But what they are really saying is, "I have a lot of fear around darkness, and I prefer to ignore it, or push it away." But as a Light worker it is important to recognise that there has to be a balance of Light and dark. You have to know your way around both systems. And the only way you can do that is by acknowledging that you have been part of both systems and know the darker side of life. For most of us down here *have* been part of the darker side whether we like to acknowledge it or not.

Although ideally you might want to only focus on the Light because it makes you feel good, there comes a time when you have to look at the darker side and recognise that it has got to be sorted out as well. And that time is now!

Certain people have a role of being 'sewer workers'. They transmute and absorb the darker energies and move them on to a higher level of awareness. I am one of them. I work with slow frequency energy quite often, but I also work with a lot of very high frequency energy. In order to be able to play your role in helping to transmute the darker energies on Earth, you need to build up your circuitry, and develop the flexibility of moving your vibration up and down to match whatever frequency is presented to you. The role of the Light workers is to now sing the high notes as well as the low notes. Some people are singing the high notes all the time and don't want to come down to the low notes because this is too much of a strain on their systems. But flexibility in moving up and down is needed now more than ever before, and many of the meditations in this book will help to train you in this.

When to heal

When you heal someone, it may not always be constructive for them if you transmute and release any slow frequency energy which they actually need to keep and work with as part of their karmic contract.

If you are engaged in healing, doing hands-on healing in a positive sense for example, and someone comes along with a terminal disease, always review the information you have from the group unconscious before doing any healing. Look at their heart chakra and wings as a means of assessing whether they are part of the negativity which now needs to be removed from the planet.

Schizophrenic people can be helped but they have to be willing. Normally they are very angry and stuck in their intellect and are not willing to accept the spiritual explanation because they need proof. So they stay caught up with all the voices in their head which is the equivalent of astral rape.

What they don't realise is that they are just psychometrising. It is their motivation which is going into another person's energy system, cording into that person who is coming in as a voice. Astral entities see this happening and think, "Ah, I can manifest as ..." So the astral entities manipulate the schizophrenic person's system as well.

Schizophrenic people can stop this happening. But they have to have enough courage to recognise that the power of their will can close the doorways, and a lot of them don't want to do it.

If you give healing to a schizophrenic person, your healing energy often goes straight through them and the little energy pirates will immediately take off with it. The best way to give them healing is to work just on the top of their head or the base of their feet. To work with all their chakra centres hurts them too much as they are far too open.

As we all become aware of the bigger picture, a lot more understanding of schizophrenic experiences will soon start to come in, and Light workers can then start to heal them by working with their higher bodies on the inner planes.

* * *

Healing Work: meditations

65. Meditation to help you feel the energy vibration of colours and to start feeling the vibrations of colours in the aura
66. Meditation to help you develop your ability to sense and see dark energies, and transmute them
67. Meditation to transmute negative dark energy during a healing session

65. Meditation to help you feel the energy vibration of colours and to start feeling the vibrations of colours in the aura

Preparation
For this meditation you need two to five satin ribbons, or pieces of silk, each one a different colour. Choose strong, clear shades of blue, red, green, yellow and mauve.

Meditation
Sit with your coloured ribbons or silks in your lap. Close your eyes, do a few cycles of gentle breathing and move into a place of inner stillness. Then, still with your eyes closed, pick up one ribbon or silk. Hold it, stroke it, feel it, and try to become aware of its particular frequency and see if you can recognise the colour from its vibration. Give yourself time and don't rush the process. Just sit quietly with each colour and allow yourself to connect with it on every level, other than normal eyesight.

When you have spent time with that colour, put it down and pick up another ribbon or silk and see if you can recognise that colour in the same way.

Do not get discouraged if initially you find this difficult. With practice you will find you can intuitively feel each colour with your eyes closed, just by its vibrational essence. Blind people are very good at feeling colours!

Once you have worked with these initial colours, add other colours until you are working with 20 different ribbons or silks, from black through the whole spectrum to white. This time introduce pastel and more subtle colours, and introduce two or three shades of one colour. Again work with your eyes closed, and feel into the different colours until you can intuit each one just by holding it in your hands.

As you learn to identify colours purely by their vibrational package, you will develop an intuitive knowledge of the precise information, vibration and sound within each different colour. Once you have learnt to identify colours in this way, you will be able to intuitively recognise the frequency vibrations of colours within the human aura. You will then find it much easier to feel into the vibratory package within the auric space of yourself and others.

66. Meditation to help you develop your ability to sense and see dark energies and transmute them

This exercise will help you become aware of multiple level frequency chakra settings. Although this meditation is focused to help you look at and transmute dark energies within a person, you can also use this meditation to look at and transmute dark energies in a room, or within an organisation - the technique is exactly the same.

If you have never done this type of work before, or feel hesitant about working with another person's negative energy, you might prefer to initially practise by transmuting toxic energy in a house plant as in Meditation 32, Chapter 6, *Communicating With Nature*. House plants always hold some negative energy but the level is low and is ideal as a starter to develop your confidence.

Preparation

As preparation for this exercise, locate and focus on your hara, your centre of gravity and drop it down to your feet. Then breathe into your feet, and as you breathe in feel a rhythm and expansion of awareness in your feet as they become transparent. Visualise them growing out sideways to about a yard (1m) in width. As you breathe out, release any tension in your feet, any anxiety, any patterns of energy which might be destructive to the meditation sequence which follows.

Bring down white Light, root yourself in and put on your Light body

Bring white Light down through the top of your head and see it flowing through your body into each chakra centre. Then root yourself in and visualise dark blue roots from your feet going deep down into the planet. Dark blue automatically heals and instigates a healing sequence.

Now put on your Light body and intuitively take on the appropriate archetypal form, then raise your hara up to your heart centre.

Look at the chakra system of the person you are working with

Visualise the person you want to work with as being external to yourself, and visualise their chakra centres from the crown down to the base chakra.

If you are working with a room or organisation, visualise it in front of you as an egg-shaped energy form and give it a chakra system with seven chakras as in the human body. Then work in the same way as below.

Focus on the crown chakra

Now focus on the crown chakra. Visualise it as nine chakra centres one behind each other which represent the nine filters - the multi-level frequency settings - of that chakra. So you have an outer crown chakra which is at the front and eight more crown chakras behind that. These filters are all the same size. Each one is circular with a small aperture of white Light in the centre.

As you peer at the nine filters of the crown chakra you should see a straight beam of white Light travelling directly through all the aperture points of all nine filters. It should be like looking through a tunnel filled with white Light. But if, as you intuitively peer down this alignment, the Light doesn't flow all the way from filter one to filter nine, then look to see which filter is out of alignment.

Then close your arms over your heart chakra, refocus on the white Light coming down through the top of your head, bring it into your heart chakra and build up an energy charge. When your energy charge is up to a point of efficiency, *do not* form a triangle of energy, but just open your arms and project your white Light directly out from your heart as a beam of Light.

So if for example you find that filter five is out of alignment, in your visualisation remove the first four filters, cleaning up each one as you go by projecting your beam of white Light from your heart centre at each filter. When you get to filter five, use your visualisation to enlarge the area of darkness on that filter.

Direct your beam of Light at that filter so that it acts like a torch to illuminate that level, and to clearly show you whatever areas of darkness are there.

Refocus on the white Light coming in through the top of your head, close your arms again over your heart chakra and amplify your energy charge. Reopen your arms and now form your triangle of white Light between your third eye and both palms.

Project this triangle of Light energy into filter five in short bursts of five seconds. As you do this, your energy charge will transmute and dissolve whatever darkness is there.

When filter five has been cleaned up, look again down the centre of all nine filters and see if the white Light is now running all the way through the central aperture points. If not, look to see which other filter is out of alignment and repeat the process.

As you do this try to spontaneously become aware of the whole chakra on a one to nine level basis. A bit like an optician testing a patient, you can actually remove different filters, then amplify or contract the energies which might be there.

As you transmute the negativity in this chakra, check that the negativity released by your outpouring of love has been fully released from your physical body. Check your treacle count and if it is over 3%, release it by pulling the plugs which you should now be well versed in doing. Do this for each chakra before moving onto the next.

Work to clean up the other chakras

When you have completely cleaned up all nine filters in the crown chakra, and can see the Light running freely through the centre of all the aperture points with all nine filters nicely aligned, move your focus down to the third eye chakra and repeat the process. Continue working in this way on a nine level basis, moving down through each chakra one at a time, cleaning up each one until the beam of white Light passes freely through the centre of each chakra.

When you come to the heart chakra, if the beam of white Light flows freely through the centre of all nine levels, or nine filters, you know that person is working with Light and hasn't been tainted or targeted. But if the Light doesn't flow all the way through you know that in some way they have been targeted and you can look to see where the darkness is. This will give you the data you need to work with.

If you are doing this meditation to cleanse a room or organisation, any sewer smell which might be there when you start the exercise will change into a pleasant flower smell. You will feel a lifting of the energies and a deeper sense of relaxation within yourself.

If you are working with a person, it can take up to 36 hours for a representation of what you have done to manifest within them. For an organisation it can take up to two to three weeks. It depends on what levels you are working and how long the energy takes to work its way into the appropriate frequency before it neutralises the energy and you get an overall uplifting of the situation.

Initially you always start working from the crown chakra as the frequencies there are easier to work with. Once you have some working knowledge of dark frequency energy, you can if you wish, work upwards from the base chakra, although doing this will mean that you will have to accept and work with a much stronger negative charge. You might want to work this way out of curiosity. Or because it gives you more information in relation to yourself, because as you focus on anything dark, anything similar inside your system will also pop up to the surface to be inspected.

To come out of the meditation

When you have worked with all seven chakras, bring the white Light back into your heart centre, draw your roots up from the planet and close down each chakra, using the gold rose process, going from a gold rose to a bud, from a bud to a point of white Light. Then fold your arms, and close down your Light body, but keep it on as an ongoing protective sequence. Do a final check to make sure your treacle count is down to 3% or less.

67. Meditation to transmute negative dark energy during a healing session

With this meditation you work with unconditional love and the God force. This is the ruthless type of healing which is now needed to break negative entities from the wheel of life and push them into a new pattern. This is why those connected with the darker side are usually quite frightened of Light workers because they recognise their ruthless performance. Don't forget there are now speciality guides and healers who will overshadow you to help you when necessary.

The following meditation is given as a guide, and as you work through it follow your own intuitive instructions as they come through. First intuitively assess the chakra system of the person who has come to you for healing. If you realise the person is polarised with negativity, follow your own intuitive working dialogue and reassure them in the normal way. Give them whatever information is necessary for their well-being so they can become more intuitively aware of the opportunity being presented to them.

Start at the crown

Start working with the crown chakra, and in your visualisation intuitively see the crown centre as an open doorway with six doorways behind that. You need to go through the outer doorway in your visualisation and seal and dedicate the doorway entrance by placing a Christian cross in it and filling it with Light.

If the doorway is guarded by slow frequency astral entities, or a pattern of negative energy in whatever way it might manifest, simply allow your will and unconditional love to force an entrance through that doorway. This can normally be done fairly quickly using your own rhythm of white Light energy and whatever intuitive instructions come to you.

Generally as you go through doorway number one, you will be confronted with a corridor or tunnel where latent negative energy might reside. You clean up whatever is there. This is something akin to removing a filling in a tooth, cleaning out the old mercury and bacteria in the cavity, then putting in a new white filling so that it becomes sterile. But in this case you are filling it with white Light. You do this to the first corridor, then duplicate this process with the other six doorways and corridors. Dedicating and blessing each doorway as you clean it up.

When you get to the last corridor, invite in the angels of Light, understanding and mercy to establish a presence within the frequencies of the person you are working with.

Work through the other chakras

Repeat the above sequence with all the other chakra centres, moving onto the third eye and working down through each chakra centre in turn. By working through each of the seven main planes within each of these centres in turn, you will see off any negative energy which this darker entity-cum-being had contracted to come in on.

In this way you are using your love, care and understanding to buy out the contract of this negative entity. As you work with the 'mind of one' and swamp the mechanism of this slow frequency energy by sending in high frequency Light, you block off and deny the essence of this negative entity the opportunity to go back to its source. It can then move on into a new setting.

If you wish, as you work from the crown down to the base, you can visualise all the negative energy being collected and put into a large catch-net like the large nets fishermen use to hold all the fish until they are ready to take the catch out of water at the end of the day. So as you trawl through each chakra centre, you put the negative energy into your net, and at the end of the healing you will have this one net holding all the astral entities, or negative energy in whatever diversity it comes. You use your will and Light to contain them in the net until the healing is complete and you are ready to hand them over.

Then visualise a big pair of white hands, which are the hands of the God force, and place all the negative energy in your net into the hands of the God force who will transmute it and dispose of it in whatever way is best.

Each chakra centre of the person being healed should then be dedicated and blessed. You can do this by visualising the chakra-closing sequence using the gold rose, closing it into a bud, and from a bud reducing it down to a point of white Light, sealing each one with a Celtic cross. You can close down someone's chakras for them in this way.

By implementing the Celtic cross on the outside of each chakra, you are cording the person you have just healed into a source of pure energy which can be labelled the divine, and as you do that you activate cosmic law in a healing, harmonious way. This gives that person an opportunity to move forward extremely quickly into the opportunities now available which might not have previously been part of their life pattern.

CHAPTER 18
WORKSHOPS AND GROUP WORK

People can be physically manoeuvred by their guides, sometimes over many years, in order to bring the right people together at the right time within a workshop setting. It is like a giant cosmic chess game being played on the inner planes! This is done to create a particular combination of people and a specific vortex of energy to allow certain individuals, or the group as a whole, to intuitively and spontaneously manifest the answer to a problem which might have been holding them back for a long time. That problem might be karmic, physical or emotional. As the group energy can last for a day or for a longer period of time, the problem might be cleared during the workshop, or it might just be seen in a new light during the workshop, then some days later the answer required will suddenly become clear.

All workshops create their own package of energy which is often interlinked with unfinished emotional energy from previous lives. So the hidden agenda within a workshop is for you to recognise which person you need to work with - and on occasions you might find you have unfinished business with the group as a whole.

The purpose of these group encounters is to transmute and release any slow frequency toxic waste you might have had from a tyranny situation in a previous life with any member of that group. As your vibration in this lifetime is the highest it has ever been, the aim is to transmute that past life situation with unconditional love and give it back to the planet and not hand it back to the person concerned.

Of course there are always exceptions! Sometimes that energy *does* have to be handed back to the person concerned as part of their karmic contract, as they may have come full circle and need to receive the energy package back again. As you develop your intuitive knowing you will know what needs to be done.

In a workshop setting, if someone has a lot of karma, they may be physically chatting to other people in the group but will also be etherically chatting and swapping contracts. They might be saying, etherically, "What have you got in your contract for the next six months? Would you like to swap something for this bit of my contract?"

One person might hesitate, "Oh, I don't know about that. I'll have a quick look at the small print first . . . Oh! you must be joking!"

Another person might reply, "Well, OK, I'll swap with you this bit of my contract for that bit of yours."

If they do agree to swap bits of their karmic contracts then an alignment of energy can take place which allows flexibility in a situation which may have previously been inflexible. For example, a person in that workshop may have been going round and round on a circuit, repeating the same problem over and over again, and may have been stuck through the influence of planetary alignment, geopathic stress points, peer conditioning, or training in previous lives as well as in this life. They may have been finding it immensely difficult to break that magnetic pull, but by swapping bits of their karmic contracts on a more refined level basis with someone in a workshop setting, the person who has been stuck has an opportunity to break the circuit and move on by creating an alignment and an entrance into a higher frequency setting.

From a karmic point of view, someone in the workshop group might also say, etherically, "OK, we'll go over to China for the next three years to do some work, do you want to come and help me?"

Several people might agree and all go over to China, astrally, as a small group. They will work intensively, either with groups over there as their guides, or work on an astral level on certain polarity points to bring about a different renaissance within the pattern of that country. In this way they open up an entrance gateway for Light to work.

Workshops happening on the same day are also now being linked into each other by those on the inner planes. So if 57 workshops are taking place around the world at the same time, all with similar karmic connotations, those 57 workshops will be astrally tapped into each other to create a sharing mechanism within the same circuitry.

This type of group input is becoming more popular with those on the inner planes, as the release mechanism created is one way of sorting out any irregularities which need to be worked on there and then. Sometimes it is comparatively easy for the transference of energy between these groups to take place. Sometimes it is immensely difficult if several people within different groups are in a stubborn mode, or have a great deal of structural fear.

When several workshops are linked into the same circuitry, the first programmed action is to release the negative input of magnetic energy which is blocking the different lines of communication. This frees the attunement to the higher self and creates a telepathic input. A strong signal is then sent out, first of all to make the people feel safe, and secondly to relax the normal spiky armour of thought structure which the physical bodies are wearing. This allows the more subtle alignments of the inner planes to come in, giving the telepathic interchange of energy a lot more space, movement and flexibility between all those physically present at those workshops.

Clearing karma

When you experience an instant rapport with people within a group or workshop, it is usually because you have lived multiple permutations with those people in past lives - mother, father, brother, sister, lover. In fact, within most workshop settings you will find that a lot of the group have been a nuisance to each other in many lives!

Likewise if you meet someone who annoys you, you may be responding not only to the genetics of the person, their colour and race, but also to their frequency vibration. They may also be triggering memories from a past life and you may be responding to the thought vibration which was dominant during your last encounter, and the emotional residue of whatever happened at that time.

Your astral shells are these thoughts and patterns you have had in previous lives which you carry as multiple overcoats. As you meet someone in a workshop, you may quickly stick on a 'green overcoat' which represents the astral shell of certain thoughts and emotions you had when you encountered that person in a previous life.

By working with the Sufi greeting ceremony, Meditation 69, at the end of this chapter, you can raise the potential of the energy between yourself and another person and burn off the 'overcoats' of misunderstanding, anger, fear, rage, pain - or just rejection if that person died in a past life and left you at a time when you loved them so much. As you work with this Sufi ceremony you can move into a pattern of forgiveness and lovingly accept that person back into your life.

Quite often as you do this exercise, working with a partner and linking into their physical, emotional and mental soul life, a lot of emotional feelings may flood over you. You might discover someone you knew in a previous life, you might have a release of the old anguish you felt through the loss of that person - and people have been known to mutter 'mummy' or 'daddy' during this exercise.

By incorporating the Sufi greeting ceremony into a group session you create an opportunity to break down any resistance between the people working together. This opens up a whole new octave of vibration based on their need at that moment.

As the partners come into contact with each other's energy system, their energies start to merge. As they begin to trust the encounter and transfer energy on a heart to heart basis, they often have flashbacks to past lives with each other. If these two people were in conflict during that life, or lifetimes, as their energy pushes into each other's heart chakras, these old blocks will be re-encountered and will be felt as something akin to a large brick wall beginning to crumble.

Initially a lot of resistance may be felt, and possibly also conscious fear. But as the bricks begin to diminish, the light of understanding and love at its truest level becomes focused. Areas of old conflict which have been tied up in bondage, be they subliminal or conscious, can be identified and removed during this exercise.

As you work through these old energy patterns you can reach a point of balance where your vibration with that person becomes very similar. You can work through any energy imbalance you had with that person whom you have now magnetically attracted back into your life. You can then merge and work with unconditional love without the variations of desire or lust coming in and getting in the way. You can also do the Sufi greeting ceremony on a one-to-one basis with any person you feel drawn to work with in this way.

As a Light worker, your aim is now to move beyond all the outer manifestations of the physical or emotional package of a person, and to resonate within the core and true essence of who that person really is. By tapping into their essence you can negotiate more specifically with their higher aspect and link into the core of energy transference which might need to take place. Therefore when you meet a person you had dealings with in a past life, your aim is to remove any old energies through the act of forgiveness and to just radiate love to that person.

Whatever work you do within your group, always work with the law of unconditional love, rather than with your own personal judgement. And only work with high frequency energies. Always prepare your aura before going into any group setting, whether it is a small healing group or a large workshop, irrespective of how much love there is within that group. You will then be in a position of 'knowing' rather than joining a group session with a complacent attitude assuming that the leader of the group is automatically going to take care of you - because quite often this will not be the case.

To prepare your aura, the form of preparation has to be intuitive as well as physical. Start preparing a few days before the workshop, ideally only eating food which encourages a release of toxicity from your body. A cleansing green vegetable diet is best, plus sufficient water to flush through your system so that any sludgy energy can be flushed out. You will then go to the workshop without a lot of physical toxicity in your body.

Take a bath with sea salt prior to the workshop, ideally just before, or on the morning of the workshop. If that is not possible do this last thing at night the evening before the workshop. This will ensure your aura is carrying the least amount of negative energy.

Also wear clean clothes to ensure your clothing isn't carrying any energy charge from encounters at other workshops. Magnetic charges can attach themselves to clothing and these energy charges will create a conflict of interest in a new workshop setting.

Working on other levels, prepare yourself by doing the black healing meditation as close to the start of the workshop as possible. See Meditation 4, in the section *Key Aspects Of Meditation Work.*

Then contract your auric space just prior to going into the workshop itself. Keep your aura contracted until you intuitively feel where the energies in the workshop are, until you know whether you can trust the people there or whether you have to be more vigilant and careful of your energy during the whole session.

Finally, before physically walking into the workshop room - just outside the door, or in your motor-car when you have parked it - invite your higher guides to accompany you into the workshop. Alternatively you can put on your archetypal Light body, or if you keep it on as a protective sequence just reactivate it then close your wings as a protective sequence. This will ensure that you are in a position of strength, and not open and vulnerable to any structural imbalance of energy from other people who are at various stages of development .

Before booking for a workshop you can also use the intuitive traffic light dowsing technique to see if that workshop setting is where you need to be.

Negative interference

If you work with any negative overtures, a vibratory package of energy will be set up. You could call this a karmic crossroads. Quite often from a karmic point of view, those who watch in a negative way on the inner planes will be aware that Light workers have to move through these subtle karmic crossroads to resolve the input difficulty. Using this as an opportunity to target you, these negative beings will lie in ambush and look for any karmic note of weakness which might be there. They look at the genetic background of your physical body and any emotional frequency point which hasn't been worked with. They will then amplify that in such a way to slow you, or possibly the whole group down.

This can often happen when a group is set up - sometimes with blissful ignorance - to do absent healing without consciously acknowledging or even being aware they are also creating a development group. The group starts with a very positive focus, building up an energy charge. As the permutations of energy within the group naturally resolve some old imbalances, one individual, possibly more, will start to become a lot more active on a psychic level. The lower astral levels open up and the person who is running ahead of the group becomes targeted.

Slow frequency thought forms can then be introduced into his or her essence, and that slow frequency energy filters down into the group. The result is group conflict. Maybe egotistical problems as those who are vibrating a bit slower see the person who is moving ahead as a definite threat to their awareness. As the vibrations within the group go higher, more specific information is usually made available, and that information might be deliberately coloured by those of a negative nature to ensure that a particular energy is set up which basically destroys the co-essence, or trust, of the group.

If the group continues to work together without realising they are being targeted, a lot more astral entities can be introduced into the space of the people in the group. These astral entities will follow them as they go home to their family life, or as they go into other group settings.

To understand how astral entities tap into your auric space, imagine the entity as a swimmer floating in the waters of life without any great capacity to move itself. As a sailing-boat - which is your auric space - goes sailing past, the swimmer makes a grab for the boat, hanging onto whatever part of the boat is available. It allows the boat to take it to wherever it docks. The entity will then try to infiltrate your auric space and move into your energy system.

This is why it is always useful to look around the auric space within groups, to see the presence of protection that might, or might not be there. Also to check the level of astral activity, especially after the group has finished for the evening.

To monitor and check that astral entities don't follow you home after any group session, you can use Meditation 70, at the end of this chapter. Using the above analogy of the sailing-boat, this meditation is akin to you being an observer on the boat, watching and looking around, then if you see anything grabbing the boat, giving their hands a sharp tap on the fingers to ensure they let go.

Group rescue work

Group work, and all workshops, can raise your awareness since all group work creates a frequency vibration on different vibratory levels. It all depends on the motivation of the group, on the formation of magnetic charges of the individuals within that group, and the essence of will attracted to the group as a whole.

When a group works together in spiritual formation, a tremendous amount of energy work can be achieved. The point of trust developed through the laws of faith can then move mountains within a normal group setting. It is merely a matter of the group leader, and the group as a whole, recognising that the group will has to be focused. In my workshops we work within a radius of about 5 miles (8km) and sometimes we stretch ourselves out to work within a radius of 25 miles (40km), working astrally as well as physically. We do a skim of the area by doing a mental trawl so that all negative thought forms and aspects of energy of a negative polarity can be brought into the workshop setting to be transmuted.

In these workshops we also do rescue work. This happens when the spiritual hierarchy do a trawl on the astral planes and grab, say 25,000 souls who are kicking around confused and earthbound. At the same time they look at the people present within the workshop and look at the problems those people have. The spiritual hierarchy then link those earthbound souls into the problematic area.

So if, for example, someone within the group is still feeling loss and pain from the death of a loved one, those souls who are linked into a similar vibration will be tuned into that person. This will amplify the emotions within the physical person concerned. As his or her pain comes up to the surface, and they release and dispose of that pain with the aid and love of the group, all those souls who have been tuned into that pain will be 'rescued'. The vibration of those souls will then move up and they will be freed from the magnetic pull which has been holding them back from their onward journey to the inner planes.

By doing this, the personal karma of the person working through the pain is enhanced. Also, since the group participates in the process, the group's karmic contract with each other, and possibly the karmic contracts with the earthbound souls, get enhanced.

The group as a whole moves into a position of much more flexibility. The individual contracts of the group members can then be negotiated more specifically, based on their individual need and on the need of the group. This gives them more energy, wisdom and understanding.

* * *

Workshops And Group Work: meditations

68. Meditation to work out the karmic pattern between people in a group or a workshop

69. Sufi greeting ceremony to tune into the soul life of people in a group
70. Meditation to monitor and check that astral entities do not follow you home after a group session or a workshop

68. Meditation to work out the karmic pattern between people in a group or a workshop

You can use this exercise in a group situation to see what karmic commitments there are between people within that group. For this meditation it is a good idea for one person to lead this exercise, or to prerecord this exercise onto a cassette tape, leaving sufficient pauses in-between each step, so that every person in the group is working in unison. With the group sitting in a circle, the meditation sequence is:

1. Visualise white Light passing down through the top of your head, and see it flowing down through your body, linking into each of your main chakra centres. Feel this as the love of the Father flowing down through each chakra.

2. Take your awareness down into your feet. Visualise dark blue roots travelling from your feet down into Mother Earth. As your roots go down into the Earth, feel your feet expanding to 3-6 feet (1-2m) and try to feel, or sense the love, bounty and beauty within the planet.

3. Now refocus on the white Light flowing in through the top of your head and down through your chakras. See it flowing out of your base chakra, down through your legs, into your roots and out into the Earth. You are now linked with Heaven and Earth.

4. With the power of your imagination, begin to breathe into your right arm. As you breathe into your right arm, visualise sky-blue energy which represents healing and the understanding of the group unconscious, flowing into the top of your arm.

As this sky-blue energy flows into your upper arm, down into your elbow and on into your lower arm and fingers, feel a new flexibility coming into the right side of your body which is the father side. As this blue healing energy flows in, it also expands your circuitry. You may feel this as a tingling.

5. While part of you carries on breathing into your right arm, start to breathe into your left arm. As you do this, pale green energy which

represents the soul's flexibility, the Light frequency flexible energy which you require at this moment in time, starts to flow into the top of your left arm.

This green energy flows into your upper arm, down through your elbow, into your lower arm and into your fingers. As this package of green energy flows down, it also gives you an identification with nature.

So you have white Light coming down through the top of your head, dark blue roots going into the ground, one pale blue arm and one pale green arm.

6. While part of you carries on breathing into both arms, you also begin to focus on your right thigh. Breathe into that thigh, pale amethyst which represents the key note of your own power flowing into the essence of your being. As that amethyst colour flows into the top of your right thigh, then into the lower part of your thigh and into your kneecap, it gives your kneecap a big cuddle. It then flows down through the lower part of your leg and into your foot, giving your foot a lot of love. Allow this amethyst colour to flow easily and quickly.

As this pale amethyst colour flows in, your leg fills up with your own personal power.

7. While part of you carries on breathing into the right aspect of yourself you now begin to concentrate on your left thigh. Breathe pale silver into your left thigh, giving you the flexibility of quicksilver and telepathy. In the same way as before, the silver flows into and fills up the upper leg, flowing in and around the kneecap, relaxing your knee, and flowing down through your leg into your foot.

You now have white Light flowing down through the top of your head, dark blue roots going into the ground, one blue arm, one green arm, one amethyst leg and one silver leg.

8. Using the power of your visualisation - remembering that energy follows thought - mix all these colours together. Do this by drawing all the colours into both hands, and passing them out through your hands to create a ball of Light about 9 inches (22cm) in diameter, which you hold in your hands.

9. As all the colours come together in your ball of Light, place that ball in the centre of the circle. Your ball will then automatically go to the person with whom you have a karmic link and unfinished karmic business.

So in your visualisation, merely push the ball away from you, see who that ball goes to and which chakra centre it goes towards or into. Your ball may go directly to one person, or it may go to more than one person. Just sit, observe and see where it goes.

10. If for any reason your ball doesn't want to whistle off, bring it back to you, recharge it up by holding it in your hands, and send it out again. You will then find that your ball will go directly to one person, or more.

Allow 3/4 minutes here for people to work with their balls of Light.

11. Having achieved that, call your ball back. Draw it back into your body, and reabsorb all the colours. You may feel a general absorption of colours or you may feel each colour going back to the arm or leg it originally flowed into.

Amplify the white Light coming in through the top of your head, and see it flowing through your body, washing all the colours out of your body to neutralise any negative energy you might have inadvertently picked up from anyone you karmically linked into.

12. Having washed out all the colours, bring your awareness back into your heart chakra, and close down all your chakra centres. Then bring your awareness back into your body. When you are ready gently open your eyes.

NB. The group can now make notes on who and what chakra centres their ball of Light went to. The group members can either follow this up by going straight into individual meditations focusing on the person or people their ball of Light went to. This may give them the necessary information to guide them as to what they need to do in order to work with that unfinished karma. Or the group can make notes and meditate on this at a later stage.

69. Sufi greeting ceremony to tune into the soul life of people in a group

You can do this meditation with any person you want to tune into on a soul level. You do this exercise keeping eye to eye contact throughout as this helps you tune into each other's auric space. As you gently open up your auric system to each other in a loving way you will find the point of remembrance which is needed.

Quite often, as you do this exercise and link into the physical, emotional and mental soul life of the person you are working with, you might have flashbacks to old life memories which can explain a lot about any structural difficulties, emotional or otherwise, you may be going through. As you do this exercise ask for any information or guidance which is necessary to flow into your space.

The Sufi greeting ceremony is done in pairs. It is a good idea for everyone to practise the overall sequence of physical movements before actually starting the meditation proper - see the sections *Starting position* and *Make your circular hand movement*. When you do start the actual meditation, the group works silently, although very gentle background music can be played. Each pair works in their own time, at their own pace, and when they have finished the full sequence with their partner, they stand quietly and contemplate what has been shown to them. They can then intuitively, and silently, choose another person who has finished their sequence. In this way the group can go from partner to partner, working with as many people as they wish, within the time allowed.

During your practice session, the complete circular movement of the hands can be done very quickly, but during the meditation itself, it can take five to 30 minutes, and when you have your hands over your heart chakra, you remain looking into each other's eyes for anything from a few minutes to 30 minutes. The whole meditation exercise with each partner can take anything from five minutes to an hour, depending on the capacity of the people concerned and the time and space allowed.

Initially some people might find the meditation and the closeness with another person a little threatening, and they may only feel comfortable with five minutes. But ideally, the whole sequence should take a minimum of 15 minutes, and ideally a lot longer, as this is a very sensitive exercise and can open up a lot of possibilities in a very healing and positive way. The idea and aim, with practice, is for people to relax and flow into the meditation so that it becomes a cosmic dance. This dance can then take you into the giddy heights of unconditional love where a new learning can take place.

Starting position

Face a partner. Stand quite close, about 12 inches (30cm) apart, ensuring that your feet are nicely apart, with your weight central, so that you don't have any strain on your body. Let your arms relax at your sides, make eye to eye contact. For those who wear glasses, these should be taken off. Think of white Light coming in through the top of your head and root yourself into the ground.

Bend your elbows out to the side, bring your hands together with your palms facing away from you and facing your partner, with your fingertips pointing towards each other and the middle three fingertips slightly overlapping, with your fingers splayed open.

Keeping this position, you and your partner bring your hands together with your palms touching their palms, your fingers touching their fingers. Keeping the hands in this position, drop them down to waist level or just below, but ensure that you and your partner's palms and fingers are still touching.

Then look deeply into each other's eyes, possibly one eye or the other. You normally find that the right eye is the boss eye and the left eye is a little bit more friendly. Maintain this eye contact throughout the exercise.

Make your circular hand movement

With eye contact established and keeping your fingers and hands in the starting position, you both *very slowly* start to raise your hands up the front of your body, keeping your palms and fingers touching.

As your splayed fingers start to move in front of the other person's face, keep looking into your partner's eyes. Your splayed fingers will slowly reveal segments of their mouth, nose, eyes and hairline. In this way, subliminal imprints of old packages will come up from previous lives - if it is appropriate.

Continuing to maintain eye contact, *and still moving in slow motion*, you raise your hands directly up above the top of your head, stretching up as far as you can without breaking hand contact. Still keeping palms and fingers touching, you then stretch your arms out to the sides in a circular movement, like a fan unfolding, and when your arms are outstretched at shoulder level, you then start to bend the elbows and bring your hands in towards your heart chakra. Your hands are still touching and you are still looking into each other's eyes.

When your hands come level with your heart chakra, you separate your hands. Each person places their right hand with the palm flat against their partner's heart chakra. The palm of your left hand is placed over the back of the other person's right hand. In this way you pass high frequency love energy, and spontaneous healing, heart to heart.

At the same time as you place your hands over your heart chakras - still looking into each other's eyes - you drop your elbows down to your side and take a step towards each other. Move up close to each other so that your noses are about 2 inches (5 cm) away from each other. Look deeply into each other's eyes, or into the eye you feel drawn to. As you do that, you build up an energy package very quickly. This will open up your auric system on a high frequency footing, and open up the opportunity to merge and meld with each other. As the eyes are the window to the soul, this may result in flashbacks to old life experiences and you might even see the face of your partner altering. There will also be an exchange of energy in a form of intuitive knowing.

It is at this point in the exercise that old emotional patterns of energy may sweep over you. As you look deeply into each other's eyes you may find yourself releasing old unbalanced energy, or moving into a space of forgiveness, or you may find someone you have lost long ago.

As you do this exercise, be gentle with the person you are working with. Be intuitively aware of their capacity to handle and hold energy. Don't be too much of a 'thug' and push your energy in if that is going to hurt the person you are working with. Be sensitive and when you feel you have both had enough, just step back, give each other a big hug and reflect on what has just been shown to you. If necessary *very quietly* talk about the flashbacks and experiences you have just had. But remember that others are still working in silence.

70. Meditation to monitor and check that astral entities do not follow you home after a group session or a workshop

You can do this meditation privately as you are walking or travelling home after any group session or workshop. Or the whole group can do it as a gentle exercise at the end of the day. With practice you can also cultivate the approach given in this meditation, so that the quality of Light created within this meditation is perpetually around you.

We offer you the main meditation sequence, then four variations. Allow your intuition and higher self to guide you to the right one for you. You may find yourself drawn to a different variation each time you do this meditation, depending on what negative energy is there, and on planetary influences at that time.

Bring down white Light and root yourself in

First bring white Light down through the top of your head. Then root yourself in by visualising your main taproot as an extension of your spine, going down into the planet to earth you.

Focus on your aura

To help you visualise your aura, see this as being a package of energy three feet (1m) around your body in all directions, above, below and on either side. The outer line of your aura - the outer skin - should be smooth and free from wrinkles. Visualise your buffer zone as an outer layer of energy around your aura, about 15 feet (4.5m) in all directions.

The total space between your outer aura and the outer edge of your buffer zone should be clear. It should be transparent in energy terms and there shouldn't be any input from external sources.

Fill up your auric space with flames

To check whether anything unwanted is within your auric space, first of all refocus on the white Light coming down through the top of your head, bring this white Light into your heart centre, and expand that white Light outwards into your aura. As you do this, visualise this Light becoming pure white flames of fire representing unconditional love and protection. These flames will flow up and down your body, filling up your whole aura.

Once your aura is filled with flames, allow the flames to flow out further, filling your buffer zone to create a fiery furnace around you.

As this undiluted energy power in the form of flames expands from your heart and fills up your entire auric space, visualise it burning off your clothing which represent any structural fear.

Put on your Light body

Put on your astral overcoat, your Light body. Bear in mind that for any astral entity or slow frequency energy to follow you home, it is normally of a slow vibration frequency which needs to sit within one of your bottom three chakra centres - base, sexual or lower part of your solar plexus. So for this meditation, choose a Light body with an earthy vibration such as the brown bear, white polar bear, wolf, or any other earthy archetype you feel an affinity with. For ease of explanation, we will use the white polar bear.

As the white polar bear superimposes itself around you, physically close your arms and fold them over your chest, visualising this as closing your paws. Move your awareness to the white Light coming down through the top of your head and see it travelling down into your base chakra, filling it up with white Light. This white Light then travels upwards filling the base, sexual, solar plexus and heart chakras. Each centre should become hot, and as this happens you build up an energy charge in your heart centre.

Now open your paws and focus your will to form a triangle of white Light which radiates out from the heart linking your third eye and both palms of your hands.

Project your Light energy at any negative energy formation

Face the north, then turn slowly in a clockwise direction, looking in all directions - north, east, south and west - focusing specifically on the buffer zone outside your aura. Check to see if your buffer zone has contracted. If for example, it is now only two feet (60cm) or less you know there is a presence outside trying to push into your auric space.

See if there is a rupture in the auric field of your buffer zone. You may see or feel this quite clearly as some form of mental or emotional pressure, and you may see it clairvoyantly as a cording coming in.

Look and see if there is any energy form there. If your clairvoyance is developed, you should see a presentation of this, and will be able to have a better idea of what is manifesting.

If you cannot see or feel any of this you may become aware of something not being quite right. Just work intuitively, knowing and trusting that whatever comes into your mind is actually there. The more you do this work, the more your astral vision will open up and you will start to see in a different way.

Wherever you notice, or intuitively feel a focal point of disturbed energy, challenge it. If you are working intuitively, use your visualisation to symbolise your feeling of 'not quite right' as a specific shape, round and black. This shape represents the opposition.

To dispose of that, you focus on the triangular energy charge coming out from your heart and visualise a Christian cross of white flames in the centre of the triangle. Project this triangle of Light with its inner cross of flames into the round black shape, or into whatever you clairvoyantly see as negative. You forcefully project your triangle, in blast after blast, until that manifestation of dark energy is disposed of. When you have done that, your triangle will wrap itself around any rupture you have in your auric wall. As your unconditional love flows into that area, the rupture hole will shrink until it is repaired.

To end the meditation

Your flames can be diminished within your auric space but kept alight as an ongoing protective sequence. Close down your chakra centres, and keep your Light body on as an extra protective sequence. On the way home, if you intuitively feel anything is still lurking there trying to have a go at you, just re-energise your Light body and your circle of flames so that nothing can get you!

Variation 1:

Use the same meditation sequence, but instead of projecting your triangle of Light and cross of flames at the darker energy, you can wrap your triangle and cross of flames around it and contain it. Your triangle and cross can be small or large to match whatever size or shape of dark energy is there. As you focus your triangle and cross, the energy will be drawn into the triangle. The cross will effectively seal off any astral doorway, the triangle will magnetise and hold the negative energy in bondage and transmute it to a degree at the same time. When the energy is in its altered state, visualise a big pair of white hands, with 'God' tattooed on the back of those hands, which will represent the God force. Offer them anything negative that you have contained. In this way you don't have to bring it further into your space.

Variation 2:

You can also work with the above sequence as in Variation 1, but this time approach the negative energy through one of your chakra centres. You can intuitively work with whichever chakra feels right, or you can use the traffic light dowsing technique to tell you which chakra centre to work with.

To do this, you drop your vibration down to that chakra centre, by taking your awareness into that chakra. Build up your triangle of white Light between your third eye and both palms, then bring it back into your heart, shrink it down in size, pass it down into the chakra you are working with and project your triangle of Light with your inner cross of flames from there. Or you can just project thousands of crosses out from that chakra. These will wrap around the energy form and transmute it. Then see that energy going into the big pair of white hands as above.

Variation 3:

Working in the same way as for Variation 2, instead of sending out the cross of flames or thousands of crosses, you can send thousands and thousands of little daisies out from the chakra you are working with, to wrap around anything that is there. This works with the energy of the daisy-chain meditation whereby groups of Light workers link into the daisy symbol to form a human daisy-chain to focus a concentrated beam of healing love energy around the Earth. The daisy symbol with 14 petals has been chosen for this work as each petal represents the 12 astrological symbols plus the male and female, and the centre of the daisy symbolises the ten planets in our solar system.

Variation 4:

Alternatively you can work with your auric Light full of flames as explained in the main sequence, but this time expand your aura of flames out to 60 to 70 feet (18-21m) all around you. In this way, if you have any astral manifestation hanging around, basically you force the issue by expanding your auric field of flames and seeing off anything that might be 'lying in the wings' and wanting to have a 'freebie' on the way home!

This variation is also good to use in any crowded situation, especially in a shopping centre or an airport. So as you walk into a large area of energy, put on or reactivate your Light body and create the aura of flames around you. Then expand those flames outwards so that any astral entities and negative influences will find it almost impossible to link into your energy because you are in an active state of protection. You will feel far better as you will have much less energy loss and will feel far more in tune at all times.

CHAPTER 19
LIGHT AND DARK ON PLANET EARTH

The Earth came together in a polarity of energy through an implosion and explosion of energy, both physically and on the subtle levels. This awakening created a unit of awareness that we now know as Gaia or Mother Earth.

When this happened, three billion years ago, the Earth came into being negatively charged, into a universe which was positively focused. Our galactic neighbours both near and far, observing this phenomenon decided, whether rightly or wrongly, that they had an opportunity to dispose of their rubbish, all their negativity and imbalanced energy which were a result of growing pains within their various planetary systems and universes.

So they put all their unfinished business, all their drop-outs and unruly elements of energy into the auric space of our planet which they viewed as nothing more than an esoteric dustbin. In this way they were able to simply dispose of negative energies which they could not, or did not want to handle at that time. This was seen as a short-term opportunity but is still ongoing to a degree, and during every eclipse negative energy is still implanted into planet Earth.

Interested parties who viewed this experimentation with planet Earth as a bit of fun, also came along to create mayhem - a bit like the lager louts thinking of this as the local party in a cosmic sense!

With all those negative energies came the thought forms, motivations, desires and all the unwanted race principles which started to work and concentrate within the essence of our planet. These thought forms and desires, and all the emotional dumping from other planetary systems, first formed astrally within the thought particles that had been held within the negative charge of the planet. As those astral thought forms came into the negative charge they created a negative sphere, both etheric and astral, around the planet.

So when our planet came in negatively charged, at a certain point of balance within the polarity of itself, it became far more negative than was really necessary. A bit like stuffing a dustbin far too full! And so a point of imbalance occurred.

During the first billion years when the planet was cooling off, these astral thought forms, who were in essence astral entities, needed an outer expression. So they started to experiment by putting down key notes into matter, creating a matrix for themselves. In this way the process we know as evolution started to take place.

These astral entities started to be preprogrammed negatively by the manipulation of the mind-essence behind them. This implant of mind-substance, which you could call genetic manipulation, collated, directed and redirected energy then manipulated that energy to create the right form for astral entities to fit into. Form then manifested on Earth.

In this way, those who were drawn into the vibratory pattern of this newly forming planet were offered an opportunity to experiment, by clothing themselves in the vibrations which made up the various forms of awareness which we on Mother Earth now refer to as the animal, plant and mineral kingdoms, for there weren't any humans in matter at that time.

When astral forms first came down to Earth, they started to experiment with the gaseous states and the permutations available within minerals. Gradually as those permutations were experienced, the astral aspects went on to experiment with the vibratory patterns of energy within plant life, then animal life. When this evolutionary road had been travelled for a billion years, the energy patterns available were again genetically manipulated and human form started to emerge.

Mind games started to take place as the negative astral entities who were first put onto our planet, and who had evolved into human form, were now capable of learning by multiple experiences. But as most of their preprogramming was negative, they tended to gravitate towards negative experiences.

Light beings incarnate into the planet

The spiritual hierarchy, observing what was happening within planet Earth, recognised they had to act. The hierarchical focus of course very rarely acts unless it is a very definite necessity. So they came, some in their spaceships, some on the inner planes, to view things more closely and decide what to do.

As they came into the space around our planet, they observed the evolution and the natural law which had already taken place within the planet itself. They also observed the life forms who had started to clothe themselves in matter, both on the inner and outer planes, and who had created the astral alignments.

When they moved closer to the Earth plane, the spiritual hierarchy thought they could simply rectify a point of balance by altering the encodement and introducing a note of harmony into life forms who were now on Earth. But when they came closer to the planet, they found they were not able to achieve this balance in the way they wanted from the higher planes.

So they decided to physically incarnate into the structure of the planet. There were two main reasons for this: first, to negotiate with the negative energies who had already started to form on the planet and give them an opportunity to change. Secondly, by incarnating into the planet themselves, they planned to help those entities evolve and move on by raising their vibrations and adjusting their pattern of evolution through the physical mix. This was again genetic manipulation, but this time with a positive focus.

They planned to adjust the DNA to make it more Light-focused, as opposed to dark-focused, and then introduce new data to bring about awareness, so that free-will could take place.

When these Light beings from the spiritual hierarchy physically incarnated into the planet, they thought the negative entities would be willing to change and communicate in a way which would speed up their evolution. But instead, they found these negative entities didn't want to change at all. They were quite happy as they were! These negative entities were far from receptive, they viewed the Light beings with some trepidation and were convinced they were a threat to their way of life, their work, and the fun they were enjoying and didn't want to give up.

Prior to this current playground on Earth these negative entities had far less flexibility in other planetary systems where they had been evolving in other ways. Also, with the structure of the planet at that time all life forms, including these entities, could live for up to 1,000 to 2,000 years since the trace elements were very rich in life-giving particles. With the frequency of Light and the newness of the planet structure everything on Earth was in abundance. Therefore life expectancy was far longer than it is today. It was during the chapter on Earth known as the fifth root race, 86,000 years ago when the latter-day floods, in particular the Aztec floods, washed away a lot of these trace elements, and humanity's life focus was reduced to approximately 70 to 80 years.

Esoteric punch-up

These negative entities reasoning among themselves, reckoned they could remove the threat to their own existence by destroying the physical bodies of the Light workers as an ongoing process. They thought that by doing this, they could eliminate the new information and higher vibration which these Light beings brought in, and stop this vibration interfering with their essence which they had established on both the inner and outer planes.

This plan is, in fact, an ongoing unfulfilled one since the first core of negative entities are still trying to implement this initial aim, which is basically to make this planet totally negative and to keep the vibrations down here very slow, almost like putting in a full stop. And of course the more they push to do this, the more the Light agents push as well.

The inner planes on which the negative entities had established their essence are just the lower astral ones. These negative folk from various planetary systems, who previously had access to various astral doorways, found that once they had incarnated into Earth they were captured within a pattern of energy around this planet known as the ring-pass-not and could not pass back out again.

The Light beings connected with the spiritual hierarchy also discovered that when they passed through the ring-pass-not, the longer they stayed down on the planet the more difficult it was to remember their source. In fact quite a few of them very quickly started to forget that they were linked into the joy and love which their spiritual brothers on the inner higher planes were sending down as a form of support mechanism.

So the spiritual hierarchy decided to introduce what we now know as time, and what we know as sleep. This was done so that during the process of sleep, Light beings on Earth who were connected with the spiritual hierarchy, those we call the 'mind of one', could then pass through the ring-pass-not, merging again with their source in a form of remembrance. This gave them a sort of esoteric cuddle.

In this way they could bring that higher energy back into their essence. When they awoke the next morning, their intuitive component was re-established and they could continue working through the contract they had agreed to, under the heading of karma.

When both parties - darkness as well as Light - came down onto the planet, each resolved to bring about a point of balance. Each was interested in raising the vibration for themselves. This created an esoteric punch-up with multiple units of intelligence coming in and trying to outmanoeuvre each other. Each trying to bring about an accumulation of acquired energy, working with the karmic currents, cosmic tides and solar winds, all of which dictate the amount of Light or dark frequency available at any one point in time.

This esoteric punch-up, this pattern of planetary negotiation between aspects of Light and dark has been going on for a very long time.

Planet Earth, being situated on the edge of the galaxy, was also a very convenient drop-off point for extraterrestrial life. It was very much like the galactic library! A lot of extraterrestrial folk used to pop in from other galaxies, entering through interdimensional frequency points, stop for a 'cup of tea', catch up on the gossip and contribute to the galactic library. In this way, the lower astral levels were very much open to manipulation by this group input. The group was composed of multiple units combined together in an overall awareness spread out over a very wide front. As the vibratory input of solar rays was slowing down, this offered a unique opportunity for manipulation by those who were dedicated to slowing down evolution.

As humans were still firmly anchored in their emotional system they were also very susceptible to emotional manipulation by the group input because, with the astral levels beginning to open up, negative entities found it easy to gain access into the human emotional system.

Slow frequency informational keys were then introduced and the amplification of fear and emotional seed thought forms in relation to fear were implemented. The minds of those using this energy to their advantage were able to implant false information and create a very effective misinformation service which allowed them to break down any resistance to their negative slow frequency ideas and concepts.

Planetary raid

Some 350,000 years ago a planetary raid took place on Earth. This was an active point of interference by darker entities where highly evolved genetic manipulators from a different planetary setting entered through an interdimensional frequency entrance point, which is the star gateway above the part of our planet known as Iraq. As they came in they interfered with the ring-pass-not, putting a note of disharmony into it which changed the vibration.

As this new energy pattern came in, it caused a contraction of Light gateways and an expansion of negative ones. This created a different vibratory focus as the points of Light contracted and darker aspects expanded. In this way Light workers were blocked from physically incarnating into matter for quite some time and the Light focus which had been actively developing came to the end of its term. This new vibratory focus offered an opportunity to the alternative darker frequency to come into operation since the Earth is made up of a combination of Light and dark, and it is only by a blend and balance of both that evolution can flow forward instead of stagnating. The Earth, going through a karmic tidal change, had also indicated its willingness to go through this shift of energies in order to bring in a more masculine focus to its vibratory needs.

Then by genetic manipulation, the darker entities captured the resonating patterns within the DNA which was in the planet, stripping back the DNA from a stranding of between eight and nine, to a basic stranding of two.

Before this, when the DNA stranding was between eight and nine, folk living down here on the planet had developed the intuitive capacity for telepathy which was well established and quite normal. But when these genetic manipulators stripped back the DNA stranding to a basic two, they actually took away from the genetic memory housings within human form, the capacity for telepathic and intuitive awareness.

They had to leave in two DNA essences which were basically the sexual instincts implanted within the emotional circuitry, as this gave life its basic form and allowed procreation of the race to continue. But with only a stranding of two, society had to reform itself by starting again at basics even though some of the more subtle references were still latent and encoded within the structure of the remaining DNA.

When they stripped back the DNA the genetic manipulators also interfered with the emotional vehicle of life forms on Earth so that a vibration which was needed for their structural food could be generated. This vibration we have got to know quite well over the last 350,000 years. It is the vibration of fear.

In this way the negative manipulators not only put a stop to the expansion of the DNA, but also gained dominance within the slow frequency vibratory circuitry which they have been expanding on since then.

These genetic manipulators also had backers who, seeing the opportunities presented, offered some of their own DNA for experimentation. As this DNA was a series of strandings and reference points which could be developed or isolated, it was experimented with and stretched into a new semblance of form aspects, then shared among those who could develop it further in whatever way was available within the rules and regulations governing their planetary systems.

With that achieved, the genetic manipulators didn't physically remain within the planet. Like a managing director their interests were widespread and they were active within many galaxies and many interdimensional time zones. So they left agents behind as managers to tend the fold, cultivate the vibration they had seeded, and collect the harvest of the emotional energy required. This harvest of course isn't just collected physically, but also within the astral levels where the ring-pass-not is found. They then sold the energy which their agents collected to other parts of the galactic empire where Earth energy is at a bit of a premium, since Earth folk are evolving through a very unique aspect known as our emotional system. This emotional system is not shared by other life forms external to our planet, even though they are also evolved and are, to a degree, physically far older than ourselves.

This means of course that the DNA form captured from Earth and sold, now has its representation elsewhere within the galaxy. So insect life, reptilian life, and animal life all have a higher representation elsewhere which is far more evolved than we human folk like to think. In fact, a lot of them are now moving back into physical orbit, and some are already here, because they recognise that a new raid by Light workers is in process - which should be fully accomplished by the year 2008, if not sooner.

During the last 2,500 years when the Piscean Age was active, a great deal of deliberate cultivation of negative energy was brought about. When the Atlantean Age - the civilisation prior to this one - came to an end there was the equivalent of an esoteric vote within the awareness of those physically incarnated at that time. Since those connected with darkness outnumbered those connected with Light, this vote introduced into our planet a pattern of devic energy.

Once this esoteric vote was sent forth from Atlantis, this voting energy attracted from a more distant part of our galaxy an entity who a few people have affectionately labelled Prince Lucifer. Lucifer is an entity who has forgotten his source, so he doesn't identify with the God Source above him but rather tends to consider himself God in his own right. So Light beings on the inner planes have a great deal of sympathy for this fallen angel. Lucifer, who was attracted onto the planet 2,500 years ago, has systematically set about to deliberately cultivate fear in all its diversity - and fear of death is one example of the fear scenarios he has created.

Light beings infiltrate back to Earth

During this time various interdimensional star gateways of a positive nature started to open. This occurred through a harmonisation external to the planet which linked into a planetary wave of sub-particles of Light which were developing within the planetary core. As those particles rhythmically flowed up to the surface of the planet, small star gateway aperture points were opened, some minor and some major ones.

The 'word' that was placed within the ring-pass-not by the darker entities was therefore denied. The Light entities who were prevented from reincarnating when this note of disharmony was first put into the ring-pass-not, were now able to infiltrate back into our planet - first in ones, then in twos, then in larger groups.

This infiltration has been a gradual process. But as Light beings passed through these smaller entrance points, they gradually maintained a structural band, or hold, on these points and were able to keep these star gateways open for others like themselves to infiltrate through. But since these star gateway aperture points were quite tiny in the initial stages, only a small amount of Light beings could come in, and only at systematic time periods. Now these aperture points are quite large, far larger in fact than the darker opposite numbers.

As the astral levels now become thinner, more people are experiencing an input of astral Light. This is one of the reasons, in a positive way, where the mechanics of dying are quite useful. During the First and Second World Wars when masses of young people were killed, these young folk all released their inbuilt Light, especially astrally, and this collective outpouring of Light punched a hole in the astral glamour*. This allowed more Light to flow in and helped to speed up the whole evolutionary process.

The negative astral entities, who were initially put onto our planet and have been living in human form, were able to reincarnate back into Earth very quickly after each physical death as their essence - being mainly astral - doesn't go further than the lower astral levels. But as the vibration on the planet is becoming more refined, it is becoming too refined for these negative entities who now find it very difficult to continue physically living down here, and are unable to reincarnate and come back down again.

So these entities are currently hanging around the lower astral planes. They are blending together in a form of structural fear, creating a build-up of slow frequency negative energy within the collective unconsciousness on the lower levels which is sitting, waiting for the lower astral levels to open up in their entirety so that they can surge down into matter once again. When they do, which will have happened by the year 2008, sufficient Light workers have to be down here to absorb all this negativity and transmute it in a total and magnificent unconditional love-dance.

The lower astral levels have already opened up in some places. But the actual aperture point is still small, and this is where Light workers are already concentrating their essence to stop the flow of negativity coming back in.

This negativity and structural fear are already looking for polarity points and for particular types of vehicles which, for one reason or another, might be at a much slower frequency than would normally be the case, so that aspects of themselves can manifest back into matter again.

Although there are many folk currently down here whom we term human, many of them in actual fact are not! There are a lot of folk incarnated on the planet who are connected with the darker side of life and some whose DNA was previously stolen. When I look around aurically, I can see human faces, but I can also see lots of other faces as well - and some are quite weird!

There are also now in physical form many folk connected with Light, and many star people as well. About 5% of Light workers currently on the planet in human form are really planet hoppers - winged beings from different planetary structures whose true essence is of angelic form.

As the lower astral levels become thinner and open up, any fear we are still carrying within us has to be identified and worked with. Fear is a deliberately cultivated performance. It is a slow frequency vibration which will be attracted towards any vibration of a similar nature. If you are fearful in any way, slow frequency negative energy with a similar vibration can attach itself to your auric field - a bit like a sheep mite. It will happily sit there feeding off your energy. Every fearful thought you have feeds that slow frequency vibration, giving it more energy and making it stronger. This negative vibration then wants even more food and will amplify your fear thought forms. And so the cycle continues.

So as we now see fear in any form presented to us, we have to work far more specifically to resolve our difficulties, and open our hearts to the new rhythm of Light which can bring about a vibration that will starve this slow frequency vibration - not only within ourselves, but within our group both on the inner and outer planes, and within the life essence of Mother Earth.

As more star gateways continue to open up - and from the year 2008 this will become a normal occurrence - more Light energies will come into our planet. As more high frequency energy comes in, it will need more human bodies who can hold and retain that frequency input. As more human bodies mutate and become capable of receiving high frequency energy, then this energy will be retained on Earth creating a whole new vibrational pattern which in turn will create a shift of the planetary tide from negative to positive. It is in fact a spiritual revolution!

Light workers everywhere - and that includes you - have to now consciously work to raise their vibration to the highest possible frequency, and become aware of what they need to do in order to open up this major opportunity to move forward, for themselves and for humanity.

It is also important to intuitively recognise what is necessary for your evolution at this time. That recognition means working towards a greater harmony within yourself by becoming intuitively aware of what your higher self is saying, rather than being mesmerised by the lower aspect of yourself. So recognise that it is time to take responsibility for yourself on all levels - physical, emotional and mental.

All Light workers have to also move towards the point of awareness where they can function more as an immortal rather than working with the short-term fear wave of death, with the patterns of limitation and the expectancy that the mass of humanity still lives by. This is old conditioning and now has to go!

If we are immortal there is no end, there is just a continuance. As we move through the permutations of this planet, we have the opportunity to gain full Brownie marks and move on into a different planetary focus and cycle where we can evolve into still greater aspects of purity which our soul requires.

We all have to raise the banner of understanding, recognising that the time has come for us to be intuitively honest. Not only within ourselves when we look into the mirror of life, but also to recognise that the time has come to issue forth a new vibration which will totally dissolve all the ideas, concepts and emotions that we still take to be real but which are, in essence, an illusion.

There are now sufficient numbers of Light workers down here on Earth for this work to gather momentum. But not all Light workers are at a point of activation at the moment, in the sense that they have not yet all remembered who they are. But throughout the world at this time, all those connected with the 'mind of one' are beginning to wake up.

CHAPTER 20
MARRIAGE AND
PARTNERSHIP

Mother Earth is going through a courtship ritual where her female essence is actually courting a male essence external to herself. This is a male planet from the Andromeda system.

These two planets are now trying to communicate in the same space, while initially both coming from totally different planetary systems. This cosmic dance is creating a planetary imbalance which could be called a point of occult pressure, although eventually by the year 2035 there will be a point of balance flowing into the one space both are currently contesting.

Marriage on Earth is reflecting this greater planetary imbalance. It is also at a point of disharmony while the male essence and hormones try to come to a new arrangement with the female essence and hormones. The result is all the conflict, misinterpretation and confusion we see in so many marriages today.

In essence, the localised custom we call marriage is really a symbolic reflection of the cosmic dance these two larger planetary entities are going through. But the subtle interpretations currently being experienced by couples within marriage are actually helping Mother Earth to understand her own current difficulties as she communicates with the male Andromeda planet.

As the human female psyche builds and comes to a point of balance with the human male essence, and when the male need to conquer on all levels is transmuted, which will happen by the year 2035, a blending and cosmic marriage between Mother Earth and the masculine Andromeda planet will actually take place. When this happens male and female essences on Earth can be on a par with each other, and the structural differences which males and females on this planet are currently going through can be neutralised. A more harmonious point of understanding will then be reached.

The super glue which currently holds marriages together is, in essence, religion. Religion is based on a series of ideas and encounters with the God force as interpreted by the prophets of old. But humanity, in its awareness, is moving into a much clearer space where individuals do not need a prophet in the conventional sense as they now have the capacity to become a prophet themselves. This is what direct channelling is all about.

So the way in which the super glue has been applied in the form of religious quotations, which has become a binder for marriage in its totality, is now becoming somewhat suspect. This is reflected in a definite drop-off from the need to conform to these conventional ideas as people start to look more closely at natural laws which govern our behaviour, attitude and the planet in which we live.

Marriage is usually a contract between two people who are coming together within the dance of the energies of love and attraction, and within the more subtle energy pull of karma. When those energies have been worked through, their particular contract is nullified on the inner planes and those two people can move on, on the outer planes. Arranged marriages are somewhat different in as much as they come together within the area of opportunist karma.

When we take marriage vows, we make a vow or affirmation 'for better or for worse' which sets up an energy charge and an emotional thought form. When a couple divorce, they actually break that vow and therefore need to consciously look at and transmute the package of energy originally set up. Within this decoding process there may also be a need to transmute a lot of gungy astral energy picked up if one of the partners has been unfaithful. If a husband had a very brief affair for just two nights, for example, a lot of astral energy from all the other sexual encounters their lover has had during this lifetime would be transferred to the husband, and then to the wife when he next makes love to her. So it might take 19 months, from an astral point of view to get rid of the astral energy picked up during those two nights. So if a husband or wife has been regularly unfaithful for many years, their married partner might be in a very peculiar state, astrally. You can work to transmute this during the main meditation programme to release personal karma by working with these vows in the section on thought forms, see Meditation 20, Chapter 2, *The Awakening*.

In the future, if marriage continues to exist it will need a placement where the energies of male, female and karma can be understood more clearly, and the selective choice in relation to the partner needed can be appropriately made. That partnership may be short or long-term. This requires a new approach to marriage by those who currently have the expectancy that marriages should last for 50 to 60 years. These people have a nasty shock when in just a few years they find they have outgrown the person they married, or their partner has outgrown them.

For many people this realisation is very difficult, especially if they have built up an expectation of being together 'till death us do part'. When a marriage breaks up the old possession thought form comes in. That person gets angry. They get caught up with the legal profession with its own form of jargon which often antagonises rather than heals, and these old thought forms get stirred up even more.

As the current creed and dogma of the religious focus within marriage begins to break down, and as the purity of unconditional love begins to take over, most major religions will cease to be in a conventional sense. Two main strandings will initially continue - Christianity and Islam - and by the year 2035, these two religious focuses will blend into a more centralised religion and will supersede all known religions which currently exist.

This new religion will reap the best of everything. It will transmute everything which is currently a limitation for the awareness of both the planet and humanity. Then, with the full understanding of natural law, we will understand what the word religion really means.

Although marriage has ceased to be a useful component in the traditional sense, and partnerships need to move on in a slightly different way, we do still need the physical blending, the merging of male and female energies in order to bring in new souls.

Everyone who incarnates has to come through the normal birth package. Even Avatars have to come through the natural birth process, which is man and woman coming together and opening up an entrance point so that the soul aspect can come in and magnetise the sperm and the egg as the two future parents come together.

When you understand this pattern of energy, you also understand the need for the blend of the male and female essences, not only physically but on the more subtle levels as well. It is a beautiful dance on all levels, and the actual sexual merging is quite a profound experience. Done with awareness and understanding, it is also a religious experience, not just a physical one.

Sperm implants miss out on this vital component as the sperm is just an outer aspect. When two people make love, their energy systems open up and merge which creates a union and an alignment of male and female energies giving the required balance. If a woman has a sperm implant, the sperm misses out on this essential merging of male and female energies and a massive component is left out which puts the psyche of the baby being born at a disadvantage.

For incoming soul aspects, the process of a test tube birth creates a much narrower frequency. Test tube babies therefore incarnate with a limited opportunity because of the limitations the test tube process actually brings about. This is reflected within the psyche of a test tube baby who does not have as much flexibility on the inner planes as the average human who incarnates through the natural parental genetic mix.

Therefore, those soul aspects who choose to incarnate through the test tube process will have a more focused package of awareness, mainly extra-planetary. This puts them in a place of disadvantage which might be ideal for their evolution. Extraterrestrials might also take advantage of incarnating this way, as there is less likelihood within the test tube birth of them becoming immersed in emotional energy which is part of the package when humans incarnate through the normal course of birth.

A lot of the genetic experimentation currently being explored is quite damaging both short-term as well as long-term as extraterrestrials and other planetary folk can and will sneak into human form this way. We have been through this once before in Atlantean times and we are coming back to a crossover point once again where ethically, and intuitively, we have to indicate quite clearly what is acceptable and what is not. Otherwise we will have a new pattern or sub-breed coming in as we had in Atlantean times. There are still some of those beings lurking around at the moment, called the Greys whom some people can see clairvoyantly.

The Greys are a genetically made sub-breed. They have a degree of intelligence and are negative and destructive as they lack the components of unconditional love. Emotionally they are quite dead and are dedicated to encoding people negatively. They are also the ones who cause people to disappear in a variety of different ways.

CHAPTER 21
REALITY

As our third dimensional anticipation of bondage, mental addiction and old conditioning of society starts to break down, we see this reflected in many ways around us.

The physical roads are cracking. Sewers are cracking open. Pollution is now worldwide. Most ideas and motivations be they political, economical or religious are no longer working. Communication between governments is also showing large cracks.

As all this third dimensional reality is now being superseded by the fourth dimensional reality, and as more Light manifests and flows into the Earth in a very specific and fundamental way, massive shifts are about to take place. Not in 20 to 30 years' time, but right now.

For many Light workers, time as we know it is stopping or has already stopped. When the lower astral levels completely open, dimensional time will dominate. Inner and outer space, inner and outer time will become available within the personality mode, and the fourth dimensional interpretation will have to be applied to life. This is the multi-dimensional facet of being in many places at once with meditation naturally occurring 24 hours a day.

As this happens, probable lives and probable outcomes and futures then become very real, based on the understanding of those who are awake as opposed to those who are still asleep. Therefore the future can hold the most beautiful scenario one can possibly imagine for humanity.

Many Light workers already recognise that the motor-car, as we know it, is on the way out. Instead of a traditional motor-car we might have something like Cinderella's slippers! You might step inside a pair of gold slippers and with the right mind-imprint helped by crystals you can think yourself from England to Scotland by flowing through a stream of energy which can be described in third dimensional language as a ley line. This ley line can transport the human from one place to another without the associations of travel as we currently know it. As the lower astral levels will be open, those who have previous knowledge of how to astrally travel, will remember again.

The age of the telephone, as we know it, will also cease to be an issue as you will be able to physically speak on an astral level and will be able to pop in to say hello to your friends on any sphere of the planet within your operating frequency.

The whole scenario of third dimensional problems will cease to be an issue. Deforestation, Chernobyl and radiation left-overs, and the hole in the ozone layer will all change when the input of sufficient minds reach the right octave.

Our weather system will also change. Our weather is the direct result of outgrown thought forms and when our thoughts stabilise and become more harmonious, based on unconditional love rather than conditional greed and territorial claims, our weather system will become perfect for life in all its diversity.

Houses, as we know them, will also cease to be an issue because they will no longer be needed. We will be in a position to grow crystals overnight, according to our intuitive need. We will then be able to change the shape and geometrical pattern of what is available into a form of shelter in the truer sense of the word.

Form shifting will also be a very real facet for humanity as a whole. The oceans of life will be clear and sparkling. Diversity within the various life forms can then grow and expand in a normal way. So humanity can, if it wishes, swim like a fish, fly like a bird, focus angelic-wise by floating up into the atmosphere, astrally project within different planets in our solar system, and generally chat up various life forms. We will be able to create biological spaceships which can be in the shape of our children as we perceive them now, or in any form we choose to experiment with, to allow our awareness and love to be shared freely with our galactic neighbours.

As the Earth is becoming fourth dimensionalised, it is already preparing for its fifth dimensional days as well. This means we are moving towards a 2,000 year epic where harmony, love, beauty and Light in all its diversity will give us a calm scenario after the storm of the last 300,000 years.

As Light workers focus and become aware of this new reality - a reality that already is - and as they bring that reality in through the right ideas, concepts, emotions and interpretations based on the need to treat others as you would like to be treated yourself, so it is that Heaven will once again be an interpretation within Mother Earth. We will then experience this within all its beauty.

GLOSSARY

Astral glamour

Astral glamour is the build-up of slow frequency thought waves which collectively gather around the planet and block light forms coming in. These slow frequency thought waves are created by negative emotional experiences, and are the negative outpourings of stress, selfishness, greed, possessiveness, cruelty and anger which are released by human minds.

Chakras

The seven main chakras of the human body are the crown chakra at the top of the head, and below that the third eye, throat, heart, solar plexus, sexual and base chakras.

Chakras are energy formations, interdimensional within their energy flow. The outer physical manifestation of a chakra therefore has a representation within the chakra systems of the subtle vehicles of the body.

Chakras exist on various levels of matter as well as the physical plane. Muscle movement affects them in a very specific way, and an unfit person will quite often have a weaker expression of chakra movement, which puts them at a disadvantage.

Chakras give off a sound, a pitch, a frequency, a taste and a smell. They exist within a set sequence or vibration and are currently much more developed, far bigger, and therefore more powerful than they have ever been in our past lives.

Each chakra also has a colour which will vary from time to time. Each one is a vortex of energy more oblong in shape than round. They tend to attract anything similar to their vibratory frequency, although each chakra has latent within the sequence of its sound, various vibratory filters which slow down the impact of other vibrations from outer manifestations.

Chakras also tend to feed the lower levels of the soul's awareness through the higher vibratory flows of astral Light, as it comes down and feeds the physical body. So when we sleep and in fact when we eat and drink, we are, on an astral level, bringing in astral Light which feeds the essence of ourselves.

They can be described as something akin to batteries and sometimes, through misuse or overuse, tend to run down and need to rest. They are in the main in a constant flux as they find a new point of balance by the interpretation of data they are being subjected to.

Chakras should work in harmony with each other. The base chakra for example feeds the whole dimensional aspect of the sexual chakra above, and so on. But in reality in the Earth plane at this time, many chakra centres are not working together in harmony and are in disharmony in relationship to each other.

Chakras are the sum total of the essence and experiences the soul has gained within the permutations of the soul sound, or thrust, as it is coming down at this point in time. So each one has its own story, its own level of informational expertise and therefore, its own running order. For further information, see 'Minor chakra centres' in this glossary.

Cosmic gypsies

Most people have not yet tapped into the true essence of cosmic gypsies and view them in a solar way. But cosmic gypsies can be seen in the cloud formations across a whole stretch of sky. These beings are very big. They are 50 miles (80 km) high, 25 miles (40 km) across, with wing spans of 75 miles (120 km) each. Cosmic gypsies are part of a series of families which are colour coded. Each colour represents a frequency, a point of intuitive understanding and a telepathic quotation of immense power.

When you see these cloud formations, try to see the shapes within them. Quite often you will be pleasantly surprised to see wings within the cloud formation - then you may start to see faces as well.

At this stage it is important to trust your intuitive impressions rather than let them run the gauntlet of emotional and intellectual reasoning. Just allow these impressions to act as a focal point in your awareness. Once you link into this aspect of natural phenomena, the pattern of energy which represents cosmic gypsies will start to come in. This will then flow into your space, allowing a new dialogue to gradually expand. It is important to trust your intuitive feelings and allow your awareness to build, mainly through telepathy, as you become more focused. As you learn to focus your will specifically in one area using natural external phenomena as a focal point, as an amplifying charge, you will have very specific information coming in. In this way your awareness will expand to the true creative story of reality - and what you once termed normal behaviour will suddenly seem very different.

Dark lodge

see White lodge.

Devas

Devas are something akin to super glue. They hold cell structure together. They are an alternative life form which does not feel pain in the normal way as we experience it. They evolve in a slightly different way and are hoping to take our place in the next round once humanity, in its awareness, has actually passed on into a higher rhythm.

DNA

DNA stranding is a pattern of interrelationship between vibration and matter which builds up in light particles which can be defined as experience. This stranding genetically evolves within a pattern of awareness within itself, recording all the diversity of experiences which the survival of our race has found useful. So a rhythmical shedding, changing and moving forward occurs to only bring the best from a survival point of view, be that physical, emotional, or mental survival.

Ectoplasm

Ectoplasm is the slow frequency latent essence which is available in all life forms, in all states of awareness. It is in the main generated energy. Mediums can see ectoplasm as a mist-like substance. In olden days when mediums used to sit in trance, this mist could be seen coming from most of the major orifices of their body.

Ectoplasm can be impregnated with positive or negative energy. Those working with the slow frequency energy associated with the darker side would use the ectoplasmic content of their medium person, by putting thought forms within it, and directing it at those they were targeting. Occasionally ectoplasm is also absorbed by slow frequency astral entities who use it as a key mechanism to keep their essence anchored within the physical plane on Earth.

Hara

The hara is normally referred to as a physical point of balance within the body, just below the belly-button. But the hara which I refer to in this book is the point of balance at any one point in time, which might be in any part of your physical body or your subtle network of bodies. All life forms also have a similar hara.

Most people who have too much high frequency energy coming into their body will be vibrating too high. So their hara will be in their throat centre, or their third eye. They will be vibrating out of key with the planet since their earthing will not be adequate. People who are aggressively violent will have their hara in their base chakra centre or in the bottom part of their sexual chakra.

The ideal position of the hara for the New Age person, is the bottom part of the heart centre or the top part of the solar plexus chakra. Not in the emotional lower part of the solar plexus or any of the lower chakra centres. And certainly not above the heart because the frequency is then far too high.

Therefore the centre of balance, or hara within any life form can be in any particular chakra centre, depending on their evolution on the inner or outer planes. If you want to communicate with an aspect of awareness which has a higher or slower vibratory frequency, by raising or lowering your hara you raise or lower your vibration to match their frequency so that communication can be adequate and efficient.

High and low key notes

As high vibratory notes come into group formations, either from individuals or from the soul family these have to be negotiated by the group. But this negotiation can only take place when the forerunner of that group - the person who is vibrating higher than the rest - can raise their vibration to absorb the interpretation of the high note. They then transmute that high note into the lower operating frequency of the group in order to pass the information from that high note down to the group. At the same time, this forerunner has to subtly raise the frequency of those in the group, until they can accept the higher note. This is done through discipline, perseverance, compassion and understanding, and the use of a subtle application of energy to get the group to raise their vibration by allowing a note of enthusiasm to permeate within the essence of the group vitality.

Logos

The planetary logos are particles of awareness which have raised their vibration and already achieved illumination. They have a much more specific understanding of who they are, and also have the capacity to manipulate natural law to their advantage.

The logos use the different vehicles which manifest within their space - such as humanity and the various life forms on Earth - as a training ground to enhance their own awareness. They also use these vehicles as capacitors to trap frequencies which, in their own way, they find difficult to hold.

Minor chakra centres

Each major joint within the physical body such as knees, hands and feet, has a minor chakra centre. Each cell structure within the body also has a minor chakra centre since each cell has a duplication of the larger chakra system. In the treacle count exercise to release toxic energy from the body, you can work with the minor chakra centres in the feet, in the joints at the back of the knees, in the base of the spine and also with those in each spinal segment.

Planetary cycles

Planetary cycles are the times when the cosmic biorhythms of planets - both near to us and more distant - affect the planetary field, the ground energy, and the rhythm of energies manifesting in the magnetic attraction which our planet is going through. Solar flares, for example, is a case in point where the magnetic outpourings have a very definite effect on the wellness, or un-wellness, which people tend to go through.

Slow frequency energy

Slow frequency negative energy, or slow frequency vibration, is an energy store of vibratory sequences which represent an old disorder, an old disharmony which at one time a person might have worked through. You may also have worked with slow frequency energies in a lifetime when those vibrations were somewhat normal.

The vibration held in the Earth at sites of old battles, and the vibration held in areas of the planet where trauma, disasters and life loss have taken place are all slow frequency vibrations. In these places the impact of the event has created a frequency or sound which is in disharmony with life forms in general.

Fear, anger or negativity are also slow frequency emotions and vibrations which specifically sit in, and affect the base and sexual chakra centres.

Astral entities are basically slow frequency vibrations who need similar vibrations for their food. They feed off the bottom two chakra centres of anyone who is carrying a similar vibration to the one they need and want. These entities can be split into two main groups: quick ones and very slow ones. The slow ones can only crawl, so to speak, and therefore have to remain anchored within the vortex of fear within the physical vibration, or at a place of trauma or disaster. The quicker vibratory astral entities can actually move from A to B. For example, they can transfer their awareness and their bulk by leaping from car to car on the motorway. In this way they leap around and attach themselves to other slow frequency vibrations which offer their next meal.

These entities will sometimes put localised amplifiers into the auric system of people - if they have the opportunity - to amplify fear, to make that person feel angrier or less secure and to create more schizophrenic experiences. In this way the entities have rich pickings of food in the form of slow frequency energy from the person they are linking into.

In places where there are street gangs, such as New York, localised entities work through the gang formation, generating fear and intolerance in order to supply themselves with the ongoing focus of slow frequency vibratory food. Racialism is also a source of rich food for slow frequency astral entities.

But slow frequency vibrations not only live in places of terrorism and conflict. They can hang around in relatively peaceful areas also! As slow frequency vibrations tend to be anchored in magnetic movement, they hang around the electrical system of televisions, computers, electrical cables and pylons. Astral entities also use the slow frequency vibrations within electric trains to travel along the electrification of the train track, feeding off any slow frequency vibrations within the mass of people travelling up and down those tracks. The electrical discharge from motor-cars and motorways also create a magnetic field which entities like.

They also feed off the fear energy which hangs around abattoirs and is given off by animals during their abuse in the slaughter process. This fear becomes a high note which feeds these entities, who then grow big and fat.

The geometrical shape of the square generates slow frequency energy as opposed to the triangle which now generates high frequency energy. As humans are coming more into a triangular vibrational essence, the average square room in which we live is not in harmony with our intuitive development as it allows slow frequency energy formations to sit quite comfortably within the room, and to live off the disharmony which the square creates.

Solar Logos
see Logos

Sun spots
Sun spots are an outpouring of magnetic energy, which spirals at a particular shift in relation to the gravitational field of the sun, physically, astrally and mentally. They specifically affect our planet through the Light particles which manifest on Earth. Therefore all life forms are affected by sun spots, depending on the cycle the planet is going through, and the personal cycle of each life form. Sun spots can be positive or negative, and they tend to manifest in 11 year cycles.

Star gateways
A star gateway is a term used to describe a frequency accord where multiple particles of Light, directed by will, usually the will of the logos, actually open up a pulsation for a period of time. This pulsation known as a star gateway, can open for a few seconds, for a few minutes, or many thousands of years. These gateways can also be manipulated by those on the inner planes, either to positive or negative ends. Currently within planet Earth there are many gateways open of both hues - both light and dark. Because of the planetary vibratory change in Mother Earth, and the cosmic tides and solar winds which are now beginning to affect our planet in a very specific way, the opening of multiple star gateways is rapidly becoming the order of the day.

Soul aspects
Soul aspects are aspects of the same soul which has split itself during its downward journey away from the Source. Aspects of the same soul have the same vibratory structure within the genetic background of the soul. But since the time between each soul aspect incarnating is normally well spaced, they can hold different frequency vibrations, such as that of a child compared to an old person. Within the

permutations of the five soul aspects who may be incarnated at the same time, there is a constant ebb and flow which enables the soul to adjust what is required within the personal karma of the soul input in total. The individual aspects can then work in a very precise and specific way.

Structural slow frequency energy

Structural slow frequency energy is a thought form which has been deliberately produced and cultivated by those of the dark lodge. It vibrates within one particular energy slot to create a vibration of an upsetting nature.

It is like a large battleship flowing very majestically but very menacingly down the waters of life, and frightening people who see the silhouette whether it has the capacity to cause damage or not. The structural slowness of this energy vibration causes a remembrance within the particles of distrust which people have as part of their older belief system.

It sends out a very strong signal which enhances any other slow frequency energies, mainly of fear, resident within the genetics of body form or within the structure of thought forms around a person or group. These slow frequency energies can then be absorbed into the energy of the one initial thought form to strengthen it and give it added data about the group or individual it came from.

So another term for structural slow frequency energy is a 'seed' thought form which is deliberately cultivated to be destructive, to be a nuisance, and in essence, to target any weakness within a person or group.

Sub-planes

Sub-planes are the sub-strata of evolution in its diversity. Each sub-plane holds within its vibratory sphere information of a certain key note which can only be experienced when a person's vibration is adequate to bear the energy. When this happens, the point of understanding within that sub-plane is released into the person's awareness. As Light workers become aware of who they are from a point of immortality, finding that point of balance, that point of peace within themselves, they can at times link into their source and move up the sub-planes within their particular angle of entry - which the soul in its fullness has actually achieved. They can then find their way about, almost as if they were in an old, specialist library, where any information they require, be it about this planetary structure, or about other aspects within other galactic empires, can be introduced into their conscious awareness.

But first they have to understand the mechanics of this operation, and in the understanding to link into these key notes which is always based on a need to know rather than a want to know. Therefore the references to old life patterns which many people have are, on one level, pretty useless since it is always what is happening in the now that is important, and not what happened in the past or what will happen in the future.

As you read these words and think about the various sub-planes, you will automatically be nibbling at those sub-planes - because energy follows thought, and your subconscious will within the fullness of time be forced to give you more information about those things which your curiosity is now feeding energy into.

Subtle anatomy

The subtle anatomy is a series of experiences which give the soul aspect a point of reference as it looks in the multi-dimensional direction of its own being, both on the inner and outer planes. It can be defined as a cell structure within the physical body. As the various anatomies form together within a concentrated unit, the various organs which work within the various plane settings interpret and work in harmony with the overall pattern of the soul aspect's experiences.

It is also a series of investigational notes to experience, understand and have a form of reference as to what the soul aspect is participating in within the totality of its being. It is therefore a series of records of the soul aspect's journey which the soul aspect starts to transmute and release by the act of becoming desireless.

As a soul aspect becomes more skilled at negotiating its awareness and various permutations of experiences from past lives, so the subtle anatomy becomes more subtle.

An evolved soul aspect will, therefore, have access to an immense energy field where a new soul aspect will only have a small point of polarity to be working through. As such the subtle anatomy within the newer soul aspect might be far more gross than the refined apparatus of the soul aspect which has been around somewhat longer.

The subtle anatomy therefore is a series of equations held together by the desire which the soul aspect has met, and has imprinted on itself. As it works through that desire principle this is reflected within the experiences that bond together the subtle anatomy, normally on the inner planes.

On the downward journey, a soul aspect builds a lot of subtle anatomy and it refines that anatomy so that it becomes balanced within the duality of male and female, and within the inner and outer planes.

On one level the subtle anatomy is a series of filters which maintain the presence of the soul aspect in each dimension it has an interest in, giving it a feedback mechanism so that it can assess at any point in time, linear, conscious or interdimensional, everything necessary for its growth.

White lodge

The white lodge is a term given to high frequency energy beings who work entirely with Light, with the Cosmic Christ energies and with the formation of the plan for the development of humanity, the Earth and our galaxy.

It is an exclusive organisation on the inner planes who, from time to time, use agents on the outer planes to help them formulate their plan and bring about a point of balance within this world and within the subtle levels which this world has access to.

The white lodge works specifically with karmic laws, both on the inner and outer planes, and is dedicated to bringing about a point of focused appraisal. Their direct and opposite number are those we term the dark lodge - these are energy beings dedicated to disharmony, to working with entirely different frequency points, and their guiding rule is that of tyranny - the stronger tyrannises the weaker.

The dark lodge normally works in isolation, its members only coming together when the need dictates - and there is some evidence that this is now taking place. Members of the white lodge always work together as a group and within the group they share in a total way the understanding, love and power from a central source, and therefore the respect of all life.

The white lodge we refer to in this book has nothing to do with the various physical organisations in Great Britain and abroad whose title also bears the name 'The White Lodge'.

APPENDIX - SOURCES

RadiTech

RadiTech is a geopathic stress neutraliser. It is an electrical apparatus which utilises the electrical pattern of energy to form a magnetic package which has a swamping mechanism to contract the negative particles which cause geopathic stress. By placing different strength RadiTechs in the appropriate area of your home, you can create this swamping mechanism to neutralise any hostile or negative energy of ground problems.

For a news-sheet on RadiTech and further information on geopathic stress and its relation to sickness, ME, asthma, cot-death etc., write (requesting news-sheet no 5) to:

> *The Dulwich Health Society, 130 Gipsy Hill, London,*
> *SE19 1PL, UK. Tel: 081-670 5883. Fax: 081-766 6616.*

MagneTech

MagneTech is a magnetic healer. For leaflet and details of prices write direct to *The Dulwich Health Society* at the address given above.

Water distiller

This is available under the brand name 'Pure Water Distiller' from:

> *Pure Water Inc, 3725 Touzalin Avenue, P.O. Box 83226,*
> *Lincoln, NE 68501, USA. Tel: (402) - 476 9300.*

The Great Invocation

For a free copy of the Great Invocation printed on a small card suitable for your purse or wallet write to: *Invocation Distribution, Worldwide Goodwill.* Larger quantities are available at cost.

UK: *Invocation Distribution, Worldwide Goodwill,*
 3 Whitehall Court, Suite 54, London, SW1A 2EF, UK.

USA: *Invocation Distribution, Worldwide Goodwill,*
 113 University Place, 11th floor, P.O. Box 722,
 Cooper Station, New York, NY 10276, USA.

CH: *Invocation Distribution, Worldwide Goodwill,*
 Case Postale 31, 1 rue de Varembe (3e), 1211 Geneva 20.

INDEX OF MEDITATION SUBJECTS

For details of workshops and tapes by

David Cousins, please write to him direct c/o:

26 Pensylvania, Llanederyn, Cardiff, CF3 7LN